EDUGORILLA
PUBLICATION

NIACL

Assistant - Prelims Exam

Latest Edition
Practice Kit

12 Tests
06 Sectional Test
06 Mock Test

Based On Real Exam Pattern

✓ Thoroughly Revised and Updated

✓ Detailed Analysis of all MCQs

Title	: NIACL Assistant - Prelims Exam
Author Name	: Mr. Rohit Manglik
Published By	: EduGorilla Community Pvt. Ltd.
Publishers Address	: 12/651, First Floor Opp. Arvindo Park, Near Jama Masjid, Indira Nagar, Lucknow, Uttar Pradesh-226016, India

Copyright EduGorilla

ISBN : 978-93-90239-83-2

First Edition

Disclaimer EduGorilla

Compiled and created by EduGorilla Community Pvt. Ltd

Printed By EduGorilla Community Pvt. Ltd.

ROHIT MANGLIK
CEO, EduGorilla

Dear Applicants,

People say *"Success comes to those who work hard."* But I've seen people working hard for their exams day in and day out for marginal success. While others succeed in their examinations by putting in just half the work. So are they God Gifted? No! I believe that it's because they work *smart* and not just *hard*. Similarly, for your exams, you should strategize your preparation so as to increase the likelihood of success. Well with EduGorilla get ready to increase your *chances of selection* in your exam by *16x*.

EduGorilla helps you in not only working *hard* but also working in a *smart and strategic* manner. With EduGorilla's preparation package, you get a chance to make your exam preparation easy, and a fun learning path towards selection. Finding the right path to your preparations can be difficult if you don't know in which direction to head. Don't worry, we have you covered! EduGorilla will be your guide to success in your journey. With our Preparation Package, you can prepare strategically and beat the exam in just one attempt.

EduGorilla's Preparation Package includes-

• **Test Series**   • **Books**

Our preparation package is handcrafted as per the latest changes, expert opinions, and students' discretion. Thus, enabling you to get through each stage of the selection process for your exam.

Our Books are designed by the teachers and experts of the respective exam with a combined 150+ years of experience; to provide you with easy, efficient, and effective learning. Our books are smart, in the sense that not only do they give you the answers to the questions but also provide similar questions for practice.

EduGorilla's competent Test Series gives you real-time experience and confidence through which you can clear your offline or online exam in just one attempt. We currently host 83,000+ mock tests for 1,440+ competitive and academic exams.

Thus, EduGorilla misses no chance to assist you in your preparation and covers all stages of the exam, so that you don't have to look anywhere else.

We provide complete preparation packages for defense, banking, teaching, and other National & State-Level exams. Hence, it doesn't matter which exam you aspire to because you will reach your success.

ALL THE BEST !

Let EduGorilla be your Guide to Success.

Rohit Manglik,
Founder and CEO, EduGorilla

INTRODUCTION

EduGorilla focuses on guiding students to succeed in their examinations. With that in mind, our book, titled "NIACL : Assistant - Prelims Exam", has been drafted through the collective efforts of our distinguished experts with 150+ years of combined experience. This book consists of questions that are created following the latest changes in the syllabus and exam pattern. We compiled the book on the basis of questions that are most likely to appear in the NIACL Assistant - Prelims Exam. Through EduGorilla's "NIACL : Assistant - Prelims Exam" your chances of success will increase 16x.

EduGorilla does this through our Complete Preparation Package. This package consists of well-conceptualized and structured content in the form of questions that are tailor-made according to your needs and will help you practice for exams in a smart way by pinpointing all the necessary information. It also provides hints and solutions, along with a smart answer sheet for your self-evaluation. You can assess your shortcomings and work accordingly on areas that may require more of your attention.

EduGorilla promises to help you succeed in your examination and accomplish your dream goals. We believe in our aspirants and see them at the top of the merit list. And the first step towards the top is to start preparing with us. EduGorilla's "NIACL : Assistant - Prelims Exam" includes the following attributes.

➤ Well-Researched Content

➤ Top-Notch Quality

➤ Detailed Answers and Analysis

➤ Smart Answer Sheet

➤ Exam Relevant Questions

Therefore, EduGorilla fortifies your preparation and makes it durable enough to help you stand tall and beat the examination.

NIACL Assistant - Prelims Exam
Scan QR code for Eligibility, Exam Pattern, Syllabus and more.

Book ID: 0250

TABLE OF CONTENTS

Mock Test	1-160
Mock Test - 1	1-26
Mock Test - 2	27-54
Mock Test - 3	55-80
Mock Test - 4	81-108
Mock Test - 5	109-133
Mock Test - 6	134-160

Sectional Test	161-216
English Language Test - 1	161-168
English Language Test - 2	169-177
Reasoning Ability Test - 1	178-186
Reasoning Ability Test - 2	187-195
Quantitative Aptitude Test - 1	196-205
Quantitative Aptitude Test - 2	206-216

English Language

Ques (1-5):Direction: Read the passage and answer the questions that follow. Some words may be highlighted for you. Pay careful attention.

The Directive Principle of State Policy to provide for primary education to all children has failed in its objectives. At present, almost half of India's population is still illiterate. Through the ages, the illiterate masses have been exploited. The present-day politicians have exploited them for their perverted interests. This has resulted in the formation of unstable coalition governments at the Centre. Social evils like drug abuse, consumption of alcohol and child labour are a result of illiteracy among the masses. Kerala has concentrated on mass education and has, thus, **controlled** many social evils. With the nation hovering around the 1 billion marks and around 48 per cent of its population still illiterate, there is hardly a ray of hope for India. In the near future, the rising illiterate population would further impede the growth and development of the nation. The Directive Principles of State Policy **inter alia** provide that the State shall endeavour to provide for free and compulsory education to all children below the age of 14 years, within a period of ten years from the commencement of the Constitution of India. However, because of the lack of resources and foresight among politicians, this dream has never been realized. The **prevalence** of illiteracy among the masses has made them vulnerable to exploitation, as they are unaware of their rights and privileges. The Indian masses have throughout the age remained illiterate and naive because education had been the privilege of only the Brahmins and the upper classes. The **underprivileged** looked up to them, but never **envied** them. On the contrary, the masses resigned themselves to their fate. The Government launched the National Literacy Mission (NLM) with the objective of achieving total adult literacy in 1988. The objective was to achieve total adult literacy among 80 million adults in the age group of 15-35 by the year 1995. Non-Governmental Organization should also take part in the literacy mission to help the government in achieving its targets sooner than proposed. Though total adult literacy is a stupendous task, we must contribute our bit in achieving the desired targets.

Q.1 Why it is said that there is hardly any ray of hope for India?
A. India's population is around 1 billion
B. 48 percent of the population is illiterate
C. It will provide free education to children
D. It has an adult literacy
E. None of the above

Q.2 Why citizens are vulnerable to exploitation?
A. They are literate
B. They are unaware of their rights and privileges.
C. There's mass education
D. Lack of resources
E. None of the above

Q.3 From the options given below, select the most appropriate synonym for the word "**controlled**".
A. Loose   B. Wild
C. Rampant   D. Irrepressible
E. Administer

Q.4 From the options given below, select the most appropriate synonym for the word "**underprivileged**".
A. Deprived   B. Privileged
C. Wealthy   D. Prosperous
E. None of the above

Q.5 Who has failed in its objectives?
A. The government
B. The illiterate citizens
C. The Directive Principle of State Policy
D. The Constitution of India
E. None of the above

Ques (6-10):Direction: Read the following sentence and determine whether there is an error in it. The error, if any, will be in one part of the sentence. If the sentence is error-free, select 'No Error' as your answer.

Q.6 Samantha felt it was more better (A)/ if she chose the job in London (B)/ as compared to Dubai (C)/ as it was closer to home. (D)
A. (A)   B. (B)   C. (C)   D. (D)
E. No error

Q.7 When it comes to playing (A)/ cricket, Amisha is better then (B)/ Samuel yet no one (C)/ selects her for the team. (D)
A. (A)   B. (B)   C. (C)   D. (D)
E. No error

Q.8 Three jawans of District (A)/ Reserve Guard were killed (B)/ while ten others were injured (C)/ in an IED blast on Tuesday. (D)
A. (A)   B. (B)   C. (C)   D. (D)
E. No error

Q.9 The Delhi government has come up (A)/ with a plan that aims at making nearly 70 (B)/ essential transport services completely online (C)/ in two phases over the next few months. (D)
A. (A)   B. (B)   C. (C)   D. (D)
E. No error

Q.10 The brother-in-laws (A)/ were very helpful (B)/ and supportive of (C)/ their choices. (D)
A. (A)   B. (B)   C. (C)   D. (D)
E. No error

Q.11 Choose the wrongly spelt word from the following words.

A. Censure
B. Iconoclast
C. Amalgam
D. Profilgate
E. Auspicious

Q.12 Choose the wrongly spelt word from the following words.
A. Castigate
B. Gregarious
C. Parsimonious
D. Chastise
E. Inocuous

Q.13 Choose the wrongly spelt word from the following words.
A. Egregious
B. Laconic
C. Demare
D. Venerate
E. Ingenious

Ques (14-18):Direction: In the following question, some of the words have been left out. Read the passage carefully and select the correct answer for the given blank out of the five alternatives given in the questions that follow:

Abhinandan Varthaman, Wing Commander of Indian Air Force was ______(P) _____ by Pakistan Army recently. This news sent a turmoil in the nation and immediate provisions were being made for his rescue. Thereafter, Pakistan decided to release the Wing Commander, following which tensions between India and Pakistan may finally ______(Q)_____ . This has been called as an offer of peace and goodwill by Pakistan Prime Minister Imran Khan. Though this offer is said to be made under pressure from other countries to prevent further ______(R)_______ from India. Pakistan must realise that the time for denial and _______(S)_______ is over. Unless it begins to act on India's and the world community's concerns about Pakistan-based terror safe havens in a time-bound manner, the two nations could be back _______(T)_______ of war if there is another trigger.

Q.14 Which of the following words most appropriately fits the blank labelled (P)?
A. Released
B. Placate
C. Fanatic
D. Vitiate
E. Captured

Q.15 Which of the following words most appropriately fits the blank labelled (Q)?
A. Cracked up
B. Run for
C. Make it up
D. Bear out
E. Wind down

Q.16 Which of the following words most appropriately fits the blank labelled (R)?
A. Bridge
B. Incarcerate
C. Abdicate
D. Escalation
E. Berate

Q.17 Which of the following words most appropriately fits the blank labelled (S)?
A. Snare
B. Pupillage
C. Charlatan
D. Desiccated
E. Obfuscation

Q.18 Which of the following words most appropriately fits the blank labelled (T)?
A. Out of the brink
B. On the brink
C. In the brink
D. Inside the brink
E. Off the brink

Ques (19-23):Direction: In the question given below, a part of the sentence is bold. Below are given alternatives to the bold part which may correct the sentence. Choose the correct alternative. In case no correction is required, choose 'No Correction Required' as your answer.

Q.19 The chickens on his farm **are fatted** up nicely.
A. are fattened
B. are fattening
C. are fattying
D. are fattered
E. No Correction required

Q.20 **These flowers smell sweetly** and are sold at high prices in the market.
A. These flowers will smell sweetly
B. These flowers smelt sweetly
C. These flowers smell sweet
D. Those flowers smell sweet
E. No Correction required

Q.21 **While learning to drive**, one of the most important things is to know the traffic rules first.
A. When learned to drive
B. When learn driving
C. When learn to drive
D. When learning to drive
E. No Correction required

Q.22 Employees should **avail them the opportunity** to buy cheap shares in the company.
A. avail the opportunity
B. avail to the opportunity
C. avail themselves of the opportunity
D. avail themselves to the opportunity
E. No correction required

Q.23 **Farther discussion on** the proposal will be deferred until August.
A. Further discussion on
B. Farther discussion of
C. Next discussion on
D. Next discussion of
E. No correction required

Q.24 Direction: Choose the word that is the same in the meaning of the given word.
Ablution
A. Dirtying
B. Adulteration
C. Purification
D. Abscission
E. Bridge

Q.25 Direction: Choose the word that is opposite in the meaning of the given word.
Obsolete
A. Current
B. Archaic
C. Archive
D. Ancient
E. Outdated

Ques (26-30):Direction: Rearrange the following five sentences/group of sentences (A), (B), (C), (D), and (E) in the proper sequence to form a meaningful paragraph; then answer the questions given below them.

A. The first factory for the industrial production of cheese opened in Switzerland in 1815.

B. The mass production of cheese made it readily available to the poorer classes.

C. Earliest proposed dates for the origin of cheese making range from around 8000 BCE, when sheep were first domesticated.

D. Factory-made cheese overtook traditional cheese making in the World War II era.

E. There is no conclusive evidence indicating where cheese making originated, whether in Europe, Central Asia or the Middle East.

Q.26 Which of the following should be the FIRST sentence after rearrangement?

[SBI PO, 2021]

A. C   B. D   C. A   D. B
E. E

Q.27 Which of the following should be the THIRD sentence after rearrangement?

[IBPS PO, 2020]

A. A   B. C   C. D   D. B
E. E

Q.28 Which of the following should be the SECOND sentence after rearrangement?

A. B   B. C   C. D   D. A
E. E

Q.29 Which of the following should be the FOURTH sentence after rearrangement?

[IBPS PO, 2020]

A. A   B. D   C. B   D. E
E. C

Q.30 Which of the following should be the LAST sentence after rearrangement?

[IBPS Clerk, 2021]

A. B   B. C   C. D   D. A
E. E

Reasoning Ability

Q.31 On sports day in a school, 8 students took part in a race. They were all made to stand in a straight line. Sumit was standing 5th from the right end and there are 3 students standing in between Sumit and Ritesh. What is the rank of Ritesh from the left end of the line?

A. 6th   B. 2nd   C. 8th   D. 9th
E. 5th

Q.32 Study the following information and answer the question based on it.

(A) 'Srikanth' is younger than Neelima.
(B) Pratima is taller than Srikant.
(C) Subhash is taller than Neelima but shorter than Hembrum.
(D) 'Nilima' is taller than Pratima.

If all of them are made to stand in a row in the order of their height, then who among them will be exactly in the middle of the row?

A. Shrikant   B. Nilima
C. Pratima   D. Hembram
E. Subhash

Ques (33-35):Direction: This question is based on the following information.

There are eight members in the family A, B, C, D, E, F, G and H with four generations. F is father of A and B is grandson of E. C is the daughter-in-law of E, who is the grandmother of B. A is father of B and D which are of different gender. G is the son of H, who is the wife of B.

Q.33 How D is related to C?

A. Son
B. Sister
C. Daughter
D. Brother
E. Cannot be determined

Q.34 Who among the following is one of the couples?

A. A and C
B. E and A
C. F and C
D. D and H
E. Cannot be determined

Q.35 Which of the following statement is true?

A. C is the father of H.
B. B and D are cousins.
C. E and F are married couple.
D. D is uncle of G.
E. H is the brother-in-law of D.

Ques (36-40):Direction: Study the following information and answer the given questions.

Eight members Amar, Dinesh, Golu, Huma, Pooja, Qamrun, Raju, and Sultan are sitting in two rows with equal number of members in each row. Members of one row are facing north and those in other row are facing south. Each member in one row is sitting exactly opposite a member in the other row.

Sultan sits in the row facing south, to the immediate right of Raju. Both Sultan and Raju did not sit any extreme end of the row. Raju faces Huma, who is second to the right of Golu. Amar sits immediate left of Huma. Qamran is 3rd ro the left of Pooja. Pooja did not face Dinesh.

Q.36 Who sit at an extreme end of the row?

A. Golu, Qamrun   B. Sultan, Dinesh
C. Pooja, Huma   D. Dinesh, Raju

E. Golu, Sultan

Q.37 What is the position of Qamrun with respect to Sultan?
A. Two places to its right
B. Opposite
C. Placed diagonally opposite
D. Two places to its left
E. Immediately adjacent

Q.38 What is the position of Qamrun?
A. Opposite to Huma
B. Immediate right of Raju
C. Immediate left of Sultan
D. Second to the right of Golu
E. None of these

Q.39 What is the position of Dinesh with respect to Golu?
A. Second to the left   **B.** Third to the right
C. Immediate left   **D.** Second to the right
E. Third to the left

Q.40 Who sits between Pooja and Raju?
A. Qamrun   **B.** Golu   **C.** Sultan   **D.** Amar
E. Huma

Ques (41-45):Directions: Study the following information carefully and answer the questions based on it.

Eight people L, M, N, O, P, Q, R and S are sitting around a circular table. Each of them works in different banks viz., Canara, Bank of India (BOI), Central Bank of India (CBI), Bank of Baroda (BOB), Indian Bank (IB), Union Bank of India (UBI), Oriental Bank of Commerce (OBC) and Dena Bank (DB), not necessarily in the same order. Four of them are facing towards the center while others face outside the center.

O is third to the right of S. The one who is working in Indian Bank is to the immediate left of O; who is not working in Dena Bank. R is fourth to the left of Q. Neither R nor Q is an immediate neighbor of O. L is working in Canara Bank and sits third to the right of the one who is working in Indian Bank. The one who is working in Union Bank of India sits second to the left of the one who is working in Canara Bank. The one who is working in Oriental Bank of Commerce sits second to the right of O. The one who works in Bank of India sits exactly between L and Q and adjacent to them. The one who works in the Central Bank of India sits second to the right of the one who works in the Bank of India. P sits third to the left of L. N is facing the center and is to the immediate right of both L and Q. M and R faces the same direction. L is facing the opposite direction of N.

Q.41 In which bank does O works?
A. Oriental bank of Commerce
B. Bank of India
C. Canara Bank
D. Bank of Baroda
E. Union Bank of India

Q.42 Who is sitting to the immediate left of the one who works in the Indian Bank?
A. R   **B.** L   **C.** M   **D.** N

E. O

Q.43 Who is sitting opposite to Q?
A. R   **B.** O   **C.** L   **D.** N
E. M

Q.44 In which bank do L works?
A. Oriental bank of Commerce
B. Bank of India
C. Canara Bank
D. Bank of Baroda
E. Union Bank of India

Q.45 Who is sitting to the immediate left of the one who works in the Oriental Bank of Commerce?
A. R   **B.** L   **C.** M   **D.** N
E. O

Q.46 Direction: In the question below are given some statements followed by two conclusions numbered I and II. You have to take the given statements to be true even if they seem to be at variance with commonly known facts. Read all the conclusions and then decide which of the given conclusions logically follows from the given statements disregarding commonly known facts.

Statements:
All ice cream is chocolate.
Some mango is vanilla.
Some ice cream is vanilla.

Conclusions:
I. Some ice cream being vanilla is a possibility.
II. Some mango is chocolate.
A. Only conclusion I follow
B. Only conclusion II follows
C. Either conclusion I or II follows
D. Neither conclusion I nor II follows.
E. Both conclusions I and II follow

Q.47 Direction: In the question below are given three statements followed by four conclusions I, II and III. You have to take the given statements to be true even if they seem to be at variance from commonly known facts. Read all the conclusions and then decide which of the given conclusions logically follows from the given statements disregarding commonly known facts.

Statements:
All Clocks are Digital.
Some Watches are Calculator.
No Clock is a Watch.

Conclusions:
I. All Watches being Digital is a possibility.
II. No calculator is a Clock.
III. Some Digitals are Clocks.
A. Only II follows
B. Only III follows
C. Both I and III follow
D. Either II or III follows

E. None of these

Q.48 Direction: In the question below are given some statements followed by two conclusions numbered I and II. You have to take the given statements to be true even if they seem to be at variance with commonly known facts. Read all the conclusions and then decide which of the given conclusions logically follows from the given statements disregarding commonly known facts.

Statements:

All chairs are locks.

All locks are key.

Some key are box.

Conclusions:

I. Some chairs are key.

II. Some box are chairs.

A. Only conclusion I follow

B. Only conclusion II follows

C. Either conclusion I or II follows

D. Neither conclusion I nor II follows

E. Both conclusions I and II follow

Q.49 Direction: In the questions given below statements are followed by some conclusions. You have to take the given statements to be True even if they seem to be at variance from commonly known facts. Read all the conclusions and then decide which of the given conclusions logically follows from the given statements disregarding commonly known facts.

Statement:

Frequently Silver is Black.

None Black is White.

Occasionally Gold is Silver.

More of the White is Yellow.

Conclusion:

I) some Yellow is not Black.

II) Few silver is black.

III) All White can never be Silver.

A. Only III and II follows

B. Only I follows

C. Only I and II follows

D. All follows

E. Only II follows

Q.50 Direction: In the question below are given some statements followed by some conclusions. You have to take given statements to be true even if they seem to be at variance with commonly known facts. Read all the conclusions and then decide which of the given conclusions logically follows from the given statements disregarding commonly known facts.

Statements:

Some Painter are Artist.

Only few brush are paints.

All artists are paints.

No frame is Paints.

Conclusions:

I. Some Paints are Painter.

II. Some Brush are not Paint.

III. Some Brush are Artist.

A. Only I and II follows

B. Only I and Either II or III

C. Either II or III

D. Only III follows

E. Only I follows

Ques (51-55):Direction: Study the following information carefully to answer the given question.

F @ 5 3 R $ J P E 1 H % I 8 4 B 6 # A W 2 U G C * 9 & Z N M © C

Q.51 How many such symbols are there in the above arrangement each of which are immediately preceded by an alphabet and followed by a number?

A. Two   **B.** Three

C. None   **D.** One

E. More than three

Q.52 If all the numbers in the above arrangement are dropped, then which of the following will be the eleventh from the right end?

A. U   **B.** B

C. W   **D.** A

E. None of these

Q.53 Which of the following is 10th to the left of the 18th element from the left end of the above arrangement?

A. J   **B.** E

C. I   **D.** P

E. None of these

Q.54 Four of the following five are alike in a certain way based on their positions in the above arrangement and so form a group. Which is the one that does not belong to that group?

A. 3 J $ **B.** E % H   **C.** # 2 W   **D.** Z © M

E. U * 9

Q.55 How many such consonants are there in the above arrangement each of which is immediately preceded by a number but not immediately followed by a symbol?

A. Two   **B.** One   **C.** Three   **D.** Five

E. None

Ques (56-57):Direction: In the following question assuming the given statements to be true, find which of the conclusion among the given conclusions is/are definitely true, and then give your answers accordingly.

Q.56 Statements: P ≤ Q > W = K; K < X; X = P > L; N < L

Conclusions:

I. Q = P

II. Q > P

A. None is true

B. Both I and II are true

C. Only II is true

D. Only I is true

E. Either I or II is true

Q.57 Statements: P ≥ S < R, T = Q > P, U ≤ L < T

Conclusions:

I. T > S

II. R ≥ T

A. If only conclusion I is true.
B. If only conclusion II is true.
C. If either I or II is true.
D. If neither I nor II is true.
E. If both I and II are true.

Q.58 How many pairs of letters are there in the word "CORONAVIRUS" which have as many letters between them in the word as in the alphabet? (both forward & backward)

A. 5   B. 7   C. 6   D. 4
E. 3

Ques (59-61):Direction: In the following question assuming the given statements to be true, find which conclusion among the given conclusions is/are definitely true and then give your answers accordingly.

Q.59 Statement:

A ≥ B = C < D; D = E > F

Conclusions:

I. B < E

II. A ≥ C

A. Only I is True
B. Only II is True
C. Either I or II is true
D. Both conclusions I and II are True
E. None is True

Q.60 Statement:

P = U < H < K ≤ G > N; D ≤ K

Conclusion:

I. D ≥ U

II. P > D

[IDBI Bank Executive, 2021]

A. Neither conclusion I nor II is true.
B. Both conclusion I and II are true.
C. Only conclusion II is true.
D. Either conclusion I or II is true.
E. Only conclusion I is true.

Q.61 Statement:

T ≤ U > S; H > G ≥ M = U; S ≥ R = Q ≥ P

Conclusion:

I. S > P

II. P ≤ S

[IDBI Bank Executive, 2021]

A. Only conclusion I follow
B. Only conclusion II follow
C. Neither conclusion I nor II follow
D. Both conclusion I and II follow
E. None of these

Q.62 If it is possible to make only one meaningful English word with the first, fifth, eighth, and ninth letters of the word SKEPTICAL, which of the following will be the third letter of that word? If no such word can be made give 'X' as the answer and if more than one such word can be made give 'Y' as the answer.

A. N   B. D   C. S   D. X
E. Y

Q.63 In a certain code language, 'PAINTS' is written as 'CRPKUV'. How will 'PURITY' be written as in that language?

A. WRKSNU   B. XSISBM
C. VSKTAZ   D. WRKTAV
E. WRKTBV

Q.64 In a certain code LUCKNOW is coded as YQPMEWN, what is the code for ENGLISH?

A. JTICFKC   B. EJCPFKI
C. TJICFKC   D. JUKNIPG
E. JKCPIPG

Q.65 In a certain code language, GOOGLE is written as TLLTOV. In the same pattern, how will REALME be written in that code?

A. VNOZVI   B. VNOZIV
C. IVZONV   D. ZVIVNO
E. None of these

Quantitative Aptitude

Q.66 Raj pulls out number of balls from a bag. Each ball has some digits printed on it. If we consider only the first 9 digits, its average comes to be 11. If each of these digits is multiplied by 5 and then 8 is added to each of these resultant digits, then the average is:

A. 55   B. 20
C. 95   D. 63
E. None of the above

Ques (67-71):Direction: In the given question, two equations numbered I and II are given. Solve both the equations and mark the appropriate answer.

Q.67 I. $15x^2 - 30x - 225 = 0$

II. $12y^2 + 96y + 180 = 0$

A. x > y
B. x < y
C. x ≥ y
D. x ≤ y
E. x = y or relationship between x and y cannot be established

Q.68 I. $24x^2 + 96x + 90 = 0$

II. $28y^2 + 56y + 21 = 0$

A. x > y
B. x < y
C. x ≥ y
D. x ≤ y
E. x = y or relationship between x and y cannot be established

Q.69 (I) $x^2 + 11x + 24 = 0$

(II) $y^2 + 9y + 14 = 0$

A. x > y

B. x < y

C. x ≥ y

D. x ≤ y

E. x = y or relationship between x and y cannot be established

Q.70 I $x^2 - 9x + 20 = 0$

II $y^2 - 11y + 30 = 0$

A. x > y

B. x < y

C. x ≥ y

D. x ≤ y

E. x = y or relationship between x and y cannot be established

Q.71 I. $x^2 - 20x + 91 = 0$

II. $y^2 + 16y + 63 = 0$

[IBPS RRB Scale I, 2020]

A. x > y

B. x ≥ y

C. x < y

D. x ≤ y

E. x = y or the relation cannot be determined

Ques (72-76):Direction: Read the following line Graph carefully and answer the following questions.

The Graph shows the percentage wise breakup of students in different streams of MBA.

Total number of students = 6000

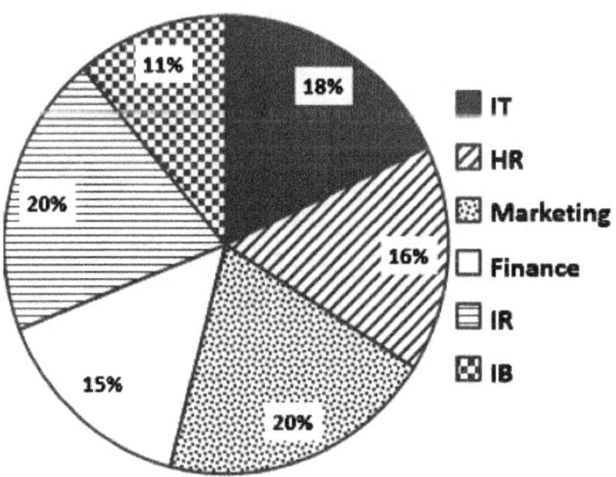

Q.72 Find the total number of students having specialization in marketing and IR?

A. 2300 **B.** 2450 **C.** 2400 **D.** 1960

E. 2100

Q.73 What is the respective ratio of students having IT as specification to the students having IB as specialization?

A. 18 : 11 **B.** 11 : 18 **C.** 14 : 19 **D.** 5 : 6

E. 4 : 7

Q.74 What is the difference between the students in HR and students in finance?

A. 70 **B.** 60 **C.** 120 **D.** 100

E. 80

Q.75 Students in HR is what percent of students in marketing?

A. 70% **B.** 50% **C.** 90% **D.** 80%

E. 75%

Q.76 If number of students increases by 2000 but the percentage distribution of students in different specialization remain same so what is difference between number of students in IB initially and after increment.

A. 330 **B.** 220 **C.** 400 **D.** 300

E. 350

Q.77 If Rs. 8544 is divides between A, B and C in ratio $6 : 11 : 15$. If B increase the rupees by 50% and A spent 20% of his rupees. Find the new ratio of rupees.

A. $16 : 55 : 50$ **B.** $17 : 58 : 49$

C. $18 : 55 : 50$ **D.** $17 : 55 : 49$

E. Data Inadequate

Q.78 A can do a work in 24 days, B can do the same work in 48 days and C can do the same work in 72 days. Unfortunately, B could not become the part of the work so the work was completed by A and C only, so in this case how much more money is earned by A than the previous situation, if total amount distributed to them in both the cases was 4400 rupees.

A. Rs. 600 **B.** Rs. 700 **C.** Rs. 800 **D.** Rs. 900

E. Rs. 1000

Q.79 The cost price of item A is equal to the cost price of item B. If the marked price of item A is Rs____ after an increase by 60% of its cost price and the marked price of B is Rs 600 after an increase by 50% of its cost price. The difference between the selling price of item B and item A is Rs____ if 10% of discount is given on the marked price of both the items.

A. 680,80 **B.** 640,36 **C.** 540,28 **D.** 720,240

E. 480,120

Ques (80-84):Direction: Given question consists of 2 statements, I and II respectively. Please read the question carefully and decide which of the statement (s) is/are sufficient/necessary to answer the question.

Q.80 Find the share of Anil.

I: Rahul, Amit, and Anil earn Rs. $24,000$.

II: Rahul and Amit completes $\left(\dfrac{1}{4}\right)$th of the work.

A. The data in statement I alone is sufficient to answer the question, while the data in statement II alone is not sufficient to answer the question.

B. The data in statement II alone is sufficient to answer the question, while the data in statement I alone is not sufficient to answer the question.

C. Either statement I or statement II alone is sufficient to

answer the question.

D. The data in both statements I and II are not sufficient to answer the question.

E. The data in both the statement I and II together are necessary to answer.

Q.81 What is the probability that 2 drawn pencils are blue when 2 pencils are drawn at random?

I: A jar contains 3 red pencils, 4 blue pencils, and 2 black pencils.

II: A jar contains 9 pencils of different colors.

A. The data in statement I alone is sufficient to answer the question, while the data in statement II alone is not sufficient to answer the question.

B. The data in statement II alone is sufficient to answer the question, while the data in statement I alone is not sufficient to answer the question.

C. Either statement I or statement II alone is sufficient to answer the question.

D. The data in both the statements I and II are not sufficient to answer the question.

E. The data in both the statement I and II together are necessary to answer.

Q.82 Find the sum.

I: The simple interest accrued at 7% rate of interest is Rs. 1190.

II: The sum is invested for 2 years.

A. The statement I alone is sufficient to answer the question, but the statement II alone is not sufficient.

B. The statement II alone is sufficient to answer the question, but the statement I alone is not sufficient.

C. Both the statements I and II together are needed to answer the question.

D. Either statement I alone or statement II alone is sufficient to answer the question.

E. Neither statement I nor statement II is sufficient to answer the question.

Q.83 I. The amount of profit earned on selling the car was Rs. $3,20,000$.

II. The selling price was twice the cost price of car.

What is the cost price of the car?

A. The statement I alone is sufficient to answer the question, but the statement II alone is not sufficient.

B. The statement II alone is sufficient to answer the question, but the statement I alone is not sufficient.

C. Both the statements I and II together are needed to answer the question.

D. Either statement I alone or statement II alone is sufficient to answer the question.

E. Neither statement I nor statement II is sufficient to answer the question.

Q.84 What is the average speed of Rohan?

I. The average speed of Rohan is double that of Ram. The average speed of Nisha is 10 km/h

II. The average speed of Ram is three times the average speed of Nisha.

A. Statement I is sufficient

B. Statement II is sufficient

C. Both statement I and statement II are sufficient individually

D. Neither statement I nor statement II is sufficient

E. Statement I and II together is sufficient

Ques (85-87): What will come in the place of the question mark ' ?' in the following question?

Q.85 $[(-251) \times 21 \times (-12)] \div ? = 63$

A. 2501   **B.** 1004   **C.** 3005   **D.** 1503

E. 1808

Q.86 22% of $4350 + 47.25 \times 4 + 17 \times 51 - 1013 = ?$

A. 1005   **B.** 900

C. 1200   **D.** 1000

E. None of these

Q.87 $888 + 88.8 + 8.88 + 8 - 1.88 - 18.8 = ?$

A. 983   **B.** 975

C. 963   **D.** 973

E. None of these

Q.88 A vessel contains a mixture of two liquids Rockford and Vodka in ratio $4:7$ respectively. When 11 liters of the mixture are taken out from the vessel and the vessel is filled with Vodka, the ratio of Rockford and Vodka becomes $1:2$ respectively. How many liters of liquid Rockford was initially there in the vessel?

A. 38 liters   **B.** 84 liters   **C.** 48 liters   **D.** 54 liters

E. 68 liters

Ques (89-93):Direction: What should come in place of the question mark '?' in the following number series?

Q.89 $1,2,6,21,88, ?$

A. 425   **B.** 435   **C.** 445   **D.** 450

E. 465

Q.90 $130,115,135,110, ?,105$

A. 120   **B.** 130   **C.** 140   **D.** 100

E. 110

Q.91 $4,2,2,3, ?,15$

A. 3   **B.** 4   **C.** 5   **D.** 6

E. 9

Q.92 $17,22,48,147, ?,2951$

A. 1024   **B.** 848   **C.** 590   **D.** 455

E. 782

Q.93 $2,10,30,68, ?,222$

A. 125   **B.** 130   **C.** 245   **D.** 155

E. 165

Q.94 What should come in place of ' x' in the following question?

$$28\frac{4}{7}\% \text{ of } 2835 + 66\frac{2}{3}\% \text{ of } 1245 = 1156 + x^2$$

A. 26   **B.** 24   **C.** 32   **D.** 22

E. 28

Q.95 What approximate value will come in the place of the question mark ' ?' in the following question?

$$90\% \text{ of } 50 + \left(\frac{1}{2}\right) \times 30 - 45 \div ? = 57$$

A. 15   **B.** 45   **C.** 30   **D.** 3

E. 12

Ques (96-100): What should come in the place of the question mark ' ?' in the following question?

Q.96 $18 + 12 \times 6 - 12 \div 3 + 77 \div 11 = ?$

A. 73   **B.** 83

C. 93   **D.** 133

E. None of these

Q.97 $(14)^2 \times 10 \div 4 - (15)^2 + 16 = ?^2 + 5^2$

A. 4   **B.** 16   **C.** 8   **D.** 10

E. 14

Q.98 $60\% \text{ of } 135 - \left(\sqrt{729} + ?\right) = 4$

A. 90   **B.** 20   **C.** 50   **D.** 30

E. 5

Q.99 $35\% \text{ of } 400 - 24\% \text{ of } 12.5 = 110 + ?$

A. 21   **B.** 37   **C.** 27   **D.** 32

E. 16

Q.100 $52\% \text{ of } 150 + 15 \times 35 - \sqrt{841} \times 8 = ?$

A. 372   **B.** 373

C. 371   **D.** 370

E. None of these

// Smart Answer Sheet //

Correct Indicates percentage of students who answered questions correctly.

Skipped Indicates percentage of students who skipped questions.

Q.	Ans.	Correct / Skipped
1	B	58.8 % / 31.79 %
2	B	45.65 % / 46.2 %
3	E	59.11 % / 30.65 %
4	A	85.29 % / 12.27 %
5	C	49.08 % / 45.73 %
6	A	79.06 % / 11.24 %
7	B	66.65 % / 30.48 %
8	E	40.09 % / 53.43 %
9	E	84.46 % / 15.29 %
10	A	83.94 % / 14.13 %
11	D	58.08 % / 38.44 %
12	E	44.65 % / 37.2 %
13	C	46.53 % / 30.36 %
14	E	52.28 % / 31.62 %
15	E	45.03 % / 42.99 %
16	D	66.81 % / 31.68 %
17	E	40.27 % / 40.38 %
18	B	62.68 % / 30.4 %
19	A	51.79 % / 46.17 %
20	C	44.69 % / 46.17 %
21	E	52.66 % / 31.38 %
22	C	60.51 % / 35.57 %
23	A	67.47 % / 30.65 %
24	C	69.05 % / 30.42 %
25	A	50.69 % / 47.66 %
26	E	57.14 % / 35.63 %
27	A	59.57 % / 40.3 %
28	B	61.61 % / 38.39 %
29	B	82.96 % / 15.82 %
30	A	18.99 % / 72.21 %
31	C	58.05 % / 34.69 %
32	B	16.18 % / 71.32 %
33	C	62.77 % / 33.57 %
34	A	49.25 % / 47.69 %
35	C	28.31 % / 67.72 %
36	A	10.21 % / 87.1 %
37	D	65.62 % / 30.05 %
38	E	84.95 % / 12.36 %
39	B	54.88 % / 39.15 %
40	C	51.42 % / 44.75 %
41	D	68.84 % / 30.11 %
42	E	46.69 % / 51.84 %
43	A	51.81 % / 42.04 %
44	C	12.96 % / 84.63 %
45	D	31.07 % / 68.09 %
46	D	47.39 % / 39.3 %
47	C	47.41 % / 38.71 %
48	A	54.71 % / 37.36 %
49	C	42.51 % / 54.83 %
50	A	43.64 % / 55.89 %
51	A	46.68 % / 34.71 %
52	C	40.47 % / 51.82 %
53	D	61.64 % / 34.2 %
54	E	64.57 % / 33.88 %
55	B	62.81 % / 37.1 %
56	E	58.21 % / 40.56 %
57	A	59.61 % / 38.43 %
58	A	69.74 % / 30.01 %
59	D	67.0 % / 32.56 %
60	D	62.58 % / 32.86 %
61	B	48.99 % / 31.78 %
62	E	43.02 % / 53.14 %
63	D	69.42 % / 30.58 %
64	D	40.07 % / 52.46 %
65	C	65.55 % / 32.49 %
66	D	49.39 % / 31.14 %
67	C	68.42 % / 31.18 %
68	D	25.97 % / 67.87 %
69	E	57.61 % / 30.44 %
70	D	77.56 % / 14.23 %
71	A	82.95 % / 16.05 %
72	C	68.13 % / 30.02 %
73	A	53.85 % / 32.98 %
74	B	86.86 % / 10.82 %
75	D	21.39 % / 77.78 %
76	B	68.87 % / 30.72 %
77	A	24.14 % / 67.89 %
78	D	13.24 % / 78.23 %
79	B	57.78 % / 33.77 %
80	E	68.65 % / 31.34 %

Q.	Ans.	Correct		Q.	Ans.	Correct		Q.	Ans.	Correct		Q.	Ans.	Correct		Q.	Ans.	Correct
		Skipped				Skipped				Skipped				Skipped				Skipped
81	A	40.34 %		85	B	61.74 %		89	C	61.57 %		93	B	43.83 %		97	B	41.53 %
		49.26 %				30.63 %				32.29 %				35.58 %				49.21 %
82	C	42.0 %		86	D	44.61 %		90	C	20.45 %		94	D	69.55 %		98	C	48.89 %
		46.26 %				44.33 %				79.24 %				30.17 %				32.14 %
83	C	49.12 %		87	D	40.98 %		91	D	82.69 %		95	A	54.75 %		99	C	42.4 %
		36.48 %				50.6 %				11.64 %				33.23 %				46.41 %
84	E	57.41 %		88	C	54.95 %		92	C	48.5 %		96	C	43.5 %		100	C	68.65 %
		35.48 %				38.82 %				45.15 %				31.98 %				30.16 %

Performance Analysis

Avg. Score (%)	44.0%
Toppers Score (%)	58.0%
Your Score	

//Hints and Solutions//

1. The given passage is about Adult Illiteracy.

- Let us refer to the line from the passage, "With the nation hovering around the 1 billion marks and around 48 percent of its population still illiterate, there is hardly a ray of hope for India".

- From the given passage we get to know India's population is around 1 billion and out of this 48 percent of the population is illiterate. This is a very large portion of the population.

- It is very hard to change this situation in a short period of time. So, it is said that there is hardly any ray of hope for India

So, '48 percent of the population is illiterate' is the correct option.

Hence, the correct option is (B).

2. The given passage is about Adult Illiteracy.

- Let us refer to the line from the passage, "The prevalence of illiteracy among the masses has made them vulnerable to exploitation, as they are unaware of their rights and privileges".

- Here, 'prevalence' means the fact or condition of being prevalent; commonness.

- From the given passage we get to know as the masses are illiterate, they lack knowledge on their rights and privileges. Due to these, they tend to become a target of exploitation.

So, 'They are unaware of their rights and privileges' is the correct option.

Hence, the correct option is (B).

3. The given passage is about Adult Illiteracy.

- The given word controlled means the power to influence or direct people's behaviour or the course of events.

- In option 5, administer means to manage or supervise the execution, use, or conduct.

So, 'administer' is the correct synonym for the word.

Let us see the meanings of the other words:

- loose - set free; release.

- wild - living or growing in the natural environment; not domesticated or cultivated.

- rampant - flourishing or spreading unchecked.

- irrepressible - not able to be controlled or restrained.

Hence, the correct option is (E).

4. The given passage is about Adult Illiteracy.

- The underlined word underprivileged means deprived through the social or economic condition of some of the fundamental rights of all members of a civilized society.

- In option (A), Deprived means suffering a severe and damaging lack of basic material and cultural benefits.

So, 'Deprived' is the correct word.

Let us see the meanings of the other words:

- Privileged - having special rights, advantages, or immunities.

- Wealthy - having a great deal of money, resources, or assets; rich.

- prosperous - successful in material terms; flourishing financially.

Hence, the correct option is (A).

5. The given passage is about Adult Illiteracy.

- Let us refer to the line from the passage, "The Directive Principle of State Policy to provide for primary education to all children has failed in its objectives. At present, almost half of India's population is still illiterate".

- From the given passage we get to know that half of India's population is still illiterate. This situation shows that the Directive Principle of State Policy has failed to achieve its objective of providing primary education to all children.

So, 'The Directive Principle of State Policy' is the correct option.

Hence, the correct option is (C).

6. The given sentence is in the past tense as can be seen from the use of the verbs 'felt' and 'chose' in the past tense.

'Better' is an adjective which means 'of a more excellent or effective type or quality'.

By referring to something as 'more' in a certain quality than something else automatically means it is a comparison.

Example: Dean was better than his brother at hunting.

'More' is also a determiner which means 'a greater or additional amount or degree of'

Example: Patrick was more talented at carrom than Stewart.

Both of them mean the same thing and thus using both of them at the same time becomes redundant.

Thus, the 'more' needs to be removed from the sentence in order to make the sentence grammatically correct.

Thus, the correct sentence: 'Samantha felt it was better if she chose the job in London as compared to Dubai as it was closer to home.'

Hence, the correct option is (A).

7. 'Then' is an adverb that is used to refers to a particular time period. Example: It was then that Ashley decided to leave her job and move to another city.

'Than' is a conjunction that means 'used to introduce the second element in a comparison. Example: Saurabh was richer than Mayuri and yet they led a very happy life.

The current sentence compares 2 people, Amisha and Samuel in terms of their cricket playing skills.

The sentence is not referring to any particular time period and thus the use of the adverb 'then' does not seem correct.

Thus, the adverb 'then' needs to be replaced with the conjunction 'than' in order to make it grammatically correct.

Thus, the correct sentence is: 'When it comes to playing cricket, Amisha is better than Samuel yet no one selects for the team.'

Hence, the correct option is (B).

8. There are no errors in the sentence.

The given sentence is in the past tense as can be seen by the use of the verbs 'killed' and 'injured' in the past tense. Thus, the correct sentence is: 'Three jawans of District Reserve Guard were killed while ten others were injured in an IED blast on Tuesday.'

Hence, the correct option is (E).

9. There are no errors in the sentence.

The given sentence is in the present perfect tense as the plan has been created in the present and the action is complete as can be seen by the usage of the verb 'has come'. Thus, the correct sentence will be: The Delhi government has come up with a plan that aims at making nearly 70 essential transport services completely online in two phases over the next few months.

Hence, the correct option is (E).

10. In the given sentence, the error in the part is the inappropriate use of the noun number.

Nouns are words used to name person, place, animal, thing, emotion, or state.

In the given statement, the incorrect plural form of 'brother-in-law' is being used.

Compound nouns are made plural by adding 's' to the main word.

For example: Commander-in-chief - Commanders-in-chief, brother-in-law - brothers-in-law etc.

Therefore, we will replace 'brother-in-laws' with 'brothers-in-law' to make the sentence grammatically correct.

The correct sentence will be: 'The brothers-in-law were very helpful and supportive to their choices.'

Hence, the correct option is (A).

11. The word 'profilgate' is correctly spelt as 'profligate' which means recklessly extravagant or wasteful in the use of resources.

Censure: express severe disapproval of (someone or something), especially in a formal statement

Iconoclast: a person who attacks or criticizes cherished beliefs or institutions

Amalgam: a mixture or blend

Auspicious: conducive to success; favourable

Hence, the correct option is (D).

12. The word 'inocuous' is correctly spelt as 'innocuous' which means not harmful or offensive.

Castigate: reprimand or rebuke (someone) severely.

Gregarious: (of a person) fond of company; sociable

Parsimonious: very unwilling to spend money or use resources

Chastise: rebuke or reprimand severely; castigate

Hence, the correct option is (E).

13. The word 'demare' is correctly spelled as 'demur' which means to raise objections or to show reluctance.

Egregious: outstandingly bad; shocking

Laconic: (of a person, speech, or style of writing) using very few words

Venerate: regard with great respect; revere

Ingenious: (of a person) clever, original, and inventive

Hence, the correct option is (C).

14. Here, knowing the meanings of the given words and the context of the statement is equally important because that will help decide the correct answer.

Released means to set someone free.

Placate means to make (someone) less angry or hostile.

Fanatic means a person filled with excessive and single-minded zeal, especially for an extreme religious or political cause.

Vitiate means to make faulty or defective, hurt

Captured means to take into one's possession. This fits in with the context because the sentence following after it tells that the reaction of the preceding statement.

Hence, the correct option is (E).

15. The context of the second sentence suggests that the tension between the two countries should reduce or lessen down. So the correct word that should fit here is 'wind down'.

The meanings of the given phrasal verbs are:

Cracked up means outburst of laughter.

Run for means to pursue something or someone.

Make it up means to compensate.

Bear out means to conform to the correctness of something.

Wind down means to draw or bring down gradually to close.

Hence, the correct option is (E).

16. Here, knowing the meanings of the given words is very important to understand the context of the sentence.

'Bridge' means to connect.

'Incarcerate' is to imprison or confine someone.

'Berate' is to scold or criticize someone angrily.

'Abdicate' is to fail to fulfill or reject a responsibility or duty.

'Escalation' means an increase in the intensity or seriousness of something.

Since the paragraph tells that further worsening of the situation has to be controlled as suggested by other countries so the word 'escalation' fits here as it makes the sentence meaningful.

Hence, the correct option is (D).

17. Here, knowing the meanings of the given words is very important to understand the context of the sentence.

A snare is a trap meant to catch birds or animals.

Pupillage is the period during which one is a student and is taught by a particular person.

Charlatan refers to a person falsely claiming to have special knowledge or skill.

Desiccated means 'completely dried out; completely devoid of any moisture.

Obfuscation refers to make something unclear or obscure (mostly intentional).

Now, reading the sentence "Pakistan must realise that the time for denial and" gives a fair idea that the word must be related to some negative trait of a personality. Since the only word that fits in is 'Obfuscation'.

Hence, the correct option is (E).

18. Here, out of the given options, only one of them is correct. Using elimination method one can easily find the correct answer.

'On the brink' means being very close or nearly close to something.

Other option are incorrect because they are grammatically incorrect sentences.

Hence, the correct option is (B).

19. Correct sentence: The chickens on his farms are fattened up nicely.

The concept is: 'Fat' is a transitive verb and it means 'to make fat' but we need an intransitive verb here because there is no object.

'Fatten' is an intransitive verb that means 'to become fat' hence we can use this verb in the present progressive tense. As this verb is an intransitive verb.

Hence, the correct option is (A).

20. The correct answer is 'These flowers smell sweet'.

The word 'sweetly' is inappropriate. Here, the smell of the flowers are being described. So, an adjective should be used instead of an adverb. The word 'sweet' should replace 'sweetly'.

Hence, the correct option is (C).

21. While means 'during', 'when', or 'at the same time'. While can also be a noun that would be translated as 'a short period of time' (this is not the case with 'whilst').

The underlined segment is absolutely free from grammatical errors. Hence, no correction is required here.

Hence, the correct option is (E).

22. Reflexive pronouns are words like myself, yourself, themselves, himself, etc.

These are used when the subject and the object of the sentence are the same.

- E.g. The poor man poisoned himself.

Certain verbs such as enjoy, avail, acquit, etc. are followed by reflexive pronouns.

- E.g. We enjoyed ourselves at the annual function of our school.

According to the rule and example that are given above, 'avail themselves of the opportunity' will be used in the underlined part of the sentence.

Correct Sentence: Employees should avail themselves of the opportunity to buy cheap shares in the company.

Hence, the correct option is (C).

23. 'Farther' and 'further' are comparative adverbs or adjectives.

Further: We use 'further' before a noun to mean 'extra', 'additional' or 'a higher level'.

- Example: She's gone to a college of further education.

Farther: When used as an adjective, 'farther' describes when one object is more distant than the other, requiring a measurement of the distance from one common point to both objects.

- Example: The red car is farther away than the blue car.

The given sentence talks about the additional discussion on a proposal.

Therefore, the usage of 'further' is the most appropriate answer in the given sentence.

The correct sentence is: Further discussion on the proposal will be deferred until August.

Hence, the correct option is (A).

24. The word Ablution means an act of washing oneself.

Purification: The act of cleaning by getting rid of impurities.

It is clear that Ablution and Purification are synonyms of each other.

Hence, the correct option is (C).

25. The word Obsolete means No longer in use.

Current: Occurring in or belonging to the present time.

It is clear that Obsolete and Current are opposite of each other, all other options are synonyms of Obsolete.

Hence, the correct option is (A).

26. The first sentence is E as it start discussing about the origination of cheese making.

The second sentence is C as it mentions the time when the process of cheese making started.

The third sentence is A as it informs about the first factory of cheese which was opened in Switzerland.

The fourth sentence is D as it mentions the consequence of preparing cheese in the factories.

The fifth sentence is B because it concludes the passage by mentioning that cheese is available to poor classes because of the mass production.

Thus the correct sequence is ECADB.

Hence, the correct option is (E).

27. The first sentence is E as it start discussing about the origination of cheese making.

The second sentence is C as it mentions the time when the process of cheese making started.

The third sentence is A as it informs about the first factory of cheese which was opened in Switzerland.

The fourth sentence is D as it mentions the consequence of preparing cheese in the factories.

The fifth sentence is B because it concludes the passage by mentioning that cheese is available to poor classes because of the mass production.

Thus the correct sequence is ECADB.

Hence, the correct option is (A).

28. The first sentence is E as it start discussing about the origination of cheese making.

The second sentence is C as it mentions the time when the process of cheese making started.

The third sentence is A as it informs about the first factory of cheese which was opened in Switzerland.

The fourth sentence is D as it mentions the consequence of preparing cheese in the factories.

The fifth sentence is B because it concludes the passage by mentioning that cheese is available to poor classes because of the mass production.

Thus the correct sequence is ECADB.

Hence, the correct option is (B).

29. The first sentence is E as it start discussing about the origination of cheese making.

The second sentence is C as it mentions the time when the process of cheese making started.

The third sentence is A as it informs about the first factory of cheese which was opened in Switzerland.

The fourth sentence is D as it mentions the consequence of preparing cheese in the factories.

The fifth sentence is B because it concludes the passage by mentioning that cheese is available to poor classes because of the mass production.

Thus the correct sequence is ECADB.

Hence, the correct option is (B).

30. The first sentence is E as it start discussing about the origination of cheese making.

The second sentence is C as it mentions the time when the process of cheese making started.

The third sentence is A as it informs about the first factory of cheese which was opened in Switzerland.

The fourth sentence is D as it mentions the consequence of preparing cheese in the factories.

The fifth sentence is B because it concludes the passage by mentioning that cheese is available to poor classes because of the mass production.

Thus the correct sequence is ECADB.

Hence, the correct option is (A).

31. Given,

On sports day in a school, 8 students took part in a race. They were all made to stand in a straight line. Sumit was standing 5th from the right end and there are 3 students standing in between Sumit and Ritesh.

As we can see,

Thus, the rank of Ritesh from the left end of the line is 8th.

Hence, the correct option is (C).

32. According to the given information, their sequence in the order of height in the queue is as follows-

Shrikant < Neelima = Neelima $>$ Shrikant ...(i)

Pratima $>$ Shrikant ...(ii)

Hembram > Subhash > Neelima...(iii)

Neelima > Pratima ...(iv)

Here ' $>$ ' means 'longer than' and '<' means 'shorter than'.

On arranging their order from equations (i), (ii), (iii) and (iv),

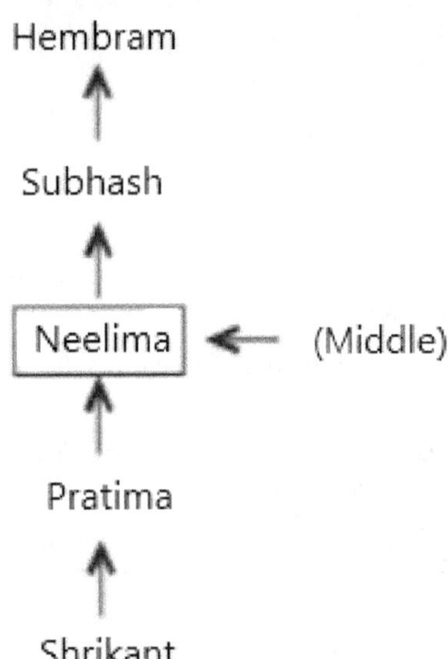

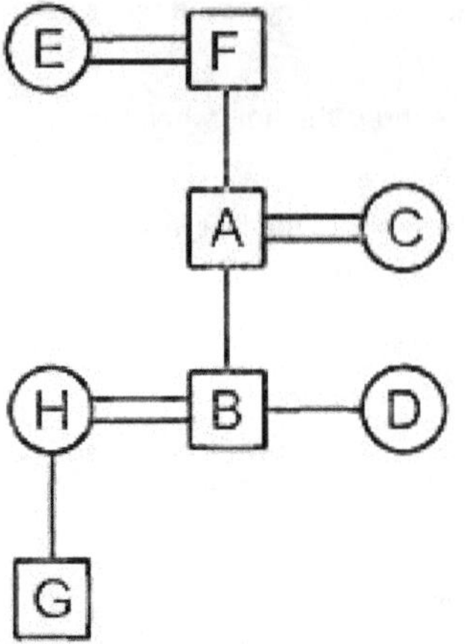

Thus, Neelima will be right in the middle of the row.

Hence, the correct option is (B).

Ques (33-35): From the given information,

Symbol in Diagram	Meaning
⃝	Female
☐	Male
═══	Married Couple
───	Siblings
│	Difference of A Generation

1. F is father of A and B is grandson of E.

2. C is daughter-in-law of E, who is grandmother of B.

3. A is father of B and D which are of different gender.

4. G is the son of H, who is the wife of B.

33. Thus, D is the daughter of C.

Hence, the correct option is (C).

34. Thus, in the family A and C is one of the couples.

Hence, the correct option is (A).

35. 1) C is the father of H - False (As C is the mother of H)

2) B and D are cousins - False (As B and D are brother and sister)

3) E and F are married couple - True

4) D is uncle of G - False (As D is aunt of G)

5) H is the brother-in-law of D - False (As H is the sister-in-law of D)

Thus, E and F are married couple is the correct statement.

Hence, the correct option is (C).

Ques (36-40): Persons: Amar, Dinesh, Golu, Huma, Pooja, Qamrun, Raju, and Sultan.

(1) Sultan sits in the row facing south, to the immediate right of Raju.

(2) Both Sultan and Raju did not sit any extreme end of the row.

(3) Raju faces Huma, who is second to the right of Golu.

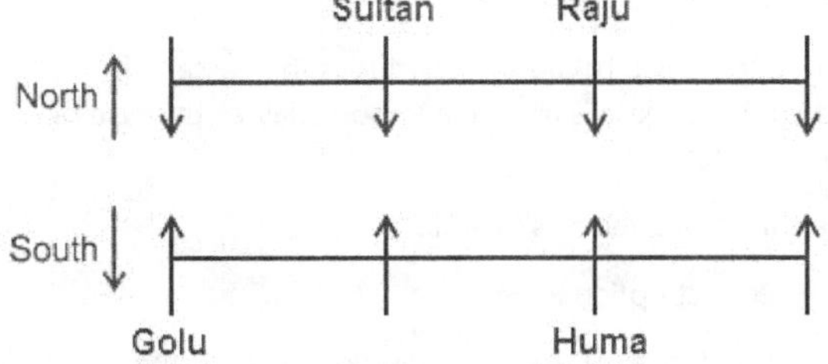

(4) Amar sits immediate left of Huma.

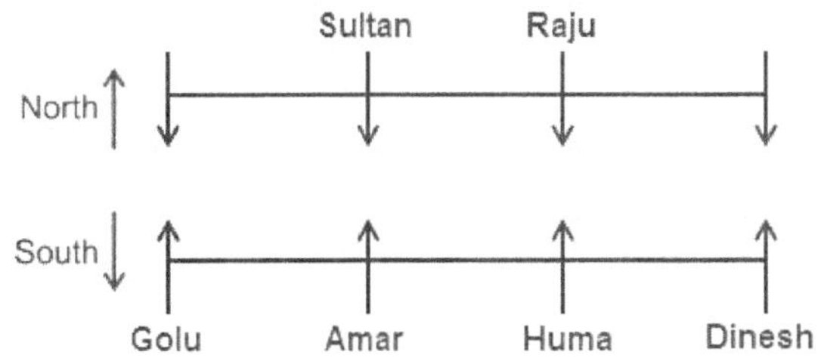

(5) Pooja did not face Dinesh.

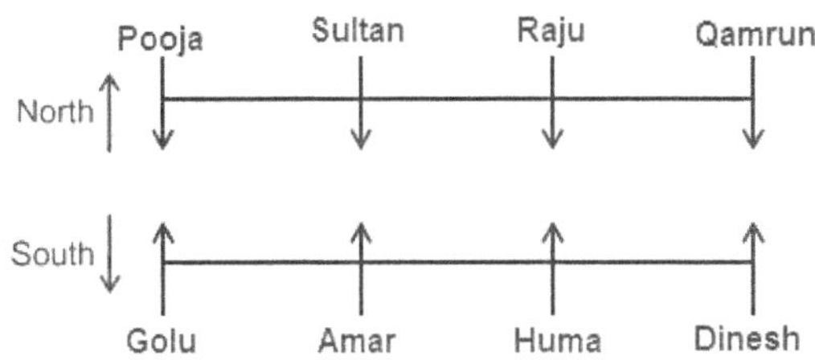

36. Therefore, Golu and Qamrun sits at an extreme end of the row.

Hence, the correct option is (A).

37. Therefore, two places to its left is the correct answer.

Hence, the correct option is (D).

38. Therefore, none of these true.

Hence, the correct option is (E).

39. Therefore, Dinesh sits third to the right of Golu.

Hence, the correct option is (B).

40. Therefore, Sultan sits between Pooja and Raju.

Hence, the correct option is (C).

Ques (41-45):Given:

People: L, M, N, O, P, Q, R, and S are sitting around a circular table. E

Bank: Canara, Bank of India (BOI), Central Bank of India (CBI), Bank of Baroda (BOB), Indian Bank (IB), Union Bank of India (UBI), Oriental Bank of Commerce (OBC) and Dena Bank (DB).

Four of them are facing towards the center while others are facing outside the center.

1) N is facing the center and is to the immediate right of both L and Q. L is facing the opposite direction of N.

2) R is fourth to the left of Q.

3) Neither R nor Q is an immediate neighbor of O.

4) L is working in Canara Bank and sits third to the right of the one who is working in Indian Bank.

5) The one who is working in Union Bank of India sits second to the left of the one who is working in Canara Bank.

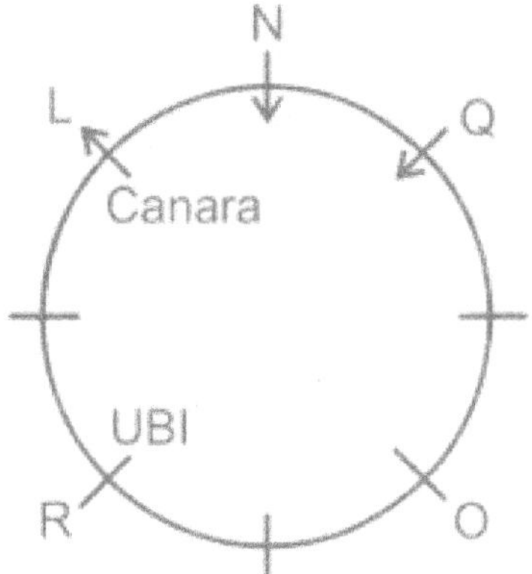

6) The one who works in Bank of India sits exactly between L and Q and adjacent to them.

7) The one who is working in Oriental Bank of Commerce sits second to the right of O.

8) P sits third to the left of L.

9) O is third to the right of S.

10) M and R faces the same direction.

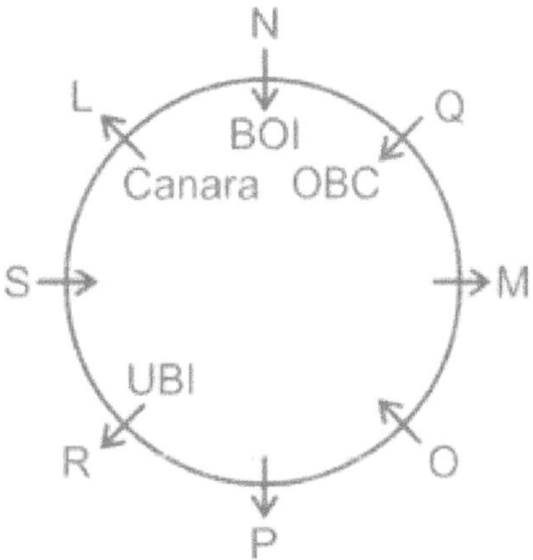

11) The one who is working in Indian Bank is to the immediate left of O, who is not working in Dena Bank.

12) The one who works in the Central Bank of India sits second to the right of the one who works in the Bank of India.

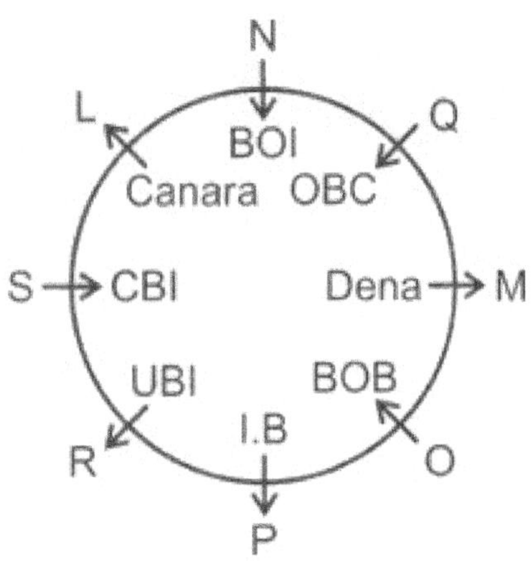

41. So, O works in the Bank of Baroda.

Hence, the correct option is (D).

42. So, O is sitting to the immediate left of the one who works in the Indian Bank.

Hence, the correct option is (E).

43. So, R is sitting opposite to Q.

Hence, the correct option is (A).

44. So, L works in the Canara Bank.

Hence, the correct option is (C).

45. So, N is sitting to the immediate left of the one who works in the Oriental Bank of Commerce.

Hence, the correct option is (D).

46. We draw the least possible Venn diagram:

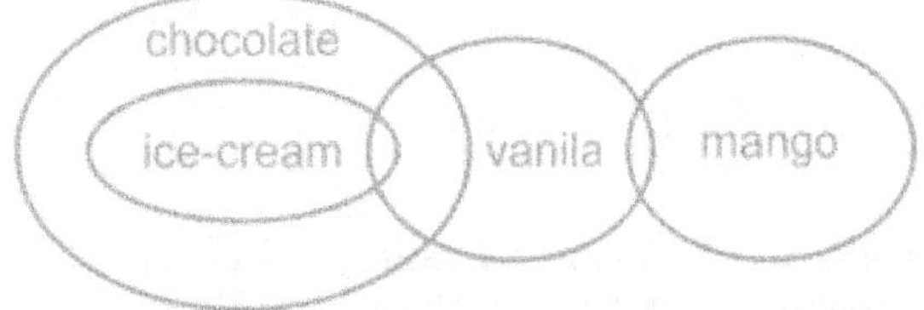

Conclusions:

I. Some ice cream being vanilla is a possibility → False (Some ice cream is definitely vanilla. Hence, the possibility is false) wrong

II. Some mango is chocolate → It's possible but not definite.

So, Neither conclusion I nor II follows.

Hence, the correct option is (D).

47. The least possible Venn diagram for the given statements is as follows,

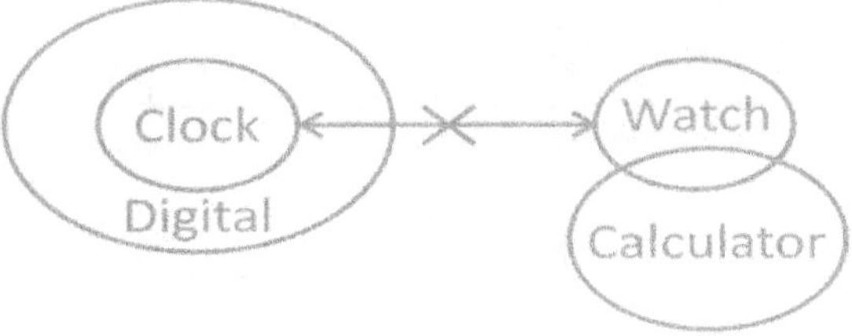

Conclusions:

I. All Watches being Digital is a possibility → Possibility is true.

II. No calculator is a Clock → False.

III. Some Digitals are Clocks → it's true.

So, the conclusion I and III follow.

Hence, the correct option is (C).

48. The possible Venn diagram is:

I. Some chairs are key → It is a definite case, hence true.

II. Some box are chairs → It is not a definite case, hence false.

Thus, only conclusion I follow.

Hence, the correct option is (A).

49. The least possible Venn diagram is given below:

I) some Yellow is not Black → True (As some yellow is white and no white is black, so some yellow is not black is true).

II) Few silver is black → True(It is True as directly seen in the figure).

III) All White can never be Silver → False

So, the correct answer is the conclusion I and II follow.

Hence, the correct option is (C).

50. The least possible Venn diagram is shown below:

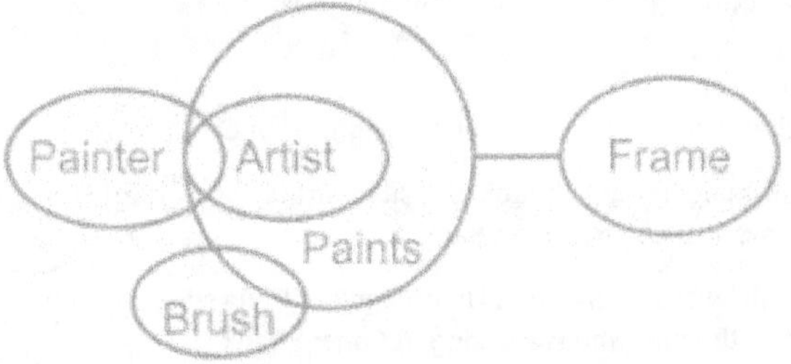

I. Some Paints are Painter → True

II. Some Brush are not Paint → True (Because in the statement it is given that strictly only a few brush are paint which indicates that there are some brush which are not paint)

III. Some Brush are Artist → false

So, the correct answer is only I and II follows.

Hence, the correct option is (A).

Ques (51-55): Given series:

Left side F @ 5 3 R $ J P E 1 H % I 8 4 B 6 # A W 2 U G C * 9 & Z N M © C Right side

51. 1) Symbols which are immediately preceded by an alphabet and followed by a number:

Required order is, Alphabet → Symbol → Number

F @ 5 3 R $ J P E 1 H % I 8 4 B 6 # A W 2 U G C * 9 & Z N M © C

Hence, there are 2 symbols which are immediately preceded by an alphabet and followed by a number: F @ 5 and C * 9.

Hence, the correct option is (A).

52. 1) If all the numbers are dropped:

Left side F @ R $ J P E H % I B # A W U G C * & Z N M © C Right side

2) 11th element from the right end is: W

Then, the letter/number that is eleventh from the right end is 'W'.

Hence, the correct option is (C).

53. As, left – Left = Left

18th from the left – 10th from the left = 8th from the left

Clearly, 8th from the left is 'P'.

Hence, the correct option is (D).

54. Here, the group is formed in which second element is third to the right of the first element, and the third element is just before the second element.

3 J $ → F @ 5 3 R $ J P E 1 H % I 8 4 B 6 # A W 2 U G C * 9 & Z N M © C

E % H → F @ 5 3 R $ J P E 1 H % I 8 4 B 6 # A W 2 U G C * 9 & Z N M © C

2 W → F @ 5 3 R $ J P E 1 H % I 8 4 B 6 # A W 2 U G C * 9 & Z N M © C

Z © M → F @ 5 3 R $ J P E 1 H % I 8 4 B 6 # A W 2 U G C * 9 & Z N M © C

U * 9 → F @ 5 3 R $ J P E 1 H % I 8 4 B 6 # A W 2 U G C * 9 & Z N M © C

So, U * 9 does not belong to the group.

Hence, the correct option is (E).

55. Consonants which are immediately preceded by a number but not immediately followed by a symbol:

The required order is: Number → Consonant → Number / Alphabet

F @ 5 3 R $ J P E 1 H % I 8 4 B 6 # A W 2 U G C * 9 & Z N M © C

So, there is only one consonant which is immediately preceded by a number but not immediately followed by a symbol: '4 B 6'

Hence, the correct option is (B).

56. Given Statements: P ≤ Q > W = K; K < X; X = P > L; N < L

On Combining: P ≤ Q > W = K < X = P > L > N

Conclusions:

I. Q = P → False (as P ≤ Q → thus the clear relation between P and Q cannot be determined.)

II. Q > P → False (as P ≤ Q → thus the clear relation between P and Q cannot be determined.)

Both Conclusion I and II are False.

Therefore, Conclusions I and II form a Complementary pair.

So, The correct answer is "Either I or II follows".

Hence, the correct option is (E).

57. Given statements: P ≥ S < R, T = Q > P, U ≤ L < T

On combining: U ≤ L < T = Q > P ≥ S < R

Conclusions:

I. T > S → True (as T = Q > P ≥ S → T > S)

II. R ≥ T → False (as T = Q > P ≥ S < R → thus clear relation between R and T cannot be determined)

So, only conclusion I is true.

Hence, the correct option is (A).

58. According to the English alphabet series and its positional value:

Alphabets	A	B	C	D	E	F	G	H	I	J	K	L	M
Positional value	1	2	3	4	5	6	7	8	9	10	11	12	13
Positional value	26	25	24	23	22	21	20	19	18	17	16	15	14
Alphabets	Z	Y	X	W	V	U	T	S	R	Q	P	0	N

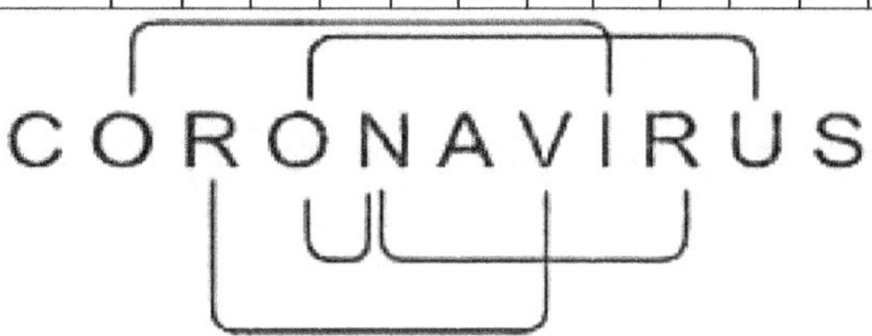

So, 5 letters between them in the word as in the alphabet (both forward & backward).

Hence, the correct option is (A).

59. Given:

A ≥ B = C < D; D = E > F

On Combining:

A ≥ B = C < D = E > F

Conclusions:

I. B < E→ True (as B = C < D = E; therefore B < E)

II. A ≥ C→ True (as A ≥ B = C; therefore A ≥ C)

So, both conclusions I and II are true.

Hence, the correct option is (D).

60. Statement:

P = U < H < K ≤ G > N; D ≤ K

Conclusion:

I. D ≥ U → False (D ≤ K > H > U = P; the clear relation between D and U cannot be determined)

II. P > D → False (P = U < H < K ≥ D; the clear relation between D and U cannot be determined)

So, the conclusion I and II forms complementary pair.

So, either conclusion I or II is true.

Hence, the correct option is (D).

61. Given Statements: T ≤ U > S; H > G ≥ M = U; S ≥ R = Q ≥ P

On Combining: T ≤ U > S ≥ R = Q ≥ P; H > G ≥ M = U

Conclusion:

I. S > P → False (As S ≥ R = Q ≥ P, clearly S ≥ P).

II. P ≤ S → True (As S ≥ R = Q ≥ P, clearly S ≥ P).

So, Only conclusion II follow.

Hence, the correct option is (B).

62. Word: SKEPTICAL

First letter = S; Fifth letter = T; Eighth letter = A; Ninth letter = L

Letters given: STAL

Words possible: LAST, SALT, SLAT

Clearly, Y is the correct answer.

Hence, the correct option is (E).

63. According to the English alphabet series and its positional value:

Alpha bets	A	B	C	D	E	F	G	H	I	J	K	L	M
Positional value	1	2	3	4	5	6	7	8	9	10	11	12	13
Positional value	26	25	24	23	22	21	20	19	18	17	16	15	14
Alpha	Z	Y	X	W	V	U	T	S	R	Q	P	O	N

bets

The pattern followed is,

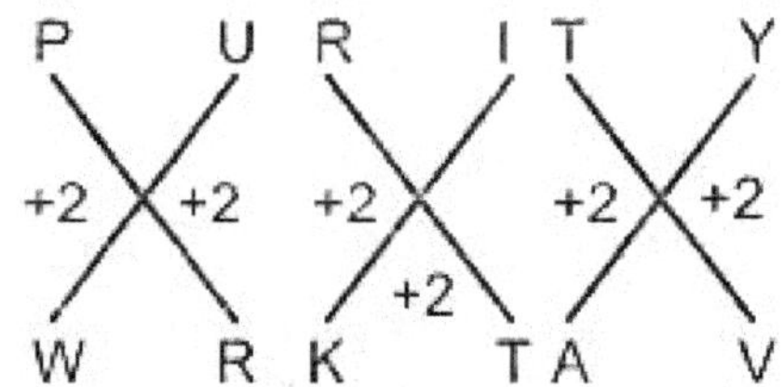

Similarly,

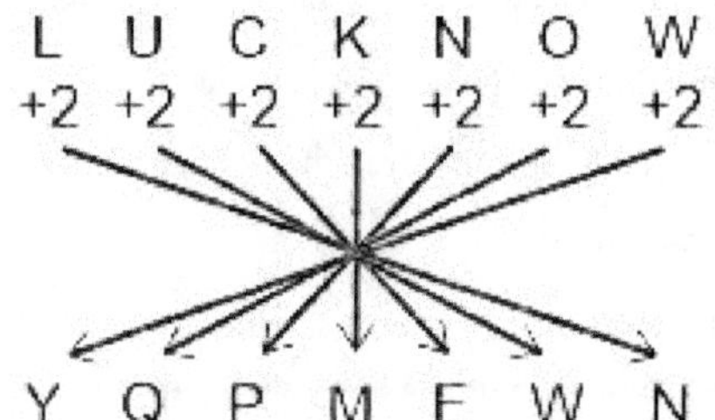

Therefore, "WRKTAV" is the correct answer.

Hence, the correct option is (D).

64. The pattern for the code is as follows;

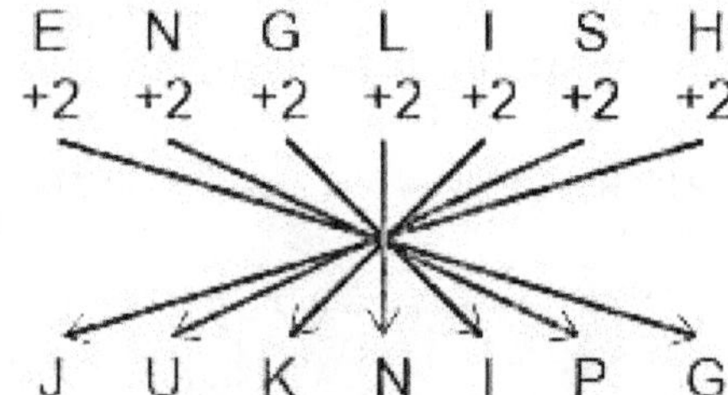

Each letter in the word is two-step ahead of the corresponding letter and also in a criss-cross format.

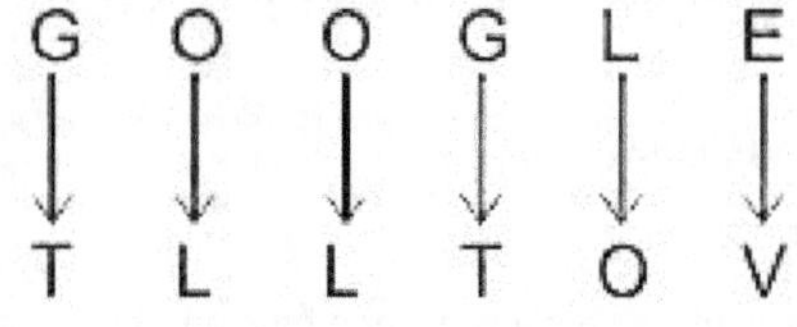

Therefore, ENGLISH is coded as JUKNIPG.

Hence, the correct option is (D).

65. The pattern for the code is as follows,

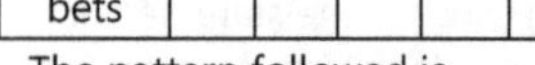

Here the combination is a reversal of the first 13 letters of the Alphabet series (A to M) to the last 13 letters (N to Z) and then changing the given letters to the facing letters in the given series.

A B C D E F G H I J K L M
Z Y X W V U T S R Q P O N

Similarly, there is a reverse alphabetical order for REALME.

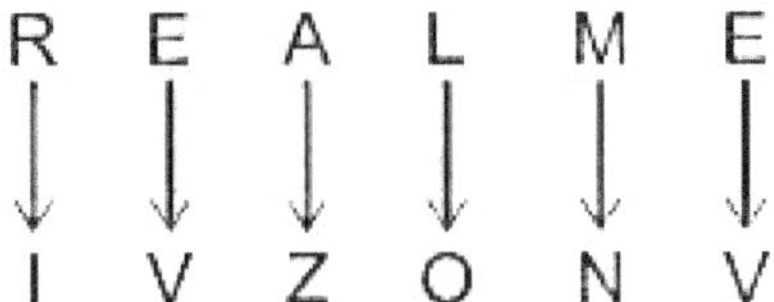

So, IVZONV is the code for REALME.

Hence, the correct option is (C).

66. The average of 9 digits is given as 11

Now, each of these digits is multiplied by 5

We know, if each quantity is multiplied by certain value 'k', then the new average is also multiplied by 'k'

Here, k = 5

New average = Old average × k

$\Rightarrow$ New average = 11 × 5

$\Rightarrow$ New average = 55

Again, each of these digits is added by 8 now

Similarly, if each quantity is increased/decreased by "k", the new average is increased/decreased by "k"

Here, k = 8

New average = Old average + k

$\Rightarrow$ New average = 55 + 8

$\therefore$ The new average is 63

Hence, the correct option is (D).

67. I. $15x^2 - 30x - 225 = 0$

$\Rightarrow 15(x^2 - 2x - 15) = 0$

$\Rightarrow x^2 - 2x - 15 = 0$

$\Rightarrow x^2 - 5x + 3x - 15 = 0$

$\Rightarrow x(x - 5) + 3(x - 5) = 0$

$\Rightarrow (x - 5)(x + 3) = 0$

$\Rightarrow x = 5, -3$

II. $12y^2 + 96y + 180 = 0$

$\Rightarrow 12(y^2 + 8y + 15) = 0$

$\Rightarrow y^2 + 8y + 15 = 0$

$\Rightarrow y^2 + 5y + 3y + 15 = 0$

$\Rightarrow y(y + 5) + 3(y + 5) = 0$

$\Rightarrow (y + 5)(y + 3) = 0$

$\Rightarrow y = -5, -3$

Value of x	Value of y	Relation
5	-5	x > y
5	-3	x > y
-3	-5	x > y
-3	-3	x = y

$\therefore x \geq y$

Hence, the correct option is (C).

68. I. $24x^2 + 96x + 90 = 0$

$\Rightarrow 6(4x^2 + 16x + 15) = 0$

$\Rightarrow 4x^2 + 16x + 15 = 0$

$\Rightarrow 4x^2 + 10x + 6x + 15 = 0$

$\Rightarrow 2x(2x + 5) + 3(2x + 5) = 0$

$\Rightarrow (2x + 5)(2x + 3) = 0$

$\Rightarrow x = \dfrac{-5}{2}, \dfrac{-3}{2}$

II. $28y^2 + 56y + 21 = 0$

$\Rightarrow 7(4y^2 + 8y + 3) = 0$

$\Rightarrow 4y^2 + 8y + 3 = 0$

$\Rightarrow 4y^2 + 6y + 2y + 3 = 0$

$\Rightarrow 2y(2y + 3) + 1(2y + 3) = 0$

$\Rightarrow (2y + 3)(2y + 1) = 0$

$\Rightarrow y = \dfrac{-3}{2}, \dfrac{-1}{2}$

Value of x	Value of y	Relation
$\dfrac{-5}{2}$	$\dfrac{-3}{2}$	x < y
$\dfrac{-5}{2}$	$\dfrac{-1}{2}$	x < y
$\dfrac{-3}{2}$	$\dfrac{-3}{2}$	x = y
$\dfrac{-3}{2}$	$\dfrac{-1}{2}$	x < y

$\therefore x \leq y$

Hence, the correct option is (D).

69. I. $x^2 + 11x + 24 = 0$

$\Rightarrow x^2 + 8x + 3x + 24 = 0$

$\Rightarrow x(x + 8) + 3(x + 8) = 0$

$\Rightarrow (x + 8)(x + 3) = 0$

$\Rightarrow x = -8, -3$

II. $y^2 + 9y + 14 = 0$

$\Rightarrow y^2 + 7y + 2y + 14 = 0$

$\Rightarrow y(y + 7) + 2(y + 7) = 0$

$\Rightarrow (y + 7)(y + 2) = 0$

$\Rightarrow y = -7, -2$

Value of x	Value of y	Relation
-8	-7	x < y
-8	-2	x < y
-3	-7	x > y
-3	-2	x < y

$\therefore$ x = y or the relationship between x and y cannot be established.

Hence, the correct option is (E).

70. I. $x^2 - 9x + 20 = 0$

$\Rightarrow x^2 - 5x - 4x + 20 = 0$

$\Rightarrow x(x - 5) - 4(x - 5) = 0$

$\Rightarrow (x - 5)(x - 4) = 0$

$\Rightarrow x = 5, 4$

II. $y^2 - 11y + 30 = 0$

$\Rightarrow y^2 - 6y - 5y + 30 = 0$

$\Rightarrow y(y - 6) - 5(y - 6) = 0$

$\Rightarrow (y - 6)(y - 5) = 0$

$\Rightarrow y = 6, 5$

Value of x	Value of y	Relation
5	6	x < y
4	6	x < y
5	5	x = y
4	5	x < y

$\therefore x \leq y$

Hence, the correct option is (D).

71. I. $x^2 - 20x + 91 = 0$

$\Rightarrow x^2 - 13x - 7x + 91 = 0$

$\Rightarrow x(x - 13) - 7(x - 13) = 0$

$\Rightarrow (x - 13)(x - 7) = 0$

$\Rightarrow x = 7, 13$

II. $y^2 + 16y + 63 = 0$

$\Rightarrow y^2 + 9y + 7y + 63 = 0$

$\Rightarrow y(y + 9) + 7(y + 9) = 0$

$\Rightarrow (y + 9)(y + 7) = 0$

$\Rightarrow y = -7, -9$

x	y	Relation
7	-7	x > y
7	-9	x > y
13	-7	x > y
13	-9	x > y

$\therefore x > y$

Hence, the correct option is (A).

72. Students in marketing $= \left(\frac{20}{100}\right) \times 6000 = 1200$

Students in IR $= \left(\frac{20}{100}\right) \times 6000 = 1200$

Total number of students in marketing and IR $= 1200 + 1200 = 2400$

$\therefore$ Total number of students having specialization in Marketing and IR is 2400.

Hence, the correct option is (C).

73. Percentage of students having IT as specialization $= 18\%$

Percentage of students having IB as specialization $= 11\%$

Required ratio $= 18\% : 11\%$

$= 18 : 11$

$\therefore$ The required ratio is $18 : 11$.

Hence, the correct option is (A).

74. Students in HR $= \left(\frac{16}{100}\right) \times 6000 = 960$

Students in Finance $= \left(\frac{15}{100}\right) \times 6000 = 900$

Required difference $= 960 - 900 = 60$

$\therefore$ The difference between the students in HR and students in finance is 60.

Hence, the correct option is (B).

75. Percentage of students in HR $= 16\%$

Percentage of students in Marketing $= 20\%$

Required percentage $= \left(\frac{16\%}{20\%}\right) \times 100 = 80$

$\therefore$ Students in HR is 80% of students in marketing.

Hence, the correct option is (D).

76. Students in IB initially $= \left(\frac{11}{100}\right) \times 6000 = 660$

Students in IB after increment $= \left(\frac{11}{100}\right) \times 8000 = 880$

Difference $= 880 - 660 = 220$

Hence, the correct option is (B).

77. Given:

Total rupees $=$ Rs. 8544

Let the ratio be x

Ratio is the smallest digits of that number

Formula:

$$\text{Percentage} = \left(\frac{\text{Actual value}}{\text{Original value}}\right) \times 100$$

So numbers ratio are $6x$, $11x$ and $15x$

According to question,

$\Rightarrow 6x + 11x + 15x = 8544$

$\Rightarrow 32x = 8544$

$\Rightarrow x = 267$

So,

A's Rupees $= 6 \times 267 = 1602$

A's spend his money $= 20\% \times 1602 = 320.4$

A's left with rupees $= 1281.6$

B's rupees $= 11 \times 267 = 2937$

B's increased his money by $50\% = 50\% \times 2937 = 1468.5$

B's rupees becomes Rs. 4405.5

C's rupees $= 15 \times 267 = 4005$

No change in C' rupees

Required ratio of new rupees in A, B and C $=$ $1281.6 : 4405.5 : 4005$

$\Rightarrow 12816 : 44055 : 40050$

$\therefore$ Ratio of rupees A, B and C $= 12816 : 44055 : 40050 = 16 : 55 : 50$

Hence, the correct option is (A).

78. Given:

A can do a work in 24 days, B can do the same work in 48 days and C can do the same work in 72 days.

In first case,

A can do the work in 24 days

B can do the work in 48 days

C can do the work in 72 days

The ratio of their efficiency will be A : B : C $= \dfrac{1}{24} : \dfrac{1}{48} : \dfrac{1}{72} = 6 : 3 : 2$

A will get $\dfrac{6}{(6+3+2)} = \dfrac{6}{11}$

$= \dfrac{6}{11} \times 4400$ of the total amount which will be equal to Rs. 2400

But in the second case only A and C work,

The efficiency of A : C $= \dfrac{1}{24} : \dfrac{1}{72} = 3 : 1$

So A will get now $\dfrac{3}{(1+3)} = \left(\dfrac{3}{4}\right)$

$= \dfrac{3}{4} \times 4400$ of the total amount which will be equal to Rs. 3300

$\therefore$ Extra money earned by A = Rs. $(3300 - 2400)$ = Rs. 900

Hence, the correct option is (D).

79. Given:

The cost price of item A is equal to the cost price of item B

MP of item A $= 160\%$ of CP

MP of item B $= 150\%$ of CP

The marked price of item B is 600 after increasing by 50%

CP of item B

CP $\times \dfrac{150}{100} = 600$

The cost price of item B $=$ Rs. 400

CP of A $=$ CP of B

Marked price of item A $= 400 \times \dfrac{160}{100}$

MP of item A $=$ Rs. 640

MP of item B $=$ Rs. 600

The selling price of item A and item B after giving a 10% discount

SP of Item A $= 640 \times \dfrac{90}{100} = 576$

SP of Item B $= 600 \times \dfrac{90}{100} = 540$

Difference between the selling price of item A and item B $= 576 - 540$

$=$ Rs. 36

Hence, the correct option is (B).

80. From statements I and II,

Let the total work be 1,

Work done by Rahul and Amit $= \dfrac{1}{4}$

Work done by Anil $= 1 - \left(\dfrac{1}{4}\right) = \dfrac{3}{4}$

Share of Anil will be proportional to work done by him,

Share of Anil $= \left(\dfrac{3}{4}\right) \times$ Rs. $24,000$

$= $ Rs. $18,000$

$\therefore$ The data in both the statement I and II together are necessary to answer.

Hence, the correct option is (E).

81. From statement I,

Let the 'E' is an event of probability,

Number of favorable outcomes: ${}^4C_2 = \dfrac{4!}{(2!\times 2!)} = 6$

Total number of outcomes $= {}^9C_2 = \dfrac{9!}{(2!\times 7!)} = 36$

$P(E) = \left(\dfrac{6}{36}\right)$

$\Rightarrow P(E) = \dfrac{1}{6}$

From statement II,

The number of pencils of each colour is not given. So, we can't get the answer.

$\therefore$ The data in statement I alone is sufficient to answer the question, while the data in statement II alone is not sufficient to answer the question.

Hence, the correct option is (A).

82. From statement I and II,

$S.I = \dfrac{PRT}{100}$

$\Rightarrow 1190 = \dfrac{(\text{Principal}\times 7\times 2)}{100}$

$\Rightarrow \dfrac{(1190\times 100)}{(2\times 7)} = \text{Principal}$

$\Rightarrow$ Rs. $8,500 = \text{Principal}$

$\therefore$ The data in both the statement I and II together are necessary to answer.

Hence, the correct option is (C).

83. From Statement I,

Profit earned $=$ Rs. $3,20,000$

It is not sufficient to answer the question,

From statement II,

The selling price was twice the cost price,

So,

Profit $= 6,40,000 \div 2$

$= 3,20,000$

Selling price $= 3,20,000 \times 2$

$= 6,40,000$

Selling price $=$ cost price $+$ profit

$\Rightarrow 6,40,000 =$ cost price $+3,20,000$

$\Rightarrow$ cost price $= 3,20,000$

So, Statement II alone is not sufficient to answer the question.

$\therefore$ Both statements are necessary to answer the question.

Hence, the correct option is (C).

84. I. We know the speed of Nisha and a relation between speed of Rohan and Ram can be established, but no relation between speed of Nisha and Rohan can be established.

So, statement I. alone is insufficient.

II. Relation between speed of Ram and Nisha can be established but no relation with the speed of Rohan can be established.

So, Statement II. alone is Insufficient.

By combining the two statements we have the speed of Nisha and a relation between speed of Nisha and Ram and subsequently Ram and Rohan can be formed.

$\therefore$ Statement I and Statement II together is sufficient.

Hence, the correct option is (E).

85. Given:

$[(-251) \times 21 \times (-12)] \div ? = 63$

$\Rightarrow \dfrac{[(-251)\times 21\times(-12)]}{63} = ?$

$\Rightarrow \dfrac{(251\times 12)}{3} = ?$

$\Rightarrow 251 \times 4 = ?$

$\Rightarrow ? = 1004$

Hence, the correct option is (B).

86. Given:

22% of $4350 + 47.25 \times 4 + 17 \times 51 - 1013 = ?$

$\Rightarrow 957 + 47.25 \times 4 + 17 \times 51 - 1013 = ?$

$\Rightarrow 957 + 189 + 867 - 1013 = ?$

$\Rightarrow 2013 - 1013 = ?$

$\Rightarrow ? = 1000$

Hence, the correct option is (D).

87. Given:

$888 + 88.8 + 8.88 + 8 - 1.88 - 18.8 = ?$

$\Rightarrow 993.68 - 1.88 - 18.8 = ?$

$\Rightarrow 993.68 - 20.68$

$\Rightarrow ? = 973$

Hence, the correct option is (D).

88. Given:

Initially, the ratio of Rockford and Vodka in the mixture $= 4:7$

11 liters of mixture is drawn off from the vessel.

After drawing off 11 liters the ratio of Rockford and Vodka becomes $= 1:2$

Now,

The initially, the ratio of Rockford and Vodka in the mixture $= 4:7$

Let the initial quantity of Rockford in the vessel be $4x$ liters and the initial quantity of Vodka in the vessel be $7x$ liters.

Now, 11 liters of mixture is drawn off from the vessel.

Quantity of Rockford in 11 liters of the mixture drawn off $=$
$11 \times \dfrac{4}{4+7} = 11 \times \dfrac{4}{11} = 4$ liters

Quantity of Vodka in 11 liters of the mixture drawn off $=$
$11 - 4 = 7$ liters

So,

Quantity of Rockford remaining in the mixture after 11 liters is drawn off $= 4x - 4$

Quantity of Vodka remaining in the mixture after 11 liters is drawn off $= 7x - 7$

Since the vessel is filled with Vodka after 11 liters of mixture is drawn off, the quantity of Vodka in the mixture,

$= 7x - 7 + 11$

$= 7x + 4$

After this the given that the ratio of Rockford and Vodka becomes $1:2$.

$(4x - 4):(7x + 4) = 1:2$

$\Rightarrow 2 \times (4x - 4) = 1 \times (7x + 4)$

$\Rightarrow 8x - 8 = 7x + 4$

$\Rightarrow x = 12$

Now the initial quantity of Rockford in the vessel $= 4x = 12 \times 4 = 48$ liters

Hence, the correct option is (C).

89. The series follows the following pattern:

$1 \times 1 + 1 = 2$

$2 \times 2 + 2 = 6$

$6 \times 3 + 3 = 21$

$21 \times 4 + 4 = 88$

$88 \times 5 + 5 = 445$

$\therefore$ The missing term in the series is 445.

Hence, the correct option is (C).

90. The series follows the following pattern:

$130 - 15 = 115$

$115 + 20 = 135$

$135 - 25 = 110$

$110 + 30 = 140$

$140 - 35 = 105$

$\therefore$ The missing term in the series is 140.

Hence, the correct option is (C).

91. The series follows the following pattern:

$4 \times 0.5 = 2$

$2 \times 1 = 2$

$2 \times 1.5 = 3$

$3 \times 2 = 6$

$6 \times 2.5 = 15$

$\therefore$ The missing term in the series is 6.

Hence, the correct option is (D).

92. The series follows the following pattern:

$17 \times 1 + 5 = 22$

$22 \times 2 + 4 = 48$

$48 \times 3 + 3 = 147$

$147 \times 4 + 2 = 590$

$590 \times 5 + 1 = 2951$

$\therefore$ The missing term in the series is 590.

Hence, the correct option is (C).

93. The series follows the following pattern:

$1^3 + 1 = 2$

$2^3 + 2 = 10$

$3^3 + 3 = 30$

$4^3 + 4 = 68$

$5^3 + 5 = 130$

$6^3 + 6 = 222$

$\therefore$ The missing term in the series is 130.

Hence, the correct option is (B).

94. Given:

$$28\frac{4}{7}\% \text{ of } 2835 + 66\frac{2}{3}\% \text{ of } 1245 = 1156 + x^2$$

$$\Rightarrow \frac{200}{7}\% \text{ of } 2835 + \frac{200}{3}\% \text{ of } 1245 = 1156 + x^2$$

$$\Rightarrow \frac{200}{7 \times 100} \times 2835 + \frac{200}{3 \times 100} \times 1245 = 1156 + x^2$$

$$\Rightarrow 2 \times 405 + 2 \times 415 = 1156 + x^2$$

$$\Rightarrow 810 + 830 = 1156 + x^2$$

$$\Rightarrow x^2 = 1640 - 1156 = 484$$

$$\Rightarrow x = \sqrt{484}$$

$$\Rightarrow x = 22$$

Hence, the correct option is (D).

95. Given:

$$90\% \text{ of } 50 + \left(\frac{1}{2}\right) \times 30 - 45 \div ? = 57$$

$$\Rightarrow 45 + 15 - 45 \div ? = 57$$

$$\Rightarrow 45 + 15 - 57 = \frac{45}{?}$$

$$\Rightarrow 60 - 57 = \frac{45}{?}$$

$$\Rightarrow 3 = \frac{45}{?}$$

$$\Rightarrow ? = \frac{45}{3}$$

$$\Rightarrow ? = 15$$

Hence, the correct option is (A).

96. Given:

$$18 + 12 \times 6 - 12 \div 3 + 77 \div 11 = ?$$

$$\Rightarrow 18 + 72 - 4 + 7 = ?$$

$$\Rightarrow 18 + 68 + 7 = ?$$

$$\Rightarrow ? = 93$$

Hence, the correct option is (C).

97. Given:

$$(14)^2 \times 10 \div 4 - (15)^2 + 16 = ?^2 + 5^2$$

$$\Rightarrow 196 \times \left(\frac{5}{2}\right) - 225 + 16 = ?^2 + 25$$

$$\Rightarrow 98 \times 5 - 209 - 25 = ?^2$$

$$\Rightarrow 490 - 234 = ?^2$$

$$\Rightarrow 256 = ?^2$$

$$\Rightarrow ? = 16$$

Hence, the correct option is (B).

98. Given:

$$60\% \text{ of } 135 - \left(\sqrt{729} + ?\right) = 4$$

$$\Rightarrow 135 \times \left(\frac{60}{100}\right) - (27 + ?) = 4$$

$$\Rightarrow 135 \times \left(\frac{3}{5}\right) - 27 - ? = 4$$

$$\Rightarrow 81 - 27 - 4 = ?$$

$$\Rightarrow 50 = ?$$

Hence, the correct option is (C).

99. Given:

$$35\% \text{ of } 400 - 24\% \text{ of } 12.5 = 110 + ?$$

$$\Rightarrow \left(\frac{35}{100}\right) \times 400 - \left(\frac{24}{100}\right) \times \left(\frac{25}{2}\right) = 110 + ?$$

$$\Rightarrow 35 \times 4 - \left(\frac{12}{4}\right) = 110 + ?$$

$$\Rightarrow 140 - 3 - 110 = ?$$

$$\Rightarrow ? = 27$$

Hence, the correct option is (C).

100. Given:

$$52\% \text{ of } 150 + 15 \times 35 - \sqrt{841} \times 8 = ?$$

$$\Rightarrow 78 + 525 - 29 \times 8 = ?$$

$$\Rightarrow 78 + 525 - 232 = ?$$

$$\Rightarrow ? = 371$$

Hence, the correct option is (C).

English Language

Ques (1-5):Direction: Select the most appropriate word to fill in the blanks.

Q.1 He plays the flute ______.
A. beautiful
B. beauty
C. beautifully
D. more beautiful
E. pretty

Q.2 I worked hard ______ that I can catch up to you.
A. there   **B.** so   **C.** by   **D.** since
E. for

Q.3 She ______ me to tie her bow.
A. say   **B.** ask   **C.** said   **D.** asked
E. asking

Q.4 He will return ______ a month.
A. in   **B.** within   **C.** into   **D.** on
E. by

Q.5 Every man and every woman ______ the right to express his or her views.
A. has   **B.** have   **C.** had   **D.** was
E. is

Q.6 Direction: Select the most appropriate ANTONYM of the given word.
Exonerate
A. Vindicate
B. Sentence
C. Acquit
D. Absolve
E. Assigned

Q.7 Direction: Choose from the options, the correct synonym of the given word:
Expediency

[Allahabad High Court ARO, 2020]

A. Expense
B. Sentence
C. Disadvantage
D. Altruism
E. Convenience

Q.8 Select the incorrectly spelt word from the given alternatives.
A. Muliebrity
B. Lalochezia
C. Verbatim
D. Toople
E. None of the above

Q.9 Select the word which is wrongly spelt.
A. Onerous
B. Tentetive
C. Deleterious
D. Parochial
E. Ostentation

Q.10 Select the correctly spelt word.
[NCHM JEE (Hotel Mgmt & Catering), 2018]

A. Manoeuvre
B. Maneuever
C. Maneuvar
D. Manuever
E. None of the above

Ques (11-15):Direction: In this question, a sentence has been given with some of its part in bold. To make the sentence grammatically and idiomatically correct you have to replace the bold part with the correct alternative given below. If the sentence is correct as it is, mark 'No correction required' as your answer.

Q.11 The man who has committed such a heinous crime **must get the mostly severe** punishment.
A. be getting the mostly severely
B. have got the most severely
C. must get the most severe
D. have been getting the severe most
E. No correction required

Q.12 I rang the Colonel and asked him to **put my name forward** for the vacancy in Zurich.
A. put my name up
B. put my name around
C. put out my name
D. put my name through
E. No correction required

Q.13 According to the International Migration Outlook 2017 report on OECD member countries, **Indians ought to be among top asylum-seekers in other countries.**
A. Indians are among top asylum-seekers in other countries
B. Indians are amidst top asylum-seekers in other countries
C. Indians are said to be among the top asylum-seekers in other countries
D. Indian's are among maximum asylum-seekers in all countries
E. No correction required

Q.14 The US and Australia have jointly test-fired a hypersonic missile capable of moving **at a speed eight times more fast** than sound, as part of $54-million research project.
A. at a speed eight times as fast as
B. at a speed eight times faster
C. with the speed eight times as faster as
D. at a speed eight times much fast
E. No correction required

Q.15 World football's governing body FIFA lifted the ban it had imposed on the Sudan Football Association (SFA) **for failed to abide to agreements** mentioned in articles 14 and 19 of the FIFA statute.
A. for having failed to abide to agreements
B. for its failure to abide by the agreements
C. for failure to abide by agreement
D. for having failed to abide by the agreement

E. No correction required

Ques (16-20):Direction: Read each sentence to find out whether there is any grammatical error in it. The error, if any will be in one part of the sentence. The number of that part is the answer. If there is no error, the answer is E. i.e. no error. (Ignore the errors of punctuation if any).

Q.16 The Renaissance was (A)/a time to 'reawakening' (B)/in both the arts (C)/and the sciences. (D)/No error (E).

A. A   **B.** B   **C.** C   **D.** D
E. E

Q.17 Nuclear waste will still be (A)/ radioactive even after twenty thousand years (B)/ so it must be disposed (C)/ of very carefully. (D)/ No error (E).

A. A   **B.** B   **C.** C   **D.** D
E. E

Q.18 From the 1970's, (A)/ William's has been the (B)/ most popular ice cream (C)/parlor in town. (D)/ No Error (E)

A. A   **B.** B   **C.** C   **D.** D
E. E

Q.19 The challenge before India is (A)/ to deepening the tactical (B)/ engagement with China (C)/ keeping strategic glitches at bay (D)/. No error.

[IBPS PO, 2019]

A. A   **B.** B   **C.** C   **D.** D
E. E

Q.20 The trip to the airport and the (A)/ flight to Singapore was both uneventful, (B)/ the hotel accommodations were better than they (C)/ could have expected on such short notice. (D)/ No error (E)

[IBPS PO, 2019]

A. A   **B.** B   **C.** C   **D.** D
E. E

Ques (21-25):Direction: Rearrange the following five segments A, B, C, D and E in the proper sequence to form a meaningful paragraph; then answer the questions given below them.

A. NPCIL is a dividend-paying company with the highest credit rating of AAA by CRISIL and CARE

B. At present, NPCIL operates 22 nuclear power reactors with an installed capacity of 6780 MW.

C. NPCIL is responsible for siting, design, construction, commissioning and operation of nuclear power reactors.

D. Nuclear Power Corporation of India Limited (NPCIL), formed in 1987, is a Public Sector Enterprise under the administrative control of Department of Atomic Energy (DAE).

E. Safety is given overriding priority in all facets of nuclear power reactors.

Q.21 Which is the first sentence according to the paragraph?

[IBPS Clerk, 2021], [SBI Clerk, 2021]

A. A   **B.** B   **C.** C   **D.** D

E. E

Q.22 Which is the second sentence according to the passage?

[IBPS Clerk, 2021], [SBI Clerk, 2021]

A. A   **B.** B   **C.** C   **D.** D
E. E

Q.23 Which is the third sentence according to the paragraph?

[IBPS Clerk, 2021], [SBI Clerk, 2021]

A. A   **B.** B   **C.** C   **D.** D
E. E

Q.24 Which is the fourth sentence according to the paragraph?

[IBPS Clerk, 2021], [SBI Clerk, 2021]

A. A   **B.** B   **C.** C   **D.** D
E. E

Q.25 Which is the fifth sentence according to the paragraph?

[IBPS Clerk, 2021], [SBI Clerk, 2021]

A. A   **B.** B   **C.** C   **D.** D
E. E

Ques (26-30):Direction: Read the passage given below and answer the question that follow by choosing the correct/most appropriate options.

In the present predicament when we are not able to adjust ourselves to the new conditions which science has brought about it is not easy to adopt the principles of non-violence, truth and understanding. But on that ground we should not give up the effort. While the obstinacy of the political leaders puts fear into our hearts, the common sense and conscience of the people of the world give us hope. With the increased velocity of modern changes we do not know what the world will be a hundred years hence. We cannot anticipate the future currents of thought and feeling. But years may go their way, yet the great principal of satya and ahimsa, truth and non-violence, are there to guide us. They are the silent stars keeping holy vigil above a tired and turbulent world. Like Gandhi we may be firm in our conviction that the sun shines above the drifting clouds. We live in an age which is aware of its own defeat and moral coarsening, an age in which old certainties are breaking down, the familiar patterns are tilting and cracking. There is increasing intolerance and embitterment. The creative flame that kindled the great human society is languishing. The human mind in all its baffling strangeness and variety produces contrary types, a Buddha or a Gandhi, a Nero or a Hitler. It is our pride that one of the greatest figures of history lived in our generations, walked with us, spoke to us, taught us the way of civilized living. He who wrongs no one fears no one. He has nothing to hide and so is fearless. He looks everyone in the face. His step is firm, his body upright, and his words are direct and straight. Plato said long ago: 'There always are in the world a few inspired men whose acquaintance is beyond price.'

Q.26 It is not easy to follow the principles of non-violence and truth because ___________.

A. scientific innovations in modern age are not free from violence.

B. science & technology have changed the perception of truth and non-violence.

C. new condition in society and religious beliefs can not exist together.

D. there is the problem of adjustment between emerging new conditions which science has brought about.

E. None of these

Q.27 What according to the writer instils fear into our heart?

A. Lack of honest and committed leaders

B. Overriding ambition of politicians

C. New condition in society and religious beliefs can not exist together

D. Declining moral statements

E. Obstinacy of our political leaders

Q.28 Which of the following is not a characteristic of modern Age?

A. Social coarseness and moral degradation

B. Breaking down of conventional values

C. Reviving of traditional familiar patterns

D. Increasing intolerance and embitterment

E. Overriding ambition of politicians

Q.29 Choose the correct antonym of the word from the given alternatives - "'obstinacy' of the political leaders puts fears into our hearts"

A. Tenacity   **B.** Obduracy

C. Tractability   **D.** Compliance

E. None of these

Q.30 It is difficult to predict the world after hundred years from today because:

A. Science has changed the world

B. Modern society is changing very rapidly

C. Life style is unpredictable

D. Breaking down of conventional values

E. Our thoughts and perceptions are subjects to change

Reasoning Ability

Q.31 Direction: In the following question assuming the given statements to be True, find which of the conclusion among given conclusions is/are definitely true and then give your answers accordingly.

Statement: A > B < C < D; K ≥ L > M = D; G > H ≥ I ≤ J < A

Conclusions:

I. G > A

II. A ≥ G

III. K > I

A. Only I is true   **B.** Only II is true

C. Only III is true   **D.** None true

E. Either I or II true

Ques (32-35):Direction: In the following question assuming the given statements to be True, find which of the conclusion among given conclusions is/are definitely true and then give your answers accordingly.

Q.32 Statements: A ≤ B < C; A ≥ E; C ≤ F

Conclusions:

I. E < C

II. F ≥ E

A. Only conclusion I is true

B. Only conclusion II is true

C. Only conclusion I or II is true

D. Neither conclusion I nor II is true

E. Both conclusions I and II are true

Q.33 Statements: X < M ≤ W; B ≥ L ≥ O; O = X

Conclusions:

I. B > M

II. M ≥ B

III. L < W

A. Only III is True

B. Both I and III are True

C. Either I or II is True

D. Both II and III are True

E. Only II is True

Q.34 Statements: R ≤ A < N ≤ I; K ≥ I; V > A

Conclusions:

I) K ≥ A

II) V > I

III) R ≤ K

A. Only I and II is true

B. Only I is true

C. Only II and III is true

D. Only III is true

E. None of these

Q.35 Statements: U ≤ W ≥ R > S; T > S = V

Conclusions:

I. W < V

II. T < V

A. Only I is true

B. Only II is true

C. Either I or II is true

D. Neither I nor II is true

E. Both I and II is true

Q.36 How many meaningful English words can be formed using the first, third, fourth, and eighth letters of the word 'MAGNIFICENT' after rearranging all the letters in alphabetical order?

A. Zero   **B.** One

C. Two   **D.** Three

E. More than three

Q.37 In the word 'MAGNIFICENT', If all the vowels are replaced with their immediate next letter as per the English alphabet series then how many pairs are there in the newly formed word (either forward or backward) which has as many letters between them as they have in the English alphabet series?

A. One   **B.** Two

C. Three   **D.** Zero

E. None of these

Ques (38-40):Direction: Study the following information carefully and answer the given questions.

In a certain code language,

'di ma ti bi' means 'sky is blue colour',

'ti ja ma pa' means 'moon colour is white',

'ma ca fo ti' means 'sun is red colour',

'ma di ko' means 'ocean is blue'.

Q.38 Which of the following means 'red' in that code language?

A. bi
B. ca
C. fo
D. Either (B) or (C)
E. ma

Q.39 Code 'ti' is for which word in the given language?

A. sky
B. blue
C. colour
D. Either (A) or (B)
E. sun

Q.40 Which of the following means 'moon' in that code language?

A. bi
B. ca
C. ja
D. pa
E. Either (C) or (D)

Q.41 In a state-level dance competition, a total of 75 people took part. Stuti's position was 13th from the top and Barkha stood 25th from the bottom. A total of how many participants stood between Stuti and Barkha?

A. 42
B. 30
C. 45
D. 37
E. 50

Q.42 In a row of children, Deepa is 9th from the left and Vijay is 13th from the right. When these two interchange their positions, Deepa becomes 17th from the left. Tell where will Vijay be from the right?

A. 9th
B. 21st
C. 20th
D. 7th
E. 14th

Ques (43-47):Directions: Read the following information carefully and answer the given questions:

Eight persons - A, E, I, J, K, L, M, and O are sitting in concentric circles in such a way that persons sitting in the inner circle are facing the persons sitting in the outer circle and the persons sitting on the same circle are facing the same direction. They all like different colors - Red, Green, Yellow, Violet, White, Pink, Grey, and Black. The one who likes Black sits immediately left to L who likes Green. The one who likes Pink sits opposite the one who likes Violet in the same circle. The one who likes Yellow faces the one who likes Violet. E sits immediately left to K who likes Grey. The one who likes Black faces the one who likes White. O likes Yellow and sits immediate right to M. The one who likes Pink is facing inside. I sit immediately right of J.

Q.43 Who likes Black?

A. J
B. M
C. E
D. K
E. A

Q.44 Who likes Red?

A. E
B. I
C. J
D. M
E. K

Q.45 Who sits opposite to the one who likes Green in the same circle?

A. E
B. J
C. The one who likes Yellow
D. The one who likes White
E. Cannot be determined

Q.46 Who faces A?

A. I
B. M
C. J
D. L
E. K

Q.47 Who sits immediate right to the one who likes Grey?

A. The one who likes Black
B. The one who likes Pink
C. O
D. E
E. None of these

Ques (48-52):Directions: Read the information given below and answer the question that follows.

Eight persons M, N, O, P, Q, R, S and T are sitting in a straight line facing north. Each of them has different number of bags among 13, 21, 25, 30, 50, 64, 70 and 90.

R has more bags than Q, who has more bags than that of M. N is not adjacent to R. M sits third to the left of one, who has 50 bags. O sits adjacent to M. Only two persons sit to the left of M. Three persons sit between O and S. T has 4 more bags than that of N. R sits immediate right of T and neither of them sits at extreme end. The one, who has 70 bags, sits immediate left of Q. O has the odd number of bags.

Q.48 How many persons sit between N and P?

A. Five
B. Four
C. Two
D. Six
E. None of the above

Q.49 What is the difference in the number of bags of T and S?

A. 22
B. 20
C. 16
D. 25
E. 30

Q.50 Who sits second to the left of T?

A. The one, who has 90 bags
B. The one, who has 21 bags
C. O
D. P
E. None of the above

Q.51 How many bags does O have?

A. 21
B. 90
C. 70
D. 13
E. 25

Q.52 How many persons sit to the right of S?

A. Three
B. Four
C. Two
D. Five

E. None of the above

Ques (53-55):Directions: Study the following information carefully and answer the given questions:

R is a female and unmarried. O is the oldest member in the family. P, who is the grandmother of S, is married to O. N is the brother of S and son of M. Q is the daughter-in-law of O, who has two children.

Q.53 Four of the following five are alike and thus form a group. Which among the following does not belong to the group?

A. O   **B.** M
C. Q   **D.** N
E. None of these

Q.54 Who among the following is the daughter of P?

A. Q   **B.** S   **C.** N   **D.** R
E. O

Q.55 How is R related to S?

A. Mother   **B.** Aunt
C. Uncle   **D.** Father
E. None of these

Ques (56-59):Direction: In each of the questions below are given some statements followed by two conclusions. You have to take the given statements to be true even if they seem to be at variance with commonly known facts. Read all the conclusions and then decide which of the given conclusions logically follows from the given statements, disregarding commonly known facts. Give answer.

Q.56 Statements:

Only a few Gmail are yahoo.

Some yahoo are windows.

Conclusions:

I. Some gmail are windows.

II. No gmail are windows.

A. Only I follows
B. Only II follows
C. Either I or II follows
D. Neither I nor II follows
E. Both I and II follows

Q.57 Statements:

Only a few speaker are special.

Only speaker are spear.

Conclusions:

I. Some spear are special is a possibility.

II. only a few spear are special.

A. Only I follows
B. Only II follows
C. Either I or II follows
D. Neither I nor II follows
E. Both I and II follows

Q.58 Statements:

All studious are student.

Some studious are teacher.

Conclusions:

I. Some teacher are student.

II. No student are teacher.

A. Only I follows
B. Only II follows
C. Either I or II follows
D. Neither I nor II follows
E. Both I and II follows

Q.59 Statements:

Only a few seven are eight.

Only eight are nine.

Conclusions:

I. Some seven are nine.

II. All nine are eight.

A. Only I follows
B. Only II follows
C. Either I or II follows
D. Neither I nor II follows
E. Both I and II follows

Q.60 Direction: In the question below are given three statements followed by three conclusions numbered I, II, and III. You have to take the given statements to be true even if they seem to be at variance with commonly known facts. Read all the conclusions and then decide which of the given conclusions logically follows from the given statements disregarding commonly known facts.

Statements:

Some men are cow.

All men and cow are genius.

Some men which are not cow are rich.

Conclusion:

I. Some genius are rich.

II. Some rich are cow.

III. Some cow are genius.

A. Only I and II follows
B. Only II and III follows
C. Only I and III follows
D. All follows
E. None follows

Ques (61-65):Direction: Study the following arrangement carefully and answer the questions given beside.

A 3 * 4 @ E 2 > I O 9 % G & 6 K P $ U 8 F # 1 O T X / 7 V ^ 5

Q.61 If all the symbols and numbers are dropped from the sequence, what will be the second alphabet to the left of the seventh alphabet from the right end?

A. I   **B.** O   **C.** K   **D.** F
E. &

Q.62 Which term will be the tenth term to the right of nineteenth term from the left end?

A. /   **B.** *   **C.** V   **D.** 7
E. X

Q.63 Four of the following five are alike in a certain way based on their positions in the above arrangement and hence form a group. Which term does not belong to that group?

A. 4EA   **B.** >O@   **C.** KU6   **D.** %&I

E. %VI

Q.64 How many numbers are there in the sequence which are immediately preceded by a symbol and immediately followed by an alphabet?

A. One   **B.** Two   **C.** Three   **D.** Four

E. Five

Q.65 How many Vowels are there that are immediately preceded by a symbol and immediately followed by a number?

A. Three   **B.** Four

C. Two   **D.** One

E. None of these

Quantitative Aptitude

Q.66 Direction: Solve the given quadratic equations and mark the correct option based on your answer.

(i) $x^2 + 4x - 32 = 0$

(ii) $y^2 - 13y + 40 = 0$

A. $x > y$

B. $x \geq y$

C. $x < y$

D. $x \leq y$

E. $x = y$ or no relation can be established between x and y

Q.67 Direction: In the given question, two equations numbered I and II are given. You have to solve both the equations and mark the appropriate answer:

(I) $2m^2 - 11m + 14 = 0$

(II) $3n^2 - 7n - 3 = 8n - 3n^2 - 9$

A. $m > n$

B. $n \leq m$

C. $n \geq m$

D. $m < n$

E. Either $m = n$ or Relationship between m and n cannot be established.

Q.68 Direction: In the following question, two equations are given. Find the correct answer after solving the equations.

I. $x^2 + x(\sqrt{5} + \sqrt{7}) + \sqrt{35} = 0$

II. $y^2 + y(\sqrt{3} + \sqrt{5}) + \sqrt{15} = 0$

A. $x > y$

B. $x < y$

C. $x \geq y$

D. $x \leq y$

E. $x = y$ or no relation can be obtained

Q.69 Direction: In the following question, two equations numbered I and II are given. You have to solve both the equation and given answer.

I. $(24 - 10x)^{\frac{1}{2}} = 3 - 4x$

II. $6y^2 - 5y - 25 = 0$

A. If $x > y$

B. If $x < y$

C. If $x \geq y$

D. If $x \leq y$

E. If $x = y$ or no relation can be established.

Q.70 Direction: In the following question two equation numbered I and II are given. Solve the equation and answer the question.

(i) $2x^2 - (6 + \sqrt{15})x + 3\sqrt{15} = 0$

(ii) $5y^2 - (9 + 5\sqrt{15})y + 9\sqrt{15} = 0$

A. $x > y$

B. $x \geq y$

C. $x < y$

D. $x \leq y$

E. $x = y$ or the relationship cannot be established between x and y

Q.71 Direction: What will come in place of the question mark (?) in the following question?

$$\sqrt{676} \times \sqrt{576} - ? \times 18 = 300$$

[RBI Assistant, 2020]

A. 14   **B.** 16   **C.** 18   **D.** 20

E. 22

Q.72 Direction: In the following question, two statements are numbered as A and B. On solving these statements, we get quantities A and B respectively. Solve both quantities and choose the correct option.

Quantity A: A two digit number get reversed when $\frac{1}{5}$th of it is added to it. Find 1% of the number.

Quantity B: A bag contains 5 red and 3 black balls. Another bag contains 4 red and 6 black balls. If one ball is drawn from each bag, then find the probability that one ball is red and one ball is black.

A. Quantity A > Quantity B

B. Quantity A < Quantity B

C. Quantity A = Quantity B

D. Quantity A ≥ Quantity B

E. Quantity A ≤ Quantity B

Q.73 Direction: What will come in place of the question mark (?) in the following question?

$$40\% \text{ of } 180 + 70\% \text{ of } ? = 121$$

[RBI Assistant, 2020]

A. 81   **B.** 77   **C.** 65   **D.** 70

E. 75

Q.74 A shopkeeper has two items of same cost price. One item sold at 10% profit and other sold at 5% loss. He gets total profit of Rs.200. Find the total profit percentage earned.

A. 8%   **B.** 1.5%   **C.** 3%   **D.** 2%

E. 2.5%

Q.75 Three pipes A, B, and C can fill a tank from empty to full in 30 minutes, 20 minutes, and 10 minutes respectively. When the tank is empty, all three pipes are opened. A, B, and C discharge chemical solutions P, Q, and R respectively. What is the proportion of the solution R in the liquid in the tank after 3 minutes?

A. $\frac{5}{11}$ **B.** $\frac{6}{11}$ **C.** $\frac{7}{11}$ **D.** $\frac{8}{11}$

E. $\frac{9}{11}$

Q.76 To complete a work, A takes 50% more time than B. If together they take 18 days to complete the work, how much time shall B take to do it?

A. 30 days   **B.** 35 days   **C.** 40 days   **D.** 45 days

E. 50 days

Q.77 A container contained 90 litres of milk. Then 9 litres of milk was replaced by water. The process was repeated one more time. The volume of milk in container is-

A. 72.0 litres   **B.** 72.9 litres

C. 62.9 litres   **D.** 63 litres

E. 81 litres

Q.78 The average age of workers in field and in documentation in a factory was 45 year. The average age of all the 16 documentation workers was 38 years and average age of field workers was 52 years. If 7 field workers were married then the number of unmarried field workers was:

A. 5   **B.** 6   **C.** 7   **D.** 8

E. 9

Ques (79-83):Direction: Read the following line graph carefully and answer the questions given below.

The given Line graph shows the number of shoes sold by 3 brands in 4 different months.

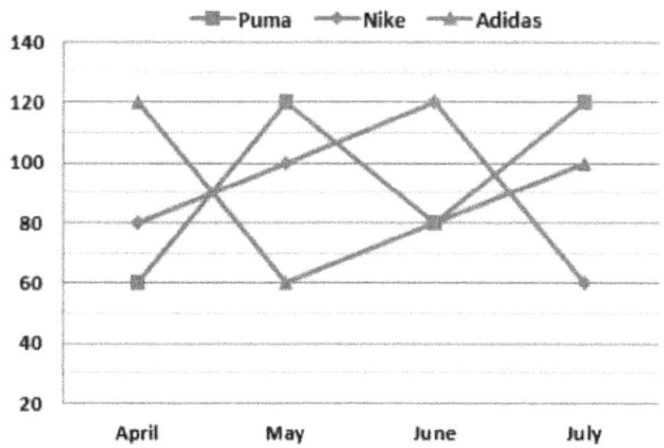

Q.79 What is the ratio of the number of total shoes sold of Puma in April and June to the number of shoes sold of Adidas in May and July?

A. 7 : 8   **B.** 7 : 9   **C.** 5 : 8   **D.** 6 : 7

E. 4 : 5

Q.80 The number of shoes sold in May and June of all companies is what percent more/less than the number of total shoes sold of Adidas in all months?

A. $64\frac{2}{7}\%$ **B.** $48\frac{5}{9}\%$ **C.** $53\frac{5}{9}\%$ **D.** $55\frac{5}{9}\%$

E. $54\frac{2}{7}\%$

Q.81 What is the average number of shoes sold of Puma in April, Nike in June, and Adidas in May?

A. 78   **B.** 80   **C.** 76   **D.** 82

E. 84

Q.82 What is the difference between the number of shoes sold by Puma in all months and the number of shoes sold by all companies in June?

A. 90   **B.** 80   **C.** 60   **D.** 120

E. 100

Q.83 The number of shoes sold in April of all companies is approximately what percent of the number of shoes sold by all companies in July?

A. 117%   **B.** 86%   **C.** 93%   **D.** 107%

E. 99%

Ques (84-85):Direction: In the following question, two statements are numbered as Quantity I and Quantity II. On solving these statements, we get quantities I and II respectively. Solve both quantities and choose the correct option.

Q.84 Quantity I: Find the missing term in the series $2, 11, 38, X, 362.$

Quantity II: Find the value of X, 125% of $X = 250$

A. Quantity I > Quantity II

B. Quantity I ≥ Quantity 2

C. Quantity I < Quantity 2

D. Quantity I ≤ Quantity 2

E. Quantity I = Quantity 2

Q.85 Quantity A: An amount is to be distributed among $A, B,$ and C in the ratio $1:3:2$ respectively, but was erroneously distributed in the ratio $2:7:9$ due to which B got Rs. 136 less. What is the amount to be distributed?

Quantity B: Rs 1228

A. Quantity A > Quantity B

B. Quantity A < Quantity B

C. Quantity A ≥ Quantity B

D. Quantity A ≤ Quantity B

E. Quantity A = Quantity B or No relation

Q.86 The squared value of the diagonal of a rectangle is $(36 + B^2)$ sq. cm, where B is less than 10 cm. what is the breadth of that rectangle?

A. 10 cm   **B.** 8 cm

C. 12 cm   **D.** 15 cm

E. None of these

Q.87 John, Jackson and Joseph enter into a partnership with Rs. 4000, Rs. 6000 and Rs. 8000 respectively. After 4 months John withdrew 25% and after 6 months Jackson add $\frac{50}{3}\%$ and after 8 months Joseph withdrew 25%. If they get a total profit of Rs. 7500 after 1 year, find the profit earned by John(approx).

A. Rs. 1456   **B.** Rs. 6194   **C.** Rs. 2048   **D.** Rs. 3066

E. Rs. 4124

Q.88 The value of $\dfrac{(0.625\times0.0729\times28.9)}{(0.0017\times0.025\times8.1)}$ is:

A. 3825   B. 3.825   C. 38.25   D. 382.5
E. 0.3825

Ques (89-90):Direction: What will come in the place of the question mark (?) in the following question?

Q.89 88.60% of 1500 + 39.25% of 800 + 63.20% of 2500 + 25.40% of 4500 = ?

A. 4856   B. 4466   C. 4256   D. 4366
E. 466

Q.90 6.67% of $225 + 6.25\%$ of $1120 = (?)^3 + 3$

A. $(-76)^{\frac{1}{2}}$ B. $(76)^{\frac{1}{2}}$ C. $(-76)^{\frac{1}{3}}$ D. $(76)^{\frac{1}{3}}$
E. $(82)^{\frac{1}{3}}$

Q.91 Direction: What will come in place of question mark (?) in the following question?

$$\frac{\left(18\times\frac{8}{15}+10\%\right)\text{of }624}{?} = 4$$

A. 16   B. 18   C. 22   D. 24
E. 26

Ques (92-95):Direction: What value should come in place of question mark (?) in the following question?

Q.92 $\sqrt{225} + (55\%\text{ of }1500) - \{(45)^2 \div 81 \times 4\} + 20 - 16 =?$

A. 744   B. 748   C. 746   D. 752
E. 742

Q.93 $(8375 \div 67)^{\frac{1}{3}} + (7.84 \times 25)^{\frac{1}{2}} = (?)^{\frac{1}{2}}$

A. 456   B. 361   C. 324   D. 338
E. 432

Q.94 $?^{\frac{1}{3}} + 47\%$ of $200 = 60\%$ of $112 + 30\%$ of 136

A. 4096   B. 1331   C. 3375   D. 2744
E. 729

Q.95 $37 \times 43 - 40^2 + \left(\frac{15}{23}\right)\%$ of $\left(\frac{11500}{3}\right) = (?)^2$

A. +4   B. -4   C. ±4   D. 0
E. 3

Ques (96-100):Direction: Which number will replace the question mark $(?)$ in the following number series?

Q.96 $24,61,122,213,?$

A. 343   B. 334   C. 337   D. 340
E. 390

Q.97 $7,8,18,57,232,?$

A. 260   B. 360   C. 1165   D. 560
E. 380

Q.98 $17,23,35,?,85$

A. 47   B. 60   C. 55   D. 53
E. 40

Q.99 $12,15,75,?,738,749$

A. 259   B. 155   C. 90   D. 82
E. 100

Q.100 $19,24,30,37,45,?$

A. 57   B. 64   C. 49   D. 82
E. 54

// Smart Answer Sheet //

Correct Indicates percentage of students who answered questions correctly.

Skipped Indicates percentage of students who skipped questions.

Q.	Ans.	Correct / Skipped	Q.	Ans.	Correct / Skipped	Q.	Ans.	Correct / Skipped	Q.	Ans.	Correct / Skipped	Q.	Ans.	Correct / Skipped
1	C	65.5 % / 33.4 %	17	E	49.99 % / 30.77 %	33	C	50.47 % / 34.35 %	49	D	59.74 % / 35.7 %	65	C	45.05 % / 35.7 %
2	B	48.82 % / 34.1 %	18	A	48.33 % / 48.25 %	34	E	31.27 % / 67.38 %	50	C	47.31 % / 49.33 %	66	C	62.44 % / 36.86 %
3	D	57.34 % / 30.71 %	19	B	48.43 % / 50.52 %	35	D	80.11 % / 12.34 %	51	D	59.72 % / 34.4 %	67	B	59.32 % / 38.68 %
4	B	58.44 % / 33.02 %	20	B	62.35 % / 32.2 %	36	B	47.83 % / 34.95 %	52	C	49.27 % / 31.31 %	68	D	52.94 % / 42.61 %
5	A	50.02 % / 38.94 %	21	D	67.53 % / 32.22 %	37	C	69.6 % / 30.12 %	53	C	63.84 % / 33.75 %	69	E	24.91 % / 67.06 %
6	B	47.85 % / 47.4 %	22	A	46.44 % / 33.06 %	38	D	58.18 % / 40.65 %	54	D	60.09 % / 35.93 %	70	E	26.61 % / 70.22 %
7	E	47.29 % / 46.8 %	23	C	43.45 % / 32.2 %	39	C	56.66 % / 31.85 %	55	B	60.96 % / 32.63 %	71	C	18.69 % / 79.18 %
8	D	62.99 % / 30.34 %	24	E	44.35 % / 39.66 %	40	E	51.45 % / 40.23 %	56	B	67.57 % / 30.96 %	72	B	49.16 % / 47.61 %
9	B	62.92 % / 35.65 %	25	B	44.66 % / 36.53 %	41	D	55.86 % / 30.59 %	57	D	44.06 % / 53.37 %	73	D	57.98 % / 33.15 %
10	A	60.85 % / 30.06 %	26	D	47.92 % / 34.27 %	42	B	47.95 % / 36.35 %	58	A	48.86 % / 46.77 %	74	E	61.76 % / 31.71 %
11	C	56.02 % / 39.59 %	27	E	60.06 % / 34.66 %	43	E	47.65 % / 34.03 %	59	B	46.25 % / 53.45 %	75	B	41.69 % / 53.0 %
12	E	58.47 % / 33.53 %	28	C	52.68 % / 33.56 %	44	D	69.4 % / 30.42 %	60	C	66.67 % / 32.05 %	76	A	44.64 % / 40.22 %
13	A	53.41 % / 41.31 %	29	D	51.3 % / 37.95 %	45	C	22.81 % / 68.57 %	61	B	65.01 % / 30.99 %	77	B	56.08 % / 37.11 %
14	B	57.8 % / 36.97 %	30	E	57.32 % / 35.64 %	46	A	54.35 % / 34.94 %	62	C	42.66 % / 46.48 %	78	E	68.09 % / 30.92 %
15	B	42.22 % / 31.2 %	31	E	40.85 % / 45.27 %	47	B	61.61 % / 35.71 %	63	C	64.75 % / 32.12 %	79	A	65.85 % / 30.02 %
16	B	46.69 % / 50.12 %	32	A	83.85 % / 11.74 %	48	A	57.56 % / 34.17 %	64	B	51.51 % / 46.72 %	80	D	53.86 % / 36.93 %

Q.	Ans.	Correct		Q.	Ans.	Correct		Q.	Ans.	Correct		Q.	Ans.	Correct		Q.	Ans.	Correct
		Skipped				Skipped				Skipped				Skipped				Skipped
81	B	45.42 %		85	B	67.97 %		89	D	55.54 %		93	B	63.98 %		97	C	63.49 %
		47.76 %				30.32 %				39.94 %				34.84 %				33.36 %
82	E	67.35 %		86	B	40.5 %		90	E	64.83 %		94	D	50.38 %		98	C	43.74 %
		30.64 %				43.67 %				32.56 %				30.09 %				34.45 %
83	C	47.03 %		87	A	44.42 %		91	B	49.13 %		95	C	65.29 %		99	D	60.76 %
		33.51 %				54.21 %				36.39 %				33.48 %				36.41 %
84	C	53.63 %		88	A	66.18 %		92	A	52.81 %		96	D	50.01 %		100	E	66.01 %
		36.93 %				30.04 %				36.42 %				32.96 %				31.06 %

Performance Analysis

Avg. Score (%)	56.0%
Toppers Score (%)	62.0%
Your Score	

//Hints and Solutions//

1. Adverb of manner- describes the manner of action. It answers the question – How is the action carried out?

Here, the blank expresses how the flute is played so 'Beautifully' is the correct solution. The other options are not adverbs.

So, The correct sentence is "He plays the flute beautifully".

Hence, the correct option is (C).

2. We have to use a conjunction in the blank that means 'with the aim that; in order that'. Hence, the correct answer is 'so'.

Eg - They whisper to each other so that no one else can hear.

Other options are rejected because :

'There' means in, at, or to that place or position.

'By' means identifying the agent performing the action. Eg - The door was opened by her.

'For' is used for a length of time whereas 'since' shows some point in time in the past as being the starting point of the action or event.

So, The correct sentence is "I worked hard so that I can catch up to you".

Hence, the correct option is (B).

3. The given sentence is in indirect speech. In indirect speech, we often use a tense which is 'further back' in the past (e.g. worked) than the tense originally used (e.g. work). This is called 'backshift'.

We have to use a verb in the past tense in the blank. The past tense is used for anything that happened before the time of speaking.

Even though a time frame is not given in the question, only 'asked' is appropriate in the sentence.

Other options are wrong because:

'Say' means 'speak'.

'Ask' is grammatically wrong as 'asked' is used in indirect speech.

'Said' is also grammatically wrong as it is the past tense and past participle of 'say'.

'Asking' is the present participle and gerund of 'ask'.

So, The correct sentence is "She asked me to tie her bow".

Hence, the correct option is (D).

4. The correct preposition to be used in the blank is 'Within' as it means 'occurring inside (a particular period of time)'.

Eg - The tickets were sold out within two hours.

Other options are rejected because:

'In' is used for expressing a period of time during which an event happens or a situation remains the case.

Eg - They met in 1999.

'Into' is used for expressing movement or action.

Eg - Put it into the fridge.

'On' means physically in contact with and supported by (a surface).

'By' is used for identifying the agent performing an action.

Eg - The door was opened by him.

So, The correct sentence is "He will return within a month".

Hence, the correct option is (B).

5. 'Man' and 'Woman' both are singular nouns.

When two singular subjects are preceded by each or every, the verb should be in the singular.

The verb 'has' is to be used in the blank as it means 'possess, own, or hold'.

Other options are rejected because :

'Have' is used with plural subjects.

'Had' is the past tense as well as the past participle of 'have'.

'Was' is the singular past tense of 'be' and 'Is' is the singular present tense of 'be'.

So, The correct sentence is "Every man and every woman has the right to express his or her views".

Hence, the correct option is (A).

6. The word 'Exonerate' means to free from a charge of wrongdoing.

The antonyms of the word 'Exonerate' are "sentence, accuse, convict".

From the antonym of the given word, we can say that the word 'sentence' is the opposite in meaning.

The word 'sentence' means the punishment assigned to a defendant found guilty by a court or fixed by law for a particular offence.

Hence, the correct option is (B).

7. The correct answer is 'Convenience'.

- The word 'Expediency' means 'the quality of being convenient and practical despite possibly being improper or immoral; convenience.

- The synonyms of the word 'Expediency' are "advisability, advisableness, desirability, convenience, desirableness, expedience, judiciousness, prudence, wisdom".

- From the synonym of the given word, we can say that the word 'Convenience' is the most similar in meaning.

- The word 'Convenience' means 'the quality of being easy, useful or suitable for somebody.

Hence, the correct option is (B).

8. The correct spelling of the given option is Topple.

To topple a government or leader, especially one that is not elected by the people, means to cause them to lose power.

Hence, the correct option is (D).

9. The word which is wrongly spelt is tentetive.

The correct spelling of the marked option is 'Tentative' which means not certain or fixed; provisional.

Hence, the correct option is (B).

10. The correctly spelt word is Manoeuvre.

Manoeuvre - perform a movement in military or naval tactics to secure an advantage in attack or defence.

Hence, the correct option is (A).

11. The adverb 'mostly' which refers to 'Usually' or 'Generally' is wrongly used here and should be replaced by 'most' which refers to 'to the greatest extent' to make the sentence grammatically correct. All other parts which are in bold are correct and need no improvement.

So the correct sentence is "The man who has committed such a heinous crime must get the most severe punishment".

Hence, the correct option is (C).

12. The correct phrasal verb to be used here is 'put forward' itself.

'Put through' means to connect to someone and thus Option (D) is incorrect.

If we put out an announcement or story, we make it known to a lot of people. Thus, option (C) is also unsuitable.

If we put forward a plan, proposal, or name, we suggest that it should be considered for a particular purpose or job.

Clearly, the sentence is absolutely correct and thus needs no improvement.

Hence, the correct option is (E).

13. Option (B) is incorrect because 'among' is being replaced by 'amidst', changing the meaning of the sentence.

Option (C) is incorrect as 'the' is a definite article and is to be used when the noun is specific.

Ex: "The dog that bit me ran away." Here, we're talking about a specific dog, the dog that bit me. However, here the word 'asylum seekers' is used in general terms.

Option (D) is fallacious due to incorrect use of apostrophe (Indian's) which is used to denote only one Indian. Also, the word 'maximum' is incorrect with respect to the context.

Option (A) is grammatically correct.

So the correct sentence is "According to the International Migration Outlook 2017 report on OECD member countries, Indians are among top asylum-seekers in other countries".

Hence, the correct option is (A).

14. The presence of the preposition 'than' right after the bold part confirm that an adjective of comparative degree must be used here. Option (A) and (D) get eliminated straightaway.

Option (C) is ungrammatical as an adjective of comparative degree is not used with 'as ... as' phrase.

So the correct sentence is "The US and Australia have jointly test-fired a hypersonic missile capable of moving at a speed eight times faster than sound, as part of $54-million research project".

Hence, the correct option is (B).

15. Here, the correct phrase should be 'abide by' and not 'abide to'.

Abide by (Phrasal Verb): to follow a rule, decision, or instruction

Ex. They promised to abide by the rules of the contest.

So, option (A) can be eliminated.

Option (C) and (D) can also be eliminated as well as it's clear that there are more than one agreement and the noun 'agreement' has to be in plural to stay relevant in the context.

So the correct sentence is "World football's governing body FIFA lifted the ban it had imposed on the Sudan Football Association (SFA) for its failure to abide by the agreements mentioned in articles 14 and 19 of the FIFA statute".

Hence, the correct option is (B).

16. Replace 'to' with 'of'.

We use 'to' to show direction and here we can not find any such direction in the sentence.

The preposition 'of' is used to show the position of something/somebody in space or time. E.g. at the time of the revolution.

So the correct sentence is "The Renaissance was a time of 'reawakening' in both the arts and the sciences".

Hence, the correct option is (B).

17. The sentence is correct. So, the complete sentence is:

Nuclear waste will still be radioactive even after twenty thousand years so it must be disposed of very carefully.

So, Clearly, the sentence is absolutely correct.

Hence, the correct option is (E).

18. From time period 1 to time period 2 - indicates a length of time.

e.g: I had lived in Delhi from 2014 to 2017. (for 3 years)

Since (Prep.) indicates a past time until a later time, or until now.

e.g: I have been living in Delhi since 1964. (from 1964 until now)

The given sentence implies that William's ice-cream gained popularity for the first time in 1970 and since then its popularity still exists.

Correct sentence:

Since the 1970's, William's has been the most popular ice cream parlor in town.

Hence, the correct option is (A).

19. The error lies in part (B) of the sentence. The usage of 'deepening' is incorrect. Use 'deepen' in place of deepening.

According to grammar, whenever we have an infinitive phrase we need to use the base form of the verb with the preposition 'to' i.e., 'to + V1'

Example- I decided not to go to London.

So, the correct sentence is: The challenge before India is to deepen the tactical engagement with China keeping strategic glitches at bay.

Hence, the correct option is (B).

20. The error lies in part (B) of the sentence.

In Part (B), replace 'was' with were because here two individual subjects are connected by 'and' so the subject is in the plural and the verb should also be in plural.

When the subject of the sentence is composed of two or more nouns or pronouns connected by and, use a plural verb.

So, the correct sentence is: The trip to the airport and the flight to Singapore were both uneventful, the hotel accommodations were better than they could have expected on such short notice.

Hence, the correct option is (B).

21. Reading the given sentences we find that:

- The paragraph starts by introducing the Nuclear Power Corporation of India Limited, and my mentioning what it is; which is D.
- Then statement A provides us more information regarding NPCIL that it is a dividend-paying company.
- This is soon followed by statement C which elaborates on what NPCIL does, its responsibilities.
- This is elaborated using the second statement that is the overriding priority given to safety as mentioned in E.
- The paragraph ends by concluding the present operation of NPCIL i.e the number of power reactors and it's capacity, which is B.
- Therefore the correct sequence is DACEB.

So, D is the first sentence according to the paragraph.

Hence, the correct option is (D).

22. Reading the given sentences we find that:

- The paragraph starts by introducing the Nuclear Power Corporation of India Limited, and my mentioning what it is; which is D.
- Then statement A provides us more information regarding NPCIL that it is a dividend-paying company.
- This is soon followed by statement C which elaborates on what NPCIL does, its responsibilities.
- This is elaborated using the second statement that is the overriding priority given to safety as mentioned in E.

- The paragraph ends by concluding the present operation of NPCIL i.e the number of power reactors and it's capacity, which is B.
- Therefore the correct sequence is DACEB.

So, A is the second sentence according to the passage.

Hence, the correct option is (A).

23. Reading the given sentences we find that:

- The paragraph starts by introducing the Nuclear Power Corporation of India Limited, and my mentioning what it is; which is D.
- Then statement A provides us more information regarding NPCIL that it is a dividend-paying company.
- This is soon followed by statement C which elaborates on what NPCIL does, its responsibilities.
- This is elaborated using the second statement that is the overriding priority given to safety as mentioned in E.
- The paragraph ends by concluding the present operation of NPCIL i.e the number of power reactors and it's capacity, which is B.
- Therefore the correct sequence is DACEB.

So, C is the third sentence according to the paragraph.

Hence, the correct option is (C).

24. Reading the given sentences we find that:

- The paragraph starts by introducing the Nuclear Power Corporation of India Limited, and my mentioning what it is; which is D.
- Then statement A provides us more information regarding NPCIL that it is a dividend-paying company.
- This is soon followed by statement C which elaborates on what NPCIL does, Its responsibilities.
- This is elaborated using the second statement that is the overriding priority given to safety as mentioned in E.
- The paragraph ends by concluding the present operation of NPCIL i.e the number of power reactors and it's capacity, which is B.
- Therefore the correct sequence is DACEB.

So, E is the fourth sentence according to the paragraph.

Hence, the correct option is (E).

25. Reading the given sentences we find that:

- The paragraph starts by introducing the Nuclear Power Corporation of India Limited, and my mentioning what it is; which is D.
- Then statement A provides us more information regarding NPCIL that it is a dividend-paying company.
- This is soon followed by statement C which elaborates on what NPCIL does, its responsibilities.

- This is elaborated using the second statement that is the overriding priority given to safety as mentioned in E.
- The paragraph ends by concluding the present operation of NPCIL i.e the number of power reactors and it's capacity, which is B.
- Therefore the correct sequence is DACEB.

So, B is the fifth sentence according to the paragraph.

Hence, the correct option is (B).

26. According to the passage, "In the present predicament when we are not able to adjust ourselves to the new conditions which science has brought about it is not easy to adopt the principles of non-violence, truth and understanding. But on that ground we should not give up the effort."

So, it can be concluded that It is not easy to follow the principles of non-violence and truth because there is the problem of adjustment between emerging new conditions which science has brought about.

Hence, the correct option is (D).

27. According to the passage, "While the obstinacy of the political leaders puts fear into our hearts, the common sense and conscience of the people of the world give us hope. "

So, it can be concluded that according to the writer obstinacy of our political leaders instils fear into our heart.

Hence, the correct option is (E).

28. According to the passage, "We live in an age which is aware of its own defeat and moral coarsening, an age in which old certainties are breaking down, the familiar patterns are tilting and cracking. There is increasing intolerance and embitterment. The creative flame that kindled the great human society is languishing. The human mind in all its baffling strangeness and variety produces contrary types, a Buddha or a Gandhi, a Nero or a Hitler."

So, it can be concluded that "Reviving of traditional familiar patterns" is not a characteristic of modern Age.

Hence, the correct option is (C).

29. The meaning of the given words:

- Obstinacy: stubbornness
- Compliance: the act or process of complying to a desire, demand, proposal, or regimen or to coercion
- Tenacity: mental or moral strength to resist opposition, danger, or hardship.
- Obduracy: stubbornly persistent in wrongdoing
- Tractability: capable of being easily led, taught, or controlled

So, from the meanings of the given words, we can conclude that compliance is correct antonym of the obstinacy.

Hence, the correct option is (D).

30. According to the passage, "We live in an age which is aware of its own defeat and moral coarsening, an age in which old

certainties are breaking down, the familiar patterns are tilting and cracking. There is increasing intolerance and embitterment. The creative flame that kindled the great human society is languishing. The human mind in all its baffling strangeness and variety produces contrary types, a Buddha or a Gandhi, a Nero or a Hitler."

So, it can be concluded that "Reviving of traditional familiar patterns" is not a characteristic of modern Age.

Hence, the correct option is (E).

31. Given Statements: A > B < C < D; K ≥ L > M = D; G > H ≥ I ≤ J < A

On combining: G > H ≥ I ≤ J < A > B < C < D = M < L ≤ K

Conclusions:

I. G > A → False (Given G > H ≥ I ≤ J < A thus clear relation between G and A cannot be determined)

II. A ≥ G → False (Given G > H ≥ I ≤ J < A thus clear relation between G and A cannot be determined)

III. K > I → False (Given I ≤ J < A > B < C < D = M < L ≤ K so K> B but the relation between B and I is not clear thus clear relation between K and I cannot be determined)

Hence, the correct option is (E).

32. Statements: A ≤ B < C; A ≥ E; C ≤ F

On combining: E ≤ A ≤ B < C ≤ F

Conclusions:

I. E < C ⇒ true as C > B and B ≥ E so C > E

II. F ≥ E ⇒ false as F > B and B ≥ E so F > E

So, only conclusion I is true.

Hence, the correct option is (A).

33. Given statements: X< M ≤ W; B ≥ L ≥ O; O = X

On combining: B ≥ L ≥ O = X; W ≥ M >O = X

Conclusions:

I. B >M → False (B ≥ L ≥ O and M >O → relation between B and M cannot be determined.)

II. M ≥ B → False (B ≥ L ≥ O and M >O → relation between B and M cannot be determined.)

III. L< W → False (L ≥ O and W ≥ M >O → relation between L and W can't be determined.)

None of the conclusions are true but conclusions I and II form a complementary pair.

Thus, either conclusion I or conclusion II is true.

Hence, the correct option is (C).

34. Given Statements: R ≤ A < N ≤ I; K ≥ I; V > A

On combining: R ≤ A < N ≤ I ≤ K and V > A

Conclusions:

I) K ≥ A → False (A < N ≤ I ≤ K implies that K is greater than A)

II) V > I → False (V > A < N ≤ I here we don't have the clear relation between V and I)

III) R ≤ K → False (R ≤ A < N ≤ I ≤ K here we have R is less than K)

Thus, the correct answer is None of these.

Hence, the correct option is (E).

35. Given statements: U ≤ W ≥ R > S ; T > S = V

on combining : U ≤ W ≥ R > S = V < T

Conclusions:

I. W < V → False (as W ≥ R > S = V) it is clear that W is greater than V

II. T < V → False (as S = V < T) V is shorter than T

Both statements not follow the given statement as per statement W ≥ R > S = V it is clear W > V while in conclusion it is given

W < V so it is false .

similarly S = V < T → V < T but in conclusion it is T < V so it is false

Therefore Neither I nor II is true.

Hence, the correct option is (D).

36. The given word:

MAGNIFICIENT

Arranging in alphabetical order:

ACEFGIIMNNT

The first, third, fourth and eighth letters are A, E, F and M.

The meaningful English word that can be formed by using A, E, F and M is FAME.

Thus only one word can be made.

Hence, the correct option is (B).

37. The given word:

MAGNIFICENT

Applying the above condition the new word is:

MBGNJFJCFNT

The two-letter pairs between which there are similar words in alphabetical order are- 'B and F', 'G and N' and 'F and J'.

Hence, the correct option is (C).

Ques (38-40): According to the given information-

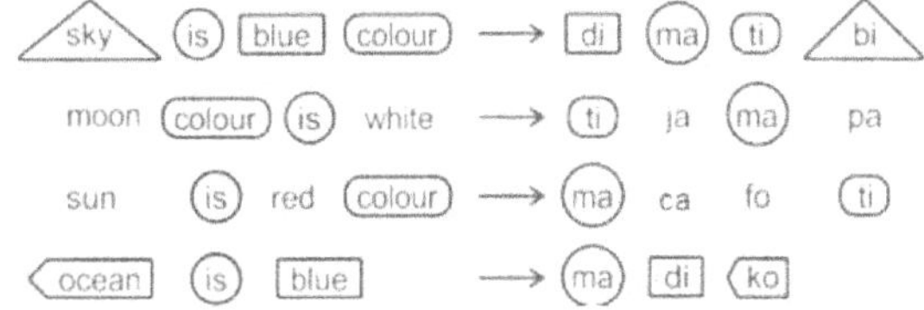

38. So, 'red' is coded as either 'ca' or 'fo'.

Hence, the correct option is (D).

39. So, 'ti' is coded for 'colour'.

Hence, the correct option is (C).

40. So, 'moon' is coded as either 'ja' or 'pa'.

Hence, the correct option is (E).

41. Given,

In a state-level dance competition, a total of 75 people took part.

Sonu's position = 13th from the top

Barkha's position = 25th from the bottom

So, the number of participants who were ranked after Stuti = 75-13 = 62

The number of participants who were ranked before Barkha = 75-25 = 50

Therefore, the number of participants who stood between both of them = 50-13 = 37

Hence, the correct option is (D).

42. Given:

In a row of children, Deepa is 9th from the left and Vijay is 13th from the right. When these two interchange their positions, Deepa becomes 17th from the left.

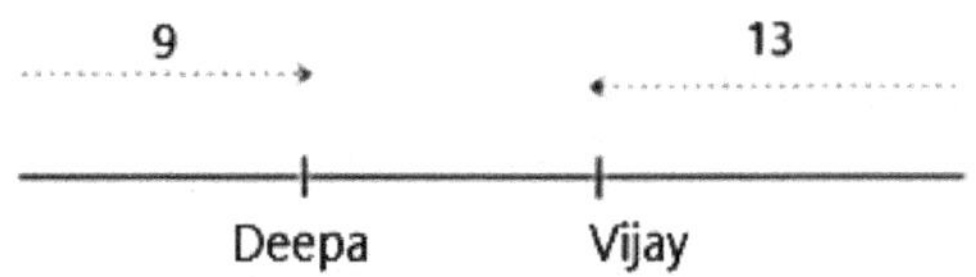

After interchanging,

Then,

Present position of Deepa = 17

Former position of Deepa = 9

Difference of present and former position of Deepa = 17 - 9 = 8

Former position of Vijay = 13

Present position of Vijay = difference of present and previous position of Deepa + former position of Vijay

$$= (17 - 9) + 13 = 21\text{st}$$

Hence, the correct option is (B).

Ques (43-47): Eight Persons: A, E, I, J, K, L, M, and O

Colors: Red, Green, Yellow, Violet, White, Pink, Grey, and Black

1) The one who likes Black sits immediately left to L who likes Green.

As it is not clear, if L sits on the inner circle or the outer circle, two cases will be formed.

Case 1:

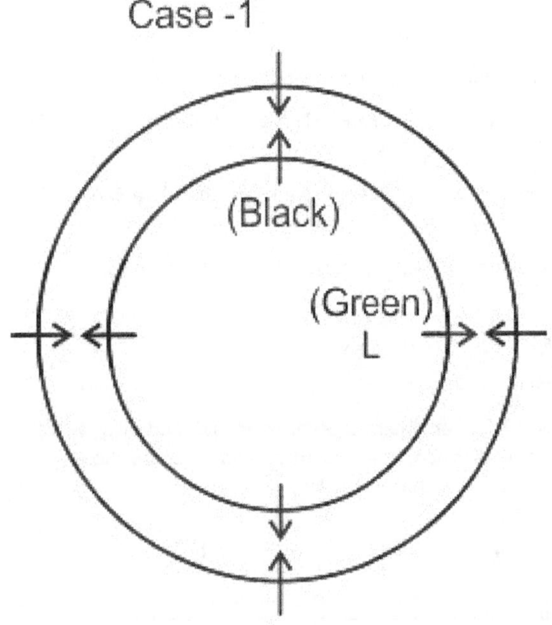

Case 2:

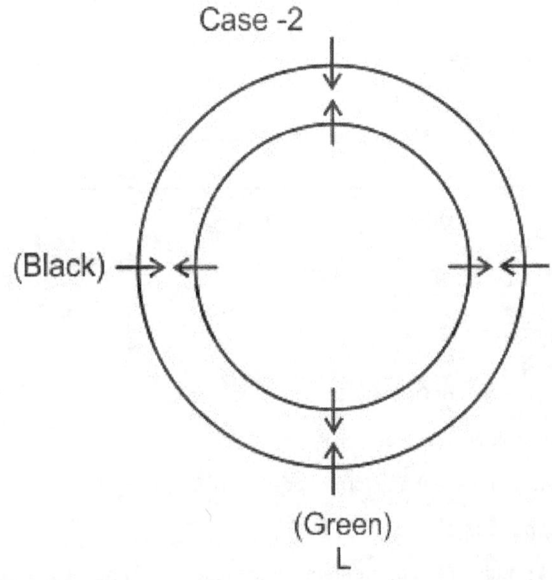

2) The one who likes Black faces the one who likes White.

Case 1:

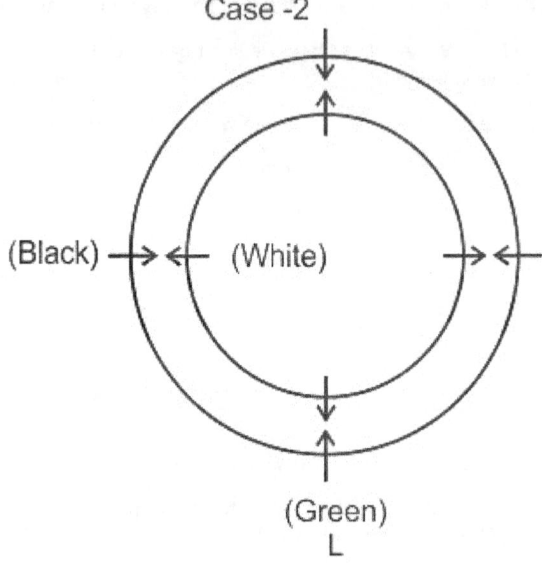

Case 2:

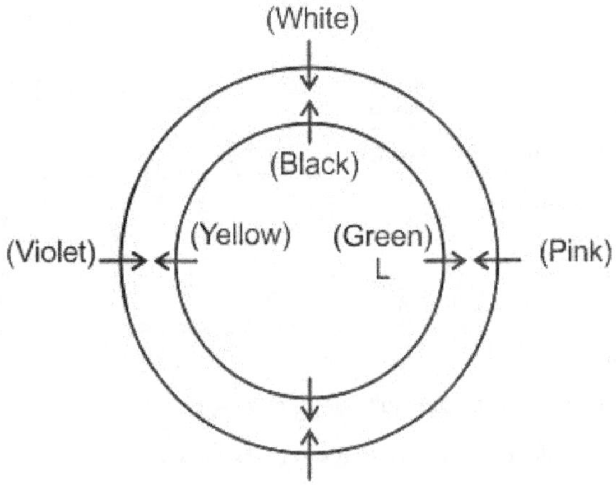

3) The one who likes Pink sits opposite the one who likes Violet in the same circle.

4) The one who likes Pink is facing inside.

As the above condition is not satisfied in case 2, it will get canceled.

5) The one who likes Yellow faces the one who likes Violet.

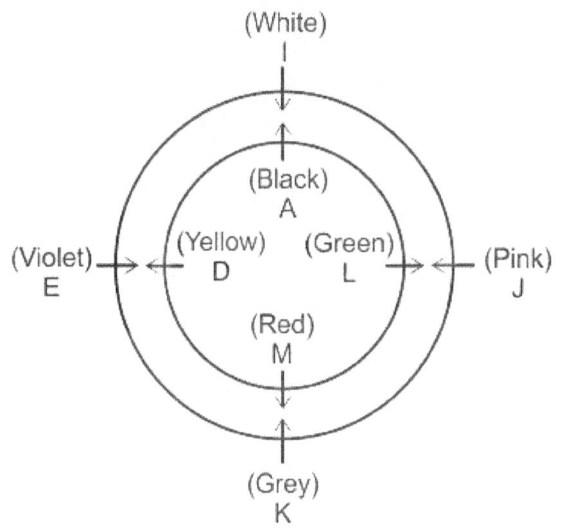

6) E sits immediately left to K who likes Grey.

7) O likes Yellow and sits immediate right to M.

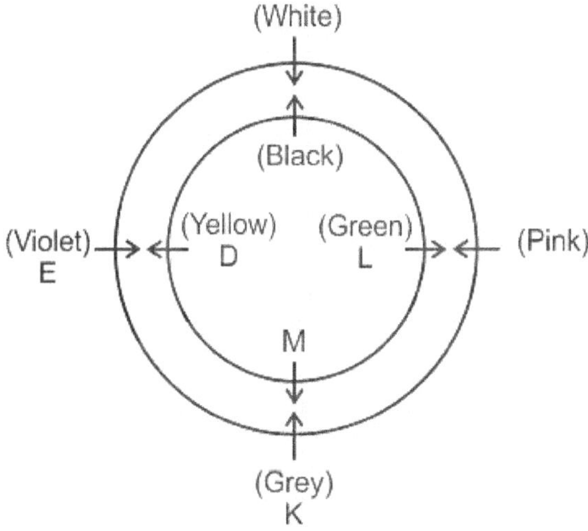

8) I sits immediate right of J.

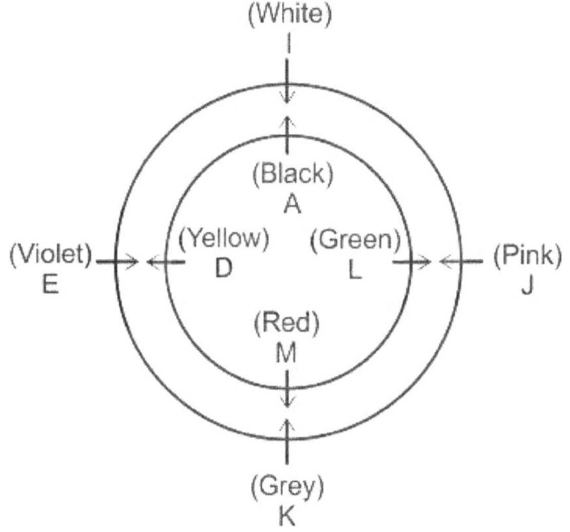

43. So, A likes Black.

Hence, the correct option is (E).

44. So, M likes Red.

Hence, the correct option is (D).

45. So, the one who likes Yellow sits opposite the one who likes Green.

Hence, the correct option is (C).

46. So, I face J.

Hence, the correct option is (A).

47. So, the one who likes Pink sits immediately right to the one who likes Grey.

Hence, the correct option is (B).

48. Persons: M, N, O, P, Q, R, S and T.

Number of bags: 13, 21, 25, 30, 50, 64, 70 and 90.

1) M sits third to the left of one, who has 50 bags.

2) O sits adjacent to M.

3) Only two persons sit to the left of M.

Case 1:

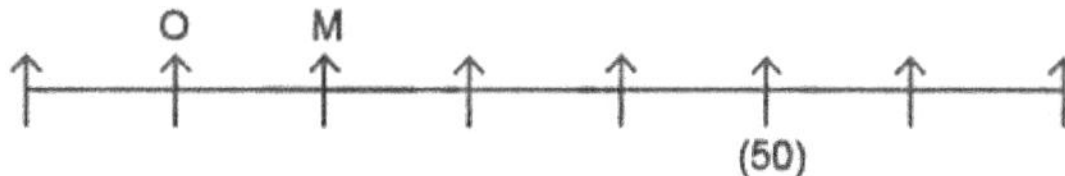

Case 2:

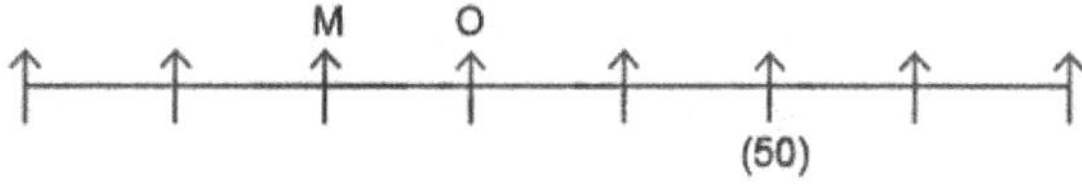

4) T has 4 more bags than that of N. So, T and N must have 25 and 21 bags or 70 and 66 bags respectively.

5) Three persons sit between O and S.

6) R sits immediate right of T and neither of them sit at extreme end.

Case 1:

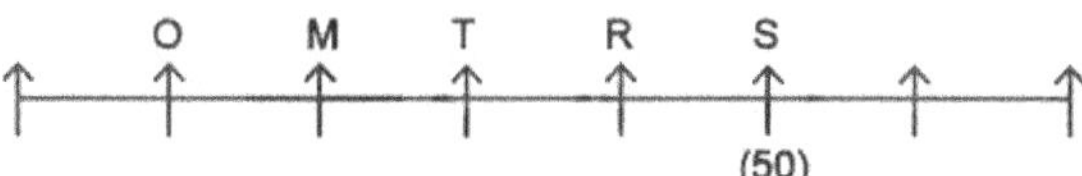

Case 2:

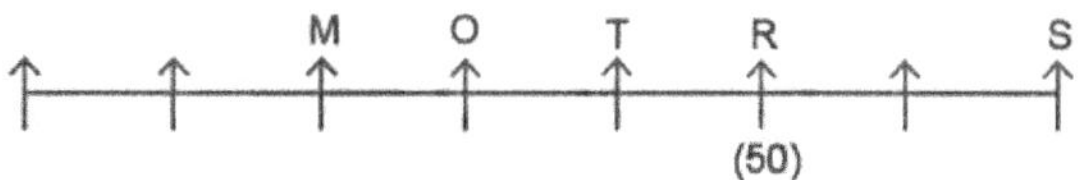

7) The one, who has 70 bags, sits immediate left of Q. Therefore, T and N must have 25 and 21 bags respectively.

8) N is not adjacent to R. So, case 2 is rejected. Also, N sits at the extreme left end.

9) O has the odd number of bags. So, O must have 13 bags.

10) R has more bags than Q, who has more bags than that of M. So, R, Q and M have 90, 64 and 30 bags respectively.

Final case:

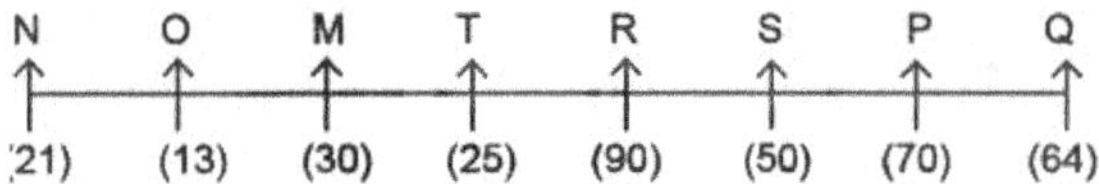

Five persons sit between N and P.

So, Five is the correct answer.

Hence, the correct option is (A).

49. Persons: M, N, O, P, Q, R, S and T.

Number of bags: 13, 21, 25, 30, 50, 64, 70 and 90.

1) M sits third to the left of one, who has 50 bags.

2) O sits adjacent to M.

3) Only two persons sit to the left of M.

Case 1:

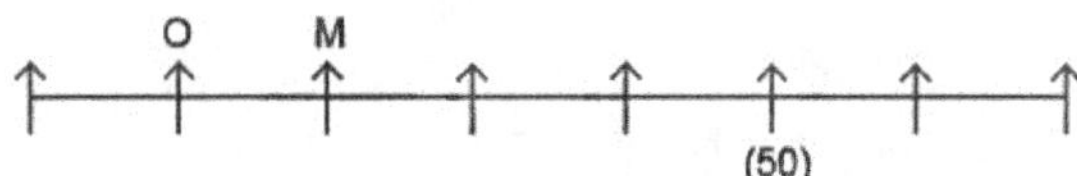

Case 2:

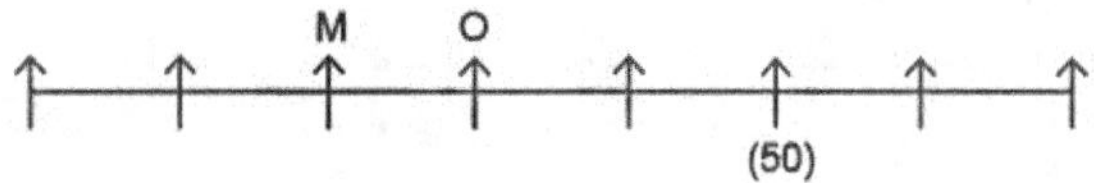

4) T has 4 more bags than that of N. So, T and N must have 25 and 21 bags or 70 and 66 bags respectively.

5) Three persons sit between O and S.

6) R sits immediate right of T and neither of them sit at extreme end.

Case 1:

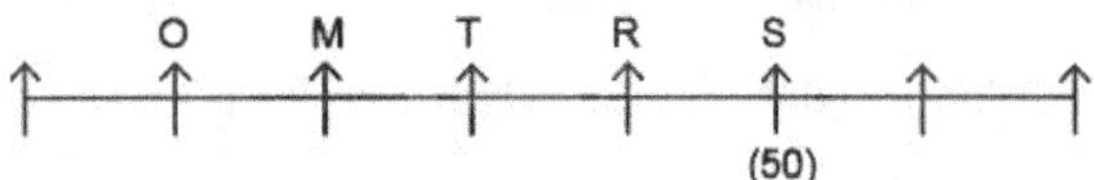

Case 2:

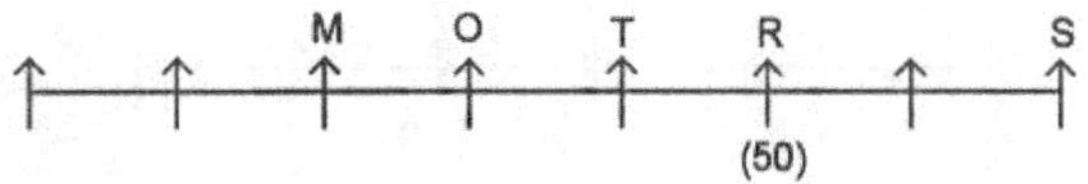

7) The one, who has 70 bags, sits immediate left of Q. Therefore, T and N must have 25 and 21 bags respectively.

8) N is not adjacent to R. So, case 2 is rejected. Also, N sits at the extreme left end.

9) O has the odd number of bags. So, O must have 13 bags.

10) R has more bags than Q, who has more bags than that of M. So, R, Q and M have 90, 64 and 30 bags respectively.

Final case:

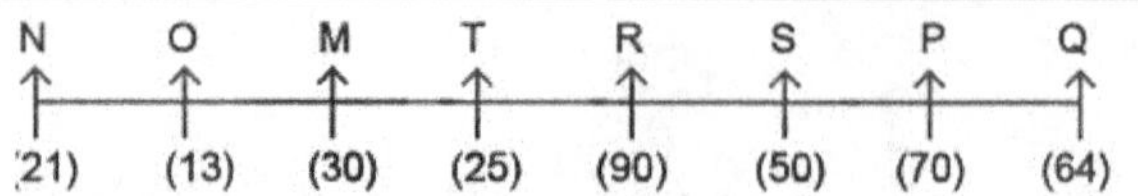

The difference in the number of bags of T and S = 50 – 25 = 25

So, 25 is the correct answer.

Hence, the correct option is (D).

50. Persons: M, N, O, P, Q, R, S and T.

Number of bags: 13, 21, 25, 30, 50, 64, 70 and 90.

1) M sits third to the left of one, who has 50 bags.

2) O sits adjacent to M.

3) Only two persons sit to the left of M.

Case 1:

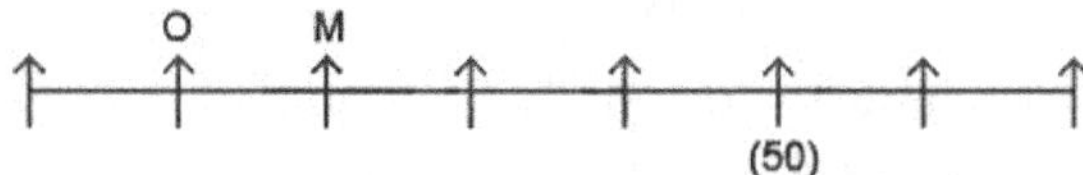

Case 2:

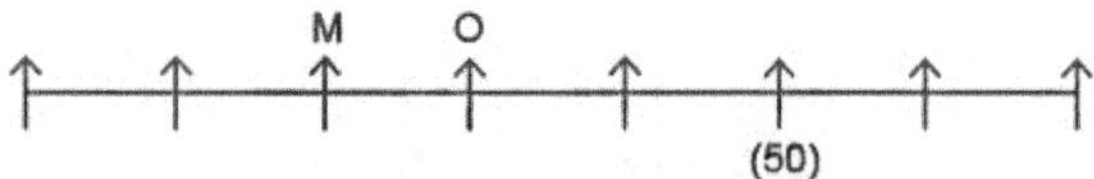

4) T has 4 more bags than that of N. So, T and N must have 25 and 21 bags or 70 and 66 bags respectively.

5) Three persons sit between O and S.

6) R sits immediate right of T and neither of them sit at extreme end.

Case 1:

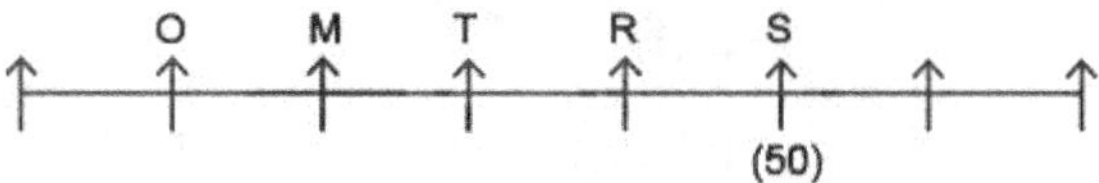

Case 2:

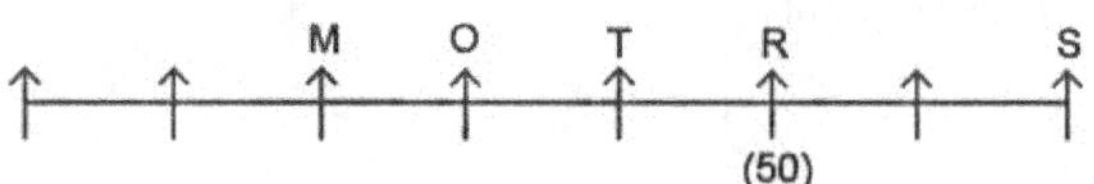

7) The one, who has 70 bags, sits immediate left of Q. Therefore, T and N must have 25 and 21 bags respectively.

8) N is not adjacent to R. So, case 2 is rejected. Also, N sits at the extreme left end.

9) O has the odd number of bags. So, O must have 13 bags.

10) R has more bags than Q, who has more bags than that of M. So, R, Q and M have 90, 64 and 30 bags respectively.

Final case:

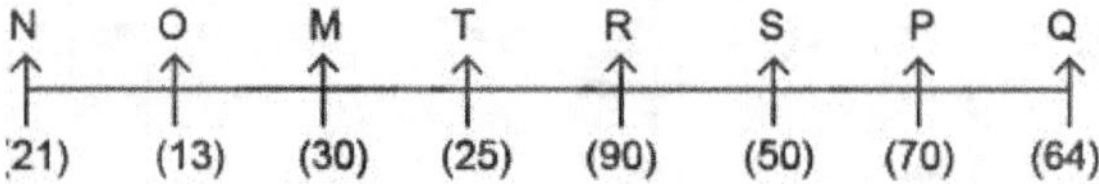

O sits second to the left of T.

So, O is the correct answer.

Hence, the correct option is (C).

51. Persons: M, N, O, P, Q, R, S and T.

Number of bags: 13, 21, 25, 30, 50, 64, 70 and 90.

1) M sits third to the left of one, who has 50 bags.

2) O sits adjacent to M.

3) Only two persons sit to the left of M.

Case 1:

Case 2:

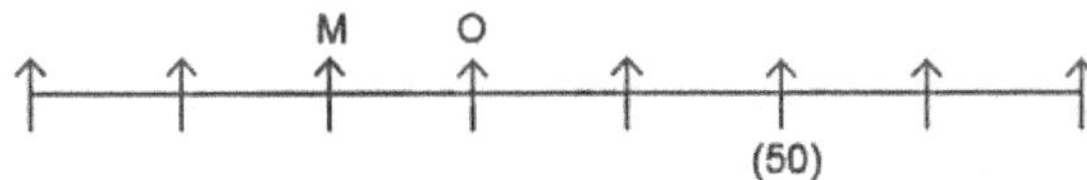

4) T has 4 more bags than that of N. So, T and N must have 25 and 21 bags or 70 and 66 bags respectively.

5) Three persons sit between O and S.

6) R sits immediate right of T and neither of them sit at extreme end.

Case 1:

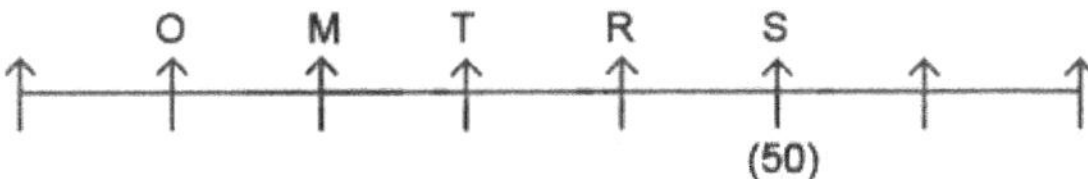

Case 2:

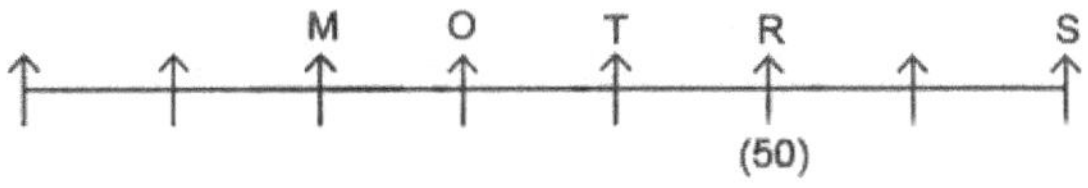

7) The one, who has 70 bags, sits immediate left of Q. Therefore, T and N must have 25 and 21 bags respectively.

8) N is not adjacent to R. So, case 2 is rejected. Also, N sits at the extreme left end.

9) O has the odd number of bags. So, O must have 13 bags.

10) R has more bags than Q, who has more bags than that of M. So, R, Q and M have 90, 64 and 30 bags respectively.

Final case:

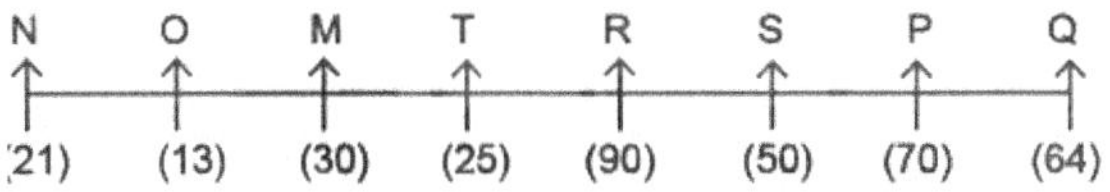

O has 13 bags.

So, 13 is the correct answer.

Hence, the correct option is (D).

52. Persons: M, N, O, P, Q, R, S and T.

Number of bags: 13, 21, 25, 30, 50, 64, 70 and 90.

1) M sits third to the left of one, who has 50 bags.

2) O sits adjacent to M.

3) Only two persons sit to the left of M.

Case 1:

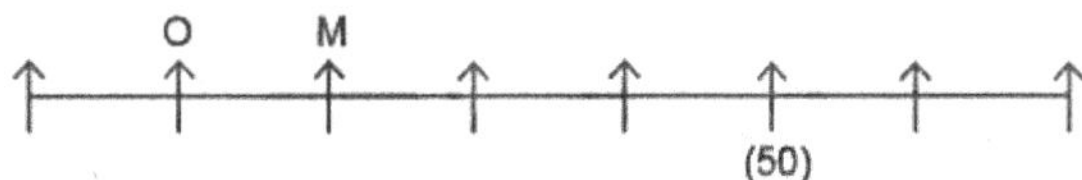

Case 2:

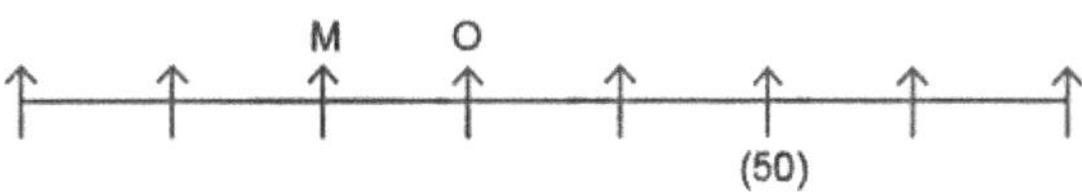

4) T has 4 more bags than that of N. So, T and N must have 25 and 21 bags or 70 and 66 bags respectively.

5) Three persons sit between O and S.

6) R sits immediate right of T and neither of them sit at extreme end.

Case 1:

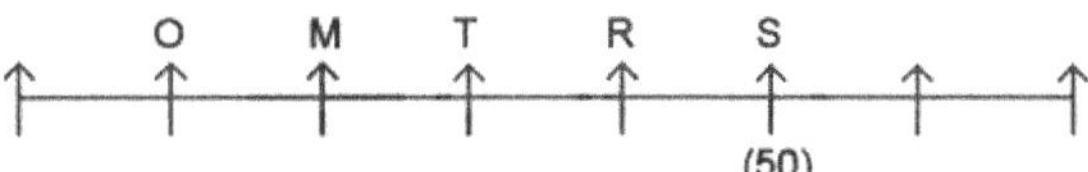

Case 2:

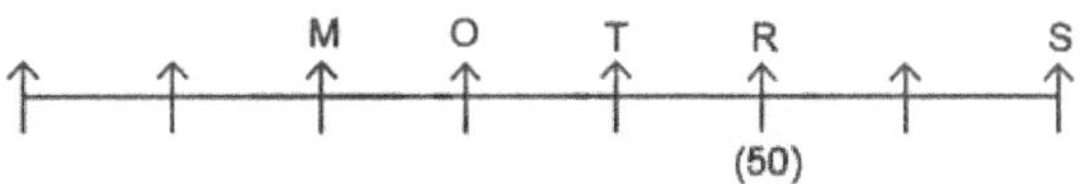

7) The one, who has 70 bags, sits immediate left of Q. Therefore, T and N must have 25 and 21 bags respectively.

8) N is not adjacent to R. So, case 2 is rejected. Also, N sits at the extreme left end.

9) O has the odd number of bags. So, O must have 13 bags.

10) R has more bags than Q, who has more bags than that of M. So, R, Q and M have 90, 64 and 30 bags respectively.

Final case:

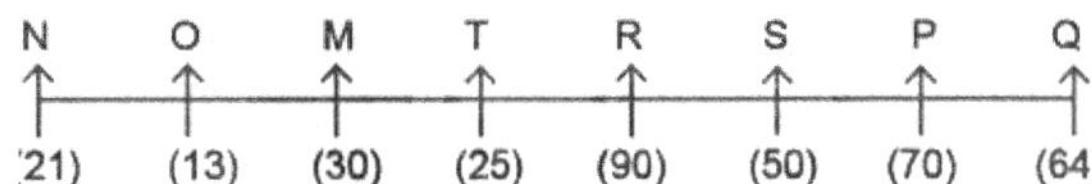

Two persons sit to the right of S.

So, Two is the correct answer.

Hence, the correct option is (C).

53. From the given information:

Symbol in Diagram	Meaning
◯	Female
☐	Male
═══	Married Couple
───	Siblings
│	Difference of A Generation

Symbol in Diagram	Meaning
◯	Female
☐	Male
═══	Married Couple
───	Siblings
│	Difference of A Generation

1. P, who is the grandmother of S, is married to O. (So, P is the wife of O)

2. O is the oldest member in the family.

3. N is the brother of S and son of M. (So, N and S are children of M)

4. R is a female and unmarried.

5. Q is the daughter-in-law of O, who has two children. (So, Q is married to M and M is the son of O and R is the daughter of O)

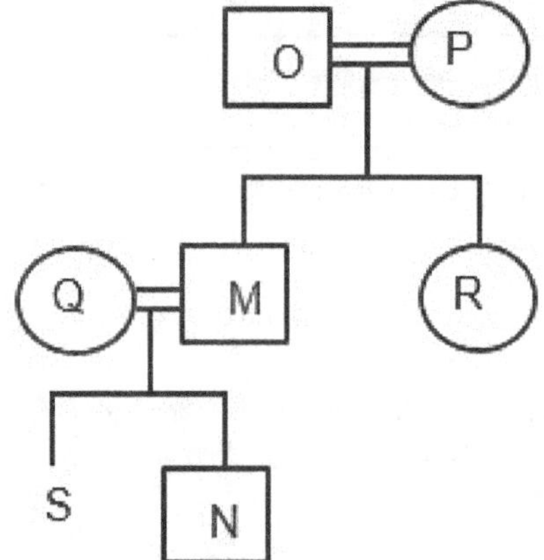

All the persons are male except Q who is female.

So, Q does not belong to the group.

Hence, the correct option is (C).

54. From the given information:

1. P, who is the grandmother of S, is married to O. (So, P is the wife of O)

2. O is the oldest member in the family.

3. N is the brother of S and son of M. (So, N and S are children of M)

4. R is a female and unmarried.

5. Q is the daughter-in-law of O, who has two children. (So, Q is married to M and M is the son of O and R is the daughter of O)

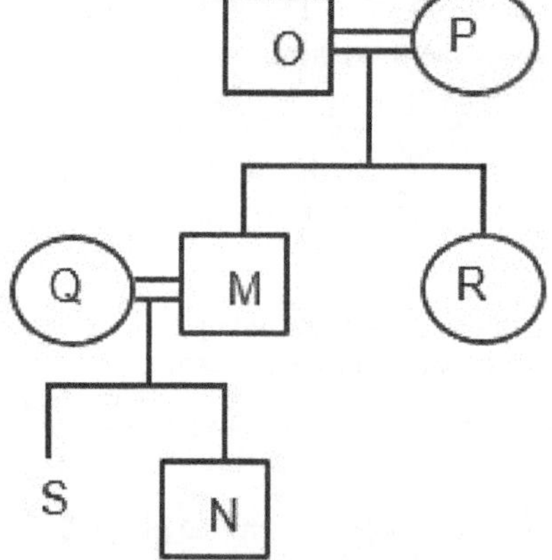

So, R is the daughter of P.

Hence, the correct option is (D).

55. From the given information:

Symbol in Diagram	Meaning
◯	Female
▢	Male
═══	Married Couple
───	Siblings
│	Difference of A Generation

1. P, who is the grandmother of S, is married to O. (So, P is the wife of O)

2. O is the oldest member in the family.

3. N is the brother of S and son of M. (So, N and S are children of M)

4. R is a female and unmarried.

5. Q is the daughter-in-law of O, who has two children. (So, Q is married to M and M is the son of O and R is the daughter of O)

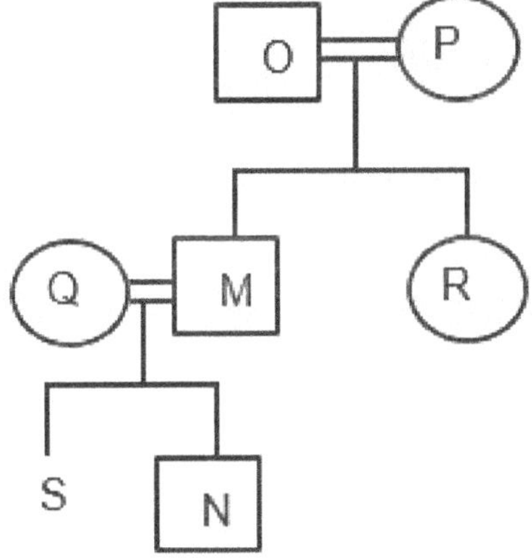

So, R is the aunt of S.

Hence, the correct option is (B).

56. The least possible Venn diagram is as follows -

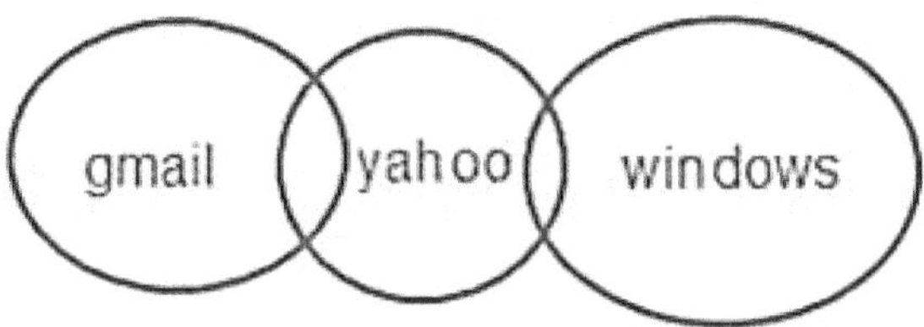

Conclusions – I Some gmail are windows – False

Conclusions – II No gmail are windows.– True

So, only II follows

Hence, the correct option is (B).

57. The least possible Venn diagram is as follows -

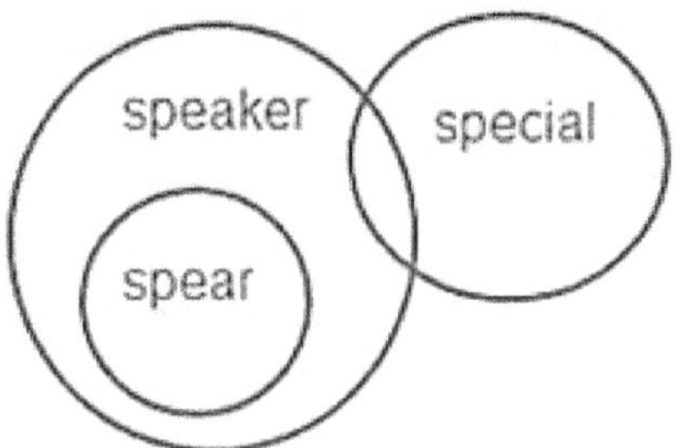

Conclusions – I some spear are special is a possibility – False (as only speaker is spear there is no relation possible between spear and any other except Speaker)

Conclusions – II only a few spear are special – False (Only a few speaker are special, Only speaker are spear)

So, neither I nor II follows.

Hence, the correct option is (D).

58. The least possible Venn diagram is as follows -

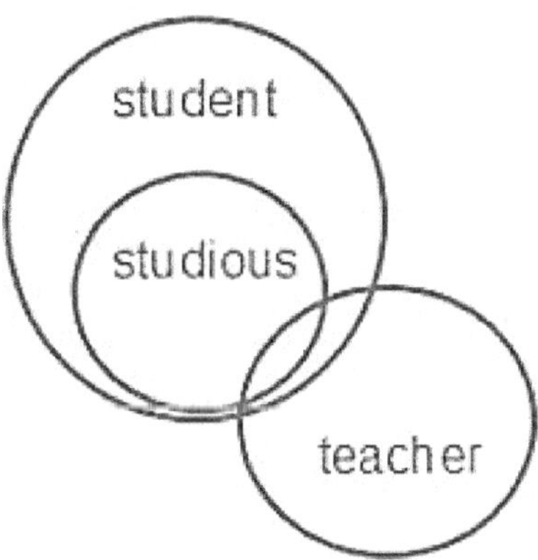

Conclusions – I Some teacher are student – True (All studious are student)

Conclusions – II No student are teacher – False (All studious are student)

So, only conclusions – I follows.

Hence, the correct option is (A).

59. The least possible Venn diagram is as follows -

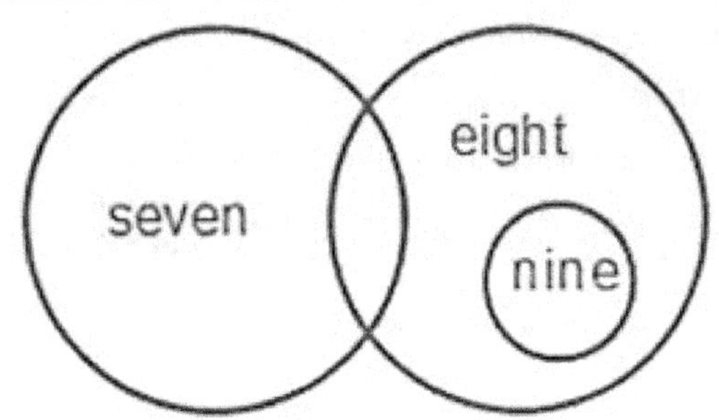

Conclusions – I some seven are nine – False (it is possible but not definite)

Conclusions – II All nine are eight – True (Only eight are nine)

So, only II follows.

Hence, the correct option is (B).

60. The least possible Venn diagram for the given statements is as follows,

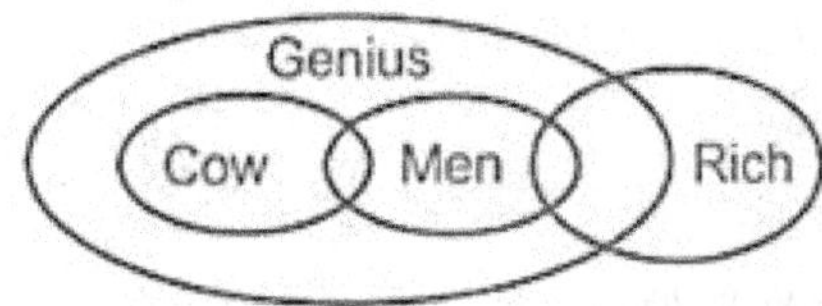

Conclusion:

I. Some genius are rich → True (All men are genius and some men which are not cow are rich)

II. Some rich are cow → False (It is possible but not definite)

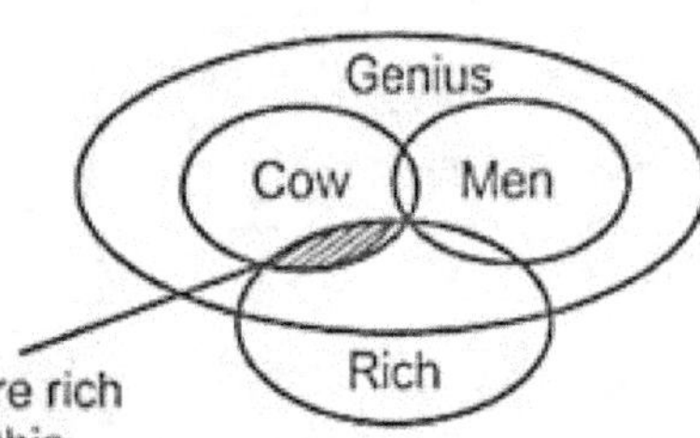

Some cows are rich is possible in this case but this case is not definite

III. Some cow are genius → True (All men and cow are genius)

Thus, only conclusion I and III follows.

Hence, the correct option is (C).

61. After dropping all the symbols and numbers, seventh alphabet from the right end is 'K'.

A E I O G **K** P U F T X V

And the second alphabet to its left is 'O'.

A E I **O** G K P U F T X V

Hence, the correct option is (B).

62. Given,

A 3 * 4 @ E 2 > I O 9 % G & 6 K P $ U 8 F # 1 O T X / 7 V ^ 5

The Nineteenth term from the Left end is 'U'.

And the tenth term to its right is 'V'.

A 3 * 4 @ E 2 > I O 9 % G & 6 K P $ **U** 8 F # 1 O T X / 7 **V** ^ 5

Hence, the correct option is (C).

63. The given sequence:

A 3 * 4 @ E 2 > I O 9 % G & 6 K P $ U 8 F # 1 O T X / 7 V ^ 5

While looking at Options 'A', 'B', 'D' and 'E', it follows the same pattern as described below:

The second term is second to the right of first term and third term is third to the left of the first term.

First term of next group in the sequence is second to the right of second term of previous group.

Hence, the correct option is (C).

64. In the given sequence , it is clear that only two numbers are there, which are immediately preceded by a symbol and immediately followed by an alphabet.

A 3 * 4 @ E 2 > I O 9 % G **& 6 K** P $ U 8 F # 1 O T X **/ 7 V** ^ 5

Hence, the correct option is (B).

65. In the given sequence, it is clear that only two vowels are there, which are immediately preceded by a symbol and immediately followed by a number.

A 3 * 4 @ **E 2** > I O 9 % G & 6 K P **$ U 8** F # 1 O T X / 7 V ^ 5

Hence, the correct option is (C).

66. $x^2 + 4x - 32 = 0$

$\Rightarrow x^2 + 8x - 4x - 32 = 0$

$\Rightarrow (x + 8)(x - 4) = 0$

Solving we get, $x = -8, 4$

$y^2 - 13y + 40 = 0$

$\Rightarrow y^2 - 8y - 5y + 40 = 0$

$\Rightarrow (y - 8)(y - 5) = 0$

Solving we get, $y = 5, 8$

x	y	Relation between x and y
-8	5	$x < y$
-8	8	$x < y$
4	5	$x < y$
4	8	$x < y$

$\therefore$ x and y are related as $x < y$.

Hence, the correct option is (C).

67. (I) $2m^2 - 11m + 14 = 0$

$$\Rightarrow 2m^2 - 7m - 4m + 14 = 0$$

$$\Rightarrow m(2m - 7) - 2(m - 7) = 0$$

$$\Rightarrow (2m - 7)(m - 2) = 0$$

$$\Rightarrow m = \frac{7}{2} \text{ or } m = 2$$

(II) $3n^2 - 7n - 3 = 8n - 3n^2 - 9$

$$\Rightarrow 6n^2 - 15n + 6 = 0$$

$$\Rightarrow 6n^2 - 12n - 3n + 6 = 0$$

$$\Rightarrow 6n(n - 2) - 3(n - 2) = 0$$

$$\Rightarrow (n - 2)(6n - 3) = 0$$

$$\Rightarrow n = 2 \text{ or } n = \frac{1}{2}$$

on comparing,

Value of m	Value of n	Result
$\frac{7}{2}$	2	$m > n$
$\frac{7}{2}$	$\frac{1}{2}$	$m > n$
2	2	$m = n$
2	$\frac{1}{2}$	$m > n$

∴ The relation between n and m is, $n \leq m$

Hence, the correct option is (B).

68. Equation I:

$$x^2 + x(\sqrt{5} + \sqrt{7}) + \sqrt{35} = 0$$

$$\Rightarrow x^2 + \sqrt{5}x + \sqrt{7}x + \sqrt{35} = 0$$

$$\Rightarrow x(x + \sqrt{5}) + \sqrt{7}(x + \sqrt{5}) = 0$$

$$\Rightarrow (x + \sqrt{7})(x + \sqrt{5}) = 0$$

$$\Rightarrow x = -\sqrt{5} \text{ and } -\sqrt{7}$$

Equation II:

$$y^2 + y(\sqrt{3} + \sqrt{5}) + \sqrt{15} = 0$$

$$\Rightarrow y^2 + \sqrt{3}y + \sqrt{5}y + \sqrt{15} = 0$$

$$\Rightarrow y(y + \sqrt{3}) + \sqrt{5}(y + \sqrt{3}) = 0$$

$$\Rightarrow (y + \sqrt{3})(y + \sqrt{5}) = 0$$

$$\Rightarrow y = -\sqrt{3} \text{ and } -\sqrt{5}$$

From (I) and (II),

x	y	Relation between x and y
$-\sqrt{5}$	$-\sqrt{3}$	$x < y$
$-\sqrt{5}$	$-\sqrt{5}$	$x = y$
$-\sqrt{7}$	$-\sqrt{3}$	$x < y$
$-\sqrt{7}$	$-\sqrt{5}$	$x < y$

∴ The relation between x and y is, $x \leq y$

Hence, the correct option is (D).

69. I. $(24 - 10x)^{\frac{1}{2}} = 3 - 4x$

$$\Rightarrow 24 - 10x = 9 + 16x^2 - 24x$$

$$\Rightarrow 16x^2 + 10x - 24x - 15 = 0$$

$$\Rightarrow 2x(8x + 5) - 3(8x + 5) = 0$$

$$\Rightarrow (8x + 5)(2x - 3)$$

$$\therefore x = \frac{-5}{8}, \frac{3}{2}$$

II. $6y^2 - 5y - 25 = 0$

$$\Rightarrow 6y^2 - 15y + 10y - 25 = 0$$

$$\Rightarrow 3y(2y - 5) + 5(2y - 5) = 0$$

$$\Rightarrow (3y + 5)(2y - 5) = 0$$

$$\therefore y = \frac{5}{2}, \frac{-5}{3}$$

x	y	Relation between x and y
$\frac{-5}{8}$	$\frac{5}{2}$	$x < y$
$\frac{-5}{8}$	$\frac{-5}{3}$	$x > y$
$\frac{3}{2}$	$\frac{5}{2}$	$x < y$
$\frac{3}{2}$	$\frac{-5}{2}$	$x > y$

∴ No relation can be established.

Hence, the correct option is (E).

70. (i) $2x^2 - (6 + \sqrt{15})x + 3\sqrt{15} = 0$

$$\Rightarrow 2x^2 - 6x - x\sqrt{15} + 3\sqrt{15} = 0$$

$$\Rightarrow 2x(x - 3) - \sqrt{15}(x - 3) = 0$$

$$\Rightarrow (x - 3)(2x - \sqrt{15}) = 0$$

$$\Rightarrow x = 3 \text{ or } \sqrt{\frac{15}{2}}$$

(ii) $5y^2 - (9 + 5\sqrt{15})y + 9\sqrt{15} = 0$

$$\Rightarrow 5y^2 - 9y - 5y\sqrt{15} + 9\sqrt{15} = 0$$

$$\Rightarrow y(5y - 9) - \sqrt{15}(5y - 9) = 0$$

$$\Rightarrow (5y - 9)(y - \sqrt{15}) = 0$$

$$\Rightarrow y = \frac{9}{5} \text{ or } \sqrt{15}$$

x	y	Relation between x and y
3	$\frac{9}{5}$	$x > y$
3	$\sqrt{15}$	$x < y$
$\sqrt{\frac{15}{2}}$	$\frac{9}{5}$	$x > y$
$\sqrt{\frac{15}{2}}$	$\sqrt{15}$	$x < y$

∴ The relationship cannot be established between x and y.

Hence, the correct option is (E).

71. Given:

$$\sqrt{676} \times \sqrt{576} - ? \times 18 = 300$$

$$\Rightarrow 26 \times 24 - ? \times 18 = 300$$

$$\Rightarrow 624 - ? \times 18 = 300$$

$$\Rightarrow ? \times 18 = 324$$

$$\therefore ? = 18$$

Hence, the correct option is (C).

72. Quantity A:

Let, the two digit number be $(10a + b)$, where 'a' is tens digit and 'b' is unit digit

So, $(10a + b) + \frac{1}{5}(10a + b) = (10b + a)$

$$\Rightarrow 11a = 8.8\, b$$

$$\Rightarrow \frac{a}{b} = \frac{4}{5}$$

Since the number is two-digit number so, the only possible no. will be 45 and reverse of it is 54

∴ 1% of number $= 1\%$ of $45 = 0.45$

Quantity B:

Probability of ball selection of red ball from first bag and black ball from the second bag =

$$\frac{5}{8} \times \frac{6}{10} = \frac{3}{8}$$

Probability of ball selection of black ball from first bag and red ball from the second bag =

$$\frac{3}{8} \times \frac{4}{10} = \frac{3}{20}$$

So, required probability $= \left(\frac{3}{8} + \frac{3}{20}\right) = \frac{21}{40} = 0.525$

So, Quantity A < Quantity B

Hence, the correct option is (B).

73. Given:

$$40\% \text{ of } 180 + 70\% \text{ of } ? = 121$$

$$\Rightarrow \left(\frac{40}{100} \times 180\right) + \left(\frac{70}{100} \times ?\right) = 121$$

$$\Rightarrow 72 + \left(\frac{70}{100} \times ?\right) = 121$$

$$\Rightarrow \left(\frac{70}{100} \times ?\right) = 49$$

$$\therefore ? = 49 \times \frac{100}{70}$$

$$= 70$$

Hence, the correct option is (D).

74. Given:

Let the cost price of an item be Rs.a

$$\Rightarrow \text{Selling price of one item} = a \times \frac{110}{100} = \text{Rs.} \frac{11a}{10}$$

$$\Rightarrow \text{Selling price of other item} = a \times \frac{95}{100} = \text{Rs.} \frac{19a}{20}$$

$$\Rightarrow \left(\frac{11a}{10} + \frac{19a}{20}\right) - 2a = 200$$

$$\Rightarrow a = 4000$$

Total cost price of two items = 4000 × 2 = Rs.8000

∴ Required percentage $= \frac{200}{8000} \times 100 = 2.5\%$

Hence, the correct option is (E).

75. Given,

Time taken by pipe A to fill the tank with chemical P = 30 minutes

Time taken by pipe B to fill the tank with chemical Q = 20 minutes

Time taken by pipe C to fill the tank with chemical R = 10 minutes

Part filled by A, B and C in 3 minutes $= 3 \times \left(\frac{1}{30} + \frac{1}{20} + \frac{1}{10}\right)$

$$= 3 \times \frac{11}{60}$$

$$= \frac{11}{20}$$

Part filled by C in 3 minutes $= \frac{3}{10}$

∴ Required ratio $= \frac{3}{10} \times \frac{20}{11}$

$$= \frac{6}{11}$$

Hence, the correct option is (B).

76. Given:

Time taken to complete a piece of work by $B = x$

Time taken to complete same work by $A = x + 50\%$

We know that,

$$\text{Efficiency} = \frac{\text{Work}}{\text{Time}}$$

Let us consider the number of days B requires to complete the work $= x$ days

So, number of days A requires to complete the work $= x + \left(\frac{50}{100}\right)x = 1.5x$

We can calculate, work done by A in 1 day $= \frac{1}{1.5}x = \frac{2}{3}x$

And work done by B in 1 day $= \frac{1}{x}$

We know that the number of days A and B together requires to do work = 18 days

So, work done by both A and B in 1 day $= \frac{1}{18}$

$$\Rightarrow \frac{2}{3}x + \frac{1}{x} = \frac{1}{18}$$

$$\Rightarrow \frac{5}{3}x = \frac{1}{18}$$

$$\Rightarrow x = \frac{(5 \times 18)}{3}$$

$$\Rightarrow x = 30$$

$\therefore$ B requires 30 days to complete the work.

Hence, the correct option is (A).

77. When first 9 litres of milk was replaced by water, then milk left in the container = 90 – 9 = 81 litres

$\therefore$ Fraction of milk in the mixture $= \frac{81}{90} = \frac{9}{10} = 0.9$

$\therefore$when next 9 litres of mixture was being replaced, amount of milk removed = 0.9 × 9 = 8.1 litres

$\therefore$ Milk left in the container = 81 – 8.1 = 72.9 litres

Hence, the correct option is (B).

78. Let the number of field workers be x.

There are 16 documentation workers.

Given total average = 45

$$\frac{Total\ age\ of\ all\ workers}{(16 + x)} = 45$$

Total age of all the workers = 45(16 + x)

The average age of 16 documentation workers = 38

Total age of documentation workers = 38 × 16

Total age of field workers = x × 52

Total age of all the workers = total age of field workers + total age of documentation workers

45(16 + x) = x × 52 + 38 × 16

$\Rightarrow$ 45 × 16 + 45x = 52x + 38 × 16

$\Rightarrow$ 720 – 608 = 7x

$\Rightarrow$ 7x = 112

$\Rightarrow$ x = 16

$\therefore$ Unmarried field workers = (16 – 7) = 9

Hence, the correct option is (E).

79. Number of shoes sold of Puma in April and June = 60 + 80 = 140

Number of shoes sold of Adidas in May and July = 60 + 100 = 160

$\therefore$ Required ratio = 140 : 160 = 7 : 8

Hence, the correct option is (A).

80. Number of shoes sold of all companies in May and June = (120 + 100 + 60) + (80 + 120 + 80)

= 560

Number of shoes sold of Adidas in all months = 120 + 60 + 80 + 100 = 360

$\therefore$ Required percent $= \frac{(560-360)}{360} \times 100 = 55\frac{5}{9}\%$

Hence, the correct option is (D).

81. Number of shoes sold of Puma in April, Nike in June, and Adidas in May = 60 + 120 + 60 = 240

$\therefore$ Required average $= \frac{240}{3} = 80$

Hence, the correct option is (B).

82. Number of shoes sold of Puma in all months = 60 + 120 + 80 + 120 = 380

Number of shoes sold in June of all companies = 80 + 120 + 80 = 280

$\therefore$ Required difference = 380 – 280 = 100

Hence, the correct option is (E).

83. Number of shoes sold of all companies in July = 120 + 60 + 100 = 280

Number of shoes sold of companies in April = 60 + 80 + 120 = 260

$\therefore$ Required percent $= \frac{260}{280} \times 100 = 92.85\% \approx 93\%$

Hence, the correct option is (C).

84. Given:

$$\text{Series} = 2, 11, 38, X, 362 \dots \dots$$

$$125\% \text{ of } X = 250$$

Calculation:

Quantity I:

$2, 11, 38, X, 362$

$\Rightarrow$ Series key $= (3 \times x) + 5$, where x is preceding term

$\Rightarrow X = (3 \times 38) + 5$

$\Rightarrow X = 119$

Quantity II:

125% of $X = 250$

$\Rightarrow \frac{125}{100} \times X = 250$

$\Rightarrow 250 \times \frac{100}{125} = X$

$\Rightarrow X = 200$

$\therefore$ Quantity I < Quantity II

Hence, the correct option is (C).

85. Given:

Real ratio $= 1 : 3 : 2$

Incorrect ratio $= 2 : 7 : 9$

B's loss $= Rs\,136$

Real ratio $= (1 + 3 + 2) = 6$

Incorrect ratio $= (2 + 7 + 9) = 18$

Let amount be $18x$ (L.C.M of 6 and 18)

Amount to be received by $B = \frac{18x}{6} \times 3 = 9x$

$\Rightarrow$ Amount erroneously received by $B = \frac{18x}{18} \times 7 = 7x$

$\therefore$ Difference $= 9x - 7x = 2x$

$\therefore 2x = 136$

$\Rightarrow x = 68$

So, amount $= 18x = 18 \times 68 = Rs.\,1224$

$\therefore$ Quantity $A <$ Quantity B

Hence, the correct option is (B).

86. Given:

The squared value of the diagonal of a rectangle $=$ $(36 + B^2)$ sq. cm

As we know, diagonal of the rectangle of length L and breadth $B = \sqrt{(L^2 + B^2)}$

$\therefore 10^2 = 36 + B^2$

$\Rightarrow 100 - 36 = B^2$

$\Rightarrow B^2 = 64$

$\therefore B = 8$

So, The breadth of the rectangle is 8 cm.

Hence, the correct option is (B).

87. Equivalent monthly investment ratio:

John : Jackson : Joseph = {(4000 × 4) + (4000 - 1000) × 8} : {(6000 × 6) + (6000 + 1000) × 6} : {(8000 × 8) + (8000 - 2000) × 4}

$\Rightarrow$ 40000 : 78000 : 88000 = 20 : 39 : 44

John $= \left\{ \frac{20}{(20+39+44)} \right\} \times 7500 = $ Rs. 1456 approx.

Hence, the correct option is (A).

88. This is a simple simplification.

$0.0729 = 8.1 \times 0.009$

$0.625 = 0.025 \times 25$

$28.9 = 0.0017 \times 17000$

$\therefore \dfrac{(0.625 \times 0.0729 \times 28.9)}{(0.0017 \times 0.025 \times 8.1)}$

$= (0.009 \times 25 \times 17000)$

$= 3825$

Therefore, the value of $\dfrac{(0.625 \times 0.0729 \times 28.9)}{(0.0017 \times 0.025 \times 8.1)}$ is 3825.

Hence, the correct option is (A).

89. Given:

88.60% of 1500 + 39.25% of 800 + 63.20% of 2500 + 25.40% of 4500 = ?

$\Rightarrow \frac{88.60}{100} \times 1500 + \frac{39.25}{100} \times 800 + \frac{63.20}{100} \times 2500 + \frac{25.40}{100} \times 4500 = ?$

$\Rightarrow$ 1329 + 314 + 1580 + 1143 = ?

$\Rightarrow ? = 4366$

$\therefore$ The value of ? is 4366.

Hence, the correct option is (D).

90. Given:

6.67% of $225 + 6.25\%$ of $1120 = (?)^3 + 3$

$\Rightarrow \frac{1}{15} \times 225 + \frac{1}{16} \times 1120 = (?)^3 + 3$

$\Rightarrow 15 + 70 = (?)^3 + 3$

$\Rightarrow 85 = (?)^3 + 3$

$\Rightarrow (?)^3 = 82$

$\Rightarrow ? = (82)^{\frac{1}{3}}$

The value of $?$ is $(82)^{\frac{1}{3}}$.

Hence, the correct option is (E).

91. Given:

$$\frac{\left(18 \times \frac{8}{15} + 10\%\right) \text{of } 624}{?} = 4$$

$$\Rightarrow 6 \times \frac{8}{5} + 624 \times \frac{10}{100} = 4 \times ?$$

$$\Rightarrow 6 \times \frac{8}{5} + 62.4 = 4 \times ?$$

$$\Rightarrow 6 \times 1.6 + 62.4 = 4 \times ?$$

$$\Rightarrow 9.6 + 62.4 = 4 \times ?$$

$$\Rightarrow 72 = 4 \times ?$$

$$\Rightarrow ? = \frac{72}{4}$$

$$\Rightarrow ? = 18$$

Hence, the correct option is (B).

92. Given:

$$\sqrt{225} + (55\% \text{ of } 1500) - \{(45)^2 \div 81 \times 4\} + 20 - 16 = ?$$

According to the BODMAS Rule,

$$\sqrt{225} + (55\% \text{ of } 1500) - \{(45)^2 \div 81 \times 4\} + 20 - 16 = ?$$

$$= 15 + 825 - 25 \times 4 + 20 - 16$$

$$= 15 + 825 - 100 + 20 - 16$$

$$= 840 - 100 + 20 - 16$$

$$= 740 + 4$$

$$= 744$$

$$\therefore \text{Answer is } 744$$

Hence, the correct option is (A).

93. Given:

$$(8375 \div 67)^{\frac{1}{3}} + (7.84 \times 25)^{\frac{1}{2}} = (?)^{\frac{1}{2}}$$

According to the BODMAS Rule,

$$(8375 \div 67)^{\frac{1}{3}} + (7.84 \times 25)^{\frac{1}{2}} = (?)^{\frac{1}{2}}$$

$$\Rightarrow (125)^{\frac{1}{3}} + (7.84 \times 25)^{\frac{1}{2}} = (?)^{\frac{1}{2}}$$

$$\Rightarrow (125)^{\frac{1}{3}} + (196)^{\frac{1}{2}} = (?)^{\frac{1}{2}}$$

$$\Rightarrow 5 + 14 = (?)^{\frac{1}{2}}$$

$$\Rightarrow (?)^{\frac{1}{2}} = 19$$

Squaring both sides,

$$? = 19^2$$

$$? = 361$$

$$\therefore 361 \text{ will come in place of '?'}$$

Hence, the correct option is (B).

94. Given:

$$?^{\frac{1}{3}} + 47\% \text{ of } 200 = 60\% \text{ of } 112 + 30\% \text{ of } 136$$

According to the BODMAS Rule,

$$?^{\frac{1}{3}} + (47 \times 2) = \left(\frac{6}{10}\right) \times 112 + \left(\frac{3}{10}\right) \times 136$$

$$\Rightarrow ?^{\frac{1}{3}} + 94 = 67.2 + 40.8$$

$$\Rightarrow ?^{\frac{1}{3}} = 108 - 94$$

$$\Rightarrow ?^{\frac{1}{3}} = 14$$

$$\Rightarrow ? = 2744$$

$$\therefore ? = 2744$$

Hence, the correct option is (D).

95. Given:

$$37 \times 43 - 40^2 + \left(\frac{15}{23}\right)\% \text{ of } \left(\frac{11500}{3}\right) = (?)^2$$

According to the BODMAS Rule,

$$37 \times 43 - 40^2 + \left(\frac{15}{23}\right)\% \text{ of } \left(\frac{11500}{3}\right) = (?)^2$$

$$\Rightarrow 37 \times 43 - 1600 + \frac{15}{23 \times 100} \times \frac{11500}{3} = (?)^2$$

$$\Rightarrow 1591 - 1600 + 5 \times 5 = (?)^2$$

$$\Rightarrow 25 - 9 = (?)^2$$

$$\Rightarrow (?)^2 = 16$$

$$\Rightarrow ? = \pm 4$$

$$\therefore \text{Value of } ? \text{ is } \pm 4$$

Hence, the correct option is (C).

96. The logic follows here is:

$$3^3 - 3 = 27 - 3 = 24$$

$$4^3 - 3 = 64 - 3 = 61$$

$$5^3 - 3 = 125 - 3 = 122$$

$$6^3 - 3 = 216 - 3 = 213$$

Similarly,

$$7^3 - 3 = 343 - 3 = 340$$

Hence, the correct option is (D).

97. In the given series, the following pattern is followed:

$$7 \times 1 + 1 = 8$$

$$8 \times 2 + 2 = 18$$

$$18 \times 3 + 3 = 57$$

$$57 \times 4 + 4 = 232$$

$$232 \times 5 + 5 = 1165$$

So, 1165 will replace the question mark.

Hence, the correct option is (C).

98. Logic is used:

$$17 + 2 \times 3 = 23$$

$$23 + 3 \times 4 = 35$$

$$35 + 4 \times 5 = 55$$

$$55 + 5 \times 6 = 85$$

$\therefore$? is 55.

Hence, the correct option is (C).

99. The logic is:

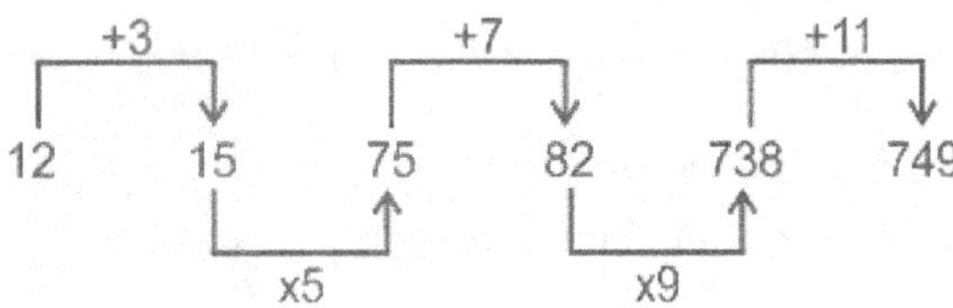

Therefore, ' 82 ' is the correct answer.

Hence, the correct option is (D).

100. Given:

$$19, 24, 30, 37, 45, ?$$

$$\Rightarrow 19 + 5 = 24$$

$$\Rightarrow 24 + 6 = 30$$

$$\Rightarrow 30 + 7 = 37$$

$$\Rightarrow 37 + 8 = 45$$

$$\Rightarrow 45 + 9 = 54$$

$\therefore$ The whole series is $19, 24, 30, 37, 45, 54$.

Hence, the correct option is (E).

English Language

Ques (1-5):Directions: Find out which part has an error and mark it as your answer. If there is no error, mark 'No error' as your answer.

Q.1 None of these (A)/ two officers (B)/ has been looking after (C)/ his department well. (D)

A. (A)   **B.** (B)   **C.** (C)   **D.** (D)
E. No error

Q.2 The strict boss (A)/ did not give her ascent (B)/ to the employee's (C)/ whimsical request. (D)

A. (A)   **B.** (B)   **C.** (C)   **D.** (D)
E. No error

Q.3 The Party Chief (A)/ and the Chief Minister (B)/ expressed his views (C)/ on demonetization in India. (D)

A. The Party Chief
B. and the Chief Minister
C. expressed his views
D. on demonetization in India.
E. No error

Q.4 Unlike Indian laws, US laws provides (A)/ for a contingency fee of lawyering (B)/ where the costs of litigation (C)/ are borne by lawyers. (D)

A. Unlike Indian laws, US laws provides
B. for a contingency fee of lawyering
C. where the costs of litigation
D. are borne by lawyers
E. No error

Q.5 India's Swachh Bharat Mission is (A)/ receiving globe praise (B)/ for attempting (C)/ to close the sanitation gap. (D)

A. India's Swachh Bharat Mission is
B. receiving globe praise
C. for attempting
D. to close the sanitation gap.
E. No error

Q.6 Select the correctly spelt word.

A. Monopolly   **B.** Monapoly
C. Monnopoly   **D.** Monopoly
E. None of these

Q.7 Select the correctly spelt word.

A. Commemorete   **B.** Comemorate
C. Commemmorate   **D.** Commemorate
E. Commeorate

Q.8 Select the correctly spelt word.

A. Hoseire   **B.** Hosier   **C.** Hosair   **D.** Hasier
E. Hesier

Ques (9-13):Direction: In the following question, some of the words have been left out. Read the passage carefully and select the correct answer for the given blank out of the five alternatives given in the questions that follow:

___________ (1) is a measure of the market value of all the final goods and services produced in a period of time. It is a very important factor in estimating the total income being produced in the country in a given year. It defines, if you will, the size of the cake. But there is a whole bunch of other ___________ (2). After all, the size of the cake is only one part of the story. How that cake is divided into different groups of people, sectors, that is equally important. When you talk of jobless growth, the growth part is coming from the GDP estimate and the ______________ (3) part is coming from employment data. The GDP data is critical to understand the pattern of growth you are seeing that is leading to the lack of jobs. ___________ (4) is another big indicator. As a country, we have neglected employment data for far too long. It's only in the last decade or so that we have started to say it is important, and finally got around to doing something about it only last year. The second, which is simply not produced, is the damage we are doing to our natural _______ (5). There is scattered data on forest cover, air pollution, water pollution, but you don't have a measure of the state of our natural capital. Are you getting high-income growth but at the cost of the environment? Is that trade-off worth it? The third is to know how income is distributed. Poverty measures, for instance, are important. Because they tell you, is this increase in income benefiting the poor?

Q.9 Which of the following words most appropriately fits the blank labelled (1)?

A. Guanosine Diphosphate
B. Gross Double Product
C. Group of Dispersed Products
D. Gross Domestic Progression
E. Gross Domestic Product

Q.10 Which of the following words most appropriately fits the blank labelled (2)?

A. Indicating   **B.** Indicators
C. Indication   **D.** Indicater
E. Indicate

Q.11 Which of the following words most appropriately fits the blank labelled (3)?

A. Conscientious   **B.** Obligation
C. Dutiful   **D.** Jobless
E. Joblessness

Q.12 Which of the following words most appropriately fits the blank labelled (4)?

A. Transport   **B.** Farming
C. Agriculture   **D.** Employment
E. Rigorous

Q.13 Which of the following words most appropriately fits the blank labelled (5)?

A. GDP   **B.** NDP   **C.** GNP   **D.** GATT
E. Growth

Q.14 Direction: Select the most appropriate synonym of the given word.

Dedicated

A. Tedious   **B.** Boring
C. Dreary   **D.** Committed
E. None of these

Q.15 Direction: In the following question, choose the word OPPOSITE in meaning to the given word.

Fastidious

A. Feckless   **B.** Fecund
C. Scrupulous   **D.** Sloppy
E. Simper

Ques (16-20):Direction: Rearrange the following sentences into a meaningful paragraph by choosing the correct sequence of the given sentences, the default order is P, Q, R, S and T, which may or may not be correct.

P. Artificial intelligence and machine learning are core drivers of how Google will pursue its 20-year-old mission

Q. The search engine focused strongly on mobile use and appeared to be growing more like Facebook, encouraging users to linger and explore topics, interests or stories

R. Google unveiled changes Monday aimed at making the leading search engine more visual and intuitive to the point it can answer questions before being asked

S. He described the latest changes as shifting from answers to journeys, providing ways to target queries without knowing what words to use and enhancing image-based searches

T. To organize the world's information and make it accessible to anyone, search vice president Ben Gomes said at an event in San Francisco

Google Images was redesigned to weave in "Lens" technology that enables queries based on what is pointed out in pictures.

Q.16 Which of the following sentences should be the FIRST sentence of the paragraph?

A. P   **B.** R   **C.** S   **D.** Q
E. T

Q.17 Which of the following sentences should be the SECOND sentence of the paragraph?

A. Q   **B.** R   **C.** S   **D.** T
E. P

Q.18 Which of the following sentences should be the THIRD sentence of the paragraph?

A. P   **B.** S   **C.** R   **D.** Q
E. T

Q.19 Which of the following sentences should be the FOURTH sentence of the paragraph?

A. S   **B.** Q   **C.** R   **D.** T
E. P

Q.20 Which of the following sentences should be the FIFTH sentence of the paragraph?

A. P   **B.** Q   **C.** S   **D.** R
E. T

Ques (21-25):Directions: In this question, a sentence has been given with some of its part in bold. To make the sentence grammatically and idiomatically correct you have to replace the bold part with the correct alternative given below. If the sentence is correct as it is, mark 'No correction required' as your answer.

Q.21 Building peace and transcending regional and global conflicts **cannot be left entirely to the action and volition of political leaders**.

A. cannot leave entirely to the action and volition of political leaders.

B. could not be left entirely for the action and volition of political leaders.

C. cannot be left entirely for the action and volition from political leaders.

D. should not be left entirely to the action and volition for political leaders.

E. No correction required

Q.22 An individual's behaviour may change over time, becoming bizarre if medication is stopped **and returns closer to normal when receiving appropriate treatment**.

A. and can return closer to normal when receiving appropriate treatment.

B. while returned closer to normal when receiving appropriate treatment.

C. and returning closer to normal when receiving appropriate treatment.

D. after returning close to normal when receiving appropriate treatment.

E. No correction required

Q.23 The book reflects the wide range of concerns and the multitude of ways **in which the United Nations touch the lives of people everywhere**.

A. in which the United Nations touches the lives of people everywhere.

B. which the United Nations touches the lives of people everywhere.

C. in which the United Nations touches all the lives of people in every place.

D. in which United Nations touches the lives of people everywhere.

E. No correction required

Q.24 Maslow's Hierarchy of needs states that we must satisfy each need in turn **starting with the first, dealing in the most obvious needs of survival itself**.

A. starting with the first, which deals with the most obvious needs of survival itself.

B. first starting with the one that deals with the most obvious needs of survival itself.

C. starting with the first, which is dealt with the most obvious needs of survival itself.

D. starting with the first one that deals in the most obvious need of survival itself.

E. No correction required

Q.25 Man and beast are struggling to live in harmony with one another **as the human population encroaches even further into the natural habitat of animals**.

A. as the human population encroaches even furthest into the natural habitat of animals.

B. with the human population encroaches further and farther into the natural habitat of animals.

C. with the human population encroaches farther into the natural habitat of animals.

D. as the human population encroach even farther into the natural habitat of animals.

E. No correction required

Ques (26-30):Direction: Read the following passage and answer the questions given below. Some words may be highlighted read carefully.

The Bronze Age in the Indian subcontinent began around 3300 BCE. Along with Ancient Egypt and Mesopotamia, the Indus valley region was one of three early **cradles** of the **civilization** of the Old World. Of the three, the Indus Valley Civilization was the most **expansive**, and at its peak, may have had a population of over five million. The civilization was primarily centered in modern-day Pakistan, in the Indus river basin, and secondarily in the Ghaggar-Hakra river basin in eastern Pakistan and northwestern India. The Mature Indus civilization **flourished** from about 2600 to 1900 BCE, marking the beginning of urban civilization on the Indian subcontinent. The civilization included cities such as Harappa, Ganeriwala, and Mohenjo-daro in modern-day Pakistan, and Dholavira, Kalibangan, Rakhigarhi, and Lothal in modern-day India. Inhabitants of the ancient Indus river valley, the Harappans, developed new techniques in **metallurgy** and handicraft (carneol products, seal carving), and produced copper, bronze, lead, and tin. The civilization is noted for its cities built of brick, roadside drainage system, and multi-storeyed houses and is thought to have had some kind of municipal organization. After the **collapse** of the Indus Valley civilization, the inhabitants of the Indus Valley civilization migrated from the river valleys of Indus and Ghaggar-Hakra, towards the Himalayan foothills of the Ganga-Yamuna basin.

Q.26 What is the meaning of the word metallurgy highlighted in the given passage?

A. Study of metals

B. Study of soil

C. Study of environment

D. Study of water

E. None of the above

Q.27 Which word is similar in meaning to the word **collapse** highlighted in the given passage?

A. Disintegration   **B.** Rise

C. Swell   **D.** Succeed

E. None of the above

Q.28 What is the main context discussed in the passage?

A. Indus Valley Civilization

B. Iron Age

C. Copper age

D. Stone age

E. None of the above

Q.29 What was the population of Indus Valley Civilization?

A. Over five million   **B.** Over two million

C. Over one million   **D.** Over three million

E. None of the above

Q.30 Which of the following cities was a part of the Indus Valley Civilization?

A. Ceylon   **B.** Sparta

C. Harappa   **D.** Rome

E. None of the above

Reasoning Ability

Ques (31-35):Directions: In the following question assuming the given statements to be True, find which of the conclusion among given conclusions is/are definitely true and then give your answers accordingly.

Q.31 Statements: $B \leq E \leq M; A > P \geq X; A = B$

Conclusions:

I. $X \leq E$

II. $M \geq P$

A. Only II is true

B. Only I is true

C. Both I and II are true

D. None is true

E. Either I or II is true

Q.32 Statements: $T < H \leq W; D > S \geq M; T > D$

Conclusions:

I. $W > D$

II. $M < T$

III. $H > S$

A. Only I is true

B. Both I and III are true

C. Either I or III is true

D. Both II and III are true

E. All are true

Q.33 Statements: $F \geq W > P; G \leq J \leq Y; W \geq Y$

Conclusions:

I. $P > J$

II. $Y < F$

III. $J \geq P$

A. Only I is true

B. Both I and III are true

C. Either I or III is true

D. Both II and III are true

E. All are true

Q.34 Statements: $Y \leq P < K; F > H \geq U \geq M; M = K$

Conclusions:

I. F ≥ K

II. Y < U

A. Only II is true

B. Only I is true

C. Both I and II are true

D. None is true

E. Either I or II is true

Q.35 Statements: C > T ≥ W; J < Q ≤ W; K > C

Conclusions:

I. C > J

II. Q ≤ T

A. Only II is true

B. Only I is true

C. Both I and II are true

D. None is true

E. Either I or II is true

Q.36 If all the letters of the word 'INTROSPECTION' are arranged in a way that all the vowels are arranged in the beginning in alphabetical order and then all the consonants are arranged in the alphabetical order, then the position of how many letters remains unchanged?

A. Zero

B. One

C. Two

D. More than two

E. None of these

Q.37 If all the letters of the word 'UNIDENTIFIED' are arranged in the alphabetical order then the position of how many letters will be remain unchanged?

A. Zero

B. One

C. Two

D. Three

E. More than three

Q.38 Direction: In a certain language, 'brown black are colors' is coded as 'po ta to la'. 'black dog is fast' is coded as 'cu da la tu'. 'fox and dog are friends' are coded as 'na da po hi pi'. 'brown fox is quick' is coded as 'pi to ra cu'.

What is the code for 'black'?

A. to

B. la

C. cu

D. ra

E. Cannot be determined

Q.39 If in a certain code language, 'MIND' is written as 'KGLB' and 'ARGUE' is written as 'YPESC'. Then, how will the word 'DIAGRAM' be written in the same code language?

[Haryana Primary Teacher (PRT), 2020]

A. BGYEYPK

B. BGYEPYK

C. GLPEYKB

D. BGEPYLK

E. GBGEPYLK

Q.40 If ABCDEF is coded ZYXWVU, then how is MERCEDES coded?

A. IVNXVHVW

B. XNVIWVHV

C. WHVVNXIV

D. NVIXVWVH

E. NNVIXVWVH

Q.41 In a row where all are facing north, Priya is 15th from the left end and Garima is 19th from the right end. They interchange their positions, and Ram who sits 24th from the left end sits at the 5th place to the left of Priya's new position. How many persons were there in the row?

A. 36   B. 42   C. 47   D. 56

E. 57

Q.42 Sahil and Gaurav are standing in a row of persons. Sahil is 12th from the left side and Gaurav is 18th from the right side of the row. If they interchanged their positions Sahil becomes 25th from left. What is the total number of persons standing in the row?

A. 42   B. 52   C. 45   D. 46

E. 56

Ques (43-45):Direction: Study the information given below carefully and answer the questions that follow.

There are 6 members in the family. There is one married couple who has only two children. N is grandson of K. P is a daughter of C. D is Paternal Aunt of P. C is maternal uncle of N. K is wife of R who is the father of D.

Q.43 Who is a brother of D?

A. K   B. C   C. R   D. N

E. P

Q.44 How is R related to C?

A. Uncle

B. Brother

C. Cousin

D. Father

E. Daughter

Q.45 Which of the following is definitely true?

A. K and R are siblings

B. D is a daughter of N

C. P is daughter of C

D. C is father of N

E. C and D are cousins

Ques (46-50):Directions: Study the given information carefully and answer the following questions below.

Eight persons S, T, U, V, W, X, Y and Z are sitting in a row facing either North or South direction but not necessarily in the same order. Z sits third to the left of X and faces opposite to that of X. Three persons are sitting between V and X. V and X are facing North direction. The immediate neighbours of Z face the same direction but opposite to that of Z. W is sitting 5th to the right of T who is facing north and neither of them is sitting at extreme positions. Y who faces the South direction sits at one of the positions at the left of V. S who is an immediate neighbour of V is sitting 4th to the right of W.

Q.46 Who sits at the extreme end of the row?

A. W   B. S   C. X   D. V

E. T

Q.47 What is the position of X with respect to U?

A. Third to the left

B. Third to the right

C. Second to the left

D. Second to the right

E. Cannot be determined

Q.48 Which of the following statements is correct?
A. S sits fifth to the left of X
B. U is an immediate neighbour of V
C. T sits at one of the extreme ends
D. Three people sit to the right of Z
E. U is neighbour of V and W

Q.49 Four are the same in a certain way thus form a group. Who among the following does not belong to the group?
A. X   **B.** W   **C.** U   **D.** V
E. T

Q.50 How many people sit to the right of S?
A. 4
B. 1
C. 2
D. 3
E. Cannot be determined

Q.51 Direction: In the question below are given some statements followed by some conclusions. You have to take the given statements to be true even if they seem to be at variance with commonly known facts. Read all the conclusions and then decide which of the given conclusions logically follows from the given statements disregarding commonly known facts.

Statements:
All vegetables are fruit
No fruit are drink
Some drink are honey.

Conclusions:
I. Some honey is not fruit.
II. No vegetables are drink.
A. Only conclusion II is true
B. Only conclusion I is true
C. Both conclusions I and II are true
D. Either conclusion I or II is true
E. Neither conclusion I nor II is true

Q.52 Direction: In the question below are given four statements followed by three conclusions I, II, III. You have to take the given statements to be true even if they seem to be at variance from commonly known facts. Read all the conclusions and then decide which of the given conclusions logically follows from the given statements disregarding commonly known facts.

Statements:
Some Pizza's are fries.
All fries are burgers.
No burger is Tacos.
Some Tacos are Wraps.

Conclusions:
I. All Pizza's being Tacos is a possibility.
II. No fries is Tacos.
III. Some Pizza are burgers.
A. Only II follows
B. Only III follows

C. Only I and III follow
D. Only II and III follows
E. None follows

Q.53 Direction: In the question below are given three statements followed by two conclusions numbered I and II. You have to take the given statements to be true even if they seem to be at variance with commonly known facts. Read all the conclusions and then decide which of the given conclusions logically follows from the given statements disregarding commonly known facts.

Statement:
All alphas are betas.
Some gammas are betas.
No gamma is a theta.

Conclusion:
I. Some theta's can be alpha's.
II. No gamma is alpha.
A. Only conclusion I follows
B. Only conclusion II follows
C. Either conclusion I or conclusion II follows
D. Neither conclusion I nor conclusion II follows
E. Both conclusion I and conclusion II follow

Q.54 Direction: In the question below are given two statements followed by two conclusions numbered I and II. You have to take the given statements to be true even if they seem to be at variance with commonly known facts. Read all the conclusions and then decide which of the given conclusions logically follows from the given statements disregarding commonly known facts.

Statement:
All short is cute.
Some cute is not tall.

Conclusion:
I. Some short is tall is a possibility
II. All tall is short is a possibility.
A. only conclusion I follows
B. only conclusion II follows
C. either I or II follow
D. neither I nor II follow
E. both conclusion I and II follow

Q.55 Direction: In the question below are given three statements followed by three conclusions numbered I, II and III. You have to take the given statements to be true even if they seem to be at variance with commonly known facts. Read all the conclusions and then decide which of the given conclusions logically follows from the given statements disregarding commonly known facts.

Statements:
Some Japaneses are Indians.
All Chinese are Mexicans.
Some Chinese are not Indians.

Conclusions:
I. Some Indians are not Mexicans.

II. Some Mexicans are not Chinese

III. Some Mexicans are Japanese.

A. Only I follows

B. Both I and II follow

C. Only II follows

D. Both I and III follow

E. None follows

Ques (56-60):Directions: Study the following information carefully to answer the given questions:

M 1 E & D 2 G 9 $ F @ 4 N Z W © 8 C Y A * 6

Q.56 How many such numbers are there in the above arrangement each of which is immediately preceded by a consonant and followed by a vowel?

A. Two

B. Three

C. One

D. None

E. More than three

Q.57 If all the numbers in the above arrangement are dropped, then which of the following will be the tenth from the right end?

A. $

B. D

C. F

D. Z

E. None of these

Q.58 Four of following five are alike in a certain way based on their positions in the above arrangement and so form a group. Which is the one that does not belong to that group?

A. ME2

B. G$4

C. NWC

D. YA6

E. None of these

Q.59 How many letters are there between the fourth element from the left end and the eleventh element from the right end of the given arrangement?

A. One

B. Two

C. Three

D. More than three

E. None

Q.60 How many such numbers are there in the above sequence which are immediately preceded by a vowel and immediately followed by a consonant?

A. One

B. Two

C. Three

D. More than three

E. None

Ques (61-65):Direction: Study the following information carefully and answer the given questions.

A teacher took her 6 students- P, Q, R, S, T & U for lunch. They went to a restaurant and sat around a circular table with students facing towards the centre and the Teacher facing away from the centre.

P, who doesn't sit next to Teacher, is second to the left of one who sits immediate left of R. At least one student sits between Q & R, taken from both the sides of R. No student sits between R & T, taken from the right of R, who is not sitting to the immediate left to the Teacher. Q and T do not sit together. U

and R do not sit together. Neither S nor U nor Q sit next to the Teacher.

Q.61 Who sits third to the left of Teacher?

A. Q

B. U

C. T

D. S

E. P

Q.62 Who sits third to the right of Q?

A. T

B. U

C. R

D. S

E. Teacher

Q.63 If Teacher and Q interchange their position and then starting from left of P, all the students sits according to English alphabetical series then, how many students sit remain at the same position excluding P?

A. 1

B. None

C. 3

D. 4

E. 2

Q.64 If another student 'X' sits in between Q & S and is facing towards the centre, then who sits 4th to the left of 'X'?

A. T

B. R

C. Teacher

D. S

E. P

Q.65 How many students are there whose names that are consonant are there in between R & P, when counted from left of R?

A. 1

B. 2

C. 3

D. No one

E. 4

Quantitative Aptitude

Q.66 The marks scored by Sam, by Geeta and by Radha in a competitive exam for Mathematics section out of 150 is 94, 85 and 120 respectively. For Science section, the scores for Sam, Geeta and Radha out of 150 is 135, 80 and 90 respectively. Find the average scores in percent of Sam, Geeta and Radha.

A. 76.33%, 55%, 70%

B. 55%, 46%, 59%

C. 78%, 57.33%, 82%

D. 70%, 60%, 62%

E. 80%, 65%, 91%

Ques (67-71):Direction: The following pie chart shows the money invested by Jeff Rhodes in different cryptocurrencies.

Total investment = 250 million dollars

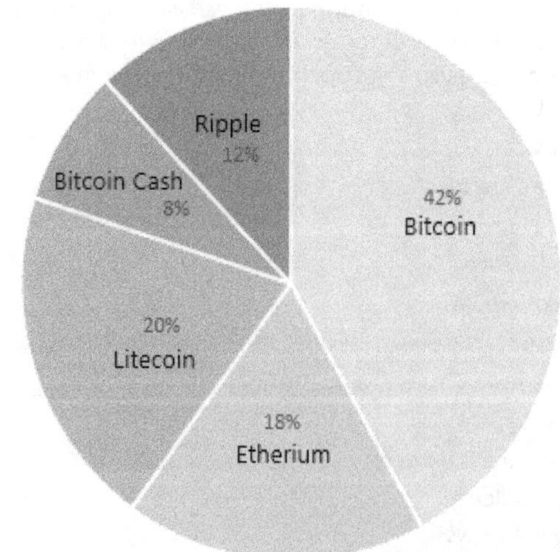

Q.67 If the total money invested in Bitcoin is 105 million dollars. What is the total worth of assets of Jeff Rhodes (in million dollars)?

A. 44 **B.** 125 **C.** 150 **D.** 250
E. 275

Q.68 How much money is invested in BTC (Bitcoin Cash) and Ripple together?

A. 20 million dollars **B.** 30 million dollars
C. 50 million dollars **D.** 150 million dollars
E. 250 million dollars

Q.69 What is the difference between the money invested in Bitcoin and the total money invested in other cryptocurrencies?

A. 10 million dollars **B.** 40 million dollars
C. 60 million dollars **D.** 105 million dollars
E. 145 million dollars

Q.70 If the price of bitcoin decreases by 40%, then the total assets of Jeff Rhodes decrease by what percentage?

A. 17% **B.** 20% **C.** 27% **D.** 40%
E. 48%

Q.71 If the price of Etherium increases by 20% and the price of Litecoin decreases by 10% then the total assets of Jeff Rhodes change by what value?

A. 4 million dollars **B.** 5 million dollars
C. 9 million dollars **D.** 14 million dollars
E. 25 million dollars

Ques (72-75):Direction: These question two equations numbered I and II are given. You have to solve both the equations and give answer.

Q.72 I. $x^2 - 16x + 63 = 0$

II. $y^2 - 2y - 35 = 0$

A. $x > y$
B. $x \geq y$
C. $x < y$
D. $x \leq y$
E. $x = y$ or no relationship can't be established between x and y

Q.73 I. $x^2 - 7x + 6 = 0$

II. $11y^2 - 13y + 2 = 0$

[IDBI Bank Assistant Manager, 2016]

A. $x > y$
B. $x < y$
C. $x \geq y$
D. $x \leq y$
E. $x = y$ or no relation can be established

Q.74 I. $x^2 - 9x + 18 = 0$

II. $y^2 - 11y + 18 = 0$

A. If $x > y$
B. If $x < y$
C. If $x = y$ or no relation is obtained
D. If $x \geq y$

E. If $x \leq y$

Q.75 I. $x^2 + x - 42 = 0$

II. $y^2 - 13y + 42 = 0$

A. $x > y$
B. $x < y$
C. $x \geq y$
D. $x \leq y$
E. $x = y$ or No relation can be established (CND)

Ques (76-84):Direction: What will come in the place of question $(?)$ mark?

Q.76 75% of $300 - 175 = 70 - ?$

[RBI Assistant, 2019]

A. 20 **B.** 25 **C.** 10 **D.** 32
E. 40

Q.77 $26 \times 15 + 310 - (15)^2 = 25\%$ of ?

[RBI Assistant, 2019]

A. 1500 **B.** 1800 **C.** 1700 **D.** 1900
E. 1600

Q.78 $? + (8)^3 = (26)^2 - 43$

[RBI Assistant, 2019]

A. 121 **B.** 119 **C.** 111 **D.** 131
E. 113

Q.79 $20 \times 168 \div 14 - 40 = ? + 110$

[RBI Assistant, 2019]

A. 84 **B.** 75 **C.** 90 **D.** 87
E. 94

Q.80 $\left(\dfrac{12}{13}\right)$ of $143 \div 6 - 12 = ?$

[RBI Assistant, 2019]

A. 14 **B.** 10 **C.** 8 **D.** 12
E. 11

Q.81 $\sqrt{625} \div \sqrt{16} \times 6 = ?\%$ of 300

[RBI Assistant, 2019]

A. 8.5 **B.** 15 **C.** 17.5 **D.** 10
E. 12.5

Q.82 $2^3 \times 4^2 \div 8 = (2)^?$

[RBI Assistant, 2019]

A. 2 **B.** 6 **C.** 4 **D.** 10
E. 16

Q.83 $\left(\sqrt{6} + 3\right)^3 = 750 + ?$

[RBI Assistant, 2019]

A. 591 **B.** 561 **C.** 581 **D.** 601
E. 461

Q.84 $? + 820 = 25\%$ of 6400

[RBI Assistant, 2019]

A. 600   B. 770   C. 760   D. 780
E. 680

Q.85 Direction: What value should come in place of the question mark '?' in the following question?

$256 \div 2^3 \times ? = 16\%$ of 3000

A. 10   B. 30   C. 20   D. 15
E. 12

Q.86 Rohan started a garage to provide the services for the old cars and after giving the labor charges of 10% per month, he was saving 15% per car which was Rs. 15000 then and on average he was selling 20 cars per month. What was the selling price of 20 cars?

A. Rs. 1200000   B. Rs. 2000000
C. Rs. 3000000   D. Rs. 2200000
E. None of these

Q.87 Soumya bought 20 kg of tea at Rs. 18 per kg and 15 kg of tea at Rs. 25 per kg. What profit did he get when he mixed the two varieties together and sold it at Rs. 30 per kg?

A. 35   B. 44.32%
C. 40.12%   D. 42.85%
E. None of these

Q.88 Direction: Each of the questions below consists of a question and two statements numbered I and II given below it. You have to decide whether the data provided in the statements are sufficient to answer the question. Read both the statements and give answer.

Is triangle ABC a right angle tringle?

Statement I: The ratio of length of sides of AB to BC is 4 : 5

Statement II: The ratio of length of sides BC to AC is 12.5 : 6.5

A. The data in statements I alone is sufficient to answer the question, while the data in statement II alone is not sufficient to answer the question.

B. The data in statements II alone is sufficient to answer the question, while the data in statement I alone is not sufficient to answer the question.

C. Either Statement I or Statement II alone is sufficient to answer the question.

D. The data in both the statements I and II is not sufficient to answer the question.

E. The data in both the statements I and II together is necessary to answer the question.

Ques (89-92):Direction: Each of the questions below consists of a question and two statements numbered I and II given below it. You have to decide whether the data provided in the statements are sufficient to answer the question. Read both the statements and give answer.

Q.89 Can a water tank of 2500 litres capacity be filled by two inlet pipes A and B together in less than 8 hours?

Statement I: If pipe A is opened alone then it takes 12 hours to fill the tank.

Statement II: Pipe B can fill 1 litres of water per minute.

A. The data in statements I alone is sufficient to answer the question, while the data in statement II alone is not sufficient to answer the question.

B. The data in statements II alone is sufficient to answer the question, while the data in statement I alone is not sufficient to answer the question.

C. Either Statement I or Statement II alone is sufficient to answer the question.

D. The data in both the statements I and II is not sufficient to answer the question.

E. The data in both the statements I and II together is necessary to answer the question.

Q.90 How much time will Ram take to cover a distance of 100 km at a uniform speed?

Statement I: The speed of Mohan is 10 km per hour more than that of Ram.

Statement II: If Mohan increases his speed by 25% then he takes 3 hours 20 minutes less to cover a distance of 500 km.

A. The data in statements I alone is sufficient to answer the question, while the data in statement II alone is not sufficient to answer the question.

B. The data in statements II alone is sufficient to answer the question, while the data in statement I alone is not sufficient to answer the question.

C. Either Statement I or Statement II alone is sufficient to answer the question.

D. The data in both the statements I and II is not sufficient to answer the question.

E. The data in both the statements I and II together is necessary to answer the question.

Q.91 What is the area of a right-angled triangle ABC?

Statement I: The length of sides AB and BC of the triangle is 12 cm and 9 cm respectively.

Statement II: The inradius of the triangle ABC is 3 cm, and the circumradius is 7.5 cm.

A. The data in statements I alone is sufficient to answer the question, while the data in statement II alone is not sufficient to answer the question.

B. The data in statements II alone is sufficient to answer the question, while the data in statement I alone is not sufficient to answer the question.

C. Either Statement I or Statement II alone is sufficient to answer the question.

D. The data in both the statements I and II is not sufficient to answer the question.

E. The data in both the statements I and II together is necessary to answer the question.

Q.92 What is the sum of x and y?

Statement I: $15x + 4y = 108$

Statement II: $y = 27 - 3.75x$

A. The data in statements I alone is sufficient to answer the question, while the data in statement II alone is not sufficient to answer the question.

B. The data in statements II alone is sufficient to answer the question, while the data in statement I alone is not sufficient to answer the question.

C. Either Statement I or Statement II alone is sufficient to answer the question.

D. The data in both the statements I and II is not sufficient to answer the question.

E. The data in both the statements I and II together is necessary to answer the question.

Q.93 If the compound ratio of $x^2 : y$ and $y^2 : z$ is $z : y$, then which of the following is true?

A. x = yz

B. y = xz

C. z = xy

D. xyz = 1

E. None of the above

Ques (94-98):Direction: What should come in place of '?' in the following number series?

Q.94 5, 10, 40, ?, 1920, 19200

A. 80   **B.** 180   **C.** 240   **D.** 120

E. 160

Q.95 0, 7, 26, 63, ?, 215, 342

A. 143

B. 168

C. 124

D. 120

E. None of these

Q.96 0, 2, 8, 18, ?, 50

A. 32   **B.** 34   **C.** 25   **D.** 48

E. 49

Q.97 123, 277, 459, 669, 907, ?

A. 1278   **B.** 1173   **C.** 1422   **D.** 1839

E. 4525

Q.98 9, 10, 22, 69, 280, (?)

A. 1321

B. 1342

C. 1405

D. 1365

E. None of these

Q.99 At its usual rowing rate, a boat can travel 32 km upstream in 2 hours more than it takes to cover the same distance in downstream. If speed of boat in still water is reduced to half of it's initial speed then it takes 8 hours more to cover a distance of 20 km in upstream than in downstream. What is the reduced speed of boat in still water?

A. 12 km/hr   **B.** 8 km/hr   **C.** 5 km/hr   **D.** 6 km/hr

E. 4 km/hr

Q.100 Direction: In the given questions, two equations numbered I and II are given. You have to solve both the equations and mark the appropriate answer.

I. $x^2 - 16x + 63 = 0$

II. $y^2 + 5y - 84 = 0$

A. x > y

B. x < y

C. x ≥ y

D. x ≤ y

E. No relation in x and y or x = y

// Smart Answer Sheet //

Correct Indicates percentage of students who answered questions correctly.

Skipped Indicates percentage of students who skipped questions.

Q.	Ans.	Correct / Skipped	Q.	Ans.	Correct / Skipped	Q.	Ans.	Correct / Skipped	Q.	Ans.	Correct / Skipped	Q.	Ans.	Correct / Skipped
1	A	48.54 % / 41.91 %	17	E	66.76 % / 30.81 %	33	C	67.47 % / 32.44 %	49	B	43.57 % / 31.37 %	65	B	45.34 % / 48.99 %
2	B	66.09 % / 31.87 %	18	E	45.63 % / 46.74 %	34	A	64.98 % / 32.13 %	50	E	67.37 % / 30.22 %	66	A	59.52 % / 31.55 %
3	C	68.81 % / 31.14 %	19	B	42.18 % / 38.0 %	35	C	42.81 % / 35.37 %	51	C	69.07 % / 30.44 %	67	D	69.55 % / 30.43 %
4	A	41.66 % / 48.69 %	20	C	66.74 % / 30.08 %	36	B	87.85 % / 10.69 %	52	D	84.17 % / 12.6 %	68	C	46.41 % / 36.78 %
5	B	48.64 % / 40.12 %	21	E	45.09 % / 34.99 %	37	B	77.32 % / 11.17 %	53	A	76.44 % / 20.66 %	69	B	64.83 % / 33.86 %
6	D	78.01 % / 12.35 %	22	C	48.13 % / 35.62 %	38	B	29.53 % / 67.78 %	54	E	57.44 % / 40.89 %	70	A	25.91 % / 68.33 %
7	D	47.19 % / 35.29 %	23	A	43.49 % / 55.09 %	39	B	42.73 % / 30.12 %	55	E	43.2 % / 53.51 %	71	A	60.91 % / 36.91 %
8	B	59.43 % / 38.47 %	24	A	67.9 % / 31.8 %	40	D	51.17 % / 44.19 %	56	C	59.62 % / 38.92 %	72	B	46.26 % / 31.8 %
9	E	80.5 % / 11.55 %	25	E	56.7 % / 41.51 %	41	C	62.89 % / 36.65 %	57	C	52.92 % / 33.52 %	73	C	40.24 % / 57.09 %
10	B	59.54 % / 39.41 %	26	A	63.77 % / 31.43 %	42	A	59.81 % / 38.14 %	58	D	53.17 % / 33.72 %	74	C	60.31 % / 34.39 %
11	E	42.41 % / 31.71 %	27	A	59.1 % / 30.96 %	43	B	82.8 % / 15.03 %	59	C	58.69 % / 35.66 %	75	D	53.3 % / 34.69 %
12	D	14.88 % / 79.77 %	28	A	28.96 % / 69.83 %	44	D	86.58 % / 11.47 %	60	E	44.7 % / 48.67 %	76	A	60.52 % / 32.96 %
13	A	43.86 % / 51.51 %	29	A	60.7 % / 34.09 %	45	C	67.29 % / 32.65 %	61	E	63.51 % / 32.97 %	77	D	61.49 % / 35.17 %
14	D	63.94 % / 32.74 %	30	C	46.9 % / 37.89 %	46	C	20.98 % / 76.76 %	62	E	62.56 % / 31.65 %	78	A	87.67 % / 12.24 %
15	C	46.22 % / 49.86 %	31	D	51.65 % / 47.5 %	47	D	61.72 % / 35.36 %	63	B	11.0 % / 78.43 %	79	C	60.74 % / 31.93 %
16	B	48.31 % / 49.44 %	32	E	57.19 % / 39.84 %	48	A	66.02 % / 31.05 %	64	A	44.25 % / 39.74 %	80	B	54.22 % / 32.61 %

Q.	Ans.	Correct / Skipped		Q.	Ans.	Correct / Skipped		Q.	Ans.	Correct / Skipped		Q.	Ans.	Correct / Skipped		Q.	Ans.	Correct / Skipped
81	E	69.46 % / 30.15 %		85	D	60.77 % / 32.45 %		89	E	69.92 % / 30.01 %		93	C	52.99 % / 41.28 %		97	B	56.61 % / 36.29 %
82	C	58.92 % / 37.76 %		86	D	49.61 % / 40.11 %		90	E	76.34 % / 12.78 %		94	C	46.11 % / 32.12 %		98	C	53.04 % / 42.12 %
83	C	58.56 % / 34.19 %		87	D	55.17 % / 31.89 %		91	B	52.92 % / 31.09 %		95	C	64.84 % / 33.44 %		99	D	50.09 % / 37.25 %
84	D	56.52 % / 34.99 %		88	E	78.19 % / 21.17 %		92	D	62.79 % / 31.04 %		96	A	50.32 % / 39.19 %		100	C	68.12 % / 31.15 %

Performance Analysis

Avg. Score (%)	57.0%
Toppers Score (%)	70.0%
Your Score	

//Hints and Solutions//

1. 'Neither' should be there in place of 'none'.

A pronoun is a word that is used instead of a noun or noun phrase. Pronouns refer to either a noun that has already been mentioned or to a noun that does not need to be named specifically.

'None of the' is used for more than two persons or objects, 'neither of the' is used for two objects.

- E.g. None of the three flowers is red.
- Neither of the two teachers is competent.

The correct sentence should be: Neither of these two officers has been looking after his department well.

Hence, the correct option is (A).

2. 'assent' should be there in place of 'ascent'.

Singular nouns are followed by singular verbs and plural nouns are followed by plural verbs.

"Ascent" means 'a climb or walk to the summit of a mountain or hill' which does not make any sense in the given context.

The correct word in place of 'ascent' would be 'assent' which means 'the expression of approval or agreement'.

- For E.g. The ascent of Fuji presents no difficulties.
- Prince Bagration bowed his head in sign of assent.

The correct sentence is: The strict boss did not give her assent to the employee's whimsical request.

Hence, the correct option is (B).

3. 'their' should be there in place of 'his'.

A pronoun is a word that is used instead of a noun or noun phrase. Pronouns refer to either a noun that has already been mentioned or to a noun that does not need to be named specifically.

When two singular nouns are joined by 'and' refer to two different persons the pronoun used for them should be 'plural'.

- E.g.: Ashwin and Hardik are brothers. They play cricket.

The correct sentence should be: The Party Chief and the Chief Minister expressed their views on demonetization in India.

Hence, the correct option is (C).

4. 'provide' should be there in place of 'provides'

Singular nouns are followed by singular verbs and plural nouns are followed by plural verbs.

A singular noun names one person. place. thing. or idea. while a plural noun names more than one person. place. thing, or idea.

The usage of the verb singular 'provides' is erroneous and needs to be replaced with the plural form of the verb 'provide' to make the sentence grammatically and contextually correct.

According to the subject-verb agreement, if the subject is singular then it is followed by a singular verb and if the subject is plural it is followed by a plural verb. Here the subject is 'US laws' which is plural and hence is followed by a plural verb.

- E.g. The dog chases the cat.
- The dogs chase the cat.

The correct sentence is: Unlike Indian laws, US laws provide for a contingency fee of lawyering, where the costs of litigation are borne by lawyers

Hence, the correct option is (A).

5. 'global' should be there in place of 'globe'

The usage of the noun 'globe' is erroneous and needs to be replaced with the adjective 'global' to make the sentence grammatically and contextually correct. This is because we need an adjective to modify the noun 'praise'. 'Globe' is a noun.

- E.g. This sacrifice was the least he could do for his friend.
- It was as if he'd tossed out a sacrificial lamb to a flock of vultures.

The correct sentence is: India's Swachh Bharat Mission is receiving global praise for attempting to close the sanitation gap.

Hence, the correct option is (B).

6. Monopoly has the correctly spelt word which means exclusive control, possession or use of something.

Hence, the correct option is (D).

7. The correctly spelt word is Commemorate. "Commemorate" means to organize or do something in memory of a past event.

Hence, the correct option is (D).

8. Hosier has the correctly spelt word. "Hosier" means a manufacturer or seller of hosiery (stockings, socks, and tights collectively).

Hence, the correct option is (B).

9. Here, a bit of general awareness is required. Upon reading the sentence will give you an idea that the paragraph is about the economy and so option (A) does not fit in.

Option (A),(B) and (C) are wrong options.

The complete sentence is:

Gross Domestic Product is a measure of the market value of all the final goods and services produced in a period of time.

Hence, the correct option is (E).

10. Here, different forms of the verb indicate are given. You have to choose the right word that is grammatically correct with the statement.

Gerund: **Indicating**

Noun: **Indication**

Noun: **Indicators**; (s) is for plural and singular is an indicator

Verb: **Indicate**

And in Indicator, there is a spelling error. So it is incorrect.

The sentence here refers to the indicators and in the latter part of the passage, employment and environment are used as indicators, not indications.

The complete sentence is:

But there is a whole bunch of other indicators.

Hence, the correct option is (B).

11. In the former part of the sentence, jobless growth is taken as a subject where growth is related to GDP and joblessness part is from the employment.

The words in options (A),(B) and (C) are somewhat similar in a sense but are incorrect for the given question.

Conscientious means to follow one's part or duty well and thoroughly.

Obligation means morally bound to something.

Only joblessness is right for the given question. One may get confused with jobless and joblessness but the thing here is the requirement of a word that tells you about the state being jobless that has already been referred in the sentence.

"A noun ending in 'ness' literally means the state of the original adjective".

The complete sentence is:

When you talk of jobless growth, the growth part is coming from the GDP estimate and the joblessness part is coming from employment data.

Hence, the correct option is (E).

12. Here, to answer this question one has to read the sentence after this. It has been clearly mentioned there that employment has been neglected for a long as an indicator. Now, for the past few years, it is being taken as an important factor and plays an essential role in GDP.

Farming and agriculture are synonyms and refer to growing crops

Transport refers to the movement of goods from place to place

Rigorous refers to hard strenuous work

The complete sentence is:

Employment is another big indicator.

Hence, the correct option is (D).

13. Here, one can understand the context of the statement and find the correct answer to the question. The blank must contain that term which is the main topic of discussion in the passage.

The Gross Domestic Product (GDP)measures the value of economic activity within a country.

The Net Domestic Product (NDP) is an annual measure of the economic output of a nation that is adjusted to account for depreciation.

Gross national product (GNP) is the value of all finished goods and services or the market value of all goods and services produced

The General Agreement on Tariffs and Trade (GATT) is a multilateral agreement regulating international trade

One can easily understand that the sentence is talking about GDP, its estimation and various other factors that involve GDP.

Hence, the correct option is (A).

14. The word 'Dedicated' refers to believing that something is very important and giving a lot of time and energy to it.

- Example: The Green Party is dedicated to protecting the environment.

The word 'committed' means loyal and willing to give your time and energy to something that you believe in.

- Example: We are committed to withdrawing our troops by the end of the year.

Therefore we can say that the word 'Committed' is the same in meaning as 'Dedicated'.

Hence, the correct option is (D).

15. Fastidious means "very attentive to and concerned about accuracy and detail." Only sloppy is the opposite of fastidious as it means "careless and unsystematic; excessively casual."

Scrupulous is cancelled as it is the synonym of fastidious and means "careful, thorough, and extremely attentive to details."

The rest of the words are incorrect too as they mean:

- Feckless: Lacking initiative or strength of character; irresponsible

- Fecund: Producing or capable of producing an abundance of offspring or new growth

- Sloppy: It shows a lack of care, thought, or effort.

- Simper: Smile in an affectedly coquettish, coy, or ingratiating manner

Hence, the correct option is (C).

16. There is no doubt that this passage is **related to technology**, and the particular organization in question is '**Google.**' This is introduced to us in **sentence R.**

The next sentence must be **P** where it says that '**the 20-year old mission**' is referring to the mission of making the search engine more intuitive. This tells us how they are going to achieve it.

The third sentence is **T as this sentence starts with 'to.'**

The fourth sentence is Q. Since the paragraph has already introduced us to 'Google' now it is referring to it as '**the search engine.**' This sentence tells us what they want to achieve and what their focus areas will be. Finally, the fifth sentence will be S.

Thus, the correct chronological order for the passage is RPTQS.

The ordered paragraph is: Google unveiled changes Monday aimed at making the leading search engine more visual and intuitive to the point it can answer questions before being asked artificial intelligence and machine learning are core drivers of how Google will pursue its 20-year-old mission to organize the world's information and make it accessible to anyone, search vice president Ben Gomes said at an event in San Francisco. The search engine focused strongly on mobile use and appeared to be growing more like Facebook, encouraging users to linger and explore topics, interests or stories. He described the latest changes as shifting from answers to journeys, providing ways to target queries without knowing what words to use and enhancing image-based searches. **Google Images was redesigned to weave in "Lens" technology that enables queries based on what is pointed out in pictures.**

Hence, the correct option is (B).

17. There is no doubt that this passage is **related to technology**, and the particular organisation in question is 'Google.' This is introduced to us in sentence R.

The next sentence must be **P** where it says that 'the **20-year old mission**' is referring to the mission of making the search engine more intuitive. This tells us how they are going to achieve it.

The third sentence is **T as this sentence starts with 'to.'**

The fourth sentence is Q. Since the paragraph has already introduced us to 'Google' now it is referring to it as '**the search engine.**' This sentence tells us what they want to achieve and what their focus areas will be. Finally, the fifth sentence will be S.

Thus, the correct chronological order for the passage is RPTQS.

The ordered paragraph is: Google unveiled changes Monday aimed at making the leading search engine more visual and intuitive to the point it can answer questions before being asked artificial intelligence and machine learning are core drivers of how Google will pursue its 20-year-old mission to organize the world's information and make it accessible to anyone, search vice president Ben Gomes said at an event in San Francisco. The search engine focused strongly on mobile use and appeared to be growing more like Facebook, encouraging users to linger and explore topics, interests or stories. He described the latest changes as shifting from answers to journeys, providing ways to target queries without knowing what words to use and enhancing image-based searches. **Google Images was redesigned to weave in "Lens" technology that enables queries based on what is pointed out in pictures.**

Hence, the correct option is (E).

18. There is no doubt that this passage is **related to technology**, and the particular organisation in question is 'Google.' This is introduced to us in sentence R.

The next sentence must be **P** where it says that '**the 20-year old mission**' is referring to the mission of making the search engine more intuitive. This tells us how they are going to achieve it.

The third sentence is **T as this sentence starts with 'to.'**

The fourth sentence is Q. Since the paragraph has already introduced us to 'Google' now it is referring to it as '**the search engine.'** This sentence tells us what they want to achieve and what their focus areas will be. Finally, the fifth sentence will be S.

Thus, the correct chronological order for the passage is RPTQS.

The ordered paragraph is: Google unveiled changes Monday aimed at making the leading search engine more visual and intuitive to the point it can answer questions before being asked artificial intelligence and machine learning are core drivers of how Google will pursue its 20-year-old mission to organize the world's information and make it accessible to anyone, search vice president Ben Gomes said at an event in San Francisco. The search engine focused strongly on mobile use and appeared to be growing more like Facebook, encouraging users to linger and explore topics, interests or stories. He described the latest changes as shifting from answers to journeys, providing ways to target queries without knowing what words to use and enhancing image-based searches. **Google Images was redesigned to weave in "Lens" technology that enables queries based on what is pointed out in pictures.**

Hence, the correct option is (E).

19. There is no doubt that this passage is **related to technology**, and the particular organisation in question is 'Google.' This is introduced to us in sentence R.

The next sentence must be **P** where it says that '**the 20-year old mission**' is referring to the mission of making the search engine more intuitive. This tells us how they are going to achieve it.

The third sentence is **T as this sentence starts with 'to.'**

The fourth sentence is Q. Since the paragraph has already introduced us to 'Google' now it is referring to it as '**the search engine.'** This sentence tells us what they want to achieve and what their focus areas will be. Finally, the fifth sentence will be S.

Thus, the correct chronological order for the passage is RPTQS.

The ordered paragraph is: Google unveiled changes Monday aimed at making the leading search engine more visual and intuitive to the point it can answer questions before being asked artificial intelligence and machine learning are core drivers of how Google will pursue its 20-year-old mission to organize the world's information and make it accessible to anyone, search vice president Ben Gomes said at an event in San Francisco. The search engine focused strongly on mobile use and appeared to be growing more like Facebook, encouraging users to linger and explore topics, interests or stories. He described the latest changes as shifting from answers to journeys, providing ways to target queries without knowing what words to use and enhancing image-based searches. **Google Images was redesigned to weave in "Lens" technology that enables queries based on what is pointed out in pictures.**

Hence, the correct option is (B).

20. There is no doubt that this passage is **related to technology**, and the particular organisation in question is 'Google.' This is introduced to us in sentence R.

The next sentence must be **P** where it says that '**the 20-year old mission**' is referring to the mission of making the search engine more intuitive. This tells us how they are going to achieve it.

The third sentence is **T as this sentence starts with 'to.'**

The fourth sentence is Q. Since the paragraph has already introduced us to 'Google' now it is referring to it as **'the search engine.'** This sentence tells us what they want to achieve and what their focus areas will be. Finally, the fifth sentence will be S.

Thus, the correct chronological order for the passage is RPTQS.

The ordered paragraph is: Google unveiled changes Monday aimed at making the leading search engine more visual and intuitive to the point it can answer questions before being asked artificial intelligence and machine learning are core drivers of how Google will pursue its 20-year-old mission to organize the world's information and make it accessible to anyone, search vice president Ben Gomes said at an event in San Francisco. The search engine focused strongly on mobile use and appeared to be growing more like Facebook, encouraging users to linger and explore topics, interests or stories. He described the latest changes as shifting from answers to journeys, providing ways to target queries without knowing what words to use and enhancing image-based searches. **Google Images was redesigned to weave in "Lens" technology that enables queries based on what is pointed out in pictures.**

Hence, the correct option is (C).

21. The sentence is absolutely correct and thus needs no improvement.

Hence, the correct option is (E).

22. Option (A) and (B) are erroneous because 'can return' and 'returned' are verb phrases which aren't parallel with the gerund phrase 'becoming bizarre'. Options (A) and (B) so get eliminated.

Option (D), though, takes care of the parallel structure yet deviates the meaning of the sentence.

Option (C) is the perfect choice among the given ones and must replace the bold part to make it a grammatically correct sentence.

Hence, the correct option is (C).

23. Option (B) is incorrect because the preposition 'in' is missing before "which". This changes the meaning of the sentence. It indicates the UN touches the ways. Option (B) so gets eliminated.

Option (C) is erroneous as well because "all" is not required. Plus, 'everywhere' is more appropriate than 'every place'.

Option (D) is also incorrect because United Nations is a world famous organization and assumes the definite article 'the' before it.

Clearly, option (A) is most suitable choice among the given ones.

Hence, the correct option is (A).

24. Option (D) can be immediately eliminated because the phrasal verb 'deal in' which refers to 'buying and selling something' is not appropriate in the context.

Option (B) is verbose as "first starting with the one" is a repetition which can be avoided with 'starting with the first'.

In option (C), usage of passive voice (which is dealt with) doesn't make any sense and is hence erroneous. This eliminates option (C) as well.

Hence, the correct option is (A).

25. The sentence is absolutely correct and thus needs no correction.

Hence, the correct option is (E).

26. Metallurgy is a domain of materials science and engineering.

It studies the physical and chemical behavior of metallic elements.

It also studies the physical and chemical behavior of inter-metallic compounds.

So, the correct answer is study of metals.

Hence, the correct option is (A).

27. Collapse means to fall or shrink together abruptly and completely.

Disintegration means breaking up into small parts.

So, the correct answer is disintegrate.

Hence, the correct option is (A).

28. Let us have a look at the following sentences given in the passage:

- After the collapse of the Indus Valley civilization, the inhabitants......
- ....the Indus Valley Civilization was the most expansive,...
- The Mature Indus civilization flourished .....
- From the above lines, we can conclude the context of the passage.

So, the correct answer is Indus Valley Civilization.

Hence, the correct option is (A).

29. Let us have a look at the following line given in the passage:

- ...may have had a population of over five million.

So, the correct answer is over five million.

Hence, the correct option is (A).

30. Refer to the following line given in the passage:

- "The civilization included cities such as Harappa, Ganeriwala, and Mohenjo-daro........"

So, the correct answer is harappa.

Hence, the correct option is (C).

31. Given statements: $B \leq E \leq M$; $A > P \geq X$; $A = B$

On combining: $X \leq P < A = B \leq E \leq M$

Conclusions:

I. $X \leq E \rightarrow$ False ($X \leq P < A = B \leq E \rightarrow X < E$)

II. $M \geq P \rightarrow$ False ($P < A = B \leq E \leq M \rightarrow P < M$)

Thus, neither conclusion I nor conclusion II is true.

Hence, the correct option is (D).

32. Given statements: T < H ≤ W; D > S ≥ M; T > D

On combining: W ≥ H > T > D > S ≥ M

Conclusions:

I. W > D → True (W ≥ H > T > D → W > D)

II. M < T → True (T > D > S ≥ M → T > M)

III. H > S → True (H > T > D > S → H > S)

Thus, all the conclusions are true.

Hence, the correct option is (E).

33. Given statements: F ≥ W > P; G ≤ J ≤ Y; W ≥ Y

On combining: F ≥ W > P; F ≥ W ≥ Y ≥ J ≥ G

Conclusions:

I. P > J → False (W > P and W ≥ Y ≥ J → relation between P and J cannot be determined.)

II. Y < F → False (F ≥ W ≥ Y → F ≥ Y)

III. J ≥ P → False (W > P and W ≥ Y ≥ J → relation between P and J cannot be determined.)

None of the conclusions are true but conclusions I and III form complementary pair.)

Thus, either conclusion I or III is true.

Hence, the correct option is (C).

34. Given statements: Y ≤ P < K; F > H ≥ U ≥ M; M = K

On combining: F > H ≥ U ≥ M = K > P ≥ Y

Conclusions:

I. F ≥ K → False (F > H ≥ U ≥ M = K → F > K)

II. Y < U → True (U ≥ M = K > P ≥ Y → U > Y)

Thus, only conclusion II is true.

Hence, the correct option is (A).

35. Given statements: C > T ≥ W; J < Q ≤ W; K > C

On combining: K > C > T ≥ W ≥ Q > J

Conclusions:

I. C > J → True (C > T ≥ W ≥ Q > J → C > J)

II. Q ≤ T → True (T ≥ W ≥ Q → T ≥ Q)

Thus, both conclusions I and II are true.

Hence, the correct option is (C).

36. The given word:

INTROSPECTION

Applying the above condition, we have a new word:

EIIOOCNNPRSTT

The final arrangements of the old and new words are:

I	N	T	R	O	S	P	E	C	T	I	O	N

E	I	I	O	O	C	N	N	P	R	S	T	T

Thus the position of only one letter i.e, "O" remains unchanged.

Hence, the correct option is (B).

37. The given word:

UNIDENTIFIED

After arranging the letters in alphabetical order:

DDEEFIIINNTU

The final arrangement of old and new words are:

U	N	I	D	E	N	T	I	F	I	E	D
D	D	E	E	F	I	I	I	N	N	T	U

On comparing both the words we will find that the position of only 1 letter viz. I is unchanged.

Hence, the correct option is (B).

38. Let's find the codes for each word by comparing the sentences. On comparing the first and the second sentences, we see that the code for 'black' is 'la'. On comparing the first and the third sentences, we see that the code for 'are' is 'po'. On comparing the first and the last sentence, we see that the code for 'brown' is 'to'. On comparing the second and the third sentences, we see that the code for 'dog' is 'da'. On comparing the second and the last sentences, we see that the code for 'is' is 'cu'.

In the second sentence, since all the codes except 'fast' are known, the code for 'fast' is 'tu'. Similarly, the codes for other words can be deduced.

The codes for 'and' and 'friends' is 'hi' or 'na' in any order.

Tabulating the results:

brown	to
fox	pi
is	cu
quick	ra
black	la
dog	da
fast	tu
are	po
colors	ta
and	hi/na
friends	na/hi

Hence, the correct option is (B).

39.

Alpha bets	A	B	C	D	E	F	G	H	I	J	K	L	M
Positi onal value	1	2	3	4	5	6	7	8	9	10	11	12	13
Positi onal value	26	25	24	23	22	21	20	19	18	17	16	15	14
Alpha bets	Z	Y	X	W	V	U	T	S	R	Q	P	O	N

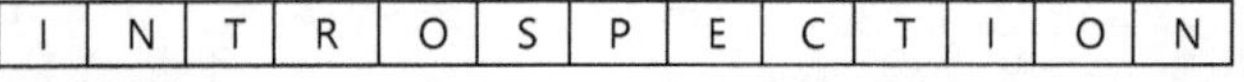

Pattern: Each letter of a given word is preceded by two places, to get the letters of the code.

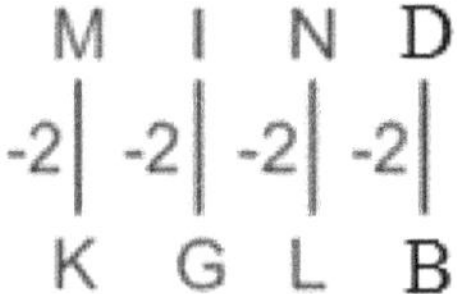

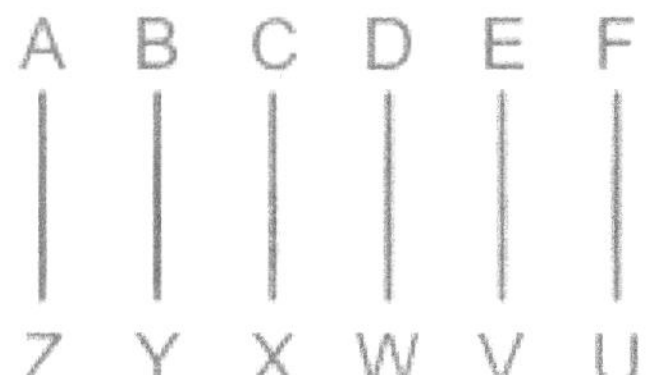

Similarly,

Hence, the correct option is (B).

40. The logic is:

Alphabets	A	B	C	D	E	F	G	H	I	J	K	L	M
Positional value	1	2	3	4	5	6	7	8	9	10	11	12	13
Positional value	26	25	24	23	22	21	20	19	18	17	16	15	14
Alphabets	Z	Y	X	W	V	U	T	S	R	Q	P	O	N

All are opposite pair letters are given:

A B C D E F
| | | | | |
Z Y X W V U

Similarly,

M E R C E D E S
| | | | | | | |
N V I X V W V H

Hence, the correct option is (D).

41. Using the given information we can create the following figure:

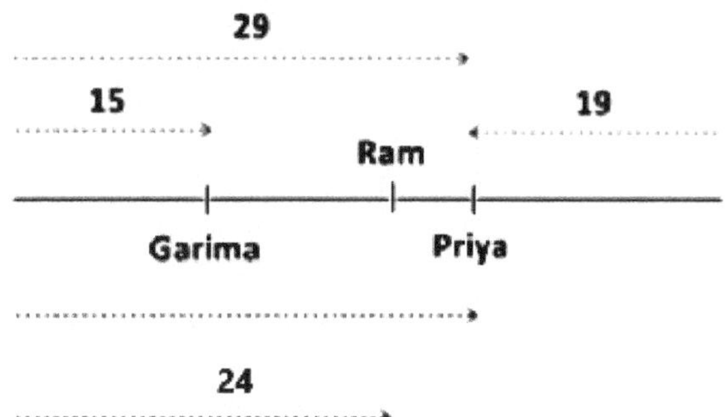

Ram's position from the left end = 24

Priya's position from Ram's position = 5

Priya's position from the left end = Ram's position from the left end + Priya's position from Ram's position

= 24 + 5 = 29

Total number of persons in the queue = [Position of Priya from right + Position of Priya from left] - 1

= (29 + 19 - 1) = 47

Hence, the correct option is (C).

42. Given,

Sahil and Gaurav are standing in a row of persons. Sahil is 12th from the left side and Gaurav is 18th from the right side of the row.

Position of Sahil from Left = 25 (after interchanging)

Total person = Position from Left + Position from right - 1

Position of Sahil from Right = 18 (position of Sahil from right end is same as Gaurav after interchanging) -1

Total person $= 25 + 18 - 1 = 42$

Thus, there are 42 persons in the row.

Hence, the correct option is (A).

Ques (43-45): Number of people: 6

There is one married couple who has only 2 children.

1) N is the grandson of K. P is a daughter of C.

2) D is a Paternal Aunt of P.

3) C is maternal uncle of N.

4) K is wife of R who is the father of D.

The family tree using the following symbols:

Symbol in Diagram	Meaning
◯	Female
☐	Male
═══	Married Couple
───	Siblings
│	Difference of A Generation

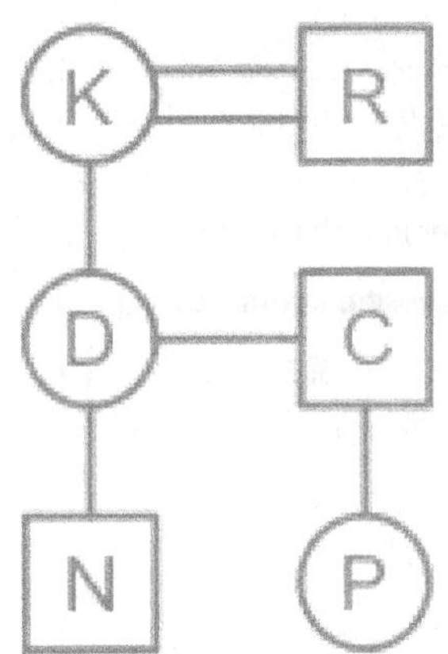

43. Thus, C is the brother of D.

Hence, the correct option is (B).

44. Thus, R is the Father of C.

Hence, the correct option is (D).

45. (A) K and R are siblings → False as K and R are a married couple.

(B) D is a daughter of N → False as D is mother of N

(C) P is daughter of C → True

(D) C is father of N → False as C is maternal uncle of N

(E) C and D are cousins → False as C and D are siblings

Thus, 'P is daughter of C' is definitely true.

Hence, the correct option is (C).

Ques (46-50): Persons: S, T, U, V, W, X, Y and Z

1) W is sitting 5th to the right of T who is facing north and neither of them is sitting at extreme positions.

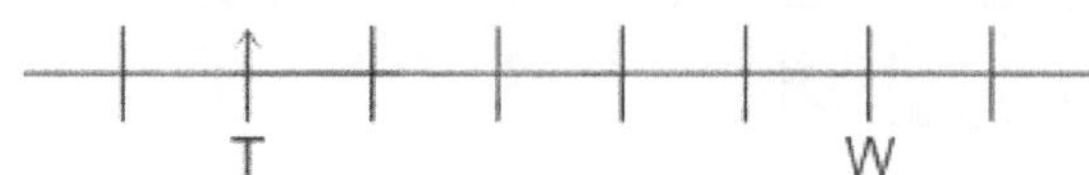

2) S who is an immediate neighbour of V is sitting 4th to the right of W.

This means W is facing south.

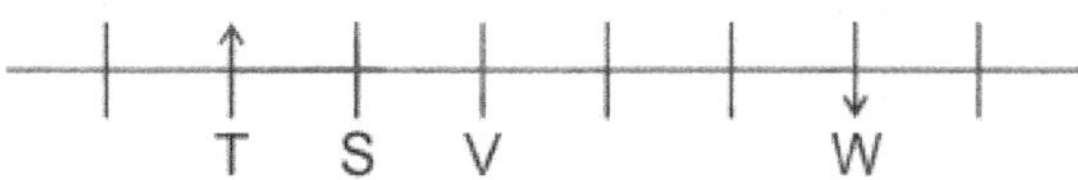

3) Three persons are sitting between V and X. V and X are facing North direction.

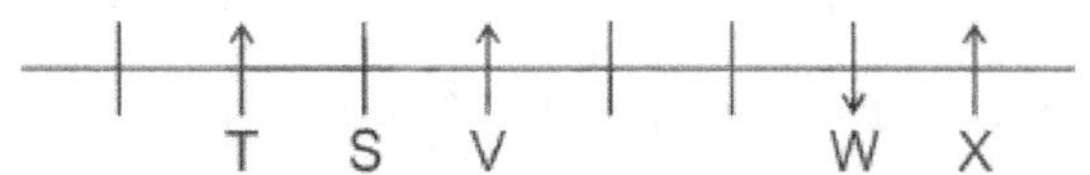

4) Z sits third to the left of X and faces opposite to that of X.

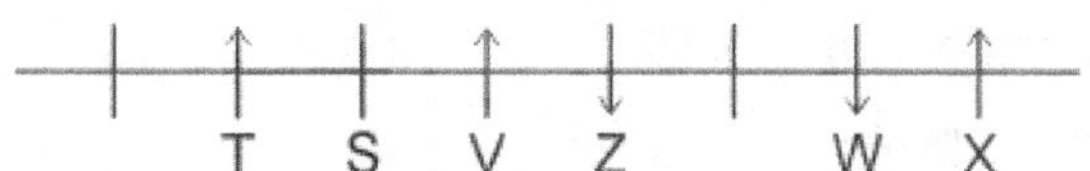

5) Immediate neighbours of Z face the same direction but opposite to that of Z.

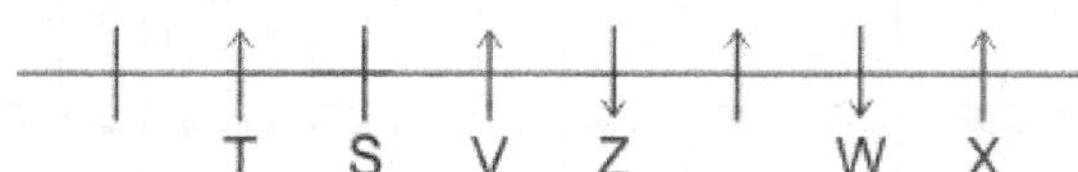

6) Y who faces the South direction sits at one of the positions at the left of V.

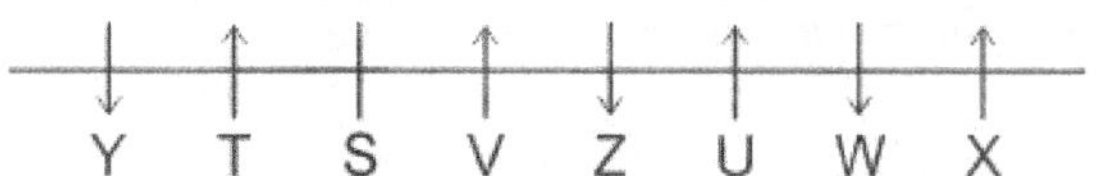

46. So, X sits at the extreme end of the row.

Hence, the correct option is (C).

47. So, X sits second to the right of U.

Hence, the correct option is (D).

48. (A) S sits fifth to the left of X - true

(B) U is an immediate neighbour of V - false (Z sits between U and V)

(C) T sits at one of the extreme ends - false (X and Y sit at the extreme ends)

(D) Three people sit to the right of Z - false (4 people sit to the right of Z)

(E) U is neighbour of V and W - false (U is the neighbour of W and Z)

So, S sits fifth to the left of X.

Hence, the correct option is (A).

49. So, W does not belong to the group as all others are facing North and W is facing South.

Hence, the correct option is (B).

50. As the direction of S cannot be determined, the number of persons sitting to the right of S cannot be determined.

Hence, the correct option is (E).

51. The Venn diagram for all the given statements:

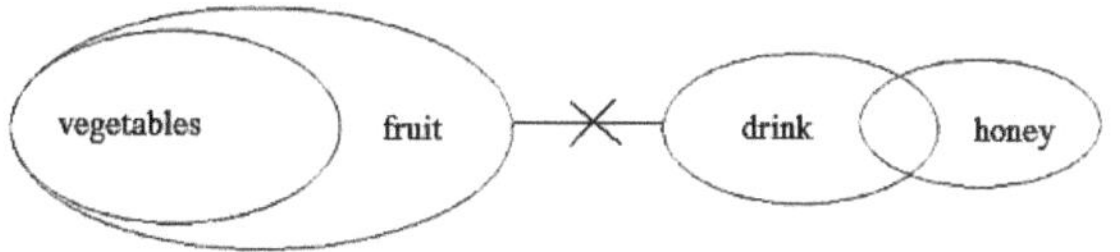

Conclusions:

I. Some honey is not fruit → definitely true.

II. No vegetables are drink → definitely true.

Clearly, both conclusions I and II follow.

Hence, the correct option is (C).

52. The least possible Venn diagram for the given statements is as follows,

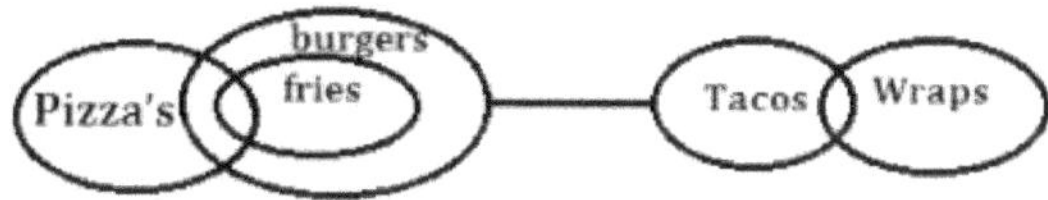

Conclusion:

I. All Pizza's being Tacos is a possibility. → False (It is not possible since no burger is Tacos)

II. No fries is Tacos → True (It is possible since no burger is Tacos)

III. Some Pizza's are burgers → True (It is possible as shown in the figure above)

So, only II and III follows.

Hence, the correct option is (D).

53. The least possible diagram of this question is as follows,

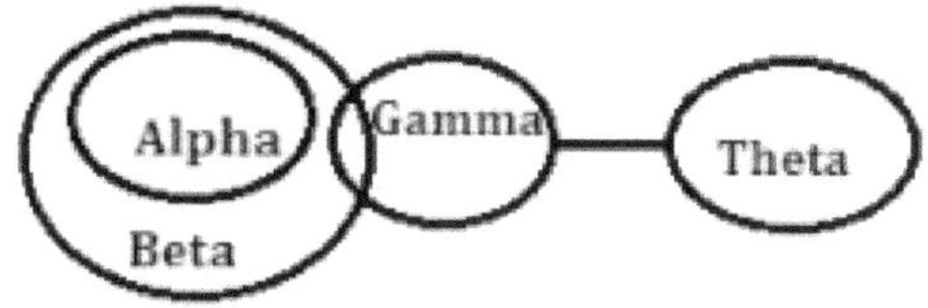

I. Some thetas can be alpha's → True (possibility is true)

II. No gamma is alpha → False (it is possible but not definite)

So, the only conclusion I follows.

Hence, the correct option is (A).

54. The given statement can be represented by using the following Venn Diagram.

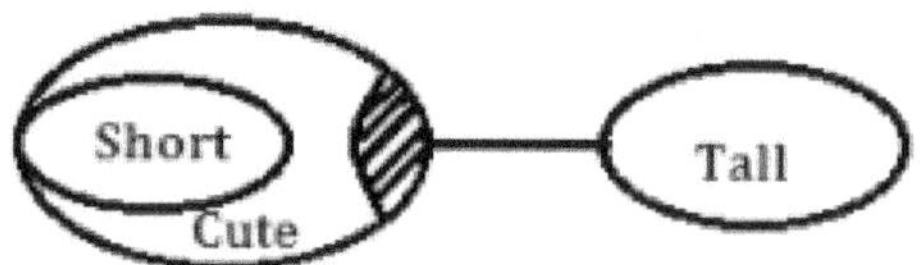

Conclusion:

I. Some short is tall is a possibility → Possibility is true.

II. All tall is short is a possibility → Possibility is true.

So, both I and II follow.

Hence, the correct option is (E).

55. The least possible Venn diagram for the given statements is as follows.

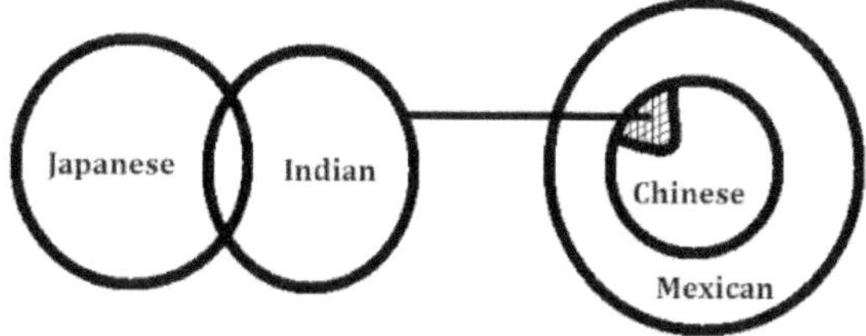

Conclusions:

I. Some Indians are not Mexicans → False (All Indians being Mexicans is a possibility, therefore the definite case is false).

II. Some Mexicans are not Chinese → False (It is possible but not definite)

III. Some Mexicans are Japaneses → False (It is possible but not definite)

So, none follows.

Hence, the correct option is (E).

Ques (56-60): Given series:

Left Side M 1 E & D 2 G 9 $ F @ 4 N Z W © 8 C Y A * 6 Right Side

56. 1) Numbers which are immediately preceded by a consonant and followed by a vowel:

M 1 E & D 2 G 9 $ F @ 4 N Z W © 8 C Y A * 6

So, there is one number that is immediately preceded by a consonant and followed by a vowel: M 1 E.

Hence, the correct option is (C).

57. 1) If all the numbers are dropped:

M E & D G $ F @ N Z W © C Y A *

2) 10th element from the right end is F

Then, letter/ symbol that is tenth from right end is 'F'.

Hence, the correct option is (C).

58. Here the group is formed in which second element is to the second next of the first element and

The third element is third next to the second.

So, YA6 does not belong to the group.

Hence, the correct option is (D).

59. 1) 4th element from the left end is '&'

2) 11th element from the right end is '4'

& D 2 G 9 $ F @ 4

So, there are 3 letters between the fourth element from the left and the eleventh element from the right end D, G and F.

Hence, the correct option is (C).

60. Any number in the above series is immediately preceded by a vowel and not immediately followed by a consonant.

Hence, the correct option is (E).

Ques (61-65):1) P, who doesn't sit next to Teacher, is second to the left of one who sits immediate left of R.

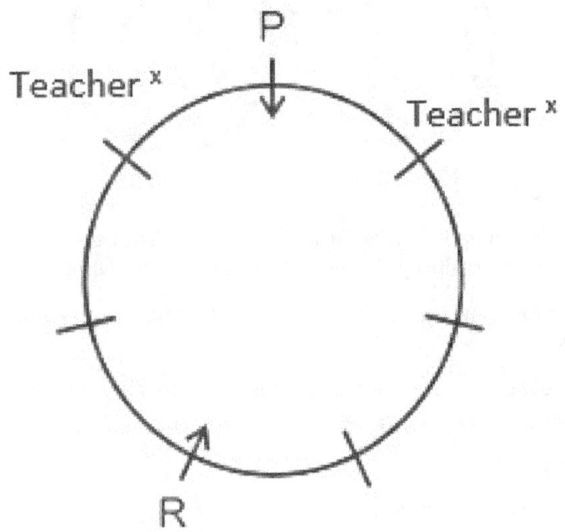

2) At least one student sits between Q & R, taken from both the sides of R.

From the above statement, we have 3 cases.

Case- 1:

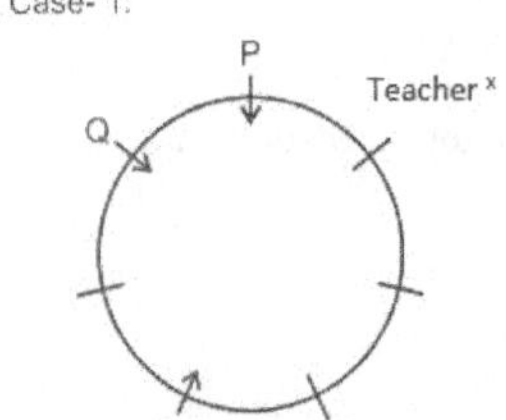

Case- 2:

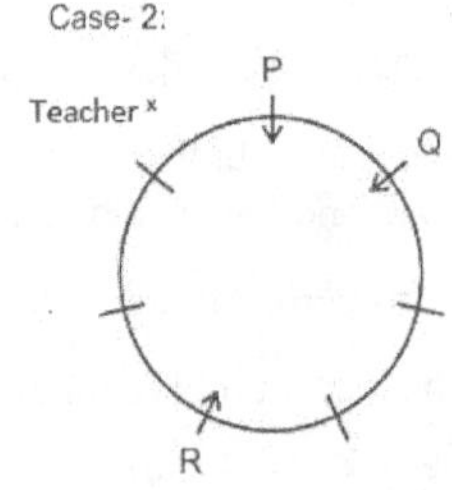

Case- 3:

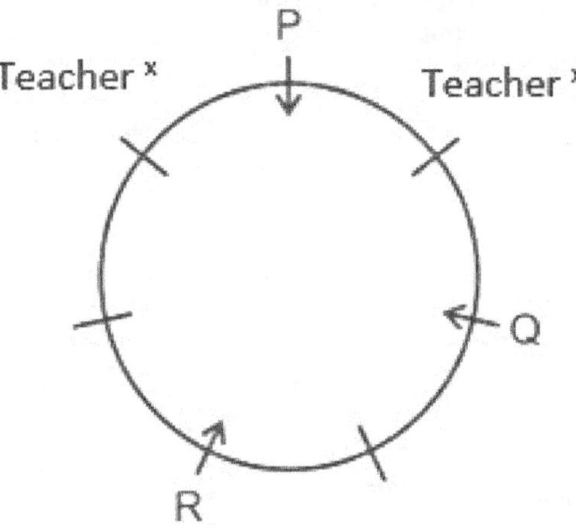

3) No student sits between R & T, taken from the right of R, who is not sitting to the immediate left to the Teacher.

That means Teacher can sit in between R & T.

4) Q and T do not sit together.

Thus case 3 gets eliminated.

5) U and R do not sit together.

6) Neither S nor U nor Q sit next to the Teacher.

Thus case 2 gets eliminated

So, the final arrangement is:

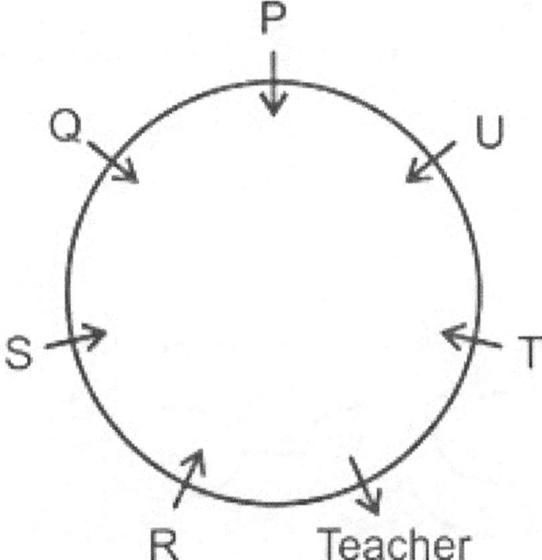

61. So, P sits third to the left of Teacher.

Hence, the correct option is (E).

62. So, Teacher sits third to the right of Q.

Hence, the correct option is (E).

63. If Teacher and Q interchange their position then there is no students whose sit remain at the same position.

Hence, the correct option is (B).

64. If another student 'X' sits in between Q & S and is facing towards the centre, then T sits 4th to the left of X.

Hence, the correct option is (A).

65. So, only 2 students are there in between R & P, whose names are consonant, when counted from left of R.

Hence, the correct option is (B).

66. Average = $\dfrac{(sum\ of\ elements)}{(number\ of\ elements)}$

Given,

The scores of Sam, Geeta and Radha out of 150

For Mathematics section = 94, 85 and 120 respectively

For Science section = 135, 80 and 90 respectively.

Sam's total score out of 300

= 94 + 135

= 229

The average percent = $\left\{\dfrac{229}{300}\right\} \times 100$

= 76.33%

Geeta's total score out of 300

= 85 + 80

= 165

The average percent = $\left(\dfrac{165}{300}\right) \times 100$

= 55%

Radha's total score out of 300

= 120 + 90

= 210

The average percent = $\left(\dfrac{210}{300}\right) \times 100$

= 70%

∴ The average percent of Sam, Geeta and Radha are 76.33%, 55% and 70% respectively.

Hence, the correct option is (A).

67. Given:

Money invested in the Bitcoin = 105 million dollars

Let the total assets be x

Percentage of money invested in the Bitcoin = 42%

⇒ 42% of x = 105 million dollars

⇒ x = $\dfrac{105 \times 100}{42}$

⇒ x = 250 million dollars

Hence, the correct option is (D).

68. Given:

Total assets = 250 million dollars

Percentage of money invested in the BTC and Ripple together = 8 + 12

= 20%

Total money invested in the BTC and Ripple together = 20% of 250 million dollars

= $250 \times \dfrac{20}{100}$

= 50 million dollars

Hence, the correct option is (C).

69. Given:

Total assets = 250 million dollars

Money invested in the Bitcoin = 42% of 250 million dollars

= $250 \times \dfrac{42}{100}$

= $\dfrac{10500}{100}$

= 105 million dollars

Money invested in the other cryptocurrencies = 250 – 105 million dollars

= 145 million dollars

Difference between the money invested = 145 – 105 million dollars

= 40 million dollars

Hence, the correct option is (B).

70. Given:

Total assets = 250 million dollars

Money invested in the Bitcoin = 42% of 250 million dollars

= $250 \times \dfrac{42}{100}$

= $\dfrac{10500}{100}$

= 105 million dollars

Total Money invested in the Bitcoin after decreasing by 40%

= $105 - \left(\dfrac{40}{100} \times 100\right)$

= $105 - \dfrac{4200}{100}$

= $105 - 42$

= 63 million dollars

Money invested in the other cryptocurrencies = 250 – 105 million dollars

= 145 million dollars

New total assets = 145 + 63

= 208 million dollars

Percentage decrease = $\dfrac{Old\ value - New\ Value}{Old\ value} \times 100$

= $\left(\dfrac{250-208}{250}\right) \times 100$

= 16.8%

Hence, the correct option is (A).

71. Given:

Total assets = 250 million dollars

Money invested in the Etherium = 18% of 250 million dollars

= $250 \times \dfrac{18}{100}$

= $\dfrac{4500}{100}$

= 45 million dollars

If the price of etherium increases by 20%

Final Money invested in the Etherium = 45 + $\dfrac{20}{100} \times 45$

= 45 + 9

= 54 million dollars

Money invested in Litecoin = 20% of 250 million dollars

= $250 \times \dfrac{20}{100}$

= $\dfrac{5000}{100}$

= 50 million dollars

The price of Litecoin decreases by 10%

Final Money invested in the Litecoin = 50 - $\dfrac{10}{100} \times 50$

= 50 - 5

= 45 million dollars

Total increase in assets = (54 − 45) + (45 − 50)

= 9 − 5

= 4 million dollars

Hence, the correct option is (A).

72. Given:

I. $x^2 - 16x + 63 = 0$

II. $y^2 - 2y - 35 = 0$

According to the given equations:

I. $x^2 - 16x + 63 = 0$

$\Rightarrow x^2 - 9x - 7x + 63 = 0$

$\Rightarrow x(x - 9) - 7(x - 9) = 0$

$\Rightarrow (x - 7)(x - 9) = 0$

$\therefore x = 7, 9$

II. $y^2 - 2y - 35 = 0$

$\Rightarrow y^2 - 7y + 5y - 35 = 0$

$\Rightarrow y(y - 7) + 5(y - 7) = 0$

$\Rightarrow (y - 7)(y + 5) = 0$

$\therefore y = 7, -5$

Value of 'x'	Relation	Value of 'y'
7	=	7
7	>	-5
9	>	7
9	>	-5

When we compared the values of 'x' and 'y' in the table above, we found that there is two relations between X and Y i.e. > and =.

So, a relation between x and y is "x ≥ y".

Hence, the correct option is (B).

73. According to the given equations:

I. $x^2 - 7x + 6 = 0$

$x^2 - 6x - x + 6 = 0$

$\Rightarrow (x - 6)(x - 1) = 0$

Thus,

$\Rightarrow x = 1, 6$

II. $11y^2 - 13y + 2 = 0$

$11y^2 - 11y - 2y + 2 = 0$

$\Rightarrow (11y - 1)(y - 2) = 0$

Thus,

$\Rightarrow y = 1, \dfrac{2}{11}$

$\therefore x \geq y$

Hence, the correct option is (C).

74. Given:

I. $x^2 - 9x + 18 = 0$

II. $y^2 - 11y + 18 = 0$

According to the given equations:

I. $x^2 - 9x + 18 = 0$

$\Rightarrow x^2 - 3x - 6x + 18 = 0$

$\Rightarrow x(x - 3) - 6(x - 3) = 0$

$\Rightarrow (x - 3)(x - 6) = 0$

$\Rightarrow x = 3, 6$

II. $y^2 - 11y + 18 = 0$

$\Rightarrow y^2 - 9y - 2y + 18 = 0$

$\Rightarrow y(y - 9) - 2(y - 9) = 0$

$\Rightarrow (y - 2)(y - 9) = 0$

$\Rightarrow y = 2, 9$

After comparison of both equations, the conclusion is $x = y$ or no relation is obtained.

Hence, the correct option is (C).

75. Given:

I. $x^2 + x - 42 = 0$

II. $y^2 - 13y + 42 = 0$

According to the given equations:

I. $x^2 + x - 42 = 0$

$\Rightarrow x^2 + 7x - 6x - 42 = 0$

$\Rightarrow x(x + 7) - 6(x + 7) = 0$

$\Rightarrow (x + 7)(x - 6) = 0$

$\Rightarrow (x + 7) = 0$ or $(x - 6) = 0$

$\Rightarrow x = -7$ or $x = 6$

II. $y^2 - 13y + 42 = 0$

$\Rightarrow y^2 - 7y - 6y + 42 = 0$

$\Rightarrow y(y - 7) - 6(y - 7) = 0$

$\Rightarrow (y - 7)(y - 6) = 0$

$\Rightarrow (y - 7) = 0$ or $(y - 6) = 0$

$\Rightarrow y = 7$ or $y = 6$

$\therefore x \leq y$

Hence, the correct option is (D).

76. Given:

75% of $300 - 175 = 70 - ?$

$\Rightarrow 75 \times \dfrac{1}{100}$ of $300 - 175 = 70 - ?$

$\Rightarrow 75 \times \dfrac{1}{100} \times 300 - 175 = 70 - ?$

$\Rightarrow ? = 70 - 225 + 175$

$= 20$

Hence, the correct option is (A).

77. Given:

$26 \times 15 + 310 - (15)^2 = 25\%$ of $?$

$\Rightarrow 26 \times 15 + 310 - 225 = 25 \times \dfrac{1}{100}$ of $?$

$\Rightarrow 390 + 310 - 225 = ? \times \dfrac{1}{4}$

$\Rightarrow ? = 475 \times 4$

$\Rightarrow ? = 1900$

Hence, the correct option is (D).

78. Given:

$? + (8)^3 = (26)^2 - 43$

$\Rightarrow ? + 512 = 676 - 43$

$\Rightarrow ? = 633 - 512$

$\Rightarrow ? = 121$

Hence, the correct option is (A).

79. Given:

$20 \times 168 \div 14 - 40 = ? + 110$

$\Rightarrow 20 \times \dfrac{168}{14} - 40 = ? + 110$

$\Rightarrow 20 \times 12 - 40 = ? + 110$

$\Rightarrow 240 - 40 = ? + 110$

$\Rightarrow 200 = ? + 110$

$\Rightarrow 200 - 110 = ?$

$= 90$

Hence, the correct option is (C).

80. Given:

$\left(\dfrac{12}{13}\right)$ of $143 \div 6 - 12 = ?$

$\Rightarrow \left(\dfrac{12}{13}\right)$ of $\dfrac{143}{6} - 12 = ?$

$\Rightarrow \left(\dfrac{12}{13}\right) \times \dfrac{143}{6} - 12 = ?$

$\Rightarrow 2 \times 11 - 12 = ?$

$= 22 - 12$

$= 10$

Hence, the correct option is (B).

81. Given:

$$\sqrt{625} \div \sqrt{16} \times 6 = ? \% \text{ of } 300$$

$$\Rightarrow 25 \div 4 \times 6 = ? \% \times 300$$

$$\Rightarrow 25 \div 4 \times 6 = ? \times \frac{1}{100} \times 300$$

$$\Rightarrow 25 \div 4 \times 6 = ? \times 3$$

$$\Rightarrow \frac{25}{4} \times 6 = ? \times 3$$

$$\Rightarrow \frac{25}{2} = ?$$

$$\Rightarrow ? = 12.5$$

Hence, the correct option is (E).

82. Given:

$$2^3 \times 4^2 \div 8 = (2)^?$$

$$\Rightarrow (2)^? = 2^3 \times 2^4 \div 2^3$$

$$\Rightarrow (2)^? = 2^{3+4-3}$$

$$\Rightarrow (2)^? = 2^4$$

On comparing power of both sides:

$$? = 4$$

Hence, the correct option is (C).

83. Given:

$$\left(\sqrt{64} + 3\right)^3 = 750 + ?$$

$$= (8 + 3)^3 - 750$$

$$= (11)^3 - 750$$

$$= 1331 - 750$$

$$= 581$$

Hence, the correct option is (C).

84. Given:

$$? + 820 = 25\% \text{ of } 6400$$

$$\Rightarrow ? + 820 = 25 \times \frac{1}{100} \text{ of } 6400$$

$$\Rightarrow ? + 820 = \frac{1}{4} \text{ of } 6400$$

$$\Rightarrow ? + 820 = 1600$$

$$\Rightarrow ? = 1600 - 820$$

$$\Rightarrow ? = 780$$

Hence, the correct option is (D).

85. Given:

$$256 \div 2^3 \times x = 16\% \text{ of } 3000$$

$$\Rightarrow 256 \div 8 \times x = 3000 \times \frac{16}{100}$$

$$\Rightarrow 32 \times x = 480$$

$$\Rightarrow x = \frac{480}{32} = 15$$

Hence, the correct option is (D).

86. Let x be the cost price of a car.

So, according to the question,

15% of x = Rs. 15000

So, x = 15000 × $\frac{100}{15}$ = Rs. 100000

On this amount, he is giving 10% labour charge.

So, selling price of 1 car = C.P + 10% of C.P = 100000 + 10000 = Rs. 110000

Therefore, total selling price of 20 cars = 110000 × 20 = Rs. 2200000

Hence, the correct option is (D).

87. Soumya bought 20 kg of tea at Rs. 18 per kg and 15 kg of tea at Rs. 25 per kg.

The total cost price of 20 kg tea at Rs. 18 per kg = Rs. 20 × 18 =Rs. 360

The total cost price of 15 kg tea at Rs. 25 per kg = Rs. 15 × 25 =Rs. 375

He mixed the two varieties together. Then total cost price of (20 + 15) = 35 kg tea mixture = Rs. 360 + 375 = Rs. 735

So, the cost price of the mixture per kg = Rs. $\frac{735}{35}$ = Rs. 21

If he sold the mixture at Rs. 30, he got the profit of Rs. (30 – 21) = Rs. 9 per kg.

∴ The required profit percentage = $\left(\frac{9}{21}\right)$ × 100 = 42.85%

Hence, the correct option is (D).

88. From the statement I, AB : BC = 4 : 5

From the statement II, BC : AC = 25 : 13

By both the statement, AB : BC : CA = 20 : 25 : 13

Therefore, by combining both the statement, we can conclude that the given triangle is not a right-angle triangle.

Hence, the correct option is (E).

89. From the statement I, the efficiency of pipe A per hour

$$= \frac{2500}{12} = \frac{625}{3} \text{ litres per hour}$$

From the statement II, the efficiency of pipe $B = 1 \times 60 = 60$ litres per hour

Pipe A and B together will fill in 1 hour

$$= \frac{625}{3} + 60 = \frac{805}{3} \text{ litres per hour}$$

The time it will take to fill 2500 litres of water = more than 8 hours

Therefore, the data in both the statements I and II together is necessary to answer the question.

Hence, the correct option is (E).

90. Let the speed of ram $= x$ km per hour

Then the speed of Mohan $= y$ km per hour

From the statement I: $y = x + 10$

From the statement II: We can find the value of y as 30, so speed of Mohan is 30 km per hour

By combining both the statement, we can get the value of x as well which is 20 km per hour

So, Ram will take 5 hours to cover 100 km at a speed of 20 km per hour

Hence, the correct option is (E).

91. From the statement I: $AB = 12\ cm$

$BC = 9\ cm$ but we could not conclude which of the angle is right angle therefore we could not get unique answer only by the statement I

From the statement II: Let the sides of the triangle $= a, b,$ and c where c is hypotenuse

Then, inradius $= \frac{a+b-c}{2} = 3$

And, circumradius $= \frac{\text{Hypotenuse}}{2} = \frac{c}{2} = 7.5, c = 15\ cm$

$a + b = 21$

By the Pythagorean theorem we can calculate the value of a and b, after that we can conclude the area.

Therefore, the data in statements II alone is sufficient to answer the question, while the data in statement I alone is not sufficient to answer the question.

Hence, the correct option is (B).

92. From the statement I, $15x + 4y = 108 \cdots$ (i)

From the statement II, $y = 27 - 3.75x$

$4y + 15x = 108 \cdots$ (ii)

Here, both the equations are same it means we have two variable and one equation therefore we could not conclude the value of two variable from one equation.

Therefore, the data in both the statements I and II is not sufficient to answer the question.

Hence, the correct option is (D).

93. As we know, compound ratio of ratios a : b and c : d is ac : bd

⇒ Compound ratio of x^2 : y and y^2 : z = x^2y^2 : yz = x^2y : z

$$\Rightarrow \frac{x^2 y}{z} = \frac{z}{y}$$

⇒ $x^2y^2 = z^2$

∴ xy = z

Hence, the correct option is (C).

94. The pattern of the given number series is as following:

⇒ 5 × 2 = 10,

⇒ 10 × 4 = 40,

⇒ 40 × 6 = 240,

⇒ 240 × 8 = 1920,

⇒ 1920 × 10 = 19200

So, the required term in place of question mark in the given number series is 240.

Hence, the correct option is (C).

95. The pattern of the given number series is as following:

$1^3 - 1 = 0,$

$2^3 - 1 = 7,$

$3^3 - 1 = 26,$

$4^3 - 1 = 63,$

$5^3 - 1 = 124,$

$6^3 - 1 = 215,$

$7^3 - 1 = 342$

So, the required term in place of question mark in the given number series is 124.

Hence, the correct option is (C).

96. The pattern of the given number series is as following:

$2 \times 0^2 = 0$

$2 \times 1^2 = 2,$

$2 \times 2^2 = 8$

$2 \times 3^2 = 18,$

$2 \times 4^2 = 32,$

$2 \times 5^2 = 50$

So, the required term in place of question mark in the given number series is 32.

Hence, the correct option is (A).

97. The pattern of the given number series is as following:

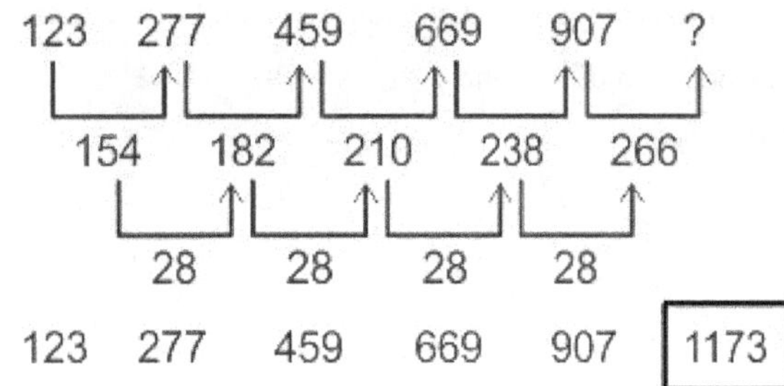

123   277   459   669   907   1173

⇒ 123,

⇒ 123 + 154 = 277,

⇒ 277 + (154 + 28 = 182) = 459,

⇒ 459 + (182 + 28 = 210) = 669,

⇒ 669 + (210 + 28 = 238) = 907,

⇒ 907 + (238 + 28 = 266) = 1173

So, the required number in place of question mark in the given number series would be 1173.

Hence, the correct option is (B).

98. The above pattern may be evaluated as:

⇒ 9

⇒ 9 × 1 + 1 = 10

⇒ 10 × 2 + 2 = 22

⇒ 22 × 3 + 3 = 69

⇒ 69 × 4 + 4 = 280

So, next number must be

⇒ 280 × 5 + 5 = 1405

∴ The required term in the given number series is 1405.

Hence, the correct option is (C).

99. Given:

A boat can travel 32 km upstream in 2 hours more than in downstream.

The difference in time = 2 hours

Formula:

Upstream = Still water speed - Current speed

Downstream = Still water speed + Current speed

Distance = Speed × Time

Let the speed of still water be 2x km/hr.

Let the speed of current be y km/hr.

According to the question,

$$\frac{32}{2x-y} - \frac{32}{2x+y} = 2$$

$$\Rightarrow 16(2x + y) - 16(2x - y) = 4x^2 - y^2$$

$$\Rightarrow 4x^2 - y^2 = 32y \quad .....(i)$$

After reducing still water speed be x.

Then, The difference in time = 8 hours

$$\Rightarrow \frac{20}{x-y} - \frac{20}{x+y} = 8$$

$$\Rightarrow 20(x + y) - 20(x - y) = 8(x^2 - y^2)$$

$$\Rightarrow x^2 - y^2 = 5y$$

$$\Rightarrow y^2 = x^2 - 5y \quad .....(ii)$$

By solving equation (i) and (ii)

x = 6 km/hr and y = 4 km/hr

Therefore, the reduced speed of boat in still water is 6 km/hr.

Hence, the correct option is (D).

100. Given:

I. x^2 - 16x + 63 = 0

II. y^2 + 5y - 84 = 0

Calculation:

From I:

x^2 - 16x + 63 = 0

⇒ x^2 - 9x - 7x + 63 = 0

⇒ x(x - 9) - 7(x - 9) = 0

⇒ (x - 9)(x - 7) = 0

⇒ x = 9, 7

From II:

y^2 + 5y - 84 = 0

⇒ y^2 + 12y - 7y -84 = 0

⇒ y(y + 12) - 7(y + 12) = 0

⇒ (y + 12)(y - 7) = 0

⇒ y = -12, 7

Comparison between x and y (via Tabulation):

Value of x	Value of y	Relation between x & y
9	-12	x > y
9	7	x > y
7	-12	x > y
7	7	x = y

∴ x ≥ y

Hence, the correct option is (C).

English Language

Ques (1-5):Direction: Some statements are given below in any random order. Rearrange the following statements in a coherent and meaningful paragraph and answer the questions that follow.

A. Microsoft's very own browser Internet Explorer was very much similar to Netscape and its new search engine Bing which is more or less similar to Google.

B. This can be evident from the fact that Windows operating system was much influenced by Unix that was used by Apple in their operating systems.

C. Similarly, Microsoft's office suite was influenced by Lotus and Word Perfect.

D. One of the key challenges that surfaced after SWOT analysis was Microsoft's lack of innovation.

E. Microsoft's lack of innovation does not stop here and in the following years, it continued to introduce products that were in some way similar to products that already existed in the market.

F. Most of the products that Microsoft has introduced in the last 25 years were influenced by existing products of its competitors.

Q.1 Which sentence should be the first sentence in the paragraph?

A. A   **B.** B   **C.** C   **D.** D
E. E

Q.2 Which sentence should be the second sentence in the paragraph?

A. B   **B.** F   **C.** C   **D.** D
E. A

Q.3 Which sentence should be the third sentence in the paragraph?

A. B   **B.** F   **C.** D   **D.** C
E. A

Q.4 Which sentence should be the fourth sentence in the paragraph?

A. B   **B.** C   **C.** D   **D.** F
E. A

Q.5 Which sentence should be the sixth sentence in the paragraph?

[IBPS PO, 2021]

A. B   **B.** C   **C.** A   **D.** F
E. D

Q.6 Direction: In the following question, five words are given, out of which only one word is wrongly spelt. Find the wrongly spelt word and indicate it by selecting the appropriate option.

A. Guarded   **B.** Cherished
C. Prevarricate   **D.** Legitimate
E. Abominate

Q.7 Direction: In the following question, five words are given, out of which only one word is wrongly spelt. Find the wrongly spelt word and indicate it by selecting the appropriate option.

A. Increment   **B.** Superficial
C. Retreat   **D.** Sustenence
E. Intensive

Q.8 Direction: In the following question, five words are given, out of which only one word is wrongly spelt. Find the wrongly spelt word and indicate it by selecting the appropriate option.

A. Shettarable   **B.** Brittle
C. Extraordinary   **D.** Crisp
E. Shivery

Ques (9-13):Direction: Read the passage and answer the questions that follow. Some words may be highlighted for you. Pay careful attention.

The number of ultra-high net worth individuals (UHNWIs), with a wealth of USD 30 million or more, is expected to rise 63 per cent over the next five years to 11,198 in India, the second-fastest growth in the world, according to property consultant Knight Frank India report. As per its Wealth Report 2021, there are currently 5,21,653 UHNWIs globally, of which India has 6,884 such individuals. According to the report, the number of UHNWIs, those with USD 30 million or more, around the world is predicted to grow by 27 per cent between 2020-2025, taking this population to 6,63,483. According to the report, the number of UHNWIs, those with USD 30 million or more, around the world is predicted to grow by 27 per cent between 2020-2025, taking this population to 6,63,483. "India is expected to see incredible growth of 63 per cent by 2025, making it the second-fastest-growing country in terms of number of UHNWIs. The number of UHNWIs in India is expected to grow by 63 per cent in the next five years to 11,198 in 2025," Knight Frank India said in a statement. The billionaires club in India is expected to increase significantly by 43 per cent to 162 by 2025 from the current 113 in 2020. The growth has outpaced the global average growth of 24 per cent and Asia average of 38 per cent during this period. The report predicts that in the regional context, Asia is likely to see the highest rise in the number of UHNWIs with an estimated growth of 39 per cent. This will be led by Indonesia (67 per cent) and India (63 per cent).

Q.9 From the given passage, what can you conclude?

A. India is leading in economy

B. Asia is leading in economy

C. India has the second-fastest-growing UHNWIs

D. It talks about UHNWIs

E. None of the above

Q.10 Why is India known as the "second-fastest growing country" in terms of the number of UHNWIs?

A. Has diversity

B. Is very intelligent

C. Has proper system

D. Shown an incredible economic growth

E. None of the above

Q.11 In whose report is the number of UHNWIs predicted?

A. India report

B. Wealth report

C. World report

D. Knight Frank

E. None of the above

Q.12 Give the antonym for the word "wealth".

A. Affluence

B. Prosperity

C. Riches

D. Poverty

E. None of the above

Q.13 Give the another word for the underlined word for the given sentence - "The number of UHNWIs in India is expected to grow by 63 per cent in the next five years to 11,198 in 2025," Knight Frank India said in a **statement**".

A. Unclear

B. Declaration

C. Indistinct

D. Definite

E. None of the above

Ques (14-18):Direction: In the following passage, some words have been deleted. Select the most appropriate option to fill in each blank.

Christmas is one of the most famous and light-hearted festivals which is ___(1)___ across the world by billions of people. People of the Christian religion celebrate Christmas to ___(2)___ the great works of Jesus Christ. 25th December is celebrated as Christmas Day ___(3)___ the world. Christians celebrate Christmas Day as the birth anniversary of Jesus Christ. Jesus Christ of Bethlehem was a spiritual leader and prophet whose teachings ___(4)___ the premise of their religion. People ___(5)___ popular customs including exchanging gifts, decorating Christmas trees, attending church, sharing meals with family and friends, and, obviously, trusting that Santa Claus will arrive. 25th December, Christmas Day, has been a federal holiday in the United States since 1870.

Q.14 Select the most appropriate option to fill in blank number 1.

A. Celebrated

B. Complicated

C. Abducted

D. Protected

E. Violated

Q.15 Select the most appropriate option to fill in blank number 2.

A. Order

B. Listener

C. Remember

D. Viewer

E. Wither

Q.16 Select the most appropriate option to fill in blank number 3.

A. Aimless

B. Address

C. Recess

D. Assess

E. Across

Q.17 Select the most appropriate option to fill in blank number 4.

A. Ensure

B. Structure

C. Secure

D. Figure

E. Assure

Q.18 Select the most appropriate option to fill in blank number 5.

A. Allow

B. Disallow

C. Fallow

D. Follow

E. Narrow

Ques (19-23):Direction: Which of the following phrases (A), (B), (C) and (D) can replace the phrase in bold so as to make the statement correct grammatically and contextually? If the statement does not need any correction, mark option E as your answer.

Q.19 Cash transfers to the poor do not **ensue accessibility**, affordability or even sustained economic security given falling real wages.

A. Ensure accessibility

B. Ensure excesses

C. Ensures accessibility

D. Assure formality

E. No correction required

Q.20 With the election **round a corner** and data revealing that the unemployment rate has hit a 45-year high, there is a spike in concern for the economic security of the people.

A. In the corner

B. Over the corner

C. Around the corner

D. For in corner

E. No correction required

Q.21 Afghanistan has **historically be an difficult place** for external invaders, thanks to its complex tribal equations and its rugged mountainous terrain.

A. historic has a difficult place

B. historically been a difficult place

C. historically being a difficult place

D. historically been a difficult places

E. No correction required

Q.22 While all rights are available to citizens, persons including foreign citizens **are entitle to the rights** to equality and the right to life, among others.

A. is entitled to the right

B. are entitled for the right

C. are entitled to a rights

D. are entitled to the right

E. No correction required

Q.23 Preserving and to restore forests are an effective step toward mitigating climate change, and comes with a host of other benefits.

A. Preserving to restore forests is

B. Preserving and restoring forests is

C. To preserve restoring of forests is

D. To preserve and to restore forests are

E. No correction required

Q.24 Direction: Select the most appropriate antonym of the given word.

Vacuous

A. Courteous

B. Exhilarated

C. Modest

D. Intelligent

E. Emergent

Q.25 Direction: Select the most appropriate synonym of the given word.

FORAY

A. Maraud

B. Contest

C. Ranger

D. Intuition

E. None of the above

Ques (26-30):Direction: Read the following sentence and determine whether there is an error in it. The error, if any, will be in one part of the sentence. If the sentence is error-free, select 'No Error' as your answer.

Q.26 The farmers, including the (A)/ village's Sarpanch were late (B)/ in paying their due to the Zamindar, (C)/ caused the Zamindar to confiscate their lands. (D)/ No error (E)

A. (A)   **B.** (B)   **C.** (C)   **D.** (D)

E. (E)

Q.27 Mark would (A)/ always remembered (B)/his dog, Molly (C)/ with fondness. (D)/ No error (E)

A. (A)   **B.** (B)   **C.** (C)   **D.** (D)

E. (E)

Q.28 His parents were very (A)/ hopeful that he would (B)/ one day achieve one's ambitions (C)/ and make them proud. (D)/ No error (E)

A. (A)   **B.** (B)   **C.** (C)   **D.** (D)

E. (E)

Q.29 "The driver will (A)/ be waiting for (B)/ you at the airport (C)/ to pick you up." (D)/ No error (E)

A. (A)   **B.** (B)   **C.** (C)   **D.** (D)

E. (E)

Q.30 Michael insisted paying (A)/ for the meal, (B)/ but Halley wanted (C)/ to split the bill. (D)/ No error (E)

A. (A)   **B.** (B)   **C.** (C)   **D.** (D)

E. (E)

Reasoning Ability

Ques (31-34):Direction: In the following question assuming the given statements to be True, find which of the conclusion among the given conclusion(s) is/are definitely True and then give your answers accordingly.

Q.31 Statements: M ≥ T; M < P; S > T

Conclusions:

I. S = M

II. T < P

III. P > S

A. Only I is true

B. I, II and III are True

C. Only II is True

D. II and III are True

E. None is true

Q.32 Statements:

X > C ≥ V > Y; U = V < T ≤ H; T < B

Conclusions:

I. Y < X

II. X ≥ B

III. V < B

A. Only conclusion II follows

B. Only conclusion I follows

C. None of these

D. Both conclusion I and III follow

E. Only conclusion III follows

Q.33 Statements:

P ≤ Q > R = S; S < T; T = P > U; V < U

Conclusions:

I. Q = P

II. Q > P

III. P < V

A. Only III is True

B. Both I and II are True

C. Only II is True

D. Only I is True

E. Either I or II is True

Q.34 Statements: A > P ≥ K; Q > M > T; P > T

Conclusions:

I. T < K

II. K > A

III. A > K

A. Only I is true

B. Only II is true

C. Only I and II are true

D. Only II and III are true

E. Only III is true

Q.35 Directions: In the following question, assuming the given statements to be true, find which of the conclusions among the given conclusions is/are definitely true, and then give your answers accordingly.

Statement:

P ≥ A > I = R; S < A > M

Conclusions:

I. M < P

II. P > S

III. M < R

A. Only I and II are True

B. Only I is True

C. Only II and III are True

D. None is True

E. Only I and III are True

Q.36 There are 25 students in a class and all of them are sitting in a row to do yoga. Meena is 11th from the top and Sneha is 6th from the bottom. Two students are sitting between Ananya and Reena. What is the position of Reena from the top?

A. 12th   **B.** 13th

C. 16th   **D.** 14th

E. Can't be determined

Q.37 In a row of girls, if Shilpa who is 8th from the left, and Reena who is 17th from the right. If they interchange their positions among themselves, Shilpa becomes 14th from the left. Find how many girls are there in this row?

A. 38   **B.** 28   **C.** 30   **D.** 25

E. 35

Ques (38-42):Direction: In the question below are given three statements, followed by some conclusions. You have to take the given statements to be true even if they seem to be at variance from commonly known facts. Read the conclusions and then decide which of the given conclusions logically follows from the given statements disregarding commonly known facts.

Q.38 Statements:

Some Lions are Tigers.

All Tigers are Bears.

No Bears are Parrot.

Conclusions:

I. Some Lions are Parrot.

II. Some Lions are Bears.

III. Some Parrot are Bears.

A. Only I follows.

B. Only II follows.

C. Only III follows.

D. All I, II and III follows.

E. None follows.

Q.39 Statement:

All cars are bikes.

Some boats are bikes.

No car is a boat.

Conclusions:

I. All bikes can be boats.

II. All bikes cannot be cars.

A. Only conclusion I follows

B. Only conclusion II follows

C. Either conclusion I or II follows

D. Neither of the conclusions follow

E. Both the conclusions follow

Q.40 Statements:

Some skies are blue.

No blue is red.

Some red are water.

Conclusions:

I. Some blue can be water.

II. All water cannot be skies.

A. Only conclusion I follows

B. Only conclusion II follows

C. Either conclusion I or II follows

D. Neither of the conclusions follow

E. Both the conclusions follow

Q.41 Statements:

All dogs are dragons.

All cats are dragons.

No dragon is a lion.

Conclusions:

I. No dog can be a lion.

II. No cat can be a lion.

A. Only conclusion I follows

B. Only conclusion II follows

C. Either conclusion I or II follows

D. Neither of the conclusions follow

E. Both the conclusions follow

Q.42 Statements:

No tree is a herb.

Some shrubs are grass.

No grass is a herb.

Conclusions:

I. No shrub can be a herb.

II. No grass can be a tree.

A. Only conclusion I follows

B. Only conclusion II follows

C. Either conclusion I or II follows

D. Neither of the conclusions follow

E. Both the conclusions follow

Ques (43-47):Directions: Read the information given below and answer the questions that follow:

Eight people A, B, C, D, L, M, N and O are sitting around a circular table with equal distance between each other but not necessarily in the same order. Some of them are facing the centre while some are facing outside. (i.e. away from the centre) B sits third to the left of A. Only three people sit between B and O. L sits to the immediate right of O. Immediate neighbor of L faces the opposite direction. Only one person sits between L and D. N sits second to the right of D. Both N and C face the same direction as O. Immediate neighbors of M face opposite directions to each other. L does not face outside. D faces a direction opposite to that of B.

Q.43 How many people sit between A and M when counted from the left of M?

A. Five   **B.** None   **C.** Four   **D.** One

E. Two

Q.44 Which of the following statements is true as per the given arrangement?

A. M faces the centre

B. Only three people sit between L and A

C. N sits to the immediate right of C

D. C is an immediate neighbour of D

E. None of these

Q.45 Who amongst the following sits third to the left of L?

A. M   **B.** C   **C.** B   **D.** A

E. N

Q.46 Which of the following pair represents the immediate neighbours of C?

A. L and A   **B.** A and N   **C.** M and B   **D.** D and N

E. D and L

Q.47 How many person sits between B and L when counted from left of L?

A. 4   **B.** 3

C. 2   **D.** 5

E. None of these

Ques (48-52):Direction: Study the following information to answer the questions.

Ten persons are sitting in two parallel rows containing five person each in such a way that there is an equal distance between adjacent persons. In row 1 P, Q, R, S, and T are seated and all of them are facing South. In row 2 A, B, C, D, and E are seated and all of them are facing North. Therefore, in the given seating arrangement each member seated in a row faces another member in the other row. S sits third to the right of Q where either of them is sitting on any of the extreme ends of the row. The one who faces Q sits second to the right of E. Two persons are sitting between B and E. Neither A nor C sits at an end of the row. The immediate neighbour of A faces the person who sits immediately to the right of Q. R and T are immediate neighbours of each other. T does not face the immediate neighbour of D.

Q.48 Who among the following is facing P?

A. S   **B.** R   **C.** Q   **D.** P

E. B

Q.49 Four of the following five are alike in a certain way and so form a group, find the one which does not belong to the group?

A. S   **B.** P   **C.** D   **D.** B

E. C

Q.50 Which of the following statements is true regarding R?

A. R faces one of the immediate neighbors of D.

B. P is one of the immediate neighbors of R.

C. None of the given statement is true.

D. R sits to the immediate right of Q.

E. All of the given statements are true.

Q.51 Who among the following is facing T?

A. D   **B.** E   **C.** B   **D.** C

E. A

Q.52 What is the position of C with respect to A?

A. Second to the left   **B.** Immediate left

C. Immediate right   **D.** Third to the right

E. Second to the right

Q.53 Each of the vowels in the word "CONCLUSION" is replaced by number "2" and each consonant is replaced by a number which is the serial number of that consonant in the word i.e., C by 1, N by 3 and so on. What is the total of all the numbers once the replacement is completed?

A. 40   **B.** 45   **C.** 37   **D.** 38

E. 36

Q.54 If it possible to make only one meaningful word with the first, sixth, seventh, and the twelfth letters of the word 'DOCUMENTATION', which would be the second letter of that word from the left? If more than one such word can be formed, give 'X' as the answer. If no such word can be formed, give 'Z' as your answer.

A. N   **B.** X   **C.** E   **D.** D

E. Z

Ques (55-59):Directions: Study the following information carefully to answer the given questions:

A F * O T & V B A # U % E @ F H E S ? M O J Q + Y C Z $ P & I @ O T F H X U Z D

Q.55 If we drop all the symbols then which letter lies at 12th position from the right end?

A. Y   **B.** Z   **C.** P   **D.** M

E. C

Q.56 How many vowels are present in the series?

A. 11   **B.** 10   **C.** 9   **D.** 8

E. 7

Q.57 How many symbols are there in the series which are immediately preceded and followed by a vowel?

A. 2   **B.** 1   **C.** 3   **D.** 5

E. 4

Q.58 If we drop all the vowels and symbols then which letter comes at the 15th place from the right end?

A. V   **B.** F   **C.** H   **D.** S

E. M

Q.59 How many consonants are immediately preceded by a symbol and followed by a vowel?

A. 0   **B.** 2   **C.** 3   **D.** 1

E. 4

Q.60 In a code language, if 'MANDATE' is coded as '2612881405' then how will 'TECHNIQUE' be coded in the same language?

[SSC Selection Post Phase IX, 2019]

A. 40106162893442   **B.** 40561614917215

C. 20561628183422   **D.** 40561628934215

E. 40561628934512

Q.61 In a code language, SKILLS is written as HPROOH. How will PLACES be written in that language?

[SSC Selection Post Phase IX, 2020]

A. KOZXVH   **B.** KOBXVG

C. LOZXVI   **D.** KPZXUH

E. KZPXUH

Q.62 In a code language, if 'MOON' is coded as '5229', 'FILM' is coded as '6315', 'ARE' is coded as '487', then in the same language How will 'INFORMER' be coded?

A. 39611578

B. 39162258

C. 79627578

D. 39628578

E. 39628587

Ques (63-65):Direction: Study the following information carefully and answer the questions given below.

H, I, J, K, L, M, N, O, P are the nine members of a family. P is the only brother of J, who is the only daughter of K. I is the mother of L, who is the niece of J. M is the maternal grand-mother of O, who is the only son of N. H is the father-in-law of the mother of O.

Q.63 How is M related to P?

A. Grandfather

B. Mother

C. Brother

D. Nephew

E. None of the above

Q.64 How is K related to O?

A. Brother

B. Mother

C. Paternal-grandfather

D. Maternal-grandfather

E. None of the above

Q.65 How is L related to P?

A. Father

B. Grandfather

C. Grandmother

D. Daughter

E. Mother

Quantitative Aptitude

Q.66 A sum of money was invested in a bank at 8% simple interest p.a. for 3 years. Had it been invested in mutual fund at 8.5% p.a. simple interest for 4 years, the earning would have been Rs. 500 more. What is the sum invested?

A. 5000

B. 5500

C. 5550

D. 4500

E. None of these

Ques (67-71):Direction: In the given question, two equations numbered I and II are given. You have to solve both the equations and mark the appropriate answer.

Q.67 I. $x^2 - 5x + 6 = 0$

II. $y^2 + y - 6 = 0$

A. x < y   **B.** x > y   **C.** x ≤ y   **D.** x ≥ y

E. x = y

Q.68 I. $2x^2 - 12x + 18 = 0$

II. $2y^2 - 19y + 39 = 0$

A. x < y   **B.** x > y   **C.** x = y   **D.** x ≥ y

E. x ≤ y

Q.69 I. $x^2 + 13x + 42 = 0$

II. $y^2 + 19y + 90 = 0$

A. x < y   **B.** x ≤ y   **C.** x > y   **D.** x ≥ y

E. x = y

Q.70 I. $3x^2 - 23x - 8 = 0$

II. $3y^2 - 32y - 11 = 0$

A. x < y

B. x > y

C. x ≤ y

D. x ≥ y

E. x = y OR the relationship cannot be determined

Q.71 I. $3x^2 - 14x - 5 = 0$

II. $6y^2 - 46y - 16 = 0$

A. x< y

B. x> y

C. x = y OR the relationship cannot be determined

D. x ≥ y

E. x ≤ y

Q.72 A book was successively sold by three book-sellers gaining a profit of 10% each. By how much percentage the price of the book has increased?

A. 10%   **B.** 15.5%   **C.** 30%   **D.** 31.2%

E. 33.1%

Ques (73-77):Directions: Read the table carefully and answer the following questions:

The following Table shows the efficiency of the 5 different machines.

Machine	Total Capacity	Efficiency
A	150	50%
B	160	40%
C	180	60%
D	120	70%
E	140	60%

Note:- If efficiency is n, then final output will be $n \times \dfrac{(n+1)}{2}$

Q.73 Find the difference between the output of the machine B and machine D.

[IBPS PO, 2020]

A. 1280   **B.** 1370   **C.** 1410   **D.** 1530

E. 1490

Q.74 Find the final output of C.

[IBPS PO, 2020]

A. 5776   **B.** 5786   **C.** 5976   **D.** 5886

E. 5676

Q.75 The output of machine A is approximately how much percent more than the output of B?

[IBPS PO, 2020]

A. 32%   **B.** 27%   **C.** 42%   **D.** 21%

E. 37%

Q.76 The output of machine D is what percent of the output of Machine E.

[IBPS PO, 2020]

A. 100%	B. 125%	C. 90%	D. 80%

E. 150%

Q.77 Find the ratio between the output of machine D and machine E.

[IBPS PO, 2020]

A. 2 : 1	B. 1 : 1	C. 1 : 2	D. 3 : 2

E. 2 : 3

Q.78 Smrita is three times as efficient as Dipti and completes the task of stitching 10 shirts in 25 min. Together, they require to stitch 500 shirts, how much time they need to complete the order?

A. 886.5 min
B. 937.5 min
C. 785 min
D. 834.5 min
E. 965 min

Q.79 A 25% gain is made by selling the mixture of two types of flour at Rs. 450 per kg. If the type one costing 620 per kg was mixed with 130 kg of the other, how many kilograms of the former was mixed?

A. 138 kg
B. 34.5 kg
C. 69.5 kg
D. 25.5 kg
E. Cannot be determined

Q.80 5 years ago, Sam was twice as old as David. 5 years from now, David's age will be two-third of Sam's age. What is the sum of the present ages of David and Sam?

A. 25	B. 35	C. 40	D. 60

E. 75

Q.81 A tank is filled by three pipes with uniform flow. The first two pipes operating simultaneously fill the tank at the same time during which the tank is filled by the third pipe alone. The second pipe fills the tank 5 hours faster than the first pipe and 4 hours slower than the third pipe. The time required by the first pipe is:

A. 6 hours	B. 10 hours	C. 15 hours	D. 30 hours

E. 5 hours

Ques (82-84):Direction: Given below are two quantities named A and B. Based on the given information, you have to determine the relationship between the two quantities. You should use the given data and your knowledge of Mathematics to choose between the possible answers.

Q.82 Quantity A: A train 100 meters long meets a man going in the opposite direction at $5\ km/h$ and crosses him in 9 seconds. What is the speed of the train?

Quantity B: $35\ m/s$

A. Quantity A > Quantity B
B. Quantity A < Quantity B
C. Quantity A ≥ Quantity B
D. Quantity A ≤ Quantity B
E. Quantity A = Quantity B or No relation

Q.83 Quantity A: A retailer makes a profit of 25% after giving a discount of 20% on the marked price of an article. If he makes a profit of Rs 1800 on the sale of the article, then the marked price is.

Quantity B: Rs 10000

A. Quantity A > Quantity B
B. Quantity A < Quantity B
C. Quantity A ≥ Quantity B
D. Quantity A ≤ Quantity B
E. Quantity A = Quantity B or No relation

Q.84 Quantity A: A can contains a mixture of two liquids A and B in the ratio $3:5$. When 12 liters of is drawn out and the can is filled with liquid B, When 12 liters of is drawn out and the can is filled with liquid B, the ratio of A and B becomes $1:3$. How many liters of liquid A were contained by the can initially?

Quantity B: 9 liters

A. Quantity A > Quantity B
B. Quantity A < Quantity B
C. Quantity A ≥ Quantity B
D. Quantity A ≤ Quantity B
E. Quantity A = Quantity B or No relation

Q.85 In a class of 60 students, 30% are girls. In a class test, the class average was 17 out of 30 marks. 50% of the girls went for an inter-school basketball match and could not take the test. Initially, the teacher assumed them to be absent and gave them 0 marks. If the teacher has to award each of the 20 marks, find the new class average.

A. 18	B. 21	C. 20	D. 17

E. 19

Ques (86-90):Direction: What should come in place of the question mark '?' in the following number series?

Q.86 4, 8, 10, 30, 33, 132, 136, 680, ?

A. 682	B. 684	C. 685	D. 690

E. 687

Q.87 40, 82, 249, 1250, ?

A. 7456	B. 6583	C. 8757	D. 3423

E. 8134

Q.88 7, 8, 14, 45, 176, ?

A. 885	B. 775	C. 475	D. 445

E. 945

Q.89 33, 47, 53, 61, 71, ?

A. 84
B. 85
C. 83
D. 81
E. None of the above

Q.90 60.5, 72, 84.5, 98, 112.5, ?

A. 125	B. 122	C. 126	D. 128

E. 132

Q.91 What value should come in place of question mark (?) in the following question?

$\sqrt{225} + (1500 \text{ of } 55\%) - \{(45)^2 \div 81 \times 4\} + 20 - 16 = ?$

A. 744   **B.** 748   **C.** 746   **D.** 752
E. 742

Q.92 What value should come in place of question mark (?) in the following question?

$(8375 \div 67)^{\frac{1}{3}} + (7.84 \times 25)^{\frac{1}{2}} = (?)^{\frac{1}{2}}$

A. 456   **B.** 361   **C.** 324   **D.** 338
E. 432

Q.93 What value should come in place of question mark (?) in the following question?

$57\frac{1}{7}\% \text{ of } 490 + 22.22\% \text{ of } 729 - \sqrt{2500} \times \sqrt{25} \div 5^2 = ?$

A. 440   **B.** 322   **C.** 432   **D.** 452
E. 462

Q.94 What value should come in place of question mark (?) in the following question?

$\sqrt{[(6.25)^2 \times 100]} + \frac{7}{2} = ? \times 11$

A. 6   **B.** 7   **C.** 8   **D.** 10
E. 12

Q.95 Direction: Simplify the given expression.

$\sqrt{1024} \times 40 + 20^2 + 0.5\% \text{ of } 9600 + 469 = ?^3$

A. 23   **B.** 13   **C.** 19   **D.** 21
E. 14

Q.96 Direction: Simplify the given expression.

$\left(\sqrt{8} \times \sqrt{8}\right)^{\frac{1}{2}} + 9^{\frac{1}{2}} = ?^3 + \sqrt{8} - 340$

A. 7   **B.** 19   **C.** 18   **D.** 9
E. 8

Q.97 What will come in the place of the question mark '?' in the following question?

$6.67\% \text{ of } 225 + 6.25\% \text{ of } 1120 = (?)^3 + 3$

A. $(-76)^{\frac{1}{2}}$ **B.** $(76)^{\frac{1}{2}}$
C. $(-76)^{\frac{1}{3}}$ **D.** $(-76)^{\frac{1}{3}}$
E. None of these

Q.98 What will come in place of the question mark '?' in the following question?

(0.1 × 0.004) + (0.02 × 0.3) − (0.04 × 0.03) = ?

A. 0.0022   **B.** 0.0034
C. 0.0046   **D.** 0.0052
E. None of these

Q.99 What will come in the place of the question mark '?' in the following question?

$25\% \text{ of } 7428 + 71.5 \times 2 = 14\frac{2}{7}\% \text{ of } ?$

A. 2000   **B.** 5000   **C.** 4000   **D.** 14000
E. 12000

Q.100 What will come in the place of the question mark '?' in the following question?

16% of 25 × 88 + 20% of 135 − 16 × (18 − 5% of 200) = ?

A. 224   **B.** 169
C. 507   **D.** 251
E. None of these

// Smart Answer Sheet //

Correct   Indicates percentage of students who answered questions correctly.

Skipped   Indicates percentage of students who skipped questions.

Q.	Ans.	Correct / Skipped	Q.	Ans.	Correct / Skipped	Q.	Ans.	Correct / Skipped	Q.	Ans.	Correct / Skipped	Q.	Ans.	Correct / Skipped
1	D	49.12 % / 38.03 %	17	B	88.28 % / 11.68 %	33	E	53.02 % / 38.11 %	49	E	87.97 % / 10.02 %	65	D	59.65 % / 37.34 %
2	B	48.58 % / 39.13 %	18	D	54.19 % / 37.36 %	34	E	86.74 % / 12.73 %	50	A	76.67 % / 14.07 %	66	D	66.77 % / 31.13 %
3	A	58.81 % / 31.69 %	19	A	54.55 % / 34.1 %	35	A	56.64 % / 30.2 %	51	D	23.46 % / 70.95 %	67	D	58.57 % / 40.78 %
4	B	62.76 % / 36.77 %	20	C	63.39 % / 33.97 %	36	E	47.48 % / 39.96 %	52	B	44.67 % / 50.06 %	68	E	50.44 % / 48.56 %
5	C	64.22 % / 30.14 %	21	B	84.77 % / 13.23 %	37	C	45.83 % / 34.77 %	53	D	40.97 % / 50.61 %	69	C	57.7 % / 40.05 %
6	C	57.75 % / 35.15 %	22	D	56.72 % / 32.53 %	38	B	42.74 % / 50.51 %	54	B	54.01 % / 30.2 %	70	E	54.04 % / 43.47 %
7	D	43.54 % / 33.16 %	23	B	32.47 % / 67.05 %	39	B	67.99 % / 30.77 %	55	E	46.62 % / 41.26 %	71	C	67.15 % / 32.15 %
8	A	50.17 % / 33.88 %	24	D	51.03 % / 32.29 %	40	A	42.69 % / 55.53 %	56	B	48.43 % / 30.42 %	72	E	68.22 % / 30.46 %
9	C	62.84 % / 35.23 %	25	A	79.68 % / 16.57 %	41	E	53.47 % / 45.61 %	57	C	53.51 % / 34.46 %	73	E	44.69 % / 39.2 %
10	D	79.19 % / 14.69 %	26	D	52.17 % / 42.24 %	42	D	66.63 % / 32.61 %	58	C	69.11 % / 30.27 %	74	D	60.0 % / 36.83 %
11	D	44.89 % / 44.95 %	27	B	87.19 % / 10.0 %	43	C	50.26 % / 30.46 %	59	D	44.39 % / 47.9 %	75	E	44.05 % / 36.85 %
12	D	69.96 % / 30.01 %	28	C	87.69 % / 10.12 %	44	A	64.58 % / 33.47 %	60	D	69.43 % / 30.56 %	76	A	45.82 % / 37.43 %
13	B	25.63 % / 69.6 %	29	E	81.01 % / 14.4 %	45	C	61.51 % / 36.99 %	61	A	53.32 % / 32.37 %	77	B	84.54 % / 12.16 %
14	A	60.71 % / 30.09 %	30	A	88.28 % / 11.04 %	46	B	69.93 % / 30.03 %	62	A	67.14 % / 31.73 %	78	B	45.13 % / 54.39 %
15	C	66.17 % / 30.32 %	31	C	61.47 % / 36.97 %	47	C	43.76 % / 46.21 %	63	B	48.92 % / 34.92 %	79	E	56.93 % / 42.99 %
16	E	69.32 % / 30.44 %	32	D	53.98 % / 33.43 %	48	E	67.58 % / 31.26 %	64	D	65.16 % / 31.57 %	80	C	77.23 % / 12.58 %

Q.	Ans.	Correct		Q.	Ans.	Correct		Q.	Ans.	Correct		Q.	Ans.	Correct		Q.	Ans.	Correct
		Skipped				Skipped				Skipped				Skipped				Skipped
81	C	44.57 %		85	C	49.9 %		89	C	81.03 %		93	C	63.42 %		97	E	58.06 %
		41.77 %				42.72 %				13.19 %				32.47 %				41.15 %
82	B	48.68 %		86	C	76.04 %		90	D	78.28 %		94	A	69.98 %		98	D	43.45 %
		44.32 %				22.19 %				18.46 %				30.01 %				33.54 %
83	A	65.99 %		87	C	57.93 %		91	A	68.27 %		95	B	64.19 %		99	D	12.69 %
		32.16 %				35.06 %				30.86 %				34.07 %				73.59 %
84	A	53.26 %		88	A	42.89 %		92	B	45.69 %		96	A	42.79 %		100	D	80.66 %
		43.89 %				40.57 %				32.08 %				52.62 %				14.66 %

Performance Analysis

Avg. Score (%)	52.0%
Toppers Score (%)	74.0%
Your Score	

//Hints and Solutions//

Ques (1-5): The given paragraph is about Microsoft's lack of innovation.

Sentence D is the first sentence as it introduces the topic of the paragraph by mentioning Microsoft's lack of innovation as one of the key challenges that surfaced after SWOT analysis.

Sentence F is the second sentence as it continues D by explaining that Microsoft lacks innovation because all its products are influenced by the existing products of its competitors.

Sentence B is the third sentence as it continues F by giving an example of how Microsoft's Windows is influenced by Apple's Unix.

Sentence C is the fourth sentence as it continues B by mentioning similarly and giving another example of how Microsoft's office suite was influenced by Lotus and Word Perfect.

Sentence E is the fifth sentence explaining more on how Microsoft's products in coming years became more similar to the already existing products.

Sentence A is the sixth sentence and it continues E by giving an example of how Microsoft's browser and search engine are similar to Netscape and Google respectively.

The correct sequence is **DFBCEA.**

1. D is the first sentence in the paragraph

Hence, the correct option is (D).

2. F is the second sentence in the paragraph

Hence, the correct option is (B).

3. B is the third sentence in the paragraph.

Hence, the correct option is (A).

4. C is the fourth sentence in the paragraph.

Hence, the correct option is (B).

5. A is the sixth sentence in the paragraph.

Hence, the correct option is (C).

6. The wrongly spelt word is Prevarricate.

The correct spelling of the word is 'prevaricate'.

It means speak or act in an evasive way.

Guarded: careful; not giving much information or showing what you feel.

Cherished: to love somebody/something and look after him/her/it carefully.

Legitimate: reasonable or acceptable.

Abominate: to feel hatred for somebody/something.

Hence, the correct option is (C).

7. The wrongly spelt word is Sustenence.

The correct spelling of the word is 'sustenance'.

It means food and drink regarded as a source of strength; nourishment.

Increment: a regular increase in the amount of money that somebody is paid for his/her job.

Superficial: not studying or thinking about something in a deep or complete way.

Retreat: to move backwards in order to leave a battle or in order not to become involved in a battle.

Intensive: involving a lot of work or care in a short period of time.

Hence, the correct option is (D).

8. The wrongly spelt word is Shettarable.

The correct spelling of the word is 'shatterable'.

It means capable of being shattered (very upset).

Brittle: hard but easily broken.

Extraordinary: very unusual.

Crisp: pleasantly hard and dry.

Shivery: shaking or trembling as a result of cold, illness, fear, or excitement.

Hence, the correct option is (A).

9. The given passage is about "Wealth report of India".

Let us refer to the line from the passage, "India is expected to see incredible growth of 63 per cent by 2025, making it the second-fastest-growing country in terms of number of UHNWIs".

From the given line we get to know that after referring to the wealth report of India we could see in all aspects India has shown a very significant growth compared to other countries.

Its incredible growth in the number of UHNWI has made India known to the world as the second-fastest-growing country in terms of UHNWIs.

Hence, the correct option is (C).

10. The given passage is about "Wealth report of India".

Let us refer to the line from the passage, "India is expected to see incredible growth of 63 per cent by 2025, making it the second-fastest-growing country in terms of number of UHNWIs".

From the given line we get to know that India has seen incredible growth than any country because of which it is known as the second-fastest-growing country in terms of the number of UHNWIs.

Hence, the correct option is (D).

11. The given passage is about "Wealth report of India".

Let us refer to the line from the passage, "The number of ultra-high nets worth individuals (UHNWIs), with a wealth of USD 30 million or more, is expected to rise 63 percent over the next five years to 11,198 in India, the second-fastest growth in the world, according to property consultant Knight Frank India report".

From the given line we get to know that a property consultant makes a wealth report. For India, the report on UHNWI was given by Knight Frank.

Hence, the correct option is (D).

12. The given passage is about "Wealth report of India".

The given word 'Poverty' means an abundance of valuable possessions or money.

In option (D), the word 'Poverty' means the state of being extremely poor.

Hence, the correct option is (D).

13. The given passage is about "Wealth report of India".

The given word 'Statment' means a definite or clear expression of something in speech or writing.

In option (B), the word 'Declaration' means a formal or explicit statement or announcement.

Hence, the correct option is (B).

14. Complete Sentence: Christmas is one of the most famous and light-hearted festivals which is **celebrated** across the world by billions of people.

The given sentence "Christmas is one of the most famous and light-hearted festivals which is ___(1)___ across the world by billions of people" is saying that Christmas is acknowledged all over the world.

Therefore, the most appropriate word to be filled in the blank is '**Celebrated**'.

Also, the use of the word "festivals" in the sentence indicates the use of the word 'celebrated' in the blank.

The word 'Celebrated' means To acknowledge a significant or happy day or event with a social gathering or enjoyable activity.

- **Example**: We celebrated the New Year with a dance party.

Hence, the correct option is (A).

15. Complete Sentence: People of the Christian religion celebrate Christmas to **remember** the great works of Jesus Christ.

The given sentence "People of the Christian religion celebrate Christmas to ___(2)___ the great works of Jesus Christ" is saying that people of the Christian religion celebrate Christmas to recall the great works of Jesus Christ.

Therefore, the most appropriate word to be filled in the blank is 'Remember'.

Also, the use of the word "works" in the sentence indicates the use of the word 'remember' in the blank.

The word '**Remember**' means To have in or be able to bring to one's mind an awareness of someone or something from the past.

- Example: The remedy for injuries is not to remember them.

Hence, the correct option is (C).

16. Complete Sentence: 25th December is celebrated as Christmas Day **across** the world.

The given sentence "25th December is celebrated as Christmas Day ___(3)___ the world" is saying that 25th December is celebrated as Christmas Day all over the world.

Therefore, the most appropriate word to be filled in the blank is '**Across**'.

Also, the use of the word "world" in the sentence indicates the use of the word 'across' in the blank.

The word '**Across**' means From one side to the other of a place, area, etc.

- **Example**: Mortality from heart disease varies widely across the world.

Hence, the correct option is (E).

17. Complete Sentence: Jesus Christ of Bethlehem was a spiritual leader and prophet whose teachings **structure** the premise of their religion.

The given sentence "Jesus Christ of Bethlehem was a spiritual leader and prophet whose teachings ___(4)___ the premise of their religion" is saying that Jesus Christ's teachings organized the premise of their religion.

Therefore, the most appropriate word to be filled in the blank is '**Structure**'.

Also, the use of the word "premise" in the sentence indicates the use of the word 'structure' in the blank.

The word '**Structure**' means The quality of being organized.

- **Example**: We shall use three headings to give some structure to the discussion.

Hence, the correct option is (B).

18. Complete Sentence: People **follow** popular customs including exchanging gifts, decorating Christmas trees, attending church, sharing meals with family and friends, and, obviously, trusting that Santa Claus will arrive.

The given sentence "People ___(5)___ popular customs including exchanging gifts, decorating Christmas trees, attending church, sharing meals with family and friends, and, obviously, trusting that Santa Claus will arrive" is talking about people going along with popular customs during Christmas.

Therefore, the most appropriate word to be filled in the blank is '**Follow**'.

Also, the use of the word "customs" in the sentence indicates the use of the word 'follow' in the blank.

The word '**Follow**' means To take an active interest in or be a supporter of someone or something.

- **Example**: The leader beckoned the others to follow her.

Hence, the correct option is (D).

19. Ensue means result/proceed and does not fit in. This does not make sense in the statement.

Excess means surplus which is opposite of what is needed.

Ensures is incorrect as it leads to subject verb disagreement.

Accessibility is correct and means ease of access.

The phrase **'ensure accessibility'** is correct and fits in well meaningfully and grammatically.

Hence, the correct option is (A).

20. The correct phrase is around/round the corner.

Around the corner: Nearby, close by, not far away.

Hence, the correct option is (C).

21. We need the adverb form of 'history'. Thus, 'historically' is correct while 'historic' is incorrect. This eliminates option A.

Being is incorrect as it is used to refer to an individual/person. Been is correct here. This eliminates option C.

Due to article 'a', the correct form is 'place' in singular.

Hence, the correct option is (B).

22. The statement talks about multiple people and thus 'are' is correct.

One is entitled 'to' something and not 'for'. This eliminates option B.

Option C is incorrect as 'a rights' is incorrect grammatically.

Option D is correct grammatically and contextually.

Hence, the correct option is (D).

23. The original sentence is incorrect.

The bold part lacks parallelism. To bring parallelism the infinitive 'to restore' has to be replaced by the gerund 'restoring' here. Secondly, as 'Preserving and restoring forests' is implying 'one' idea, the verb to be used has to be singular in number. Therefore, 'are' should be replaced by 'is' to make the sentence correct. Clearly, among the given choices, option B replaces the bold part most appropriately.

The correct sentence will therefore be:

Preserving and restoring forests is an effective step toward mitigating climate change, and comes with a host of other benefits.

Hence, the correct option is (B).

24. Vacuous: having or showing a lack of thought or intelligence; mindless.

Intelligent: having or showing intelligence, especially of a high level.

Courteous: polite, respectful, or considerate in manner.

Exhilarated: make (someone) feel very happy, animated, or elated.

Modest: not talking too much about your own abilities, good qualities, etc.

Emergent: in the process of coming into being or becoming prominent.

Therefore, "intelligent" is the opposite of "Vacuous".

Hence, the correct option is (D).

25. Foray means a sudden attack or incursion into enemy territory, especially to obtain something.

Maraud means go about in search of things to steal or people to attack.

Contest means an event in which people compete for supremacy in a sport or other activity.

Ranger means a keeper of a park, forest, or area of countryside.

Intuition means the ability to understand something instinctively, without the need for conscious reasoning.

Therefore, "Maraud" is the synonym of "Foray".

Hence, the correct option is (A).

26. The sentence is in the past continuous tense.

This can be seen from the usage of 2 separate verbs - including and paying - in their continuous form and the usage of the verb 'are' in the past form i.e. 'were'.

This means that all the verbs in the sentence need to be in the continuous tense.

Thus, 'caused' needs to be replaced with 'causing' in order to make the sentence grammatically correct.

Correct Sentence: The farmers, including the village's Sarpanch were late in paying their due to the Zamindar, causing the Zamindar to confiscate their lands.

Hence, the correct option is (D).

27. The given sentence in the past tense, this can be seen by the use of the modal verb 'would'.

Even if the verb 'would' were to be replaced by the verb 'will', 'remembered' would still be incorrect as 'will' is in the present tense.

A modal verb has to be followed by the base form of the verb.

Thus, 'remembered' needs to be replaced with 'remember'.

Correct Sentence: Mark would always remember his dog, Molly with fondness.

Hence, the correct option is (B).

28. The sentence is in the past tense as can be seen by the use of the verb 'were' and 'would' in the past tense.

The sentence already tells us that the subject of the sentence is 'he/his' and this is the pronoun that is used to refers to him in the rest of the sentence.

If the sentence already uses one specific pronoun it should be maintained throughout the sentence unless the subject of the sentence changes.

Thus, 'one's' needs to be replaced with 'his' in order to make the sentence grammatically correct.

Correct Sentence: His parents were very hopeful that he would one day achieve his ambitions and make them proud.

Hence, the correct option is (C).

29. The sentence is in the continuous tense as can be seen by the use of 'ing' form of the verb 'wait'.

The use of the construction 'will + be' before the continuous form of the verb indicates that the action is yet to occur, but will occur in the future.

This means that every verb in the sentence should comply with this format of the future continuous tense.

The given sentence has **no errors** and is grammatically correct.

Hence, the correct option is (E).

30. The sentence is in the past tense as can be seen by the use of the verb 'insisted' and 'wanted' in the past tense.

The verb 'insist' means to 'demand something forcefully or not taking no for an answer'.

This means that there usually is an idea or a point which one is being 'forceful' about.

The verb 'insisted' needs to be followed by the preposition 'on' in order to show what point someone is being forced about.

Thus, 'insisted' needs to be followed by the preposition 'on' in order to make the sentence contextually correct.

Correct Sentence: Michael insisted on paying for the meal, but Halley wanted to split the bill.

Hence, the correct option is (A).

31. Given statements: M ≥ T; M < P; S > T

On combining: P > M ≥ T < S

Conclusions:

I. S = M → False (as P > M ≥ T < S → thus clear relation between S and M cannot be determined)

II. T < P → True (as P > M ≥ T → P > T)

III. P > S → False (as P > M ≥ T < S → thus clear relation between P and S cannot be determined)

So, only conclusion II is true.

Hence, the correct option is (C).

32. Given Statements:

X > C ≥ V > Y; U = V < T ≤ H; T < B

On Combining:

X > C ≥ V > Y, X > C ≥ U = V < T ≤ H, B > T ≤ H

Conclusions:

I. Y < X → True (as X > C ≥ V > Y → X > Y)

II. X ≥ B → False (as X > C ≥ U = V < T < B → thus clear relation between X and B cannot be determined)

III. V < B → True (as U = V < T < B → V < B)

So, only conclusion I and III follow.

Hence, the correct option is (D).

33. Given statements: P ≤ Q > R = S; S < T; T = P > U; V < U

On combining: Q ≥ P = T > S = R; T = P > U > V

Conclusions:

I. Q = P → False (as R = S < T → R < T and T = P > U → U < T → thus clear relation between R and U cannot be determined)

II. Q > P → False (as Q ≥ P > U > V → Q > V)

III. P < V → False (as V < U < P = T → V < P)

Note: conclusion I and II forms complementary pair.

So, either I or II follows.

Hence, the correct option is (E).

34. Given statements: A > P ≥ K; Q > M > T; P > T

On combining: A > P > T < M < Q; P ≥ K

Conclusions:

I. T < K → False (as P > T; P ≥ K; relation between T and K cannot be determined)

II. K > A → False (as A > P; P ≥ K; A > P ≥ K; A > K)

III. A > K → True (as A > P; P ≥ K; A > P ≥ K; A > K)

So, only III is true.

Hence, the correct option is (E).

35. Given: P ≥ A > I = R; S < A > M

On Combining: P ≥ A > I = R; P ≥ A > S; P ≥ A > M

Conclusions:

I. M < P → True (as M < A ≤ P).

II. P > S → True (as P ≥ A > S).

III. M < R → False (as P ≥ A > I = R; P ≥ A > M, thus a clear relation between M and R cannot be established)

Therefore, only conclusions I and II are true.

Hence, the correct option is (A).

36. Given,

There are 25 students in a class and all of them are sitting in a row to do yoga. Meena is 11th from the top and Sneha is 6th from the bottom. Two students are sitting between Ananya and Reena.

From the above information, we cannot be sure about the position of Reena, as we don't have enough information about the position of Ananya and Reena.

Hence, the correct option is (E).

37. Given,

In a row of girls, if Shilpa who is 8th from the left and Reena who is 17th from the right interchange their positions, then Shilpa is 14th from the left She goes.

After interchanging,

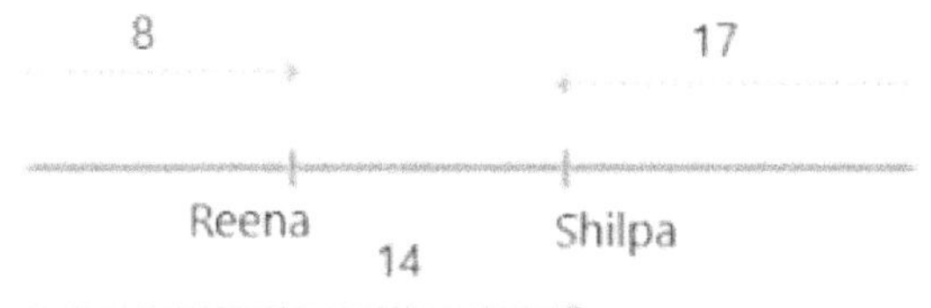

Then,

Shilpa's present position = 14

Reena's former position = 17

Total noumber of girls = (Shilpa's present position + Reena's former position) -1

$$= (14 + 17) - 1 = 30$$

Hence, the correct option is (C).

38. Following is the least possible Venn diagram for the given statements:

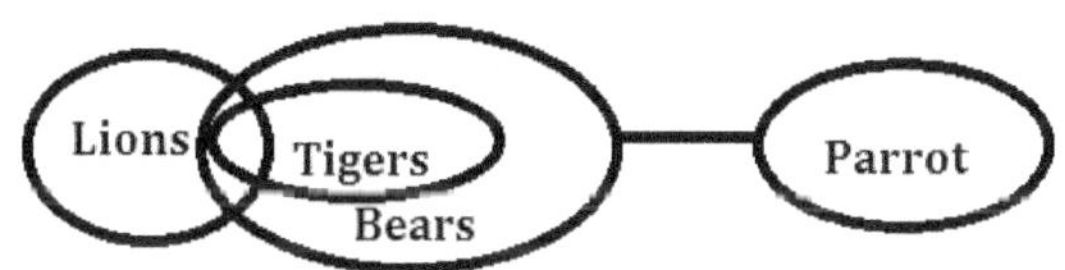

Conclusions:

I. Some Lions are Parrot → It's definitely not possible, hence false.

II. Some Lions are Bears → It's definitely possible, hence true.

III. Some Parrot are Bears → It's definitely not possible, hence false.

Thus, only conclusion II follows.

Hence, the correct option is (B).

39. The best possible Venn diagram for the given statements is as follows:

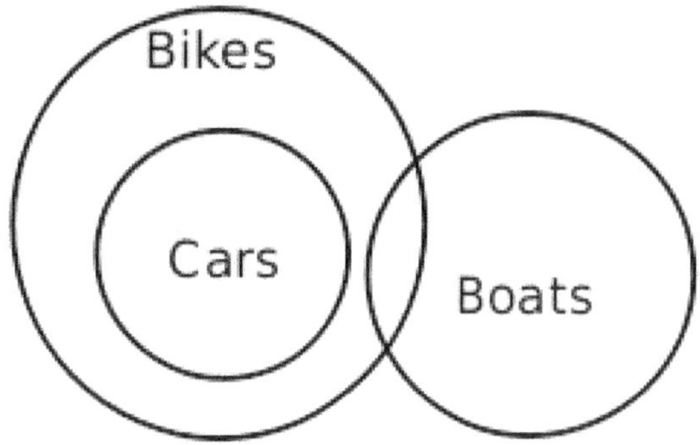

Since some bikes are cars and no car is a boat, all bikes cannot be boats. Thus, the conclusion I is not possible.

Since some bikes are boats and no car is a boat, all bikes cannot be boats. Thus, conclusion II follows.

Hence, the correct option is (B).

40.

The best possible Venn diagram for the given statements is as follows:

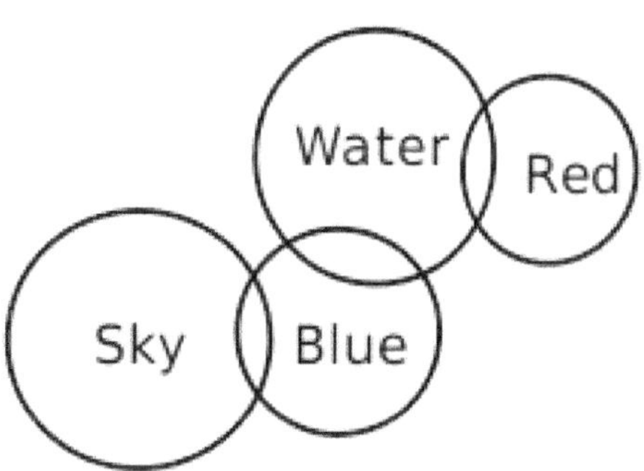

From the Venn diagram, we can see that conclusion I is possible.

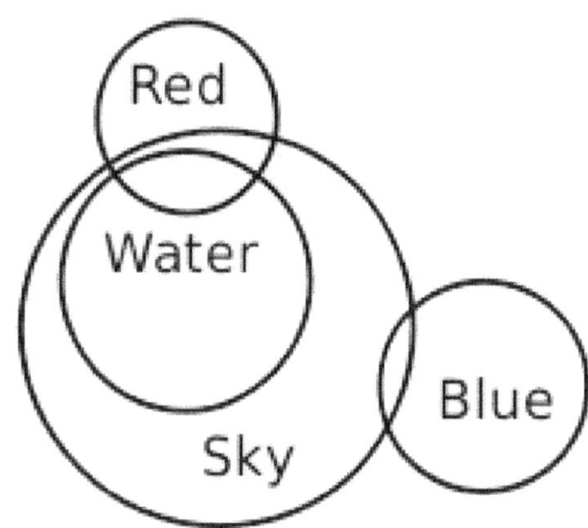

From the Venn diagram, we can see that all water can be skies. Conclusion II does not follow.

Hence, the correct option is (A).

41.

The best possible Venn diagram for the given statements is as follows:

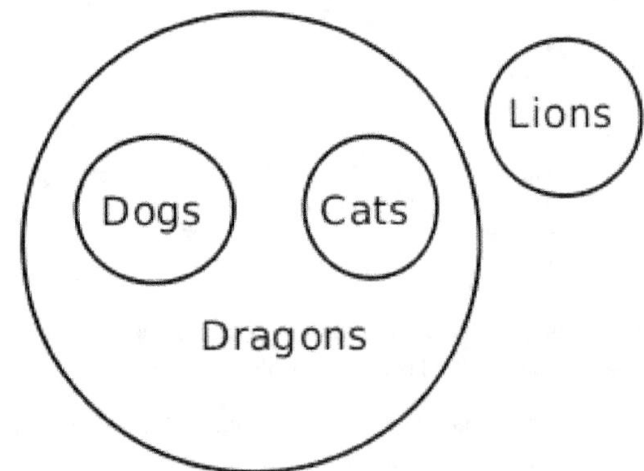

Since all cats are dragons and no dragon is a lion, no cat can be a lion. Thus, conclusion II follows.

Hence, the correct option is (E).

42. The given statements can be expressed diagrammatically as follows without violating any condition.

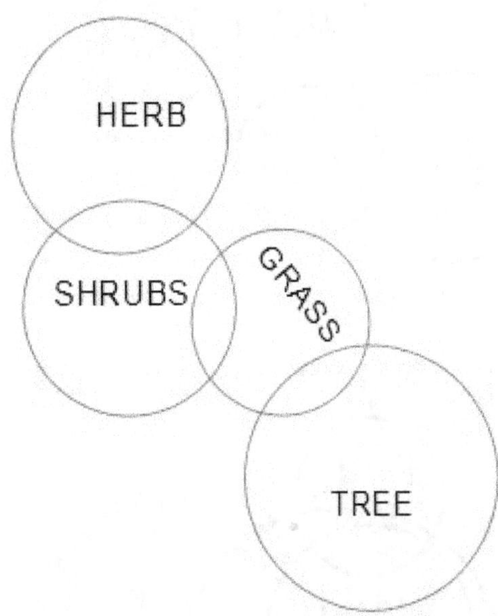

As we can see, neither of the conclusions follow.

Hence, the correct option is (D).

Ques (43-47): Eight people are A, B, C, D, L, M, N, and O. Some are facing centre, and some are facing outside.

i) Only three people sit between B and O.

ii) L sits to the immediate right of O.

iii) B sits third to the left of A.

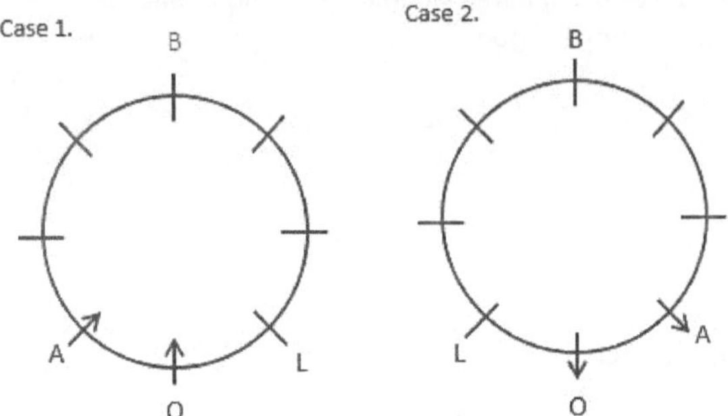

iv) Only one person sits between L and D.

v) Immediate neighbours of L face opposite directions.

vi) L does not face outside.

vii) N sits second to the right of D.

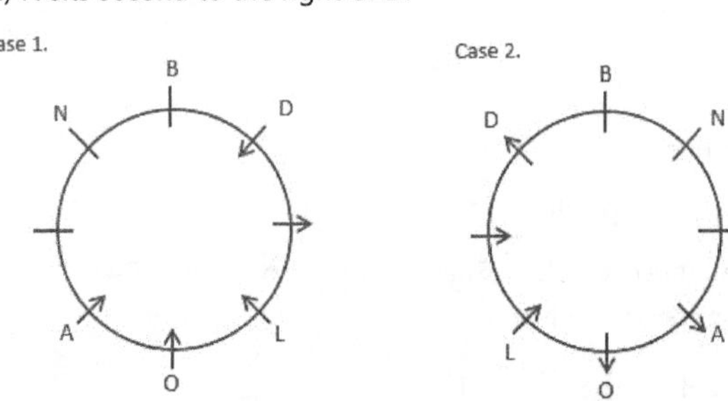

viii) Both N and C face the same direction as O.

ix) Immediate neighbours of M face opposite directions to each other.

In Case 1. Both N and C will face towards centre. Thus, M will sit between L and D. Both L and D face the same direction. So, Case 1 gets eliminated.

x) D faces a direction opposite to that of B.

Case 2.

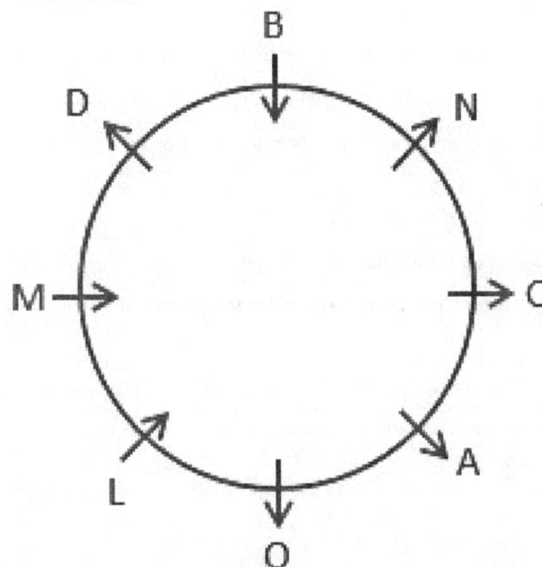

43. Clearly, 4 people sit between A and M if counted from left of M.

Hence, the correct option is (C).

44. So, M faces the centre is true.

Hence, the correct option is (A).

45. B sits third to the left of L.

Hence, the correct option is (C).

46. So, A and N are immediate neighbours of C.

Hence, the correct option is (B).

47. So, when counted from left of L two persons sits between B and L

Hence, the correct option is (C).

48. Facing South: P, Q, R, S, and T (Row 1)

Facing North: A, B, C, D, and E (Row 2)

(1) S sits third to the right of Q where either of them is sitting on any of the extreme ends of the row.

(Here, there are two possible cases, Case 1: Q sits at the extreme right end of the row, Case 2: S sits at the extreme left end of the row.)

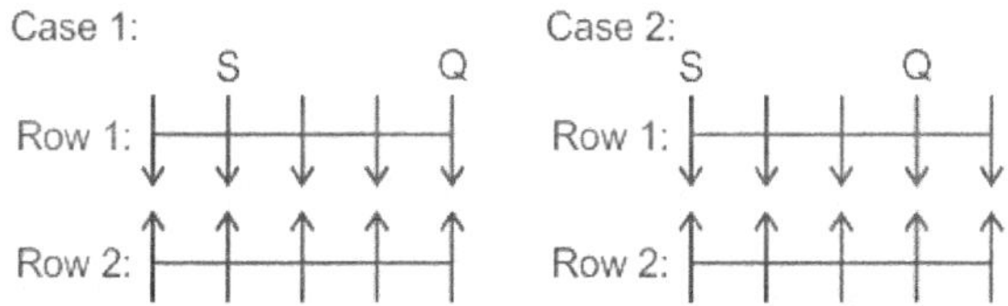

(2) The one who faces Q sits second to the right of E.

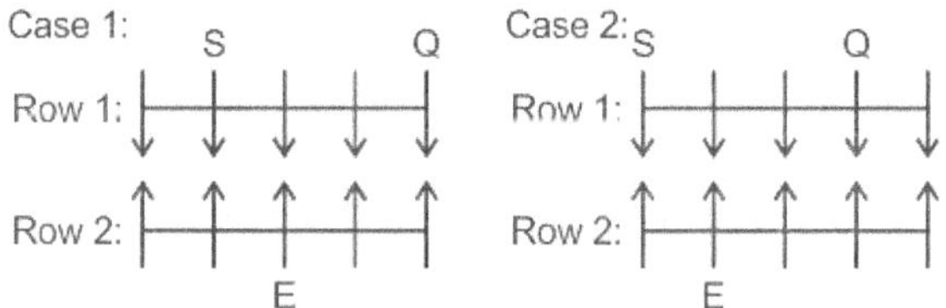

(3) Two persons are sitting between B and E.

(Here we can eliminate Case 1)

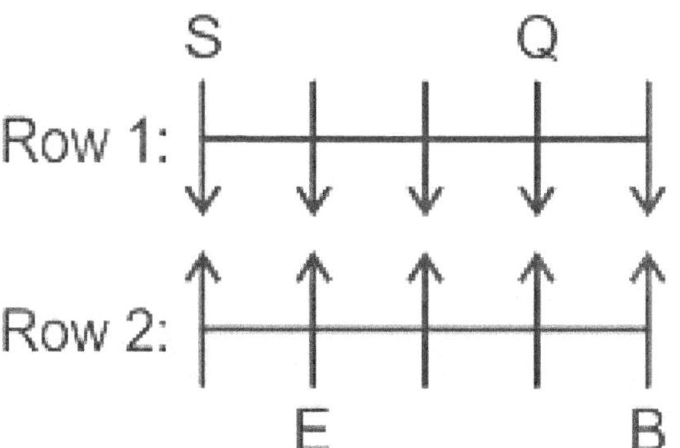

(4) Neither A nor C sits at an extreme end of the row.

(So D sits at the extreme end of row 2)

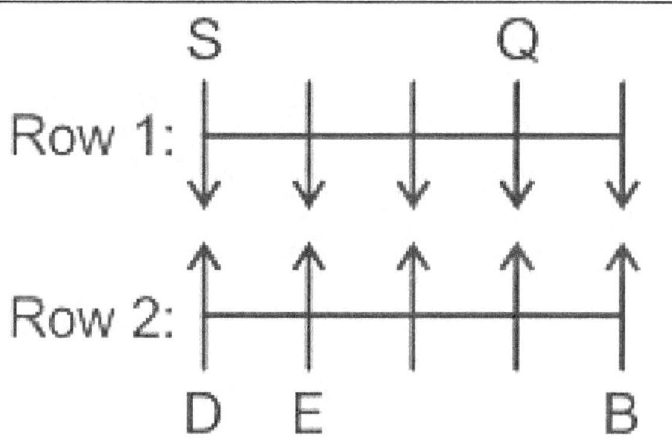

(5) The immediate neighbour of A faces the person who sits immediately to the right of Q.

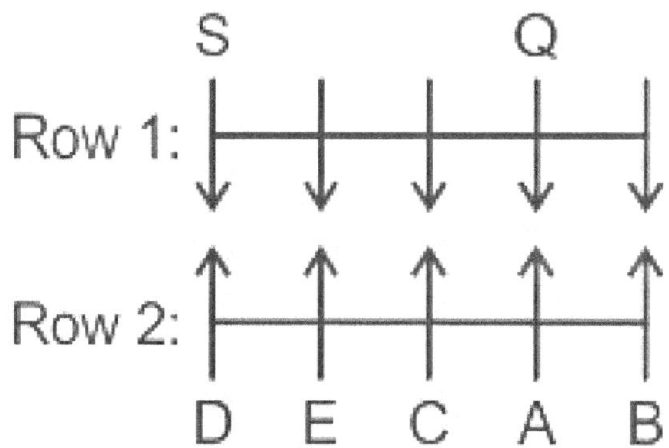

(6) R and T are immediate neighbours of each other.

(7) T does not face the immediate neighbour of D.

The final arrangement will be as follows.

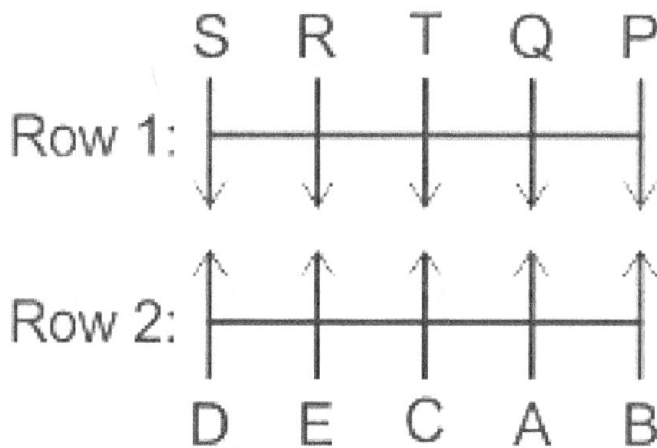

Thus, B is facing P.

Hence, the correct option is (E).

49. Facing South: P, Q, R, S, and T (Row 1)

Facing North: A, B, C, D, and E (Row 2)

(1) S sits third to the right of Q where either of them is sitting on any of the extreme ends of the row.

(Here, there are two possible cases, Case 1: Q sits at the extreme right end of the row, Case 2: S sits at the extreme left end of the row.)

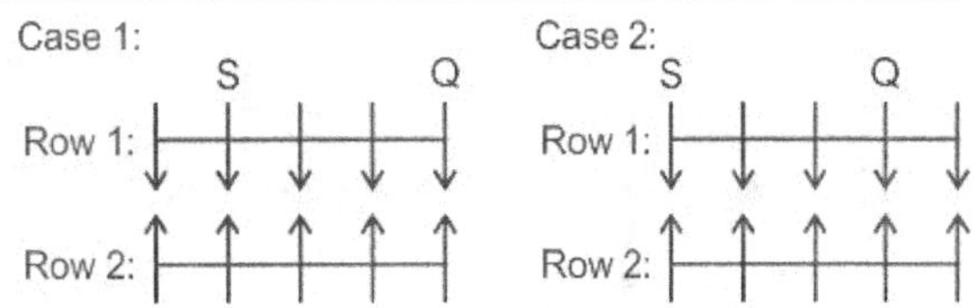

(2) The one who faces Q sits second to the right of E.

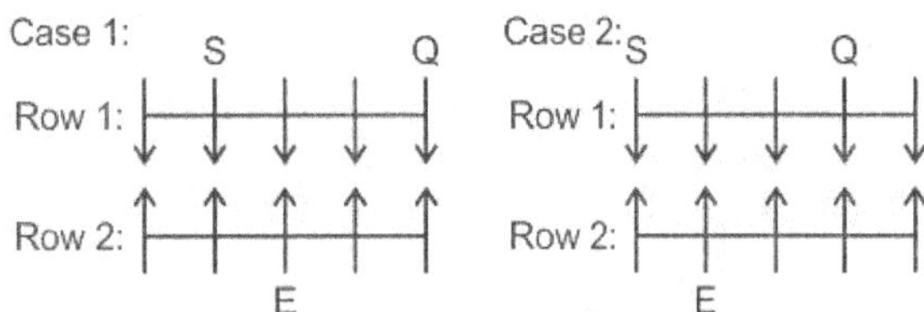

(3) Two persons are sitting between B and E.

(Here we can eliminate Case 1)

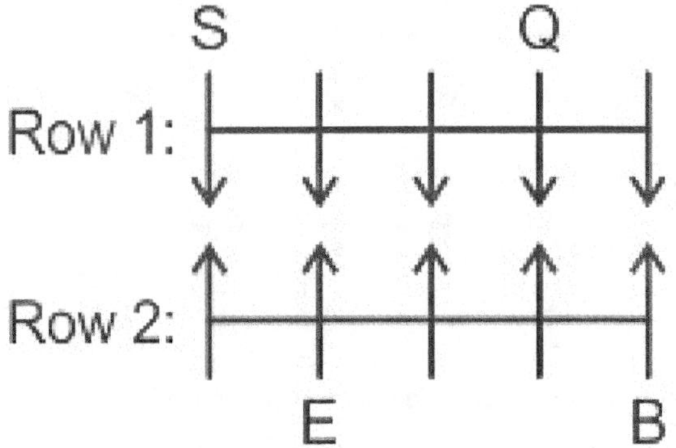

(4) Neither A nor C sits at an extreme end of the row.

(So D sits at the extreme end of row 2)

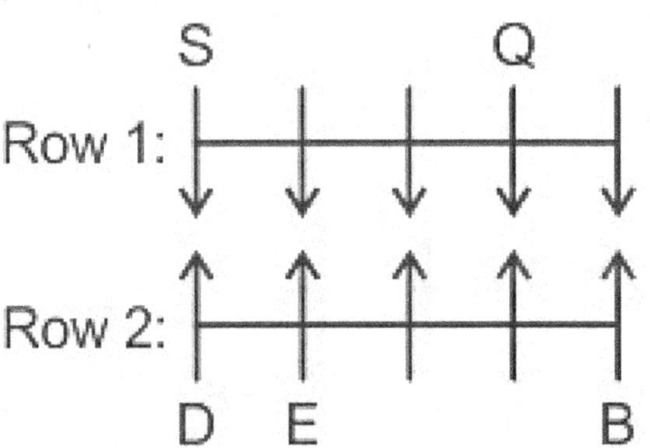

(5) The immediate neighbour of A faces the person who sits immediately to the right of Q.

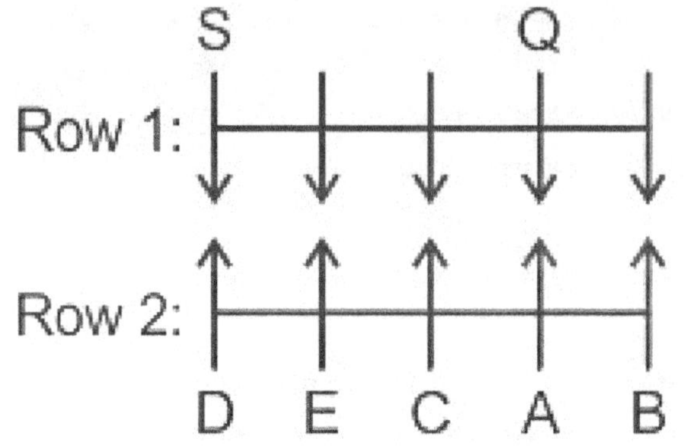

(6) R and T are immediate neighbours of each other.

(7) T does not face the immediate neighbour of D.

The final arrangement will be as follows.

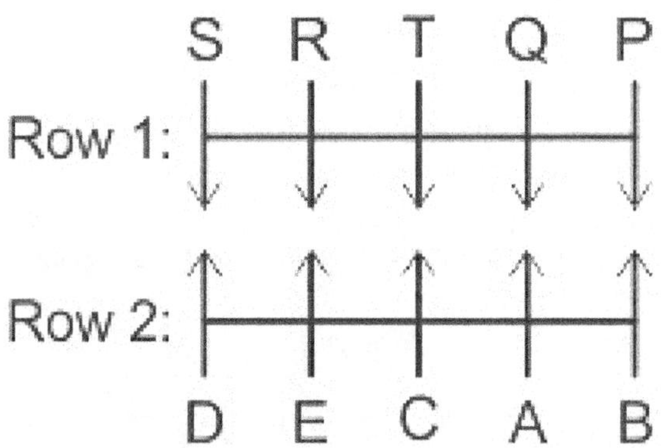

S, P, D, and B are sitting at the extreme ends of the row. C sits in the middle of the row.

Thus, C does not belong to the group.

Hence, the correct option is (E).

50. Facing South: P, Q, R, S, and T (Row 1)

Facing North: A, B, C, D, and E (Row 2)

(1) S sits third to the right of Q where either of them is sitting on any of the extreme ends of the row.

(Here, there are two possible cases, Case 1: Q sits at the extreme right end of the row, Case 2: S sits at the extreme left end of the row.)

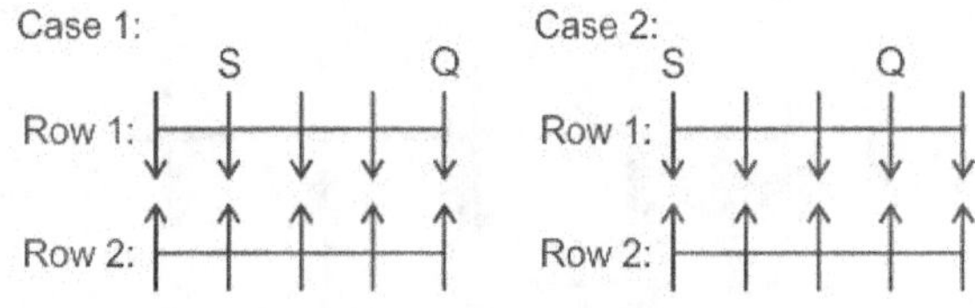

(2) The one who faces Q sits second to the right of E.

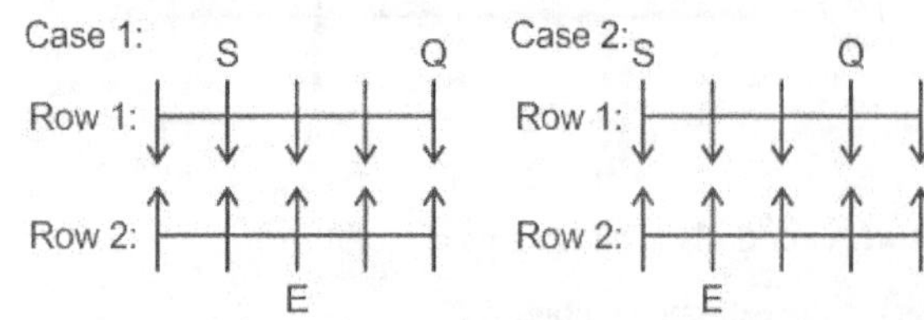

(3) Two persons are sitting between B and E.

(Here we can eliminate Case 1)

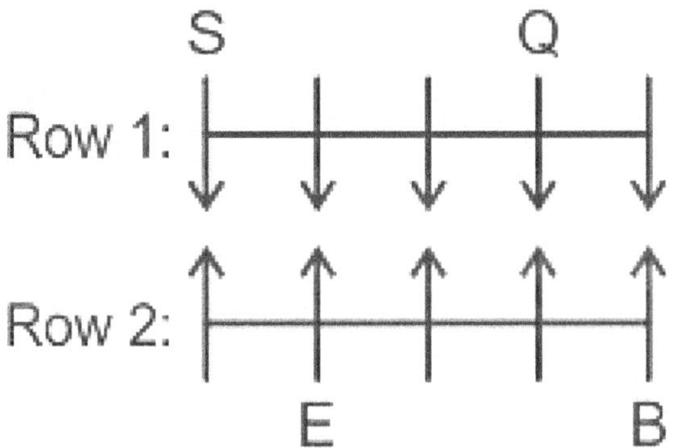

(4) Neither A nor C sits at an extreme end of the row.

(So D sits at the extreme end of row 2)

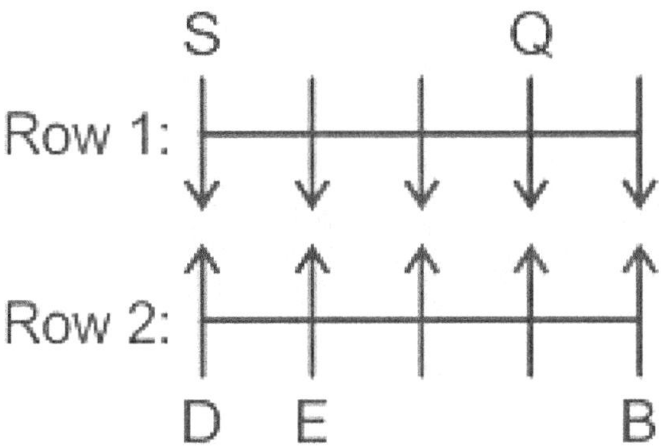

(5) The immediate neighbour of A faces the person who sits immediately to the right of Q.

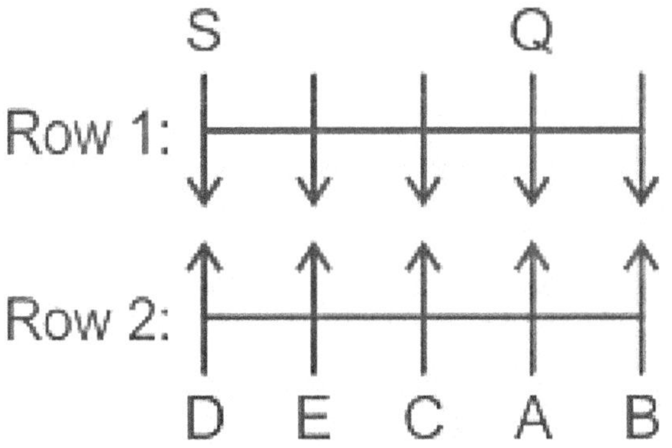

(6) R and T are immediate neighbours of each other.

(7) T does not face the immediate neighbour of D.

The final arrangement will be as follows.

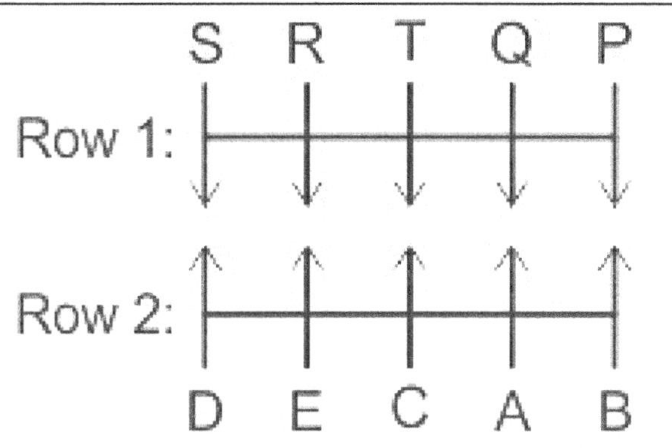

Thus, R faces one of the immediate neighbours of the D is a true statement.

Hence, the correct option is (A).

51. Facing South: P, Q, R, S, and T (Row 1)

Facing North: A, B, C, D, and E (Row 2)

(1) S sits third to the right of Q where either of them is sitting on any of the extreme ends of the row.

(Here, there are two possible cases, Case 1: Q sits at the extreme right end of the row, Case 2: S sits at the extreme left end of the row.)

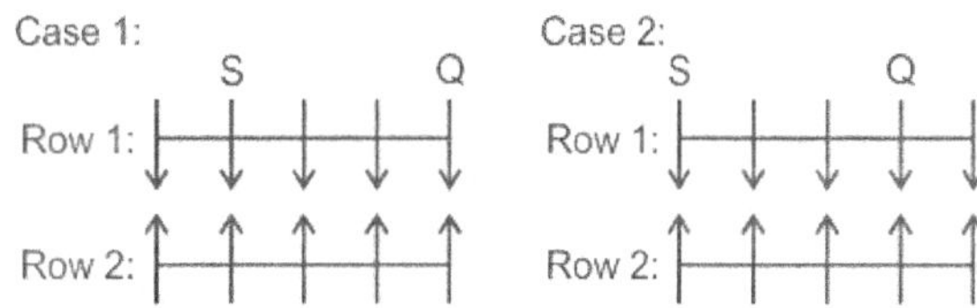

(2) The one who faces Q sits second to the right of E.

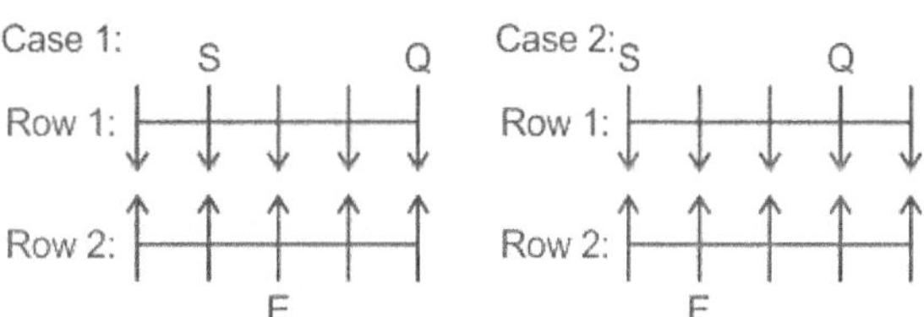

(3) Two persons are sitting between B and E.

(Here we can eliminate Case 1)

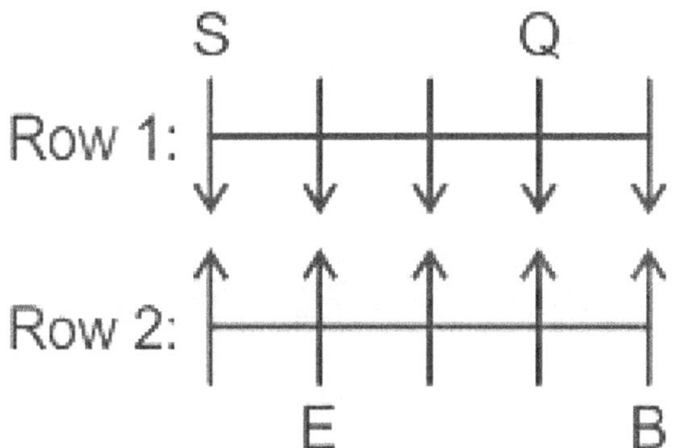

(4) Neither A nor C sits at an extreme end of the row.

(So D sits at the extreme end of row 2)

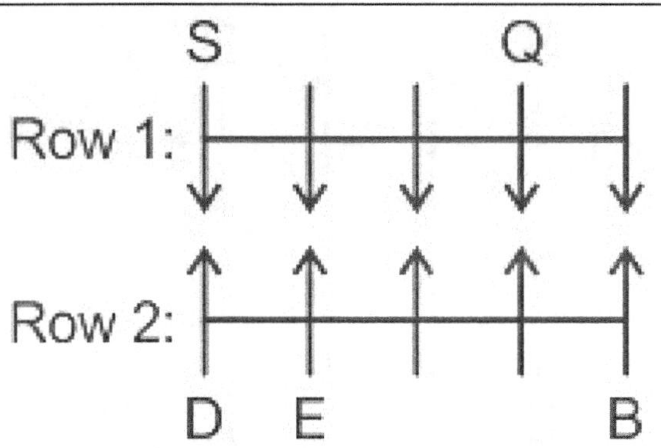

(5) The immediate neighbour of A faces the person who sits immediately to the right of Q.

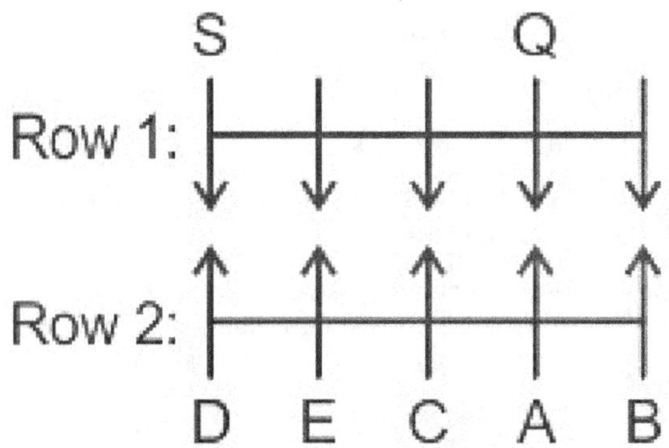

(6) R and T are immediate neighbours of each other.

(7) T does not face the immediate neighbour of D.

The final arrangement will be as follows.

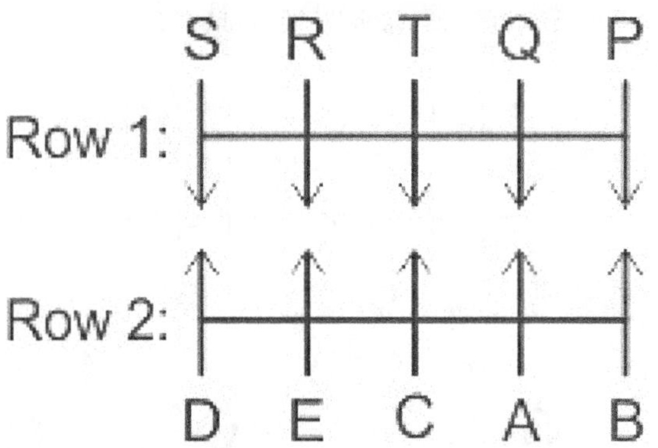

Thus, C is facing T.

Hence, the correct option is (D).

52. Facing South: P, Q, R, S, and T (Row 1)

Facing North: A, B, C, D, and E (Row 2)

(1) S sits third to the right of Q where either of them is sitting on any of the extreme ends of the row.

(Here, there are two possible cases, Case 1: Q sits at the extreme right end of the row, Case 2: S sits at the extreme left end of the row.)

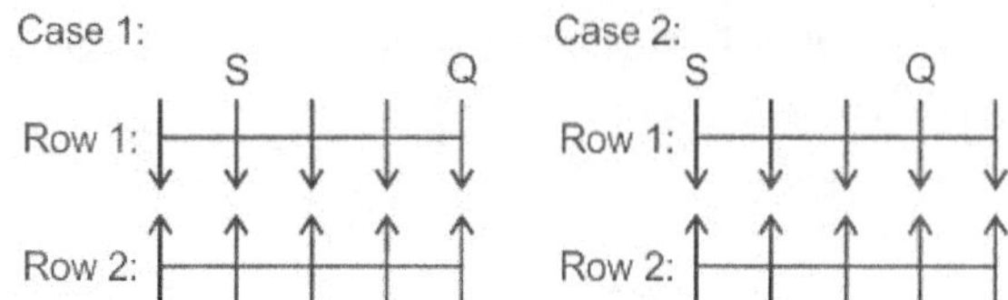

(2) The one who faces Q sits second to the right of E.

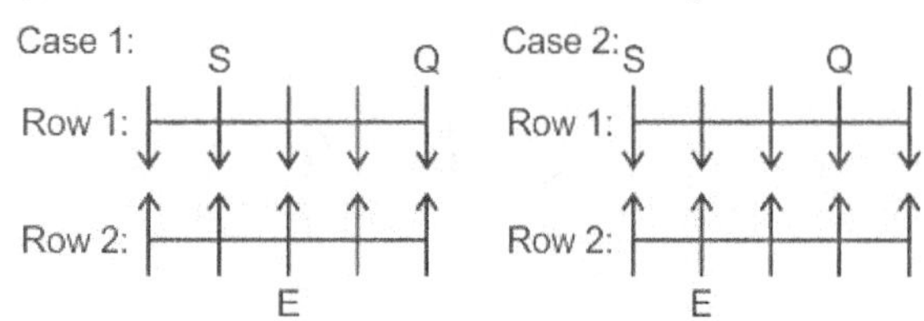

(3) Two persons are sitting between B and E.

(Here we can eliminate Case 1)

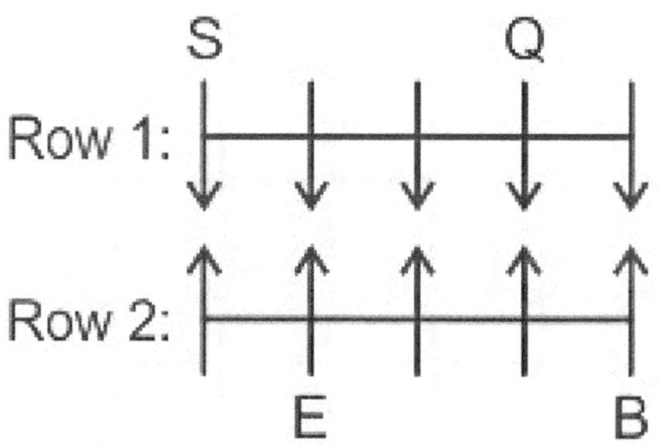

(4) Neither A nor C sits at an extreme end of the row.

(So D sits at the extreme end of row 2)

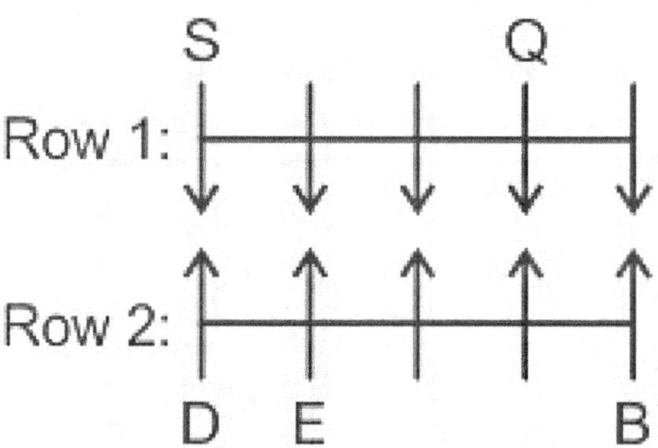

(5) The immediate neighbour of A faces the person who sits immediately to the right of Q.

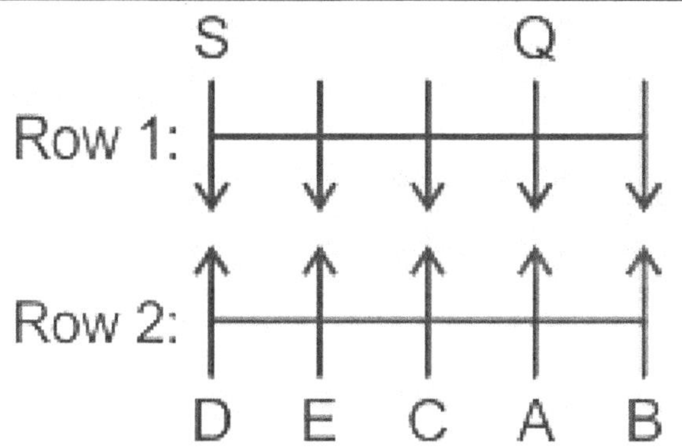

(6) R and T are immediate neighbours of each other.

(7) T does not face the immediate neighbour of D.

The final arrangement will be as follows.

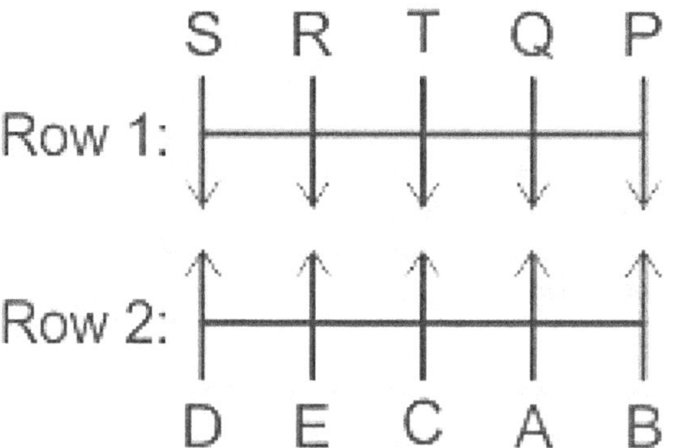

Thus, C sits immediate left of A.

Hence, the correct option is (B).

53. 1) It is given that vowels will be replaced by number "2" so all vowels in the word "CONCLUSION" is replaced by number "2" so vowels are I, O, O, U

will be replaced by number "2".

2) It is given that each consonant is replaced by a number which is the serial number of that consonant in the word so C will be replaced by 1, N by 3, L by 5, S by 7 and N by 10.

Letters	C	O	N	C	L	U	S	I	O	N
Position	1	2	3	4	5	2	7	2	2	10

Therefore, required value = 1 + 2 + 3 + 4 + 5 + 2 + 7 + 2 + 2 + 10 = 38

Hence, the correct option is (D).

54. Given word: DOCUMENTATION

First alphabet = D, Sixth alphabet = E, Seventh alphabet = N, Twelfth alphabet = O.

Letters: D, E, N, O

Thus, Possible meaningful words = DONE, NODE

So, more than 1 such word can be formed.

Hence, the correct answer is "X".

Hence, the correct option is (B).

55. Left Side A F * O T & V B A # U % E @ F H E S ? M O J Q + Y C Z $ P & I @ O T F H X U Z D Right Side

If all symbols are dropped,

A F O T V B A U E F H E S M O J Q Y C Z P I O T F H X U Z D

Now counting from the right end, we get "C" at 12th position.

Hence, "C" is the correct answer.

Hence, the correct option is (E).

56. Left Side A F * O T & V B A # U % E @ F H E S ? M O J Q + Y C Z $ P & I @ O T F H X U Z D Right Side

Dropping all the Consonants and symbols

We get, A O A U E E O I O U.

Number of vowels is 10.

Hence, the correct option is (B).

57. A F * O T & V B **A # U % E** @ F H E S ? M O J Q + Y C Z $ P & **I @ O** T F H X U Z D

So, there are three symbols which are immediately preceded and followed by a vowel.

Hence, the correct option is (C).

58. Left Side A F * O T & V B A # U % E @ F H E S ? M O J Q + Y C Z $ P & I @ O T F H X U Z D Right Side

Dropping vowels and symbols:

Left side F T V F H S M J Q Y C Z P T F H X Z D Right side

When counted from the right end, "H" is placed at 15th position from the right end.

Hence, "H" is the correct answer.

Hence, the correct option is (C).

59. A F * O T & V B A # U % E @ F H E S **? M O** J Q + Y C Z $ P & I @ O T F H X U Z D

Hence, "M" is the only consonant which is immediately preceded by a symbol and followed by a vowel.

i.e. "? M O"

Hence, the correct option is (D).

60. The logic is:

Alphabets	A	B	C	D	E	F	G	H	I	J	K	L	M
Positional value	1	2	3	4	5	6	7	8	9	10	11	12	13
Positional value	26	25	24	23	22	21	20	19	18	17	16	15	14
Alphabets	Z	Y	X	W	V	U	T	S	R	Q	P	O	N

Consonants place value is doubled and that of vowels is kept the same.

13	1	14	4	1	20	5
M	A	N	D	A	T	E
×2	×1	×2	×2	×1	×2	×1
26	1	28	8	1	40	5

Similarly,

20	5	3	8	14	9	17	21	5
T	E	C	H	N	I	Q	U	E
×2	×1	×2	×2	×2	×1	×2	×1	×1
40	5	6	16	28	9	34	21	5

Hence, the correct option is (D).

61.

Alpha bets	A	B	C	D	E	F	G	H	I	J	K	L	M
Positional value	1	2	3	4	5	6	7	8	9	10	11	12	13
Positional value	26	25	24	23	22	21	20	19	18	17	16	15	14
Alpha bets	Z	Y	X	W	V	U	T	S	R	Q	P	O	N

Opposite letters are used in code language as:

S	K	I	L	L	S
Opposite	Opposite	Opposite	Opposite	Opposite	Opposite
H	P	R	O	O	H

Similarly,

P	L	A	C	E	S
Opposite	Opposite	Opposite	Opposite	Opposite	Opposite
K	O	Z	X	V	H

Thus, KOZXVH is the correct answer.

Hence, the correct option is (A).

62. In a certain code language,

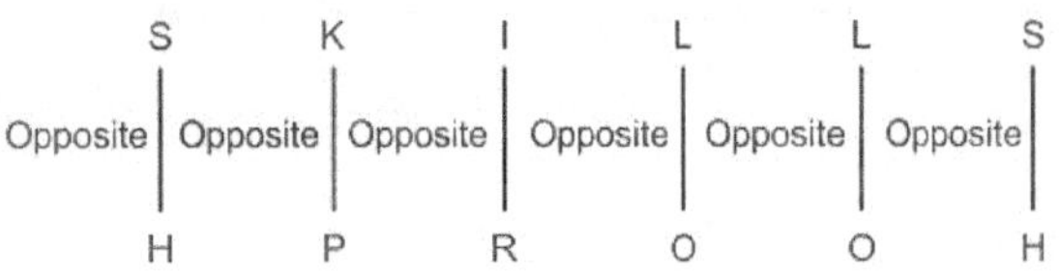

M	O	O	N
5	2	2	9

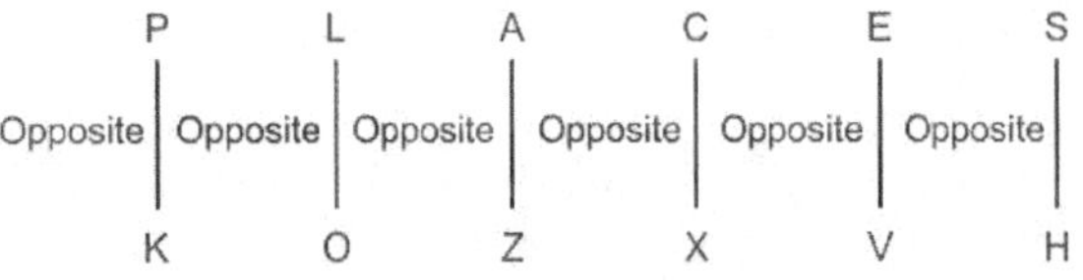

F	I	L	M
6	3	1	5

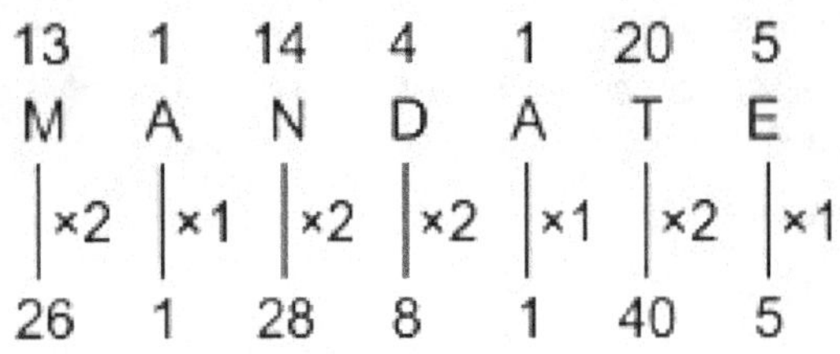

A	R	E
4	8	7

From above, the code for 'INFORMER' would be:

I	N	F	O	R	M	E	R
3	9	6	2	8	5	7	8

Hence, INFORMER is coded as '39628578'.

Hence, the correct option is (A)

Ques (63-65): Best possible figure according to the given information:

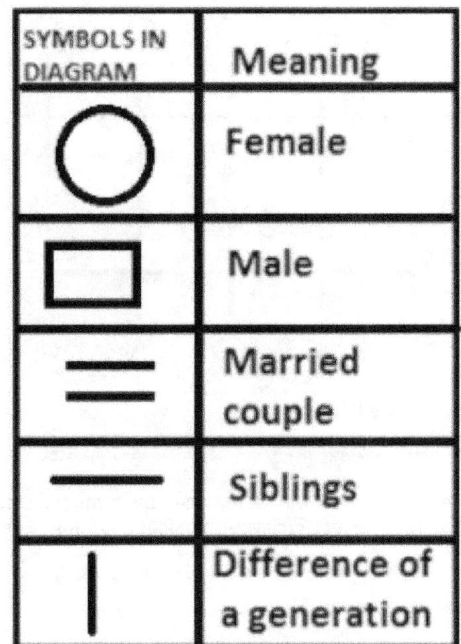

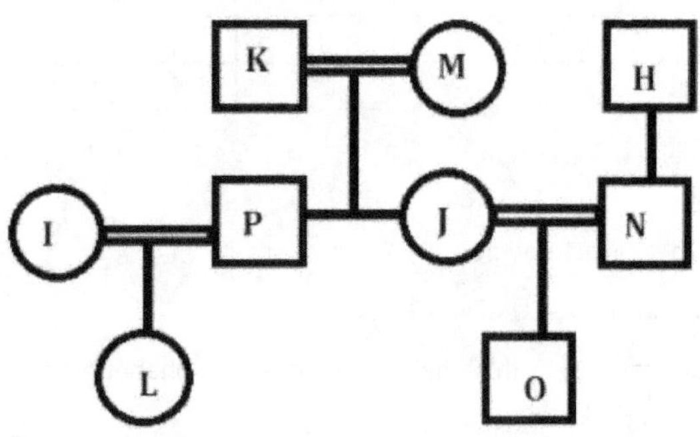

63. Clearly, M is the mother of P.

Hence, the correct option is (B).

64. Clearly, K is the Maternal-grandfather of O.

Hence, the correct option is (D).

65. Clearly, L is the daughter of P.

Hence, the correct option is (D).

66. Given:

Initial Rate $= 8\%$

Time $= 3$ years

Rate in mutual fund $= 8.5\%$ and time $= 4$ years

Simple interest $= \dfrac{P \times R \times T}{100}$

Let the sum be Rs. x

S.I from the bank $= \dfrac{x \times 8 \times 3}{100}$

$\Rightarrow \dfrac{24x}{100}$

Earnings in the form of interest from mutual fund $= \dfrac{(x \times 8.5 \times 4)}{100}$

$\Rightarrow \dfrac{34x}{100}$

According to question:

$\dfrac{34x}{100} - \dfrac{24x}{100} = \text{Rs} .500$

$\Rightarrow 10x = 50000$ or $x = 5000$

$\therefore$ The sum invested $=$ Rs. 5000

Hence, the correct option is (A).

67. According to the given information,

I. $x^2 - 5x + 6 = 0$

By middle term splitting, we get,

$\Rightarrow x^2 - 3x - 2x + 6 = 0$

$\Rightarrow x(x - 3) - 2(x - 3) = 0$

$\Rightarrow (x - 3)(x - 2) = 0$

$\Rightarrow x = 3$

$\Rightarrow x = 2$

II. $y^2 + y - 6 = 0$

By middle term splitting, we get,

$\Rightarrow y^2 + 3y - 2y - 6 = 0$

$\Rightarrow y(y + 3) - 2(y + 3) = 0$

$\Rightarrow (y - 2)(y + 3) = 0$

$\Rightarrow y = 2$

$\Rightarrow y = -3$

Here, one value of x and y are equal and the other value of x is greater than y.

Hence, the correct option is (D).

68. According to the question,

I. $2x^2 - 12x + 18 = 0$

$\Rightarrow 2x^2 - 6x - 6x + 18 = 0$

$\Rightarrow 2x(x - 3) - 6(x - 3) = 0$

$\Rightarrow (x - 3)(2x - 6) = 0$

$\Rightarrow x = 3$ and 3

II. $2y^2 - 19y + 39 = 0$

$\Rightarrow 2y^2 - 13y - 6y + 39 = 0$

$\Rightarrow y(2y - 13) - 3(2y - 13) = 0$

$\Rightarrow (2y - 13)(y - 3) = 0$

$\Rightarrow y = \dfrac{13}{2}$ and 3

So, when x = + 3, x < y for y = $\dfrac{13}{2}$ and x = y for y = 3

$\therefore$ So, we can clearly observe that x $\leq$ y.

Hence, the correct option is (E).

69. According to the question,

I. $x^2 + 13x + 42 = 0$

$\Rightarrow x^2 + 6x + 7x + 42 = 0$

$\Rightarrow x(x + 6) + 7(x + 6) = 0$

$\Rightarrow (x + 6)(x + 7) = 0$

$\Rightarrow x = -6$ or -7

II. $y^2 + 19y + 90 = 0$

$\Rightarrow y^2 + 10y + 9y + 90 = 0$

$\Rightarrow y(y + 10) + 9(y + 10) = 0$

$\Rightarrow (y + 10)(y + 9) = 0$

$\Rightarrow y = -10$ or -9

So, when x = -6, x > y for y = -10 and x > y for y = -9

And when x = -7, x > y for y = -10 and x > y for y = -9

$\therefore$ We can observe that x > y.

Hence, the correct option is (C).

70. According to the question,

I. $3x^2 - 23x - 8 = 0$

$\Rightarrow 3x^2 - 24x + x - 8 = 0$

$\Rightarrow 3x(x - 8) + 1(x - 8) = 0$

$\Rightarrow (x - 8)(3x + 1) = 0$

$\Rightarrow x = + 8$ or $-\dfrac{1}{3}$

II. $3y^2 - 32y - 11 = 0$

$\Rightarrow 3y^2 - 33y + y - 11 = 0$

$\Rightarrow 3y(y - 11) + 1(y - 11) = 0$

$\Rightarrow (y - 11)(3y + 1) = 0$

$\Rightarrow y = 11$ or $-\dfrac{1}{3}$

So, when x = 8, x < y for y = 11 and x > y for y = $-\dfrac{1}{3}$

and when x = $\dfrac{1}{3}$, x < y for y = 11 and x = y for y = $-\dfrac{1}{3}$

∴ So, we can observe that no clear relationship cannot be determined between x and y.

Hence, the correct option is (E).

71. According to the question,

I. $3x^2 - 14x - 5 = 0$

$\Rightarrow 3x^2 - 15x + x - 5 = 0$

$\Rightarrow 3x(x - 5) + 1(x - 5) = 0$

$\Rightarrow (x - 5)(3x + 1) = 0$

$\Rightarrow x = + 5$ or $-\dfrac{1}{3}$

II. $6y^2 - 46y - 16 = 0$

$\Rightarrow 6y^2 - 48y + 2y - 16 = 0$

$\Rightarrow 6y(y - 8) + 2(y - 8) = 0$

$\Rightarrow (y - 8)(6y + 2) = 0$

$\Rightarrow y = + 8$ or $-\dfrac{1}{3}$

So, when x = 5, x < y for y = 8 and x > y for y = $-\dfrac{1}{3}$

and when x = $-\dfrac{1}{3}$, x < y for y = 8 and x = y for y = $-\dfrac{1}{3}$

∴ So, we can observe that no clear relationship cannot be determined between x and y.

Hence, the correct option is (C).

72. Let the original price of the painting be Rs. 'x'

Selling price of 1st seller = (100 + 10)% of x

$\Rightarrow$ 110% of x

$\Rightarrow$ 1.1x

Selling price of 2nd seller = (100 + 10)% of 1.1x

$\Rightarrow$ 110% of 1.1x

$\Rightarrow$ 1.1 × 1.1x

$\Rightarrow$ 1.21x

Selling price of 3rd seller = (100 + 10)% of 1.21x

$\Rightarrow$ 110% of 1.21x

$\Rightarrow$ 1.1 × 1.21x

$\Rightarrow$ 1.331x

∴ The price of the book increased by = 1.331x - x = 0.331x = 33.1% of x

Hence, the correct option is (E).

73. Efficiency of machine D = 70% and Total capacity of D = 120 units

$\Rightarrow$ Efficiency of machine D = 70% of 120 = 84 units

Output of machine D $= 84 \times \left(\dfrac{85}{2}\right)$ = 3570 units

Efficiency of machine B = 40% and Total capacity of B = 160 units

$\Rightarrow$ Efficiency of machine B = 40% of 160 = 64 units

Output of machine B $= 64 \times \left(\dfrac{65}{2}\right)$ = 2080 units

$\Rightarrow$ Difference = (3570 – 2080) = 1490 units

∴ The required difference is 1490 units.

Hence, the correct option is (E).

74. Given:

Total capacity of machine C = 180 units

Efficiency of machine C = 60%

Efficiency of machine C = 60% of 180 units

$\Rightarrow$ 108 units

Output of machine C $= 108 \times \left(\dfrac{109}{2}\right)$

$\Rightarrow$ 5886 units

∴ The final output of C is 5886 units.

Hence, the correct option is (D).

75. Given:

If efficiency is n, then final output will be $n \times \dfrac{(n+1)}{2}$

Machine	Total Capacity	Efficiency%	Efficiency	Machine Output
A	150	50%	75	$\left[\dfrac{(75\times76)}{2}\right]$ = 2850
B	160	40%	64	$\left[\dfrac{(65\times64)}{2}\right]$ = 2080

Difference in machine outputs = (2850 – 2080) units = 770 units

$\Rightarrow$ Percentage of difference $= \left(\dfrac{770}{2080}\right) \times 100 \approx 37\%$

∴ Output of A is 37% more than the output of B.

Hence, the correct option is (E).

76. Given:

Total capacity of machine D = 120 units

Efficiency of machine D = 70%

Total capacity of machine E = 140 units

Efficiency of machine E = 60%

⇒ Efficiency of machine D = 70% of 120 units = 84 units

⇒ Output of machine D $= 84 \times \left(\dfrac{85}{2}\right)$ = 3570 units

⇒ Efficiency of machine E = 60% of 140 units = 84 units

⇒ Output of machine E $= 84 \times \left(\dfrac{85}{2}\right)$ = 3570 units

⇒ Required percentage $= \left(\dfrac{3570}{3570}\right) \times 100\%$

⇒ 100%

∴ The output of machine D is 100% of the output of Machine E.

Hence, the correct option is (A).

77. Output of machine D = 70% and Total capacity of D = 70% of 120 = 84 units

Output of machine E = 60% and Total capacity of E = 60% of 140 = 84 units

∴ Required ratio = 1: 1

Hence, the correct option is (B).

78. For Smrita,

Time taking to stitch 10 shirt by Smrita = 25 min,

⇒ Time taken to stitch 1 shirt by Smrita = $\dfrac{25}{10}$ = 2.5 min

For Dipti,

Smrita is 3 times efficient as Dipti,

1 shirt stitch by Dipti = 3 shirt stitch by Smrita

Time taken by Dipti to stitch one shirt,

⇒ Time for Dipti = 3 × time taken by Smrita for each shirt = 3 × 2.5 = 7.5 min

By working together,

number of shirt stitch by them in one minute = $\dfrac{1}{2.5} + \dfrac{1}{7.5}$

$= \dfrac{(7.5 + 2.5)}{(7.5 \times 2.5)} = \dfrac{10}{18.75}$

Time taken to stitch 1 shirt = 1.875

For 500 shirt,

∴ Time taken for 500 shirt = 500 × 1.875 = 937.5 min

Hence, the correct option is (B).

79. We cannot determine the answer because we don't know the price per kg of the other flour.

So, we cannot find the ratio of mixing which would be required to further solve the question.

Hence, the correct option is (E).

80. Let the present age of David be D and that of Sam be S.

According to the question,

(S - 5) = 2 (D - 5)

⇒ S - 2D = -5 ...(1)

Similarly,

2(S + 5) = 3(D + 5)

⇒ 2S - 3D = 5 ...(2)

So, solving equations (1) and (2), we get:

S = 25, D = 15

So the sum of present ages of Sam and David = 25 + 15 = 40

Hence, the correct option is (C).

81. Given,

Time taken by first two pipes = Time taken by third pipe alone

Let the first pipe alone takes x hours to fill the tank.

Then, time taken by second pipe = $(x - 5)$ hours

Time taken by third pipe = $(x - 9)$ hours

According to question,

Time taken by first two pipes = Time taken by third pipe alone

$\dfrac{1}{x} + \dfrac{1}{x-5} = \dfrac{1}{x-9}$

$\Rightarrow \dfrac{x-5+x}{x(x-5)} = \dfrac{1}{x-9}$

$\Rightarrow (2x - 5)(x - 9) = x(x - 5)$

$\Rightarrow x^2 - 18x + 45 = 0$

$\Rightarrow (x - 15)(x - 3) = 0$

We will not take x as 3 because this will give the negative value of an hour which is not possible.

Therefore,

$x - 15 = 0$

$\Rightarrow x = 15$

∴ The time required by the first pipe is 15 hours.

Hence, the correct option is (C).

82. Given:

Train's length $= 100 \; m$

Man's speed $= 5 \; km/h$

Time to cross $= 9$ seconds

We know,

Speed $= \dfrac{Distance}{Time}$

Let the speed of the train be $x km/h$

$\therefore$ Relative speed $= (x + 5)km/h$

$D = \dfrac{1}{10}\ km$, where, D= Distance

$T = \dfrac{9}{3600}\ hr$, where, T= Time

$\Rightarrow (x + 5) = \dfrac{\frac{1}{10}}{\frac{9}{3600}}$

$\Rightarrow x + 5 = 40$

$\Rightarrow x = 35\ km/h$

$\therefore$ Speed of the train is $35\ km/h$.

Quantity B is in m/s and quantity A is in km/h.

$\therefore 35 \times \dfrac{18}{5} = 126\ km/h$

$\therefore$ Quantity $A < $ Quantity B

Hence, the correct option is (B).

83. Given:

Profit $= 25\%$

Discount $= 20\%$

Profit $= Rs1800$

Quantity A:

Let the M.P. is Rs 100

$\therefore$ S.P. $= 80\%$ of $100 = Rs80$

Now, S.P. is 125% of C.P.,

$\therefore C.P. = \dfrac{80}{125} \times 100 = Rs64$

We know,

Profit = S.P. - C.P.

$\Rightarrow$ Profit $= 80 - 64 = Rs16$

So, Profit is Rs 16 for M.P Rs 100

For profit to be Rs 1800 ,

M.P. $= \dfrac{100}{16} \times 1800 = 25 \times 450$

$\Rightarrow$ M.P.= Rs 11250

$\therefore$ The M.P is Rs 11250

Now, **Quantity** $B = $ Rs. 10,000

$\therefore$ Quantity $A > $ Quantity B

Hence, the correct option is (A).

84. Given:

Initial ratio $(A:B) = 3:5$

Amount of liquid drawn $= 12$ litres

Final ratio $(A:B) = 1:3$

Let the initial quantity of A and B be $3x$ and $5x$.

Quantity of A left $= 3x - \left(\dfrac{3}{8}\right) \times 12 = \left(3x - \dfrac{9}{2}\right)$ litres

Quantity of B left $= 5x - \left(\dfrac{5}{8}\right) \times 12 = \left(5x - \dfrac{15}{2}\right)$ litres

According to question,

$\dfrac{3x - \frac{9}{2}}{5x - \frac{15}{2}} + 12 = \dfrac{1}{3}$

$\Rightarrow \dfrac{3x - \frac{9}{2}}{5x + \frac{9}{2}} = \dfrac{1}{3}$

$\Rightarrow 9x - \dfrac{27}{2} = 5x + \dfrac{9}{2}$

$\Rightarrow 4x = \dfrac{36}{2}$

$\Rightarrow 4x = 18$

$\Rightarrow x = 4.5$

A's initial quantity $= 3x = (3 \times 4.5)$ liters

$\Rightarrow$ A's Initial quantity $= 13.5$ litres

$\therefore$ Quantity $A > $ Quantity B

Hence, the correct option is (A).

85. According to the question,

The total number of students = 60

Number of girls = 60 $\times$ $\dfrac{30}{100}$ = 18

Number of girls that did not give the test = 18 $\times$ $\dfrac{50}{100}$ = 9

Initial class average = 17

Total marks = 17 $\times$ 60 = 1020

Marks awarded to 9 girls = 9 $\times$ 20 = 180

New total = 1020 + 180 = 1200

$\therefore$ Class average = $\dfrac{1200}{60}$ = 20

Hence, the correct option is (C).

86. The pattern is as follows:

4 $\times$ 2 = 8

8 + 2 = 10

10 $\times$ 3 = 30

30 + 3 = 33

33 $\times$ 4 = 132

132 + 4 = 136

136 × 5 = 680

680 + 5 = 685

∴ The value of ? is 685.

Hence, the correct option is (C)

87. Given series:

40, 82, 249, 1250, ?

The pattern is:

40 × 2 + 2 = 82

82 × 3 + 3 = 249

249 × 5 + 5 = 1250

1250 × 7 + 7 = 8757

So, the missing number is 8757.

Hence, the correct option is (C).

88. The pattern is as follows:

7 × 1 + 1 = 8

8 × 2 − 2 = 14

14 × 3 + 3 = 45

45 × 4 − 4 = 176

176 × 5 + 5 = 885

∴ The value of ? is 885.

Hence, the correct option is (A).

89. Given series:

$33, 47, 53, 61, 71, ?$

The pattern is:

$33 + 2^2 + 10 = 47$

$33 + 3^2 + 11 = 53$

$33 + 4^2 + 12 = 61$

$33 + 5^2 + 13 = 71$

$33 + 6^2 + 14 = 83$

So, the missing number is 83 .

Hence, the correct option is (C).

90. The pattern is as follows:

60.5   72   84.5   98   112.5   128

+11.5   +12.5   +13.5   +14.5   +15.5

∴ The value of ? is 128.

Hence, the correct option is (D).

91. Using the BODMAS rule:

$$\sqrt{225} + (1500 \text{ of } 55\%) - \{(45)^2 \div 81 \times 4\} + 20 - 16 = ?$$

$$= 15 + 825 - 25 \times 4 + 20 - 16$$

$$= 15 + 825 - 100 + 20 - 16$$

$$= 840 - 100 + 20 - 16$$

$$= 740 + 4$$

$$= 744$$

Hence, the correct option is (A).

92. Using the BODMAS rule:

$$(8375 \div 67)^{\frac{1}{3}} + (7.84 \times 25)^{\frac{1}{2}} = (?)^{\frac{1}{2}}$$

$$\Rightarrow (125)^{\frac{1}{3}} + (7.84 \times 25)^{\frac{1}{2}} = (?)^{\frac{1}{2}}$$

$$\Rightarrow (125)^{\frac{1}{3}} + (196)^{\frac{1}{2}} = (?)^{\frac{1}{2}}$$

$$\Rightarrow 5 + 14 = (?)^{\frac{1}{2}}$$

$$\Rightarrow (?)^{\frac{1}{2}} = 19$$

Squaring both sides,

$$? = 19^2$$

$$= 361$$

∴ 361 will come in place of '?'

Hence, the correct option is (B).

93. According to BODMAS:

$$57\frac{1}{7}\% \text{ of } 490 + 22.22\% \text{ of } 729 - \sqrt{2500} \times \sqrt{25} \div 5^2 = ?$$

$$\Rightarrow \left(\frac{4}{7}\right) \times 490 + \left(\frac{2}{9}\right) \times 729 - 50 \times 5 \div 25 = ?$$

$$\Rightarrow 4 \times 70 + 2 \times 81 - 10 = ?$$

$$\Rightarrow 280 + 162 - 10 = ?$$

$$\Rightarrow 442 - 10 = ?$$

$$\Rightarrow ? = 432$$

∴ The value of '?' Is 432 .

Hence, the correct option is (C).

94. According to BODMAS:

$$\sqrt{[(6.25)^2 \times 100]} + \frac{7}{2} = ? \times 11$$

$$\sqrt{[(6.25)^2 \times 100]} + 3.5 = ? \times 11$$

$\Rightarrow \sqrt{(6.25 \times 6.25 \times 100)} + 3.5 = ? \times 119$

$\Rightarrow \sqrt{(6.25 \times 6.25 \times 10 \times 10)} + 3.5 = ? \times 11$

$\Rightarrow 62.5 + 3.5 = ? \times 11$

$\Rightarrow 66 = ? \times 11$

$\Rightarrow 6 = ?$

$\therefore$ The required value is 6.

Hence, the correct option is (A).

95. Given,

$\sqrt{1024} \times 40 + 20^2 + 0.5\%$ of $9600 + 469 = ?^3$

$\Rightarrow 32 \times 40 + 400 + 9600 \times \dfrac{0.5}{100} + 469 = ?^3$

$\Rightarrow 32 \times 40 + 400 + 48 + 469 = ?^3$

$\Rightarrow 1280 + 400 + 48 + 469 = ?^3$

$\Rightarrow 1280 + 448 + 469 = ?^3$

$\Rightarrow 2197 = ?^3$

$\Rightarrow ? = \sqrt[3]{2197}$

$\Rightarrow ? = 13$

Hence, the correct option is (B).

96. Given,

$\left(\sqrt{8} \times \sqrt{8}\right)^{\frac{1}{2}} + 9^{\frac{1}{2}} = ?^3 + \sqrt{8} - 340$

$\Rightarrow \left(\left(\sqrt{8}\right)^2\right)^{\frac{1}{2}} + 9^{\frac{1}{2}} = ?^3 + \sqrt{8} - 340$

$\Rightarrow (8)^{\frac{1}{2}} + 9^{\frac{1}{2}} = ?^3 + \sqrt{8} - 340$

$\Rightarrow (4 \times 2)^{\frac{1}{2}} + 9^{\frac{1}{2}} = ?^3 + \sqrt{(4 \times 2)} - 340$

$\Rightarrow 2\sqrt{2} + 3 = ?^3 + 2\sqrt{2} - 340$

$\Rightarrow 3 = ?^3 + (-340)$

$\Rightarrow ?^3 = 340 + 3$

$\Rightarrow ?^3 = 343$

$\Rightarrow ? = \sqrt[3]{343}$

$\Rightarrow ? = 7$

Hence, the correct option is (A).

97. Given:

6.67% of $225 + 6.25\%$ of $1120 = (?)^3 + 3$

$\Rightarrow \dfrac{1}{15} \times 225 + \dfrac{1}{16}$ of $1120 = (?)^3 + 3$

$\Rightarrow 15 + 70 = (?)^3 + 3$

$\Rightarrow 85 = (?)^3 + 3$

$\Rightarrow (?)^3 = 82$

$\Rightarrow ? = (82)^{\frac{1}{3}}$

Hence, the correct option is (E).

98. Given

$(0.1 \times 0.004) + (0.02 \times 0.3) - (0.04 \times 0.03) = ?$

$\Rightarrow 0.0004 + 0.006 - 0.0012 = ?$

$\Rightarrow 0.0064 - 0.0012 = ?$

$\therefore ? = 0.0052$

Hence, the correct option is (D).

99. We know that $25\% = \dfrac{1}{4}$ and $14\dfrac{2}{7}\% = \dfrac{1}{7}$

$\Rightarrow \dfrac{1}{4} \times 7428 + 143 = \dfrac{1}{7} \times ?$

$\Rightarrow ? = 7 \times 2000$

$\Rightarrow ? = 14000$

Hence, the correct option is (D).

100. Given,

16% of $25 \times 88 + 20\%$ of $135 - 16 \times (18 - 5\%$ of $200) = ?$

$\Rightarrow \left(\dfrac{16}{100}\right) \times 25 \times 88 + \left(\dfrac{20}{100}\right) \times 135 - 16 \times (18 - 10) = ?$

$\Rightarrow 4 \times 88 + 27 - 16 \times 8 = ?$

$\Rightarrow 352 + 27 - 128 = ?$

$\Rightarrow 379 - 128 = ?$

$\Rightarrow 251 = ?$

$\therefore$ The value of ? is 251

Hence, the correct option is (D).

English Language

Q.1 Which of the following is MOST OPPOSITE in meaning to the word 'Covert'?

A. Cunning   **B.** Violent
C. Sly   **D.** Overt
E. Cloistered

Q.2 Which of the following is MOST OPPOSITE in meaning to the word 'PRUDENT'?

A. Hasty   **B.** Cautious   **C.** Reckless   **D.** Rude
E. Pastoral

Ques (3-7):Direction: A passage is given below with five blanks labelled (A)-(E). Below the passage, five options are given for each blank. Choose the word that fits each blank most appropriately in the context of the passage, and mark the corresponding answer.

Almost one-third of the world's population consists of children. Therefore they need to be cared for and __(A)__. Children are an important component of the social __(B)__. Finding a single definition to describe a 'child' is becoming an __(C)__ task. The dictionary defines the word 'child' as a young person, especially __(D)__ infancy and youth.

Biologically, a child is anyone between the stages of infancy and adulthood, or a child is a human being between the stages of birth and puberty. The legal definition of 'child' refers to a minor, or somebody who is yet to become an adult. The only __(E)__ is that the child should be unable to maintain himself. Hence a child, though not a minor, is still a child as long as it is unable to maintain himself.

Q.3 Which of the following words most appropriately fits the blank labelled (A)?

A. Emotional   **B.** Protected
C. Democratic   **D.** Abused
E. None of these

Q.4 Which of the following words most appropriately fits the blank labelled (B)?

A. Structure   **B.** Fullness
C. Statutory   **D.** Contrast
E. None of these

Q.5 Which of the following words most appropriately fits the blank labelled (C)?

A. Qualified   **B.** Pleasant
C. Uphill   **D.** Untoward
E. None of these

Q.6 Which of the following words most appropriately fits the blank labelled (D)?

A. Between   **B.** Among
C. Amidst   **D.** Along

E. None of these

Q.7 Which of the following words most appropriately fits the blank labelled (E)?

A. Surprise   **B.** Policies
C. qualification   **D.** adopt
E. None of these

Ques (8-12):Direction: Read the sentence to find outwhether there is any error in it. The error,if any, will be in one part of the sentence.The number corresponding to that part isyour answer. If the given sentence iscorrect as given, mark the answer as "Noerror". Ignore the errors of punctuation,if any.

Q.8 The defence minister thought (1)/that each veteran (2)/ was as respectfulas himself and (3)/ should be given duepreference as well. (4)

[RBI Assistant, 2017]

A. 1   **B.** 2   **C.** 3   **D.** 4
E. No error

Q.9 Unfortunately, India continues to beone of the backward countries (1)/ withrespect to literacy, despite of the fact (2)/that successive governments have beentrying (3)/ their best to promoteeducation. (4)

[RBI Assistant, 2017]

A. 1   **B.** 2   **C.** 3   **D.** 4
E. No error

Q.10 The first lady took it upon (1)/ herselfto make sure that the (2)/ governmentrun smoothly while the (3)/ President wasrecuperating from the surgery. (4)

[RBI Assistant, 2017]

A. 1   **B.** 2   **C.** 3   **D.** 4
E. No error

Q.11 Cases of malignant melanoma arerising (1)/ faster among men thanwomen, but men are (2)/ often worsethan their female counterpart at (3)/protecting themselves from the Sun. (4)

[RBI Assistant, 2017]

A. 1   **B.** 2   **C.** 3   **D.** 4
E. 5

Q.12 Appropriation of assets have become(1)/ increasingly important due to (2)/the willingness of those in power (3)/ toabuse authority for personal gains. (4)

[RBI Assistant, 2017]

A. 1   **B.** 2   **C.** 3   **D.** 4
E. No error

Q.13 Choose the correctly spelt word.

A. Monotheeism   **B.** Misogynist
C. Morotorium   **D.** Momentery
E. None of these

Q.14 Select the wrongly spelt word

A. Cautiously
B. Consequantly
C. Completely
D. Concurrently
E. None of the above

Q.15 Select the Incorrectly spelt word.

A. Delicious
B. Journy
C. Furious
D. Failure
E. Ruthless

Ques (16-20):Directions: Read the passage given below and answer the questions that follow by choosing the correct/most appropriate options:

Nearly a decade and a half since its inception, the Indian Premier League (IPL) has struck deep roots and acquired nimble feet. General elections in 2009, 2014, and 2019, and the pandemic lasting over two years, have never stymied the league. Irrespective of the external challenges, the tournament's organizers have always conducted the IPL. Even as India remains the base, at varying points South Africa and the United Arab Emirates have chipped in as hosts. Cut to the present, the 15th edition will commence at Mumbai's Wankhede Stadium on Saturday with defending champion, Chennai Super Kings, (CSK) taking on last year's runner-up, Kolkata Knight Riders. And over two months, the IPL will monopolize prime-time television while its caravan will shuttle between Mumbai and Pune due to COVID-19 bio-bubble protocols. Mumbai's Wankhede, Brabourne, DY Patil Stadiums, and Pune's MCA Stadium will conduct the games while the venue for the play-offs, including the final on May 29, will be announced later. Ever since that summer night at Bengaluru's M. Chinnaswamy Stadium in 2008, when the IPL made its debut, its commercial value has found incremental gains. The latest outing has Tata as the title sponsor while multiple brands will jostle for space through the tournament and its 10 teams. Meanwhile, the two new squads — Gujarat Titans and Lucknow Super Giants — will enhance the novelty factor.

The IPL's current version will have a transition as an underlying theme. Most units have had a change of personnel and in some cases, there are new captains too. CSK, until now led by the talismanic M.S. Dhoni, will have a fresh skipper in Ravindra Jadeja. At 40, Dhoni will continue as a player but with him having relinquished the reins of captaincy, an era has ended in the league's history. Having led CSK to four titles, the legend from Ranchi remains the IPL's biggest player. While CSK will look at replicating its triumphs, Mumbai Indians, the most successful franchise with five trophies, will hope to excel in its backyard. Led by Rohit Sharma, who is now India's all-format skipper, the outfit has Kieron Pollard in its ranks, reflective of the championship's international flavor. However, the event isn't just about youngsters grabbing attention, it is also about seniors reiterating their credentials. Virat Kohli is now seeking a fresh wind as a mere player. And this IPL will also help leading players such as Kane Williamson to finesse their craft ahead of the ICC T20 World Cup in Australia, later this year.

Q.16 According to the passage, who is the title sponsor for the IPL 2022?

A. VIVO
B. BYJU'S
C. HERO
D. TATA
E. None of these

Q.17 Choose the antonym of the word '**Inception**'.

A. Commencement
B. Cessation
C. Genesis
D. Outset
E. None of these

Q.18 Which of the following is/are incorrect according to the given passage?

A. Gujarat and Lucknow are the two new IPL teams.

B. Chennai Super Kings has won the maximum titles of IPL.

C. The 2022 ICC Men's T20 World Cup is in Australia.

A. Only A
B. Both A and B
C. Only B
D. Both B and C
E. None of these

Q.19 What is the central theme of the passage?

A. IPL – The money-making machine
B. IPL – Growing Ignorance of COVID-19
C. IPL's Dark Side – A Rise in Suicide Cases due to betting
D. IPL – Underworld connection
E. None of these

Q.20 Choose the synonym of the word 'Nimble'.

A. Clumsy
B. Lumbering
C. Stiff
D. Agile
E. None of these

Ques (21-25):Direction: Rearrange the following six sentences/ group of sentences (A), (B), (C), (D), (E) and (F) in the proper sequence to form a meaningful paragraph; then answer the questions given below them.

A. His story is truly inspirational and has a strong moral for kids and adults alike.

B. Despite the rejection by Guru Dronacharya, Eklavya mastered the skill of archery on his own.

C. He aspired to learn archery and become one of the finest archers in the world.

D. One of the popular Indian mythological stories is that of Eklavya.

E. His act of offering his thumb to his Guru as Dakshina labeled him as an ideal disciple.

F. He practised tirelessly in front of a statue of his teacher.

Q.21 Which is the FIRST sentence of the paragraph?

A. A
B. B
C. D
D. F
E. E

Q.22 Which is the SECOND sentence of the paragraph?

A. D
B. E
C. F
D. B
E. A

Q.23 Which is the THIRD sentence of the paragraph?

A. E
B. F
C. B
D. D
E. A

Q.24 Which is the FOURTH sentence of the paragraph?

A. A   **B.** B   **C.** F   **D.** D

E. E

Q.25 Which is the FIFTH sentence of the paragraph?

A. F   **B.** D   **C.** A   **D.** B

E. C

Ques (26-30):Directions: In each of the following questions a sentence is given with some part of it marked in bold. You have to identify the option that would replace the bold part and make the sentence contextually and grammatically correct. If no correction is required, then mark option 'E' as your answer.

Q.26 The new government needs to **call off** the good work so that the popular sentiment remains positive.

A. Cancel

B. Continue

C. Require

D. Accomplish

E. No correction required

Q.27 There is an argument that it is health that Mr. Modi does not bargain with caste, linguistic and region-oriented interests groups.

A. There is an argument that is healthy

B. There is an argumentative that it is healthy

C. There is an argument that health

D. There is an argument that it is healthy

E. No correction required

Q.28 Karim's father **does not like him hanging around** with rowdy boys who cause trouble.

A. does not like his hanging around

B. does not like him hang around

C. does not like his hang around

D. does not like he hanging around

E. No correction required

Q.29 The Japanese army **fell out only after the** devastating attack on Nagasaki.

A. fall out only after the

B. fell back only after the

C. fell in only after the

D. fell upon only after the

E. No correction required

Q.30 The minister didn't **respond to an email requesting** an interview, and a call to her office wasn't answered.

A. respond to an email request

B. respond to a email requesting

C. respond with an email requesting

D. responded to an email requesting

E. No correction required

Reasoning Ability

Q.31 Direction: In the following question assuming the given statements to be True, find which of the conclusion among given conclusions is/are definitely true and then give your answers accordingly.

Statements: A > B > C = D; D ≤ E ≤ F ≥ G ≥ H; I ≥ H

Conclusions:

I. C > G

II. F > I

A. None is true

B. Both I and II are true

C. Only II is true

D. Only I is true

E. Either I and II is true

Ques (32-35):Direction: In the following question assuming the given statements to be true, find which of the conclusion among given conclusions is/are definitely true and then give your answers accordingly.

Q.32 Statements:

A > B > C = P, R < B > Q, P ≥ S = T

Conclusions:

I. A > R

II. C = T

III. B > S

A. All follow

B. Only I follow

C. Only II follows

D. Only I and III follow

E. None follow

Q.33 Statement:

N ≥ T > J ≤ R, J ≥ P ≥ M

Conclusions:

I. M < R

II. N = P

III. R = M

A. Only III is true

B. Only either I or III is true

C. Only II is true

D. Only I is true

E. None is true

Q.34 Statements:

B ≥ Q, O = M, E ≤ O, Q ≤ E

Conclusions:

I. O ≥ Q

II. O < B

III. B < E

A. Neither I nor II conclusion are true

B. Neither I nor III conclusion are true

C. Only III is true

D. Only I is true

E. Only II is true

Q.35 Statements: K ≤ L ≤ M = N, P ≥ O ≥ N

Conclusions:

I. K < O

II. K = N

III. K ≤ M

A. None is true

B. Only I is true

C. Only I and II is true

D. Only II and III is true

E. Only III is true

Q.36 Each consonant of the word 'TERMINATION' is changed to the previous letter in the English alphabetical series and each vowel is changed to the next letter in the English alphabetical series. If the new alphabets thus formed are arranged in alphabetical order (from left to right), which of the following will be the sixth letter from the right end?

A. M

B. S

C. P

D. L

E. None of these

Q.37 If in the word 'FAVOURITE' all the consonants are arranged on the left in reversed alphabetical order after that on the right of these consonants all the vowels are arranged in alphabetical order then how many letters are there in alphabetical series between third letter from right end and fourth letter from left end?

A. 2   B. 5   C. 6   D. 8

E. 9

Q.38 Height of five students A, K, L, M and T are compared. Height of K is more than only two students. Height of M is greater than T and Height of T is greater than K. How many students are smaller than T ?

A. 3   B. 4   C. 5   D. 1

E. 2

Q.39 Direction: Read the following information carefully and answer the question that follows.

In a row of 35 children, M is 15th from the right and there are 10 children between M and R. What is the position of R from the left end of the row?

A. 15th

B. 5th

C. 30th

D. 20th

E. Cannot be determined

Ques (40-42):Direction: Study the following information and answer the below-given questions.

In a family, there are six members Ajay, Kavya, Vivek, Omkar, Shruti, and Kajal. Ajay and Kavya are a married couple, Ajay being a male member. Omkar is the only son of Vivek, who is the brother of Ajay. Shruti is the sister of Omkar. Kavya is the daughter-in-law of Kajal, whose husband has died.

Q.40 How is Kajal related to Kavya?

A. Mother   B. Mother-in-law

C. Sister-in-law   D. Sister

E. Aunt

Q.41 How many female members are there in the family?

[IBPS RRB Scale I, 2020]

A. One   B. Two

C. Three   D. Four

E. Can't be determined

Q.42 How is Kajal related to Shruti?

A. Maternal grandmother

B. Paternal grandmother

C. Aunt

D. Mother-in-law

E. Can't be determined

Ques (43-47):Direction: Study the information carefully and answer the given questions below.

Seven Students viz. Ganga, Arnav, Swati, Anup, Samita, Prakash, Parul are sitting around a circle to form a circle facing inside. Anup is sitting second to the left of Arnav. Only two students will sit between Samita and Ganga. Parul is not sitting next to Swati and Samita. Arnav is sitting second to the left of Parul. Ganga is not a neighbour of Anup and Swati.

Q.43 Who is sitting to the immediate right of Parul?

A. Ganga   B. Arnav

C. Prakash   D. No one

E. None of these

Q.44 If they are made to sit in linear arrangement starting from Arnav at the extreme left followed by Ganga, then who will be sitting third from extreme right end.

A. Parul   B. Swati   C. Samita   D. Ganga

E. Prakash

Q.45 Who is sitting between Swati and Samita?

A. Parul   B. Anup   C. Arnav   D. No one

E. Prakash

Q.46 Who is sitting second to left of the one who is immediate right of Anup?

A. Samita   B. Swati

C. Parul   D. Prakash

E. None of these

Q.47 How many persons are sitting between Prakash and Parul taking clockwise from Parul?

A. One   B. Four   C. Three   D. Five

E. No one

Ques (48-51):Direction: In the questions, two statements are given, followed by two conclusions, I and II. You have to consider the statements to be true even if it seems to be at variance from commonly known facts. You have to decide which of the given conclusions, if any, follows from the given statements.

Q.48 Statements:

No computer is a tablet.

Only a few bands are computers.

Conclusions:

I: Some bands are tablets.

II: All bands are computers.

A. Only conclusion I follows

B. Only conclusion II follows
C. Either conclusion I or II follows
D. Neither conclusion I nor II follows
E. Both conclusion I and II follow

Q.49 Statements:

All cages are bars.

Only few fences are bars.

Conclusions:

I: All cages are fences.

II: Some fences are cages.

A. Only conclusion I follows
B. Only conclusion II follows
C. Either conclusion I or II follows
D. Neither conclusion I nor II follows
E. Both conclusion I and II follow

Q.50 Statements:

Only few buildings are chalks.

No chalk is toffee.

Conclusions:

I: Some buildings are toffee

II: All buildings being chalks is a possibility

A. Only conclusion I follows
B. Only conclusion II follows
C. Either conclusion I or II follows
D. Neither conclusion I nor II follows
E. Both conclusion I and II follow

Q.51 Statements:

Only few colleagues are smart.

All fathers are smart.

Conclusions:

I: Some colleagues are fathers.

II: Some smart are colleagues.

A. Only conclusion I follows
B. Only conclusion II follows
C. Either conclusion I or II follows
D. Neither conclusion I nor II follows
E. Both conclusion I and II follow

Q.52 Direction: In the question below are given three statements followed by two conclusions numbered (i) and (ii). You have to take the given statements to be true even if they seem to be at variance with commonly known facts. Read all the conclusions and then decide which of the given conclusions logically follows from the given statements disregarding commonly known facts.

Statements:

Only A are B.

Only C are D.

Some A are C.

Conclusions:

(i) Some B can be C.

(ii) Some D are A.

A. Only (i) follows
B. Only (ii) follows
C. Either (i) and (ii) follows
D. Both (i) and (ii) follow
E. None follows

Q.53 In a certain code language, 'BLANCH' is written as 'YIXKZE'. What will be the code for 'DEFAME' in that code language?

[SSC MTS, 2019]

A. CDEJKL
B. ABCXJB
C. BCDXJC
D. ABDXIB
E. None of these

Q.54 In a certain code language, 'FRAUD' is written as 'KWFZI'. What will be the code for 'GLAIR' in that code language?

[SSC MTS, 2019]

A. KRHOX
B. LQFNW
C. KQGMX
D. LRHMX
E. None of these

Q.55 If the code for MOTHER is JRQKBU then what is the code for PRINCIPAL?

A. MRFKZLMXI
B. SULQFLSDO
C. MUFQZLMDI
D. MRFKZFMXI
E. None of these

Ques (56-60):Directions: Study the following information carefully and answer the questions that follow.

A certain number of people are sitting in a row facing towards the north. Ankit is sitting second from the right end of the row. Five persons are sitting between Ankit and Abhi. Pihu is sitting immediate right of Abhi. Shweta is sitting third to the right of Pihu. Seven persons are sitting to the left of Shweta. Neha is sitting on one of the extreme ends but not sitting immediately right of Ankit. Sikha is sitting eighth to the right of Neha and immediately left of Ankit. Anu is sitting second to the right of Sikha. Four persons are sitting between Anu and Riya.

Q.56 What is position of Shweta from the right end of the line?
A. Second   B. Third   C. Fourth   D. Fifth
E. Sixth

Q.57 Who is sitting immediate left of Riya?
A. Anu   B. Abhi   C. Ankit   D. Pihu
E. Neha

Q.58 How many persons are sitting between Pihu and Sikha?
A. One   B. Two   C. Three   D. Four
E. Five

Q.59 How many persons are sitting in the row?
A. 8   B. 9   C. 10   D. 11
E. 12

Q.60 Who is sitting at the extreme left end of the row?
A. Ankit   B. Abhi   C. Pihu   D. Riya
E. Neha

Ques (61-65):Directions: Study the following information carefully to answer the given question:

H 8 & 5 T O 9 # V 6 P $ 7 W F * 1 N L 4 ? 3 / C Q U ! A 2 > J

Q.61 How many symbols in the given series are immediately preceded by a number but not immediately followed by a letter?

A. None   **B.** 1
C. 2   **D.** 3
E. More than 3

Q.62 If all the even numbers are skipped from the series then find the product of the numbers that come between second vowel from right end and $?

A. 63   **B.** 21
C. 48   **D.** 84
E. None of these

Q.63 If all the symbols are skipped from the series then which of the following element will be fifth to the right of the highest number of the series?

A. W   **B.** F   **C.** 1   **D.** 7
E. N

Q.64 Four of the following five are alike in a certain way and thus form a group. Which of the following does not belong to the group?

A. OV5   **B.** C!3   **C.** FN7   **D.** 4/L
E. 96T

Q.65 How many odd numbers are immediately followed by a symbol but not immediately preceded by a letter?

A. None   **B.** 1
C. 2   **D.** 3
E. More than 3

Quantitative Aptitude

Ques (66-70):Direction: Following bar graph show the number of units produced and sold by different companies.

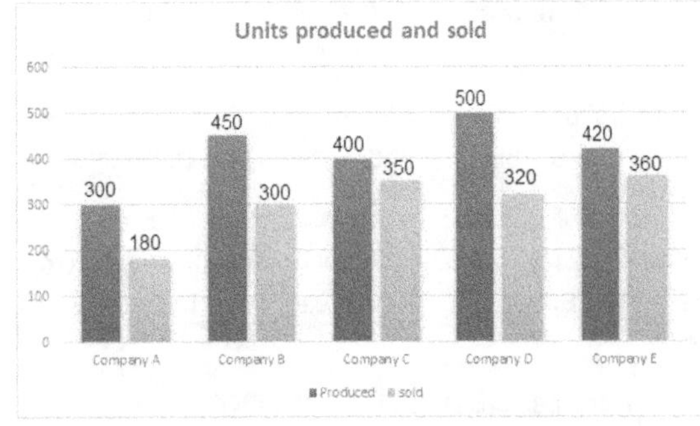

Q.66 What is the ratio of unsold units of Company E and D together to the sold units of company A and B together?

A. 1 : 2   **B.** 2 : 1   **C.** 3 : 2   **D.** 4 : 3
E. 5 : 7

Q.67 Units produced by company C is how much percent more/less than that of the units sold by company B?

A. 25%   **B.** 20%   **C.** 30%   **D.** 33.33%
E. 37.5%

Q.68 What is the average unit of all the companies that remain unsold?

A. 118   **B.** 120   **C.** 112   **D.** 150
E. 130

Q.69 If company F produces 10% more unit that was produced by company A and sells 20% fewer units that were sold by Company C. How many units of company F remain unsold?

A. 60   **B.** 50   **C.** 70   **D.** 90
E. 80

Q.70 What is the difference between the total produced and total sold units by all the companies?

A. 500   **B.** 560   **C.** 550   **D.** 600
E. 650

Ques (71-74):Direction: Each of the questions below consists of a question and two statements numbered I and II given below it. You have to decide whether the data provided in the statements are sufficient to answer the question. Read both the statements and give answer.

Q.71 How much amount Rina will get at the end of two years if the rate of interest is compounded annually?

Statement I: Rohan invests the same of amount of money under simple interest at the rate of 10% per annum and receives a total amount of Rs.1560 at the end of 3 years.

Statement II: The difference between the simple interest and compound interest on the same sum of money at the same rate of interest at the end of 2 years is Rs 12.

A. The data in statements I alone is sufficient to answer the question, while the data in statement II alone is not sufficient to answer the question.

B. The data in statements II alone is sufficient to answer the question, while the data in statement I alone is not sufficient to answer the question.

C. Either Statement I or Statement II alone is sufficient to answer the question.

D. The data in both the statements I and II is not sufficient to answer the question.

E. The data in both the statements I and II together is necessary to answer the question.

Q.72 How much time train P will take to cover a distance of 532 km?

Statement I: The ratio of speed at which train P and train Q runs is 4 : 5 respectively.

Statement II: The average speed of the train P and train Q is $\frac{400}{9}$ km per hour.

A. The data in statements I alone is sufficient to answer the question, while the data in statement II alone is not sufficient to answer the question.

B. The data in statements II alone is sufficient to answer the question, while the data in statement I alone is not sufficient to answer the question.

C. Either Statement I or Statement II alone is sufficient to answer the question.

D. The data in both the statements I and II is not sufficient to answer the question.

E. The data in both the statements I and II together is necessary to answer the question.

D. The data in all the statements I, II and III is not sufficient to answer the question.

E. The data in all the statements I, II and III together is necessary to answer the question.

Q.73 The population of a city in the year 2018 was 219615 then what was the population of city exactly 4 years ago?

Statement I: The population of city in the year 2018 is exactly 1.4641 times of that in the year 2014.

Statement II: The population of the city increased by 10% each year.

A. The data in statements I alone is sufficient to answer the question, while the data in statement II alone is not sufficient to answer the question.

B. The data in statements II alone is sufficient to answer the question, while the data in statement I alone is not sufficient to answer the question.

C. Either Statement I or Statement II alone is sufficient to answer the question.

D. The data in both the statements I and II is not sufficient to answer the question.

E. The data in both the statements I and II together is necessary to answer the question.

Q.74 In a triangle abc, which of the sides among ab, bc, and ca is the longest side?

Statement I: The ratio of angle a to angle B is 3 : 2 that is the same as the ratio of angle b to angle c.

Statement II: The perimeter of the triangle is 144 cm.

A. The data in statements I alone is sufficient to answer the question, while the data in statement II alone is not sufficient to answer the question.

B. The data in statements II alone is sufficient to answer the question, while the data in statement I alone is not sufficient to answer the question.

C. Either Statement I or Statement II alone is sufficient to answer the question.

D. The data in both the statements I and II is not sufficient to answer the question.

E. The data in both the statements I and II together is necessary to answer the question.

Q.75 Direction: Each of the questions below consists of a question and three statements numbered I, II and III given below it. You have to decide whether the data provided in the statements are sufficient to answer the question. Read all the statements and give answer:

At what time will the train reach point X from point Y?

I. The train crosses another train of equal distance of 250 m in 25 sec. running opposite direction.

II. The train of 250 m crosses a signal pole in 10 sec.

III. The distance between point X and point Y is 360 km.

A. The data in statements I alone is sufficient to answer the question, while the data in statement II and III is not sufficient to answer the question.

B. The data in statements II and III is sufficient to answer the question, while the data in statement II alone is not sufficient to answer the question.

C. The data in any two of the statements out of three is sufficient to answer the question.

Q.76 What value should come in place of the question mark '?' in the following question?

$45^2 - 100 - 25^2 = ?$

[Union Bank of India Clerk, 2019], [Indian Bank Clerk, 2019], [Central Bank of India Clerk, 2019]

A. 1200 **B.** 1100 **C.** 1300 **D.** 1700
E. 1500

Q.77 What value should come in place of the question mark '?' in the following question?

$$\sqrt[3]{1728} + \sqrt[3]{1331} + \sqrt{?} + 12 = 49$$

[Union Bank of India Clerk, 2019], [Indian Bank Clerk, 2019], [Central Bank of India Clerk, 2019]

A. 256 **B.** 225 **C.** 196 **D.** 169
E. 324

Q.78 What value should come in place of the question mark '?' in the following question?

$120 \div x = 14 \times 6 - 4^3$

[Union Bank of India Clerk, 2019], [Indian Bank Clerk, 2019], [Central Bank of India Clerk, 2019]

A. 4 **B.** 6 **C.** 12 **D.** 8
E. 10

Q.79 What value should come in place of the question mark '?' in the following question?

$$\sqrt{81 + ? + 95} = 16$$

[Union Bank of India Clerk, 2019], [Indian Bank Clerk, 2019], [Central Bank of India Clerk, 2019]

A. 90 **B.** 70 **C.** 60 **D.** 80
E. 110

Q.80 What value should come in place of the question mark '?' in the following question?

$$\sqrt{1024} \times 11 + 8 \times ? = 32 \times 16$$

[Union Bank of India Clerk, 2019], [Indian Bank Clerk, 2019], [Central Bank of India Clerk, 2019]

A. -30 **B.** 24 **C.** -16 **D.** 20
E. -32

Q.81 What value should come in place of the question mark '?' in the following question?

$12^2 + 16^2 - ?^2 = 10^2 \times 3$

[Union Bank of India Clerk, 2019], [Indian Bank Clerk, 2019], [Central Bank of India Clerk, 2019]

A. 15 **B.** 20 **C.** 10 **D.** 12
E. 8

Ques (82-83): What will come in place of the question mark (?) in the following equation?

Q.82 $185\% \text{ of } 500 - 46\% \text{ of } 1650 = 4 \times ?$

A. 42.5 **B.** 35.5

C. 53.5   **D.** 41.5
E. None of these

Q.83 $2\frac{5}{13}\%$ of $5200 + 1\frac{1}{17}\%$ of $5100 =?$

A. 17800   **B.** 1780
C. 178   **D.** 17.8
E. None of these

Q.84 A shopkeeper sells 12 pens at a price for which he bought 14 pens. If he has to pay a tax of 10% on the profit obtained, what is his net profit on the overall transaction?

A. 15.33%
B. 16%
C. 16.67%
D. 15%
E. Cannot be determined

Q.85 In an election, 80% of the people casted their votes and 45% of the voters who casted votes are employed and 66.67% of employed voters are engineers. Find the percentage of non-engineers among total voters?

A. 12%   **B.** 24%   **C.** 50%   **D.** 76%
E. 48%

Q.86 Direction: In the given question, two equations numbered I and II are given. Solve both the equations and mark the appropriate answer.

I. $x^2 - 13x + 30 = 0$

II. $y^2 + 5y + 4 = 0$

A. x > y
B. x < y
C. x ≥ y
D. x ≤ y
E. x = y or relationship between x and y cannot be established

Q.87 Direction: In the given question, two equations numbered I and II are given. Solve both the equations and mark the appropriate answer.

I. $x^2 + 17x + 72 = 0$

II. $y^2 + 11y + 30 = 0$

A. x > y
B. x < y
C. x ≥ y
D. x ≤ y
E. x = y or relationship between x and y cannot be established

Q.88 Direction: In the given question, two equations numbered I and II are given. Solve both the equations and mark the appropriate answer.

I. $2x^2 - 39x + 189 = 0$

II. $y^2 - 16y + 63 = 0$

A. x > y
B. x < y
C. x ≥ y

D. x ≤ y
E. x = y or relationship between x and y cannot be established

Q.89 Direction: In the given question, two equations numbered I and II are given. Solve both the equations and mark the appropriate answer.

I. $x^2 - 27x + 180 = 0$

II. $y^2 - 31y + 240 = 0$

A. x > y
B. x < y
C. x ≥ y
D. x ≤ y
E. x = y or relationship between x and y cannot be established

Q.90 Direction: In the given question, two equations numbered I and II are given. Solve both the equations and mark the appropriate answer.

I. $5x^2 + 29x - 42 = 0$

II. $20y^2 - 9y - 18 = 0$

A. x > y
B. x < y
C. x ≥ y
D. x ≤ y
E. x = y or relationship between x and y cannot be established

Q.91 What should come in place of the question mark '?' in the following number series?

68, 71, 65, 74, 62, ?

A. 72   **B.** 82   **C.** 79   **D.** 83
E. 77

Q.92 What should come in place of the question mark '?' in the following number series?

63, 80, 99, ?, 143, 168

A. 121   **B.** 122   **C.** 124   **D.** 126
E. 120

Q.93 What should come in place of the question mark '?' in the following number series?

12, 15, 24, 39, 60, ?

A. 77   **B.** 81   **C.** 83   **D.** 87
E. 91

Q.94 What should come in place of the question mark '?' in the following number series?

7, 8, 17, 52, ?, 1046

A. 209   **B.** 316   **C.** 329   **D.** 263
E. 291

Q.95 What should come in place of the question mark '?' in the following number series?

16, 160, 281, 381, ?, 526

A. 432   **B.** 442   **C.** 462   **D.** 452
E. 472

Q.96 A man can travel 50 km in 2.5 hours and 200 km in 4 hours. Find his average speed.

A. 38 km/hr   **B.** 37.5 km/hr

C. 36.4 km/hr   **D.** 38.46 km/hr

E. 34 km/hr

Q.97 A mixture of 20 litres of alcohol and water contains 15% of alcohol. How much alcohol should be added to the mixture so that the mixture contains 20% of alcohol.

A. 2.25 litres   **B.** 1.50 litres

C. 1.25 litres   **D.** 2.50 litres

E. 3.50 litres

Q.98 Direction: What approximate value should come in the place of the question mark '?' in the following question?

$$(17.76)^2 + (20.99)^2 = (2)^7 + ?$$

A. 581   **B.** 650   **C.** 532   **D.** 648

E. 637

Q.99 What will come in the place of the question mark '?' in the following question?

$$\sqrt{676} \times 12 - 864 \div 36 = ? + 61$$

A. 224   **B.** 169   **C.** 507   **D.** 227

E. 223

Q.100 Average of 40 numbers is 71. If the number 100 replaced by 140, then average is increased by :

A. 3   **B.** 4   **C.** 2   **D.** 1

E. 6

// Smart Answer Sheet //

Correct Indicates percentage of students who answered questions correctly.

Skipped Indicates percentage of students who skipped questions.

Q.	Ans.	Correct / Skipped	Q.	Ans.	Correct / Skipped	Q.	Ans.	Correct / Skipped	Q.	Ans.	Correct / Skipped	Q.	Ans.	Correct / Skipped
1	D	69.1 % / 30.06 %	17	B	46.4 % / 33.44 %	33	B	16.9 % / 68.41 %	49	D	66.44 % / 30.11 %	65	B	45.15 % / 36.62 %
2	B	28.45 % / 67.68 %	18	C	25.87 % / 69.16 %	34	D	69.03 % / 30.95 %	50	D	62.54 % / 37.31 %	66	A	83.34 % / 15.44 %
3	B	61.01 % / 36.69 %	19	A	56.18 % / 36.75 %	35	E	26.91 % / 70.93 %	51	B	68.15 % / 31.65 %	67	D	87.96 % / 12.0 %
4	A	40.91 % / 34.31 %	20	D	66.57 % / 32.59 %	36	A	83.02 % / 15.79 %	52	D	88.45 % / 10.97 %	68	C	84.15 % / 14.7 %
5	C	67.93 % / 31.62 %	21	C	43.32 % / 47.27 %	37	A	10.26 % / 78.7 %	53	B	78.25 % / 10.14 %	69	B	64.75 % / 30.32 %
6	A	69.73 % / 30.06 %	22	E	44.9 % / 50.23 %	38	A	45.57 % / 43.65 %	54	B	79.59 % / 14.62 %	70	B	80.11 % / 15.2 %
7	C	49.95 % / 32.24 %	23	D	13.0 % / 76.97 %	39	E	49.97 % / 45.7 %	55	C	53.5 % / 30.85 %	71	E	67.19 % / 30.52 %
8	E	80.34 % / 19.56 %	24	B	24.68 % / 71.38 %	40	B	40.49 % / 49.69 %	56	C	45.89 % / 48.64 %	72	E	79.93 % / 11.35 %
9	B	51.38 % / 35.52 %	25	A	47.01 % / 44.08 %	41	C	54.92 % / 34.72 %	57	D	59.21 % / 31.7 %	73	C	51.01 % / 45.75 %
10	C	66.66 % / 32.6 %	26	B	42.18 % / 47.5 %	42	B	51.5 % / 46.72 %	58	C	67.58 % / 31.29 %	74	A	10.02 % / 79.84 %
11	C	65.38 % / 31.64 %	27	D	60.25 % / 33.05 %	43	C	60.05 % / 30.38 %	59	D	47.86 % / 40.5 %	75	B	57.59 % / 42.12 %
12	A	16.6 % / 70.54 %	28	A	48.33 % / 44.41 %	44	C	68.78 % / 30.97 %	60	E	47.64 % / 49.0 %	76	C	61.83 % / 35.94 %
13	B	67.02 % / 30.51 %	29	B	40.82 % / 32.73 %	45	B	51.65 % / 41.27 %	61	C	60.57 % / 31.96 %	77	C	59.28 % / 40.54 %
14	B	54.66 % / 32.45 %	30	E	55.49 % / 39.64 %	46	A	62.26 % / 34.25 %	62	B	61.73 % / 32.32 %	78	B	64.87 % / 33.96 %
15	B	54.75 % / 35.17 %	31	A	42.61 % / 36.34 %	47	D	54.45 % / 44.74 %	63	A	66.57 % / 30.64 %	79	D	83.69 % / 10.12 %
16	D	58.91 % / 34.89 %	32	D	61.58 % / 31.79 %	48	D	48.85 % / 37.59 %	64	D	57.99 % / 34.99 %	80	D	40.64 % / 54.3 %

Q.	Ans.	Correct / Skipped
81	C	51.81 %
		41.9 %
82	D	85.02 %
		13.74 %
83	C	56.42 %
		34.69 %
84	D	52.27 %
		37.77 %

Q.	Ans.	Correct / Skipped
85	A	63.31 %
		35.16 %
86	A	65.05 %
		31.77 %
87	B	46.02 %
		34.68 %
88	C	20.57 %
		76.07 %

Q.	Ans.	Correct / Skipped
89	D	22.06 %
		77.34 %
90	E	66.97 %
		32.65 %
91	E	60.71 %
		35.34 %
92	E	50.49 %
		31.35 %

Q.	Ans.	Correct / Skipped
93	D	81.67 %
		18.07 %
94	A	31.11 %
		68.48 %
95	C	52.55 %
		40.85 %
96	D	55.13 %
		44.86 %

Q.	Ans.	Correct / Skipped
97	C	47.43 %
		48.78 %
98	E	63.83 %
		32.06 %
99	D	47.02 %
		36.1 %
100	D	48.26 %
		35.7 %

Performance Analysis

Avg. Score (%)	56.0%
Toppers Score (%)	58.0%
Your Score	

//Hints and Solutions//

1. Overt is MOST OPPOSITE in meaning to the word 'Covert'.

Covert means not openly shown, engaged in, or avowed.

Overt means done or shown openly; plainly apparent.

Hence, the correct option is (D).

2. Cautious is MOST OPPOSITE in meaning to the word 'PRUDENT'.

The given word 'Prudent' means sensible and careful when making judgements and decisions; avoiding unnecessary risks.

- Let's see the meaning of other given options:-
    - 'Hasty' means said or done too quickly.
    - 'Cautious' means taking great care to avoid possible danger or problems.
    - 'Reckless' means not thinking about possible bad or dangerous results that could come from your actions.
    - 'Rude' means not polite.

Hence, the correct option is (B).

3. The sentence mentions 'need to be cared for', therefore, ruling-out the word 'abused' as it would make the sentence vague. The word 'democratic' disturbs the meaning of the sentence. Using the word 'emotional' would be grammatically incorrect. The word 'protected' that means to keep someone safe from any kind of harm or injury fits the blank best.

Almost one-third of the world's population consists of children. Therefore they need to be cared for and (A) protected.

Hence, the correct option is (B).

4. The words 'statutory' and 'contrast' cannot be used with the word 'social' mentioned in the sentence. Using the word 'fullness' would not provide any meaning to the sentence, therefore, making 'structure' as the best fit to fill the blank.

Children are an important component of the social (B) structure.

Hence, the correct option is (A).

5. The sentence mentions the word 'task', which should be used as a hint while picking up the word fitting the blank. As the sentence indicates a negative remark, 'qualified' and 'pleasant' gets omitted for being positive words. 'Untoward' does not make a proper sentence. When used with 'task', it does not convey an appropriate meaning to the sentence in the above passage. The word 'uphill' fits the word 'task' along with appropriately conveying the meaning of the sentence too.

Finding a single definition to describe a 'child' is becoming an (C) uphill task.

Hence, the correct option is (C).

6. The reading of the sentence with the inclusive phrase 'infancy and youth' gives us the hint that the word that needs to fit the blank must be talking about both these terms i.e. 'infancy' and 'youth' separately. Out of the given words, 'among' is used to talk about a group or crowd or mass of objects and thus, is rejected. 'Along' means to move in a constant direction and thus, it does not fit the context of the sentence. 'Amidst' means to be in the middle of or to be surrounded by something and therefore, gets ruled out. The word 'between' makes the best fit for the blank as it is used to refer to two separate things.

The dictionary defines the word 'child' as a young person, especially (D) between infancy and youth.

Hence, the correct option is (A).

7. The words 'policies' and 'adopt' gets omitted due to being grammatically incorrect. 'Surprise' cannot be used as it makes the sentence vague and does not provide an appropriate meaning.The word 'qualification' carries the required message fitting the sense of the statement.

The only (E) qualification is that the child should be unable to maintain himself.

Hence, the correct option is (C).

8. There is no error in the given sentence.

Therefore the correct sentence is "The defence minister thought that each veteran was as respectful as himself and should be given due preference as well."

Hence, the correct option is (E).

9. The error lies in the second part of thestatement because 'of' cannot be used with 'despite'. "Despite" itself means 'inspite of'.

Unfortunately, India continues to be one of the backward countries with respect to literacy, despite the fact that successive governments have been trying their best to promote education.

Hence, the correct option is (B).

10. The error lies in the part (3) of the sentence. The sentence has a past context, hence 'run' needs to be replaced with 'ran'.

The correct sentence will be "The first lady took it upon herself to make sure that the government ran smoothly while the President was recuperating from the surgery.

Hence, the correct option is (C).

11. The error lies in the third part of the sentence. Since the comparison is between men and women, the plural form of the word 'counterpart' (counterparts).

The correct sentence will be "Cases of malignant melanoma are rising faster among men than women, but men are often worse than their female counterparts at protecting themselves from the Sun.

Hence, the correct option is (C).

12. The error lies in the first part of thesentence. The subject is 'appropriation',which is singular, thus the helping verb'have' should be replaced with 'has'.

The correct sentence will be "Appropriation of assets has become increasingly important due to the willingness of those in power to abuse authority for personal gains.

Hence, the correct option is (A).

13. The correctly spelt word is misogynist means a man who hates women. The correct spellings of the other words are momentary, monotheism, moratorium.

Hence, the correct option is (B).

14. Consequantly has the wrongly spelt word. The correct spelling is 'Consequently' which means accordingly.

Cautiously means careful.

Completely means totally or utterly.

Concurrently means occurring at the same time, simultaneously.

Hence, the correct option is (B).

15. Journy has the incorrectly spelt word. The correct word is a journey which refers to the act of travelling from one place to another.

Meaning of other words:

Delicious means greatly pleasing or entertaining.

Furious means marked by extreme and violent energy.

Failure means an event that does not accomplish its intended purpose.

Ruthless means having no pity, cruel or merciless.

Hence, the correct option is (B).

16. The given passage is all about the Indian Premier League.

The second-last sentence of the first paragraph says "The latest outing has Tata as the title sponsor while multiple brands will jostle for space through the tournament and its 10 teams."

From the above sentence, we can say that according to the passage, TATA is the title sponsor for the IPL 2022.

Hence, the correct option is (D).

17. The word 'Inception' means The establishment or the point at which something begins.

- Example: The club has grown rapidly since its inception in 1990.

Let's look at the meaning of the given options:-

Commencement - The beginning of something.

- Example: She had to get all her stuff ready before the commencement of her course.

Cessation - The fact or process of ending or being brought to an end.

- Example: The cessation of the war will save the lives of millions.

Genesis - The beginning or origin of something.

- Example: The project had its genesis two years earlier.

Outset - The start or beginning of something.

- Example: Since the doctor discovered cancer during the outset of its stage, the person would fully recover.

Dawn - The beginning of something.

- Example: People have talked about the weather since the dawn of civilization.

Hence, the correct option is (B).

18. The last sentence of the first paragraph says "Meanwhile, the two new squads — Gujarat Titans and Lucknow Super Giants — will enhance the novelty factor" and the last sentence of the passage says "And this IPL will also help leading players such as Kane Williamson to finesse their craft ahead of the ICC T20 World Cup in Australia, later this year".

From the above sentences, we can say that statements A and C are correct according to the given passage.

The sixth sentence of the second paragraph says "While CSK will look at replicating its triumphs, Mumbai Indians, the most successful franchise with five trophies, will hope to excel in its backyard".

From the above sentence, we can say that statement B is incorrect according to the given passage.

Hence, the correct option is (C).

19. The first sentence of the passage says "Nearly a decade and a half since its inception, the Indian Premier League (IPL) has struck deep roots and acquired nimble feet", the eighth sentence of the first paragraph says "Ever since that summer night at Bengaluru's M. Chinnaswamy Stadium in 2008 when the IPL made its debut, it's commercial value has found incremental gains" and the ninth sentence of the first paragraph says "The latest outing has Tata as the title sponsor while multiple brands will jostle for space through the tournament and its 10 teams".

From the above sentences, we can say that the central theme of the passage is "IPL – The money-making machine".

Hence, the correct option is (A).

20. The meaning of the given words:

- Nimble. Quick and light in movement or action; agile.
- Agile: Able to move quickly and easily.
- Clumsy - Awkward in movement or in handling things.
- Lumbering - Moving in a slow, heavy, awkward way.
- Stiff - Not easy to move.

So, it is concluded that Agile is the synonym of the word 'Nimble'.

Hence, the correct option is (D).

21. The first sentence of the passage should introduce the topic and it is the story of 'Eklavya' which is sentence D

- The second sentence mentions why this story is special and this is sentence A.
- The third sentence tells us more about Eklavya, who Ekklavya was and this is sentence C.
- Eklavya's first step towards achieving his goal is mentioned in sentence B.
- Sentence F then states the way by which Eklavya learnt archery.
- The last sentence is E as it concludes the passage.

The correct order is DACBFE.

D is the FIRST sentence of the paragraph.

Hence, the correct option is (C).

22. The first sentence of the passage should introduce the topic and it is the story of 'Eklavya' which is sentence D

- The second sentence mentions why this story is special and this is sentence A.
- The third sentence tells us more about Eklavya, who Ekklavya was and this is sentence C.
- Eklavya's first step towards achieving his goal is mentioned in sentence B.
- Sentence F then states the way by which Eklavya learnt archery.
- The last sentence is E as it concludes the passage.

The correct order is DACBFE.

The second sentence is A.

Hence, the correct option is (E).

23. The first sentence of the passage should introduce the topic and it is the story of 'Eklavya' which is sentence D

- The second sentence mentions why this story is special and this is sentence A.
- The third sentence tells us more about Eklavya, who Ekklavya was and this is sentence C.
- Eklavya's first step towards achieving his goal is mentioned in sentence B.
- Sentence F then states the way by which Eklavya learnt archery.
- The last sentence is E as it concludes the passage.

The correct order is DACBFE.

The third sentence is C.

Hence, the correct option is (D).

24. The first sentence of the passage should introduce the topic and it is the story of 'Eklavya' which is sentence D

- The second sentence mentions why this story is special and this is sentence A.
- The third sentence tells us more about Eklavya, who Ekklavya was and this is sentence C.
- Eklavya's first step towards achieving his goal is mentioned in sentence B.
- Sentence F then states the way by which Eklavya learnt archery.
- The last sentence is E as it concludes the passage.

The correct order is DACBFE.

The fourth sentence is B.

Hence, the correct option is (B).

25. The first sentence of the passage should introduce the topic and it is the story of 'Eklavya' which is sentence D

- The second sentence mentions why this story is special and this is sentence A.
- The third sentence tells us more about Eklavya, who Ekklavya was and this is sentence C.
- Eklavya's first step towards achieving his goal is mentioned in sentence B.
- Sentence F then states the way by which Eklavya learnt archery.
- The last sentence is E as it concludes the passage.

The correct order is DACBFE.

The last sentence is F.

Hence, the correct option is (A).

26. According to the given context we are talking about the need for the government to carry on with the good work so that the people remain with the government.

Call off (Phrasal Verb): Cancel something

Therefore, it is not correct in the given context and it should be corrected. Among the given words, continue fits perfectly here and it is our pick as the correct answer.

The correct statement is:

The new government needs to continue the good work so that the popular sentiment remains positive.

Hence, the correct option is (B).

27. There is an error in the bold part of the sentence since it is not expressing the correct meaning that it is healthy for the democracy of India that Mr Modi does not take into account the caste, language and region oriented issues while deciding on any policy.

Option A can be eliminated since it is not expressing the desired meaning whereas Option B is not making any sense. Same can be said regarding Option C also. Only Option D is there that explains the correct meaning of the statement.

The correct statement is:

There is an argument that it is healthy that Mr. Modi does not bargain with caste, linguistic and region-oriented interest groups.

Hence, the correct option is (D).

28. The original sentence is erroneous.

Reason: The noun or pronoun relating to a gerund should always be in the possessive case. A gerund is a verb form which functions as a noun. It is present in verb+ing form. Hence the possessive pronoun 'his' should be used in place of the objective pronoun 'him' to make the sentence grammatically correct.

Among the given choices, only option A replaces the given bold part most appropriately.

The sentence after replacement becomes:

Karim's father does not like his hanging around with rowdy boys who cause trouble.

Hence, the correct option is (A).

29. The original sentence is erroneous.

Reason: Usage of the phrasal verb 'fall out' which means 'have an argument' is inappropriate in this sentence.

'Fall back' which means 'withdraw or retreat' would be suitable in this context.

E.g.: The infantry fell back in disarray.

Hence 'fell back' should be used in place of 'fell out' to make the sentence grammatically and contextually correct.

Among the given choices, only option B replaces the given bold part most appropriately.

The sentence after replacement becomes:

The Japanese army fell back only after the devastating attack on Nagasaki.

Hence, the correct option is (B).

30. The original sentence is absolutely correct and hence the bold part needs no replacement.

Hence, the correct option is (E).

31. Given statements: A > B > C = D; D ≤ E ≤ F ≥ G ≥ H; I ≥ H

On combining: A > B > C = D ≤ E ≤ F ≥ G ≥ H ≤ I

Conclusions:

I. C > G → False (as C = D ≤ E ≤ F ≥ G → therefore we cannot determine the relationship between C and G)

II. F > I → False (as F ≥ G ≥ H ≤ I → therefore we cannot determine the relationship between F and I)

Thus, none is true.

Hence, the correct option is (A).

32. Given statements: - A > B > C = P, R < B > Q, P ≥ S = T

On combining: A > B > C = P ≥ S = T, R < B > Q

Conclusions:

A > R → True (because A > B > R, implies A > R)

C = T → False (as C = P ≥ S =T, implies C ≥ T, thus C = T is not definite)

B > S → True (because B > C = P ≥ S, implies B > S)

So, only I and III follow.

Hence, the correct option is (D).

33. Given: N ≥ T > J ≤ R, J ≥ P ≥ M

On Combining: R ≥ J ≥ P ≥ M, N ≥ T > J ≥ P ≥ M

Conclusions:

I. M < R → False (as R ≥ J ≥ P ≥ M, therefore R ≥ M).

II. N = P → False (as N ≥ T > J ≥ P, therefore N > P).

III. R = M → False (as R ≥ J ≥ P ≥ M, therefore R ≥ M)

Conclusion I and III form a complementary pair.

So, either conclusion I or III is true.

Hence, the correct option is (B).

34. Given statement: B ≥ Q, O = M, E ≤ O, Q ≤ E

On Combining: B ≥ Q ≤ E ≤ O = M

Conclusions:

I. O ≥ Q → True (as Q ≤ E ≤ O → O ≥ Q)

II. O < B → False (as B ≥ Q ≤ E ≤ O → clear relation between O and B cannot be determined

III. B < E → False (as B ≥ Q ≤ E → clear relation between B and E cannot be determined)

Since only conclusion I is true and conclusion II and III are false.

Hence, the correct option is (D).

35. Given statements: K ≤ L ≤ M = N, P ≥ O ≥ N

On combining: K ≤ L ≤ M = N ≤ O ≤ P

Conclusions:

I. K < O → False (as K ≤ L ≤ M = N ≤ O → K ≤ O)

II. K = N → False (this can only be true if K = L and L = M, and so K = N is not definitely true)

III. K ≤ M → True (as K ≤ L and L ≤ M→ thus it can be concluded that K ≤ M)

Therefore, only conclusion III is true.

Hence, the correct option is (E).

36. The given word:

T E R M I N A T I O N

Applying the above condition, we have new word:

S F Q L J M B S J P M

Now, arranging in alphabetical order (from left to right)

B F J J L M M P Q S S

So, M is sixth from the right.

Hence, the correct option is (A).

37. The given word:

FAVOURITE

After arranging all the consonants on the left in reversed alphabetical order, we get:

VTRF

Now, arranging all the vowels on the right of these consonants, we get:

VTRFAEIOU

Here, the third letter from the right end is I and the fourth letter from the left end is F.

And, we know that there are two letters between F and I in alphabetical series.

Hence, the correct option is (A).

38. Given,

Height of five students A, K, L, M and T are compared. Height of K is more than only two students. Height of M is greater than T and Height of T is greater than K.

Five students -A, K, L, M and T are compared.

1. Height of K is more than only two students.

_ > _ > K > _ > _

2. Height of M is greater than T and Height of T is greater than K.

M > T > K

From condition 1 and 2, we get

M > T > K > _ > _

So, 3 students are smaller than T.

Hence, the correct option is (A).

39. Given,

In a row of 35 children, M is 15th from the right and there are 10 children between M and R.

According to the given information,

$$
\begin{array}{c}
 M R \\
\rule{6cm}{0.4pt} \\
20 15th 10 4
\end{array}
$$

(Left end)   (Right end)

Or,

$$
\begin{array}{c}
 R M \\
\rule{6cm}{0.4pt} \\
9 10th 10 15th 14
\end{array}
$$

(Left end)   (Right end)

Thus, the position of R cannot be determined.

Hence, the correct option is (E).

Ques (40-42):1) Ajay and Kavya are a married couple.

2) Ajay is the male member means Ajay is the husband and Kavya is the wife.

3) Omkar is the only son of Vivek, who is the brother of Ajay.

4) Shruti is the sister of Omkar means daughter of Vivek.

5) Kavya is the daughter-in-law of Kajal means Kajal is the mother of Ajay and Vivek.

Symbol in Diagram	Meaning
○	Female
□	Male
══	Married Couple
──	Siblings
│	Difference of A Generation

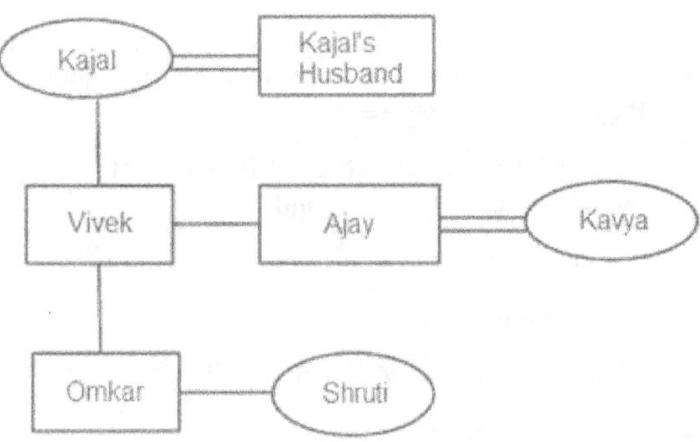

40. So, Kajal is the mother-in-law of Kavya.

Hence, the correct option is (B).

41. So, there are three female members in the family.

Hence, the correct option is (C).

42. So, Kajal is the paternal grandmother of Shruti.

Hence, the correct option is (B).

Ques (43-47):1) Anup is sitting second to the left of Arnav.

2) Arnav is sitting second to the left of Parul.

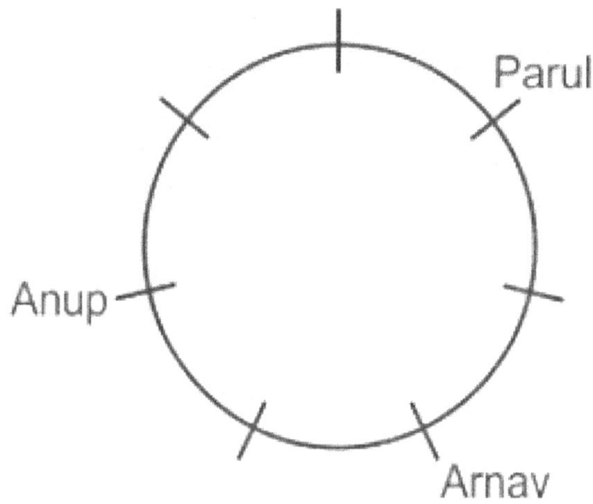

3) Parul is not sitting next to Swati and Samita.

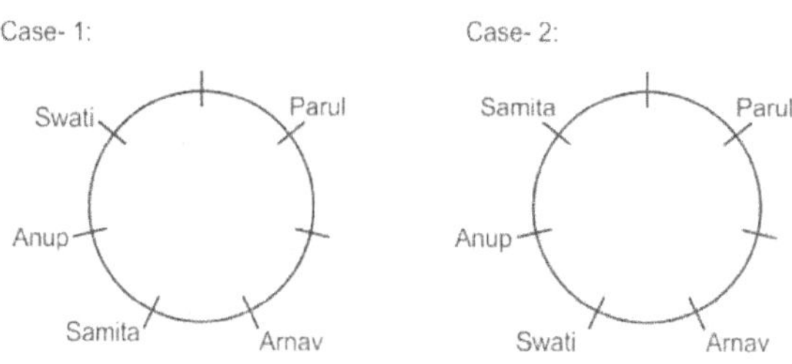

4) Ganga is not a neighbour of Anup and Swati(So, case 1 will be eliminated).

5) Only two students will sit between Samita and Ganga.

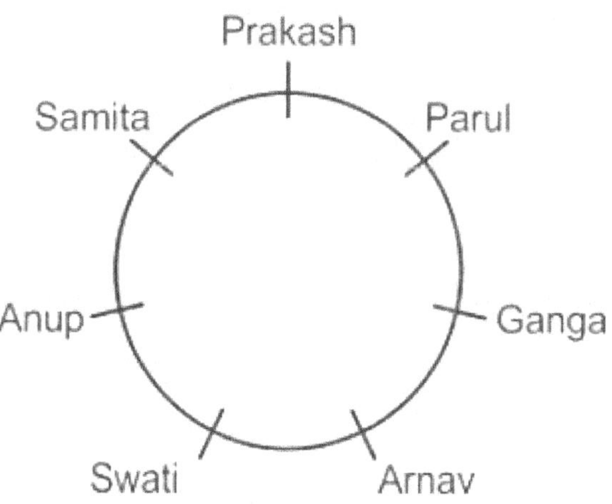

43. So, Prakash is sitting to the immediate right of Parul.

Hence, the correct option is (C).

44. If they are seated in a linear arrangement starting with Arnav at the left end.

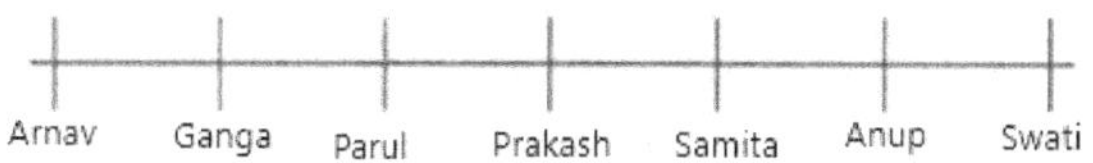

So, Samita is sitting in the third position from the right end.

Hence, the correct option is (C).

45. So, Anup is sitting between Swati and Samita.

Hence, the correct option is (B).

46. Samita is sitting second to the left of the one who is the immediate right of Anup.

Hence, the correct option is (A).

47. Five people are sitting between Prakash and Parul taking clockwise from Parul.

Hence, the correct option is (D).

48. The least possible Venn diagram is given below:

Conclusions:

I: Some bands are tablets → False (it is possible but not definite)

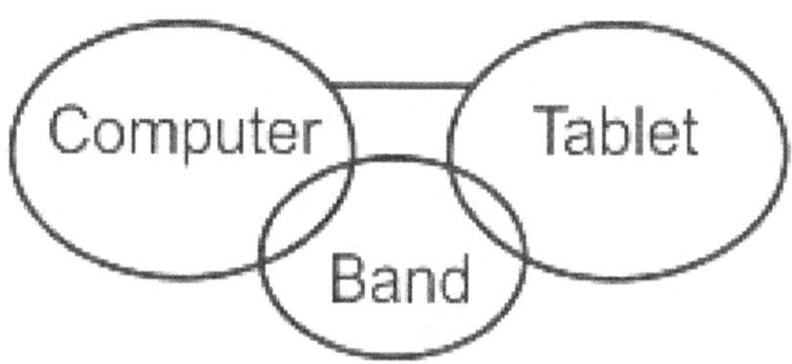

This diagram shows that some band being tablet is a possibility.

II: All bands are computers → False (only a few bands are computers)

So, neither conclusion I nor II follows.

Hence, the correct option is (D).

49. The least possible Venn diagram is given below:

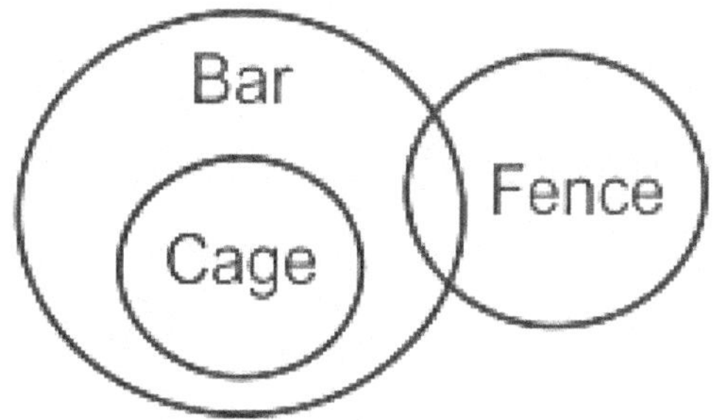

Conclusions:

I: All cages are fences → False (it is possible but not definite)

The possibility diagram is shown below:

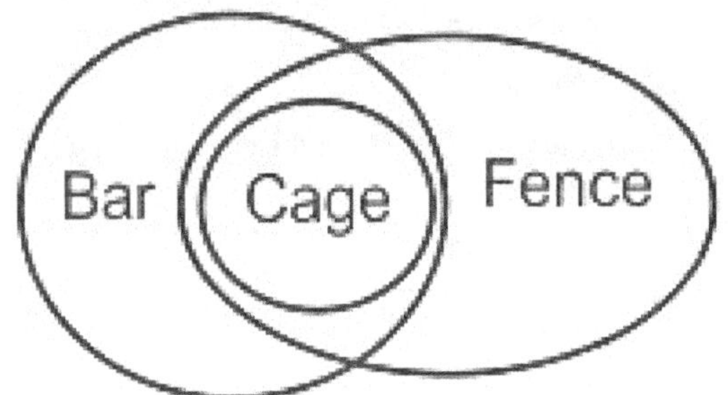

II: Some fences are cages → False (it is possible but not definite)

The possibility diagram is shown below:

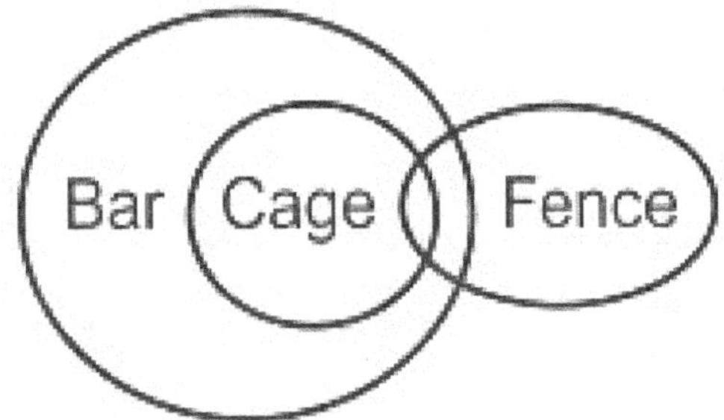

So, neither conclusion I nor II follows.

Hence, the correct option is (D).

50. The least possible Venn diagram is given below:

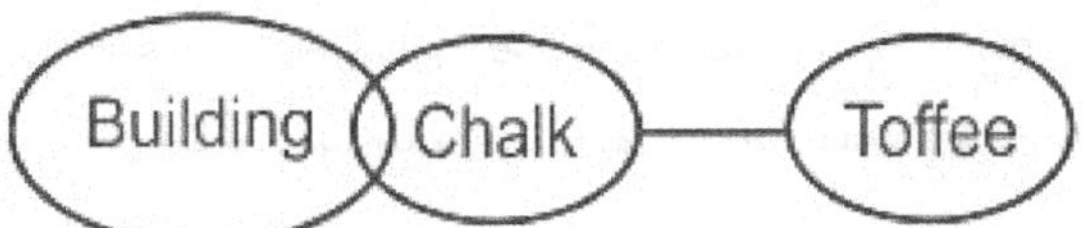

Conclusions:

I: Some buildings are toffee → False (it is possible but not definite)

The possibility diagram is shown below:

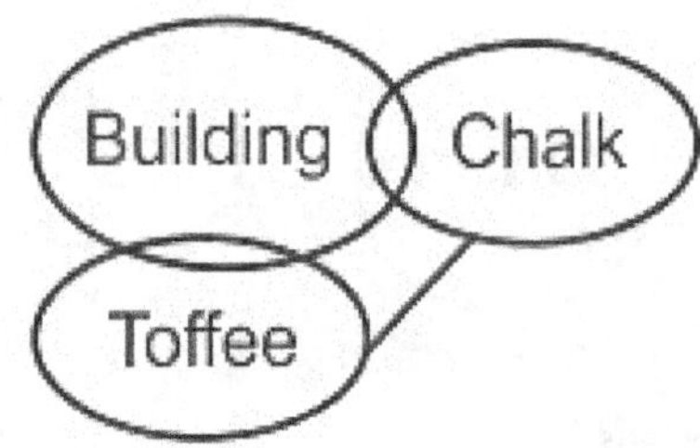

II: All buildings being chalks is a possibility → False (only few buildings are chalks)

So, neither conclusion I nor II follows.

Hence, the correct option is (D).

51. The least possible Venn diagram is given below:

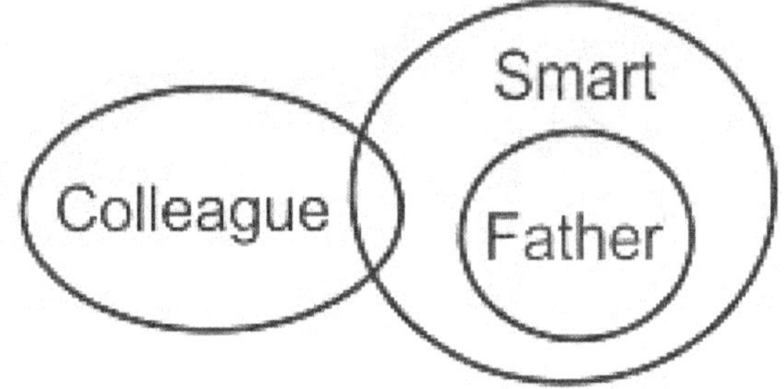

Conclusions:

I: Some colleagues are fathers → False (it is possible but not definite)

The possibility diagram is shown below:

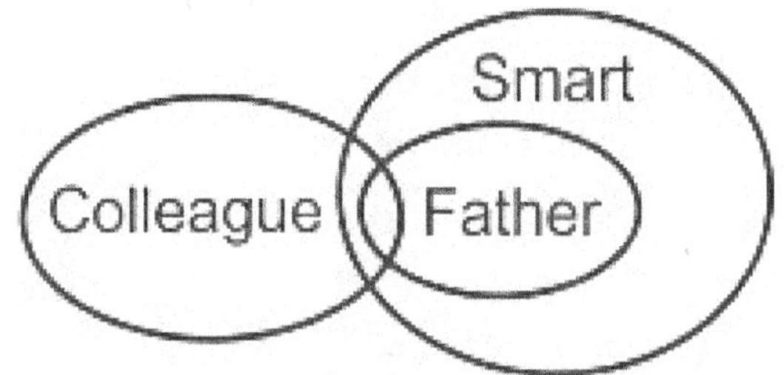

II: Some smart are colleagues → True (only few colleagues are smart)

So, only conclusion II follows.

Hence, the correct option is (B).

52. The least possible Venn diagram for the given statements is as follows

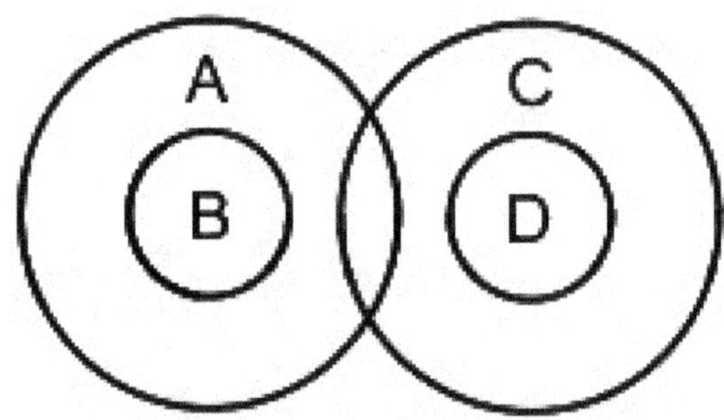

Conclusions:

(i) Some B can be C → False (only A are B, nothing else can be B)

(ii) Some D are A → False (Only C are D, nothing else can be D)

Therefore, both conclusion (i) and (ii) follow.

Hence, the correct option is (D).

53. The pattern is:

Alphabets	A	B	C	D	E	F	G	H	I	J	K	L	M
Positional value	1	2	3	4	5	6	7	8	9	10	11	12	13
Positional value	26	25	24	23	22	21	20	19	18	17	16	15	14
Alphabets	Z	Y	X	W	V	U	T	S	R	Q	P	O	N

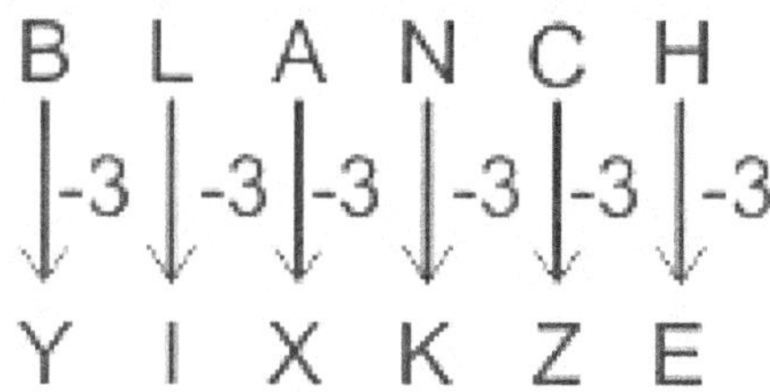

Similarly,

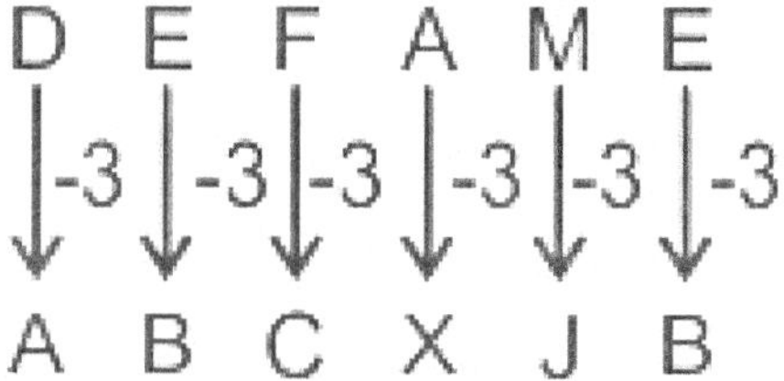

Thus, 'ABCXJB' is the correct answer.

Hence, the correct option is (B).

54. The pattern is:

Alphabets	A	B	C	D	E	F	G	H	I	J	K	L	M
Positional value	1	2	3	4	5	6	7	8	9	10	11	12	13
Positional value	26	25	24	23	22	21	20	19	18	17	16	15	14
Alphabets	Z	Y	X	W	V	U	T	S	R	Q	P	O	N

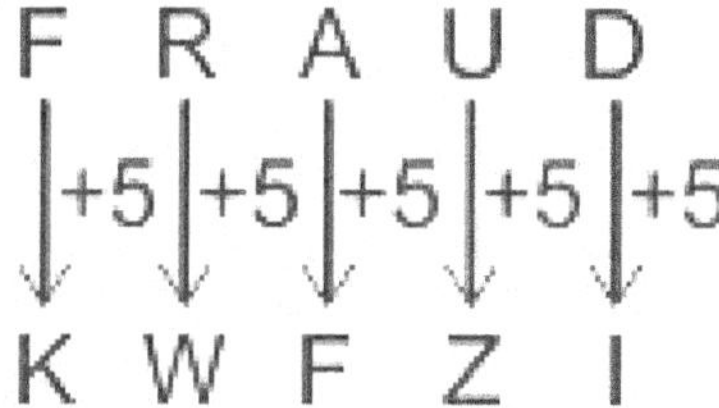

Similarly,

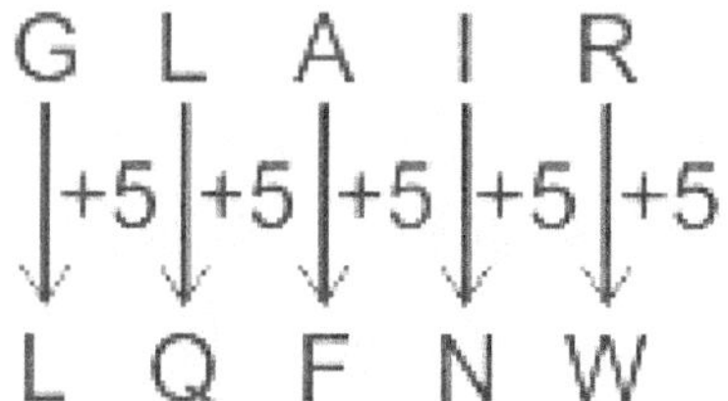

Therefore, 'LQFNW' is the correct answer.

Hence, the correct option is (B).

55. The relation between the given words is as follows,

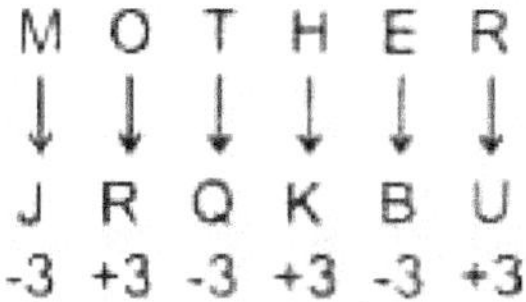

Similarly,

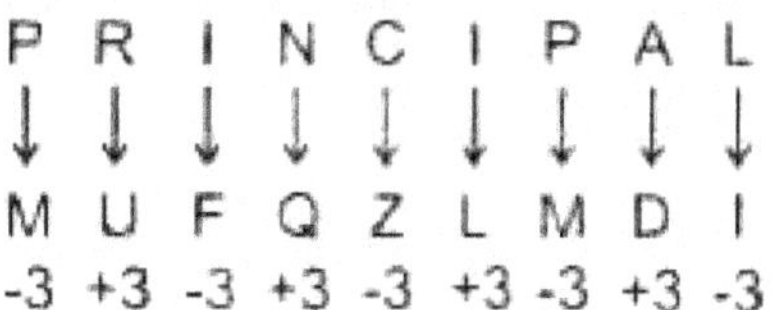

Thus code for PRINCIPAL is MUFQZLMDI.

Hence, the correct option is (C).

Ques (56-60): Given,

Facing direction - North

1. Ankit is sitting second from the right end of the row.

2. Five persons are sitting between Ankit and Abhi.

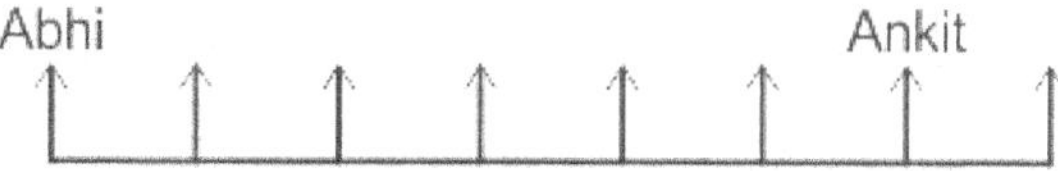

3. Pihu is sitting immediate right of Abhi.

4. Shweta is sitting third to the right of Pihu.

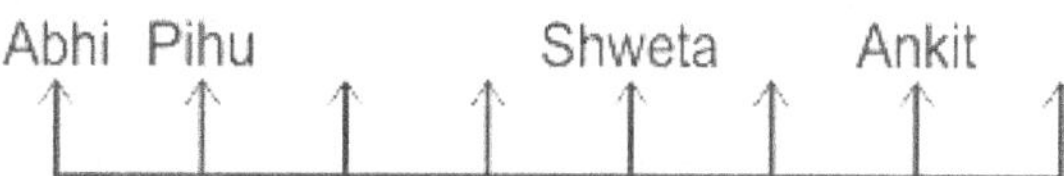

5. Seven persons are sitting to the left of Shweta.

6. Neha is sitting on one of the extreme ends but not sitting immediately right of Ankit.

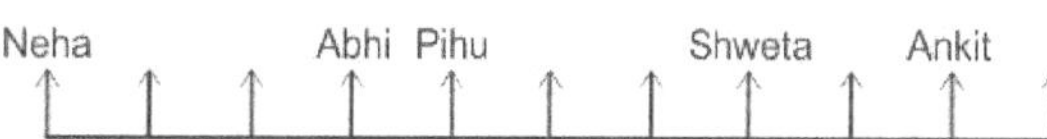

7. Sikha is sitting eighth to the right of Neha and immediately left of Ankit.

8. Anu is sitting second to the right of Sikha.

9. Four persons are sitting between Anu and Riya.

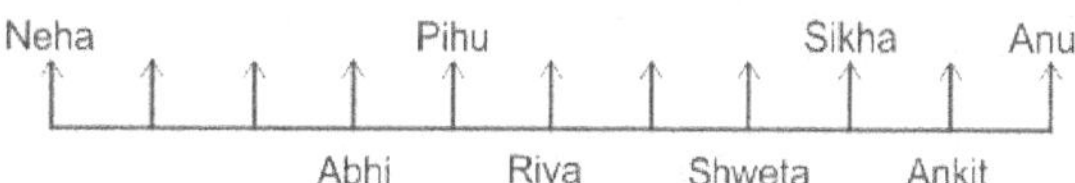

56. So, Shweta is fourth from the right end of the line.

Hence, the correct option is (C).

57. So, Pihu is sitting immediate left of Riya.

Hence, the correct option is (D).

58. So, Three persons are sitting between Pihu and Sikha.

Hence, the correct option is (C).

59. So, 11 persons are sitting in the row.

Hence, the correct option is (D).

60. So, Neha is sitting at the extreme left end of the row.

Hence, the correct option is (E).

61. Series given: H 8 & 5 T O 9 # V 6 P $ 7 W F * 1 N L 4 ? 3 / C Q U ! A 2 > J

H 8 & 5 T O 9 # V 6 P $ 7 W F * 1 N L 4 ? 3 / C Q U ! A 2 > J

Clearly, 2 such symbols are there.

Hence, the correct option is (C).

62. Series given: H 8 & 5 T O 9 # V 6 P $ 7 W F * 1 N L 4 ? 3 / C Q U ! A 2 > J

New series : H & 5 T O 9 # V P $ 7 W F * 1 N L ? 3 / C Q U ! A > J

The numbers between $ and U(second vowel from right end) are – 7,1 and 3.

Thus the required product is 21.

Hence, the correct option is (B).

63. Series given: H 8 & 5 T O 9 # V 6 P $ 7 W F * 1 N L 4 ? 3 / C Q U ! A 2 > J

New series : H 8 5 T O 9 V 6 P 7 W F 1 N L 4 3 C Q U A 2 J

The highest number in the series is 9, so the element fifth to the right of 9 when all the symbols are skipped is – 'W'.

Hence, the correct option is (A).

64. Series given: H 8 & 5 T O 9 # V 6 P $ 7 W F * 1 N L 4 ? 3 / C Q U ! A 2 > J

Logic: The second element is third to the right of first element and the third element is second to the left of first element.

All others except option (D) follows the above mentioned logic.

Hence, the correct option is (D).

65. Series given: H 8 & 5 T O 9 # V 6 P $ 7 W F * 1 N L 4 ? 3 / C Q U ! A 2 > J

Now,

H 8 & 5 T O 9 # V 6 P $ 7 W F * 1 N L 4 ? 3 / C Q U ! A 2 > J

From the above series we can get only one odd number (? 3 /) is immediately followed by a symbol but not immediately preceded by a letter.

Explicitly, only one such odd number is there.

Hence, the correct option is (B).

66. Unsold unit of company E $= 420 - 360 = 60$

Unsold unit of company D $= 500 - 320 = 180$

Unsold units of Company E and D together $= 180 + 60 = 240$

Sold units of company A $= 180$

Sold units of company B $= 300$

Sold units of company A and B together $= 180 + 300 = 480$

Required ratio $= 240 : 480$

$= 1 : 2$

Hence, the correct option is (A).

67. Unit produced by Company C $= 400$

Units sold by Company B $= 300$

$\therefore$ Required percentage $= \dfrac{(400 - 300)}{300} \times 100$

$= 33.33\%$

Hence, the correct option is (D).

68. Unsold unit of company A $= 120$

Unsold unit of company B $= 150$

Unsold unit of company C $= 50$

Unsold unit of company D $= 180$

Unsold unit of company E $= 60$

Average unit remain unsold $= \dfrac{(120 + 150 + 50 + 180 + 60)}{5}$

$= 112$

Hence, the correct option is (C).

69. Units produced by A = 300

So, units produced by company F $= 300 \times \dfrac{110}{100} = 330$

Units sold by company C = 350

So, units sold by company F $= 350 \times \dfrac{80}{100} = 280$

Unsold unit of company F = 330 - 280

$= 50$

Hence, the correct option is (B).

70. Total produced units = 300 + 450 + 400 + 500 + 420 = 2070

Total sold units = 180 + 300 + 350 + 320 + 360 = 1510

$\therefore$ Required difference = 2070 - 1510

$= 560$

Hence, the correct option is (B).

71. From the statement I, we can conclude the sum of money Rina had invested but nowhere it is mentioned the rate of interest Rina had invested her money. Therefore we can not reach theanswer by the statement alone.

From the statement II, Difference between CI and SI is Rs.12 at the end of 2 years. But as the principal is not given here, we can't deduce the rate of interest using statement II alone.

But, from the statement I, we concluded the sum of money and to this statement we can conclude the rate of interest.

Therefore, if we combine statement I and statement II then we can conclude that the rate of interest was 10% per annum and the sum of money was Rs. 1200 now we can calculate the amount Rina will receive al the end of 2 years

Therefore, the data in both the statements I and II together is necessary to answer the question

Hence, the correct option is (E).

72. In the question, the distance is given.

In the statement I, the ratio of speed is given.

From the statement I we can conclude that P's speed : Q's speed = 4 : 5 but we cannt find out speed of individual trains.

In statement II the average speed of both the trains is given so we cannot find out speed of individual trains.

If we combine statement I with statement II, then we can get as P's speed = 40 km per hr Q's speed = 50 km per hr

Therefore, the data in both the statements I and II is necessary to answer the question.

Hence, the correct option is (E).

73. Let the population of the city 4 years ago i.e. in the year $2014 = x$

Then, from the statement I, $1.4641 \times x = 219615$

$x = 150000$

From the statement II,

If it was increased by 10% each year then,

$$x \times \frac{110}{100} \times \frac{110}{100} \times \frac{110}{100} \times \frac{110}{100} = 219615$$

From here, we can get the value of $x = 150000$

therefore, Either Statement I or Statement II alone is sufficient to answer the question.

Hence, the correct option is (C).

74. From the statement I, we can conclude the ratio of the angle $a : b : c = 9 : 6 : 4$

We know that in a triangle the side opposite to the bigger angle is largest.

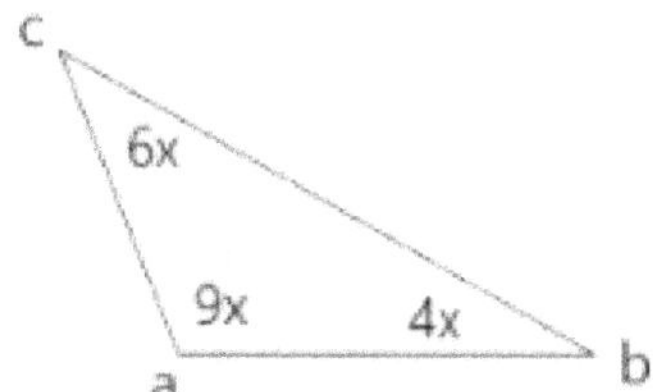

From here we can conclude that the side bc will be the largest.

From the statement II, only perimeter is given but, in the question, we need to find the largest side therefore, nothing can be concluded by this statement alone.

Therefore, the data in statements I alone is sufficient to answer the question, while the data in statement II alone is not sufficient to answer the question.

Hence, the correct option is (A).

75. Statement I:

Relative Speed $= \dfrac{D}{T}$

$$S_1 + S_2 = \frac{250+250}{25}$$

$$= \frac{500}{25} = 20 \ m/s$$

Statement II:

$$S = \frac{D}{T}$$

$$= \frac{250}{25} = 10 \ m/s$$

Statement II:

$$S = \frac{D}{T}$$

$$= \frac{250}{25} = 10 \ m/s$$

Statement III:

Distance from point X to point $Y = 360 \ km$

Statement II and III:

Speed $= 10 \ m/s$

or $10 \times \dfrac{18}{5} = 36 \ km/h$

$$S = \frac{D}{T}$$

$$36 = \frac{360}{T}$$

$T = 10$ hours.

Hence, the correct option is (B).

76. Given:

$45^2 - 100 - 25^2 = ?$

$\Rightarrow 2025 - 100 - 625 = ?$

$\Rightarrow 1300 = ?$

Hence, the correct option is (C).

77. Given,

$$\sqrt[3]{1728} + \sqrt[3]{1331} + \sqrt{x} + 12 = 49$$

$\Rightarrow 12 + 11 + \sqrt{x} = 37$

$\Rightarrow \sqrt{x} = 37 - 23$

$\Rightarrow \sqrt{x} = 14$

Squaring on both side,

$\Rightarrow x = 196$

Hence, the correct option is (C).

78. Given:

$120 \div x = 14 \times 6 - 43$

$\Rightarrow \dfrac{120}{x} = 84 - 64$

$\Rightarrow \dfrac{120}{x} = 20$

$\Rightarrow x = \dfrac{120}{20}$

$\Rightarrow x = 6$

Hence, the correct option is (B).

79. Given:

$\sqrt{(81 + ? + 95)} = 16$

$81 + x + 95 = 256$

$x = 256 - 176$

$x = 80$

Hence, the correct option is (D).

80. Given:

$\sqrt{1024} \times 11 + 8 \times x = 32 \times 16$

Follow BODMAS rule to solve this question, as per the order is given below,

$\Rightarrow 32 \times 11 + 8x = 512$

$\Rightarrow 32 \times 11 + 8x = 512$

$\Rightarrow 8x = 512 - 352$

$\Rightarrow x = \dfrac{160}{8}$

$\Rightarrow x = 20$

Hence, the correct option is (D).

81. Given:

$12^2 + 16^2 - ?^2 = 102 \times 3$

Follow BODMAS rule to solve this question, as per the order is given below,

$\Rightarrow 144 + 256 - ?^2 = 100 \times 3$

$\Rightarrow ?^2 = 400 - 300 = 100$

$\Rightarrow ? = \sqrt{100} = \sqrt{(10 \times 10)}$

$\Rightarrow ? = 10$

Hence, the correct option is (C).

82. Given:

$185\% \text{ of } 500 - 46\% \text{ of } 1650 = 4 \times?$

$\Rightarrow 185\% \text{ of } 500 - 46\% \text{ of } 1650 = 4 \times?$

$\Rightarrow (925 - 759) = 4 \times?$

$\Rightarrow 166 = 4 \times?$

$\Rightarrow ? = 41.5$

Hence, the correct option is (D).

83. Given expression:

$2\dfrac{5}{13}\% \text{ of } 5200 + 1\dfrac{1}{17}\% \text{ of } 5100 =?$

$\left(\dfrac{31}{1300}\right) \times 5200 + \left(\dfrac{18}{1700}\right) \times 5100 =?$

$? = 31 \times 4 + 18 \times 3$

$? = 124 + 54$

$= 178$

Hence, the correct option is (C).

84. According to the question,

Selling price of 12 pens = Cost price of 14 pens

$12 \times SP = 14 \times CP$

$\Rightarrow SP = \left(\dfrac{7}{6}\right) \times CP$

$Profit = \dfrac{(SP-CP)}{CP} \times 100\% = 16.67\%$

So, if the cost price is 100, the profit is 16.67

$Tax = 10\% = \left(\dfrac{10}{100}\right) \times 16.67 = 1.67$

So, net profit = 16.67 - 1.67 = 15

So, the shopkeeper is making a net profit of 15 when the cost price is 100.

$\Rightarrow$ Net profit percentage = 15%

Hence, the correct option is (D).

85. Given:

80% of the people casted their votes.

45% of the voters who casted votes are employed.

66.67% of employed voters are engineers.

Let the total number of voters be 100.

80% of the voters casted their votes

$= \left(\dfrac{80}{100}\right) \times 100 = 80$

80 people casted their votes

$= 45\% \text{ of } 80 = \left(\dfrac{45}{100} \times 80\right) = 36$

36 voters were employed.

Among employed voters 66.67% are engineers

$\Rightarrow$ 36 × 66.67% = 24

24% voters were the engineer

= Number of non – engineers among total voters = 36 – 24 = 12

$\therefore$ Required percentage = $\dfrac{12}{100}$ × 100 = 12%

Hence, the correct option is (A).

86. I. $x^2 - 13x + 30 = 0$

$\Rightarrow x^2 - 3x - 10x + 30 = 0$

$\Rightarrow (x - 3)(x - 10) = 0$

$\Rightarrow x = 3, 10$

II. $y^2 + 5y + 4 = 0$

$\Rightarrow y^2 + y + 4y + 4 = 0$

$\Rightarrow (y + 4)(y + 1) = 0$

$\Rightarrow y = -4, -1$

Value of x	Value of y	Relation
3	−4	x > y
3	−1	x > y
10	−4	x > y
10	−1	x > y

So, x > y

Hence, the correct option is (A).

87. 1. $x^2 + 17x + 72 = 0$

$\Rightarrow x^2 + 9x + 8x + 72 = 0$

$\Rightarrow (x + 8)(x + 9) = 0$

$\Rightarrow x = -8, -9$

II. $y^2 + 11y + 30 = 0$

$\Rightarrow y^2 + 5y + 6y + 30 = 0$

$\Rightarrow (y + 5)(y + 6) = 0$

$\Rightarrow y = -5, -6$

Value of x	Value of y	Relation
−8	−5	x < y
−8	−6	x < y
−9	−5	x < y
−9	−6	x < y

So x < y

Hence, the correct option is (B).

88. I. $2x^2 - 39x + 189 = 0$

$\Rightarrow 2x^2 - 18x - 21x + 189 = 0$

$\Rightarrow 2x(x - 9) - 21(x - 9) = 0$

$\Rightarrow (x - 9)(2x - 21) = 0$

$\Rightarrow x = 9, \dfrac{21}{2}$

II. $y^2 - 16y + 63 = 0$

$\Rightarrow y^2 - 7y - 9y + 63 = 0$

$\Rightarrow y(y - 7) - 9(y - 7) = 0$

$\Rightarrow (y - 7)(y - 9) = 0$

$\Rightarrow y = 7, 9$

Value of x	Value of y	Relation
9	7	x > y
9	9	x = y
$\frac{21}{2}$	7	x > y
$\dfrac{21}{2}$	9	x > y

$\therefore$ x ≥ y

Hence, the correct option is (C).

89. I. $x^2 - 27x + 180 = 0$

$\Rightarrow x^2 - 12x - 15x + 180 = 0$

$\Rightarrow (x - 12)(x - 15) = 0$

$\Rightarrow x = 12, 15$

II. $y^2 - 31y + 240 = 0$

$\Rightarrow y^2 - 15y - 16y + 240 = 0$

$\Rightarrow (y - 15)(y - 16) = 0$

$\Rightarrow y = 15, 16$

Value of x	Value of y	Relation
12	15	x < y
12	16	x < y
15	15	x = y
15	16	x < y

So, x ≤ y

Hence, the correct option is (D).

90. I. $5x^2 + 29x - 42 = 0$

$\Rightarrow 5x^2 + 35x - 6x - 42 = 0$

$\Rightarrow 5x(x + 7) - 6(x + 7) = 0$

$\Rightarrow (x + 7)(5x - 6) = 0$

$\Rightarrow x = -7, \dfrac{6}{5}$

II. $20y^2 - 9y - 18 = 0$

$\Rightarrow 20y^2 + 15y - 24y - 18 = 0$

$\Rightarrow (5y - 6)(4y + 3) = 0$

$\Rightarrow y = \dfrac{-3}{4}, \dfrac{6}{5}$

Comparison between x and y (via Tabulation):

Value of x	Value of y	Relation
-7	$\dfrac{-3}{4}$	x < y
-7	$\dfrac{6}{5}$	x < y
$\dfrac{6}{5}$	$\dfrac{-3}{4}$	x > y
$\dfrac{6}{5}$	$\dfrac{6}{5}$	x = y

So, relationship between x and y cannot be established.

Hence, the correct option is (E).

91. The series follows the following pattern:

68 + 3 = 71

71 - 6 = 65

65 + 9 = 74

74 - 12 = 62

62 + 15 = 77

Hence, the correct option is (E).

92. The series follows the following pattern:

$8^2 - 1 = 63$

$9^2 - 1 = 80$

$10^2 - 1 = 99$

$11^2 - 1 = 120$

$12^2 - 1 = 143$

$13^2 - 1 = 168$

Hence, the correct option is (E).

93. The series follows the following pattern:

12 + 3 = 15

15 + 9 = 24

24 + 15 = 39

39 + 21 = 60

60 + 27 = 87

Hence, the correct option is (D).

94. The series follows the following pattern:

7 × 1 + 1 = 8

8 × 2 + 1 = 17

17 × 3 + 1 = 52

52 × 4 + 1 = 209

209 × 5 + 1 = 1046

Hence, the correct option is (A).

95. The series follows the following pattern:

16 + 144 = 160

160 + 121 = 281

281 + 100 = 381

381 + 81 = 462

462 + 64 = 526

Hence, the correct option is (C).

96. Given:

Time taken to travel 50 km = 2.5 hours

Time taken to travel 200 km = 4 hours

Average speed $= \dfrac{\text{Total distance}}{\text{total time}} = \dfrac{250}{6.5}$

Average speed = 38.46 km/hr

∴ The average speed is 38.46 km/hr.

Hence, the correct option is (D).

97. Given:

Quantity of mixture = 20 litres

Quantity of alcohol in mixture = 15%

Let x litres of alcohol is added to mixture.

Quantity of alcohol in 20 litres = 15% of 20

$= 20 \times \dfrac{15}{100} = 3$ litres

As per question,

$\Rightarrow \dfrac{(3+x)}{(20+x)} = \dfrac{20}{100}$

$\Rightarrow 5(3 + x) = 20 + x$

$\Rightarrow 4x = 5$

$\Rightarrow x = 1.25$ litres

∴ 1.25 litres of alcohol is added in the mixture to make 20% alcohol in mixture.

Hence, the correct option is (C).

98. Given:

$(17.76)^2 + (20.99)^2 = (2)^7 + ?$

Calculation:

$(17.76)^2 + (20.99)^2 = (2)^7 + ?$

$\Rightarrow (18)^2 + (21)^2 = (2)^7 + ?$

$$\Rightarrow 324 + 441 = 128 + ?$$

$$\Rightarrow ? = 765 - 128$$

$$\Rightarrow ? = 637$$

$\therefore$ The value of $?$ is 637.

Hence, the correct option is (E).

99. Given:

$$\sqrt{676} \times 12 - 864 \div 36 = ? + 61$$

Follow the BODMAS rule to solve this question, as per the order given below,

$$\Rightarrow 26 \times 12 - 24 = ? + 61$$

$$\Rightarrow 312 - 24 = ? + 61$$

$$\Rightarrow 312 - 85 = ?$$

$$\Rightarrow ? = 227$$

Hence, the correct option is (D).

100. Given:

Average of 40 numbers = 71

Formula:

Average = Sum of all observations/Total number of all observations

Calculation:

Sum of 40 numbers = 40 × 71 = 2840

New sum of 40 numbers = 2840 – 100 + 140 = 2880

New average of 40 numbers = $\dfrac{2880}{40}$ = 72

$\therefore$ The average increased = 72 – 71 = 1

Hence, the correct option is (D).

English Language

Q.1 Select the incorrectly spelt word.

A. Deliquescence   **B.** Pertinacious

C. Pisiculture   **D.** Renaissance

E. Renegade

Q.2 Select the incorrectly spelt word.

A. Millennium   **B.** Millionaire

C. Millenerian   **D.** Manageable

E. None of these

Q.3 Four words are given, out of which only one word is spelt correctly?

A. Dysorientation   **B.** Desorientation

C. Disorientation   **D.** Disorientetion

E. None of the above

Ques (4-8):Direction: Rearrange the following six sentences (A), (B), (C), (D), (E) and (F) in the proper sequence to form a meaningful paragraph and then answer the question given beside.

(A) Last June, ISRO had come close to NASA's record by launching 20 satellites in one mission.

(B) The Indian Space Research Organisation boosted its reputation further when it successfully launched a record 104 satellites in one mission from Sriharikota a few days ago.

(C) Of the 101 foreign satellites launched, 96 were from the U.S. and one each from the other five countries.

(D) An earth observation Cartosat-2 series satellite and two other nano satellites were the only Indian satellites launched: the remaining were from the United States, Israel, the UAE, the Netherlands, Kazakhstan and Switzerland.

(E) The launch is particularly significant as ISRO now cements its position as a key player in the lucrative commercial space launch market by providing a cheaper yet highly reliable alternative.

(F) But ISRO views the launch not as a mission to set a world record but as an opportunity to make full use of the capacity of the launch vehicle.

Q.4 Which of the following would be the first sentence after rearrangement?

A. (E)   **B.** (A)   **C.** (C)   **D.** (B)

E. (D)

Q.5 Which of the following would be the second sentence after rearrangement?

A. (D)   **B.** (E)   **C.** (A)   **D.** (F)

E. (B)

Q.6 Which of the following would be the third sentence after rearrangement?

A. (D)   **B.** (C)   **C.** (A)   **D.** (F)

E. (E)

Q.7 Which of the following would be the fourth sentence after rearrangement?

A. (D)   **B.** (F)   **C.** (E)   **D.** (A)

E. (C)

Q.8 Which of the following would be the last but one sentence after rearrangement?

A. (A)   **B.** (C)   **C.** (D)   **D.** (E)

E. (F)

Ques (9-13):Directions: The sentence given below has blank, the blank indicating that something has been omitted. Choose the word that would fit the blank appropriately.

Q.9 South Africa finds itself in the middle of a _______ third-wave of the COVID with people losing their lives faster than any wave before.

A. mesmerizing   **B.** tantalizing

C. crippling   **D.** stabilizing

E. sloping

Q.10 The Louvre pyramid is one of the most ______ landmarks in France.

A. dismal   **B.** shallow

C. iconic   **D.** crude

E. contempt

Q.11 China's computing machine is 20000 times faster than its international counterparts and may ______ the processing power of supercomputers.

A. hinder   **B.** boost   **C.** decrease   **D.** diminish

E. destroy

Q.12 The ______ nature of the employee was unacceptable to the boss because the work kept piling up with time.

A. genius   **B.** diligent

C. indolent   **D.** indefatigable

E. None of these

Q.13 I despise ______ people as they have a tendency to blow their own trumpet.

A. garrulous   **B.** reticent

C. generous   **D.** pragmatic

E. None of these

Q.14 Direction: Choose the word which best expresses nearly the same meaning of the given word.

OCCULT

A. Religious   **B.** Unnatural

C. Supernatural   **D.** Strong

E. None of these

Q.15 Direction: Choose the word which best expresses the opposite meaning of the word.

COUNTERFEIT

A. Destructive **B.** Genuine
C. Affirm **D.** Harmonize
E. None of these

Ques (16-20):Direction: Read the following sentence and determine whether there is any error in it. The error, if any, will be in one part of the sentence. If the sentence is error-free, then select 'No Error' as your answer.

Q.16 Despite of the rain, the parade went(A)/on uninterrupted which was followed by(B)/ the President's address and other formal (C)/ festivities of the Republic Day. (D)

[SBI Clerk, 2021]

A. (A) **B.** (B) **C.** (C) **D.** (D)
E. No Error

Q.17 "Lisa is more stronger than(A)/ her opponent", said the coach(B)/ during the press briefing(C)/ ahead of the Asian Games.(D)

[SBI Clerk, 2021]

A. (A) **B.** (B) **C.** (C) **D.** (D)
E. No Error

Q.18 I lost the bag in which I had my all documents, certificates, and academic records. /(A) I have a job interview tomorrow where I need all these things, /(B) and I have no clue what will happen. I lodged /(C) a police complaint, but within this short time, nothing is possible. /(D)

[SBI Clerk, 2021]

A. (A) **B.** (B) **C.** (C) **D.** (D)
E. No error

Q.19 The fabric is as softer as cotton, but it is /(A) not pure cotton. That's why she got so many /(B) allergic reactions on her face after using that mask /(C) and is now under proper medication and care. /(D)

[SBI Clerk, 2021]

A. (A) **B.** (B) **C.** (C) **D.** (D)
E. No error

Q.20 Kiva has loaned out (A) nearly a quarter of (B) a billion dollars to (C) small and medium businesses for 2005. (D)

[SBI Clerk, 2021]

A. (A) **B.** (B) **C.** (C) **D.** (D)
E. No error

Ques (21-22):Direction: In the following sentence, a part of the sentence is underlined. Below are given alternatives to the underlined part, which may improve the sentence. Choose the correct alternative. In case no improvement is needed, choose the alternative that indicates 'No improvement'.

Q.21 Covid treatment in this hospital is <u>very low expensive that</u> they had to sell off their land to pay for it.

[IBPS Clerk, 2021]

A. quite expensive and **B.** too expensive for
C. so expensive but **D.** more expensive
E. No improvement

Q.22 The entire town was <u>set on the ears</u> when it was announced that a giant megastore would be closing itself.

[IBPS Clerk, 2021]

A. Set by the eyes **B.** Set by the ears
C. Set at the ears **D.** Set on the eyes
E. No Improvement

Ques (23-24):Direction: A sentence/part of the sentence is emboldened. Five alternatives are given to the embolden part which will improve the sentence. Choose the correct alternative and choose the option corresponding to it. In case no improvement is needed, click the option corresponding to 'No improvement required'.

Q.23 He slapped the team into action and they headed for the town at a **more leisure pace**.

[IBPS PO, 2021]

A. many leisurely
B. many leisured
C. more leisure paced
D. more leisurely pace
E. No improvement required

Q.24 Although both the United States and China are formidable world powers, **India should side with the later.**

[IBPS PO, 2021]

A. India should side along the later
B. India should side with the latter
C. India should side along the latter
D. India should be siding with the later
E. No Improvement required

Q.25 Direction: In the following sentence, a part is underlined. Below are given alternatives to the underlined part, which may improve the sentence. Choose the correct alternative. In case no improvement is needed, choose the alternative that indicates 'No improvement'.

The new captain's poker face made them <u>unable for gauge his mood</u>.

A. unable in gauge his mood

B. unable to assess his mood

C. unable to gauge his mood

A. Only A **B.** Only C
C. Only B **D.** Both B and C
E. No improvement

Ques (26-30):Direction: Read the passage and answer the following questions.

The economic and labour crisis created by the COVID-19 pandemic could increase global unemployment by almost 25 million, according to a new assessment by the International Labour Organization (ILO). However, if we see an internationally coordinated policy response, as happened in the global financial crisis of 2008/9, then the impact on global unemployment could be ______ lower.

The preliminary assessment note, COVID-19 and the world of work: Impacts and responses, calls for urgent, large-scale and coordinated measures across three pillars: protecting workers in the workplace, stimulating the economy and employment, and supporting jobs and incomes. These measures include extending social protection, supporting employment retention (i.e. short-time work, paid leave, other subsidies), and financial and tax relief, including for micro, small and medium-sized enterprises. In addition, the note proposes fiscal and monetary policy measures, and lending and financial support for specific economic sectors.

Based on different scenarios for the impact of COVID-19 on global GDP growth, the ILO estimates indicate a rise in global unemployment of between 5.3 million ("low" scenario) and 24.7 million ("high" scenario) from a base level of 188 million in 2019. By comparison, the 2008-9 global financial crisis increased global unemployment by 22 million. Underemployment is also expected to increase on a large scale, as the economic consequences of the virus outbreak translate into reductions in working hours and wages. Self-employment in developing countries, which often serves to cushion the impact of changes, may not do so this time because of restrictions on the movement of people (e.g. service providers) and goods.

Fall in employment also means large income losses for workers. The study estimates these as being between USD 860 billion and USD 3.4 trillion by the end of 2020. This will translate into falls in the consumption of goods and services, in turn affecting the prospects for businesses and economies. Working poverty is expected to increase significantly too, as "the strain on incomes resulting from the decline in economic activity will devastate workers close to or below the poverty line". The ILO estimates that between 8.8 and 35 million additional people will be in working poverty worldwide, compared to the original estimate for 2020 (which projected a decline of 14 million worldwide).

Q.26 Which options best fits the given blank in the passage "However, if we see an internationally coordinated policy response, as happened in the global financial crisis of 2008/9, then the impact on global unemployment could be _______ lower."

[IBPS Clerk, 2021]

A. significantly
B. obsessed
C. aggravated
D. mitigating
E. None of these

Q.27 What could be the most similar in meaning to the word "**restrictions**"?

[IBPS Clerk, 2021]

A. Liberation
B. Limitation
C. Freedom
D. Permission
E. All of the above

Q.28 What does the fall in employment mean?

[IBPS Clerk, 2021]

A. Large income losses for workers
B. Rise in inflation
C. No pay for employees
D. Decline in economy
E. None of these

Q.29 According to a new assessment by the International Labour Organization (ILO), unemployment could globally increase by:

[IBPS Clerk, 2021]

A. 20 million
B. 22 million
C. 23 million
D. 24 million
E. 25 million

Q.30 The ILO estimates indicate a rise in global unemployment of between 5.3 million and 24.7 million from a base level of 188 million in which year?

[IBPS Clerk, 2021]

A. 2020
B. 2021
C. 2019
D. 2022
E. None of these

Reasoning Ability

Ques (31-34):Directions: In the following question assuming the given statement to be true, find which of the conclusion(s) among given conclusions is/are definitely true and then give your answers accordingly.

Q.31 Statement: $B < S \leq Q < Y = X > C \geq J$
Conclusion:
I. $S < Y$
II. $X > B$
A. Only I is true
B. Either I or II is true
C. Only II is true
D. Both I and II are true
E. None of these

Q.32 Statements: $A < C = D \leq E; B = A > F$
Conclusions:
I. $D > F$
II. $B > E$
A. Only II is true
B. Only I is true
C. Both are true
D. Neither I nor II is true
E. Either I or II is true

Q.33 Statement: $D = X \geq C > S = F; D > Y \geq H \geq G$
Conclusion:
I. $G \leq X$
II. $D > F$
A. Only conclusion I follows
B. Both conclusion I or II follows
C. Only conclusion II follows
D. Either I or II follows
E. Neither conclusions I nor II follows

Q.34 Statements: $G \geq M = P > C; Q < R = B < C$

Conclusions:

I. M > R

II. G ≥ B

A. Only I follows

B. Only II follows

C. Both follows

D. Either I or II follows

E. None follows

Q.35 Directions: In the following question assuming the given statements to be true, find which of the conclusion among given conclusions is /are definitely true and then give your answers accordingly.

Statements:

M < N < U; R = T; U ≤ R ≥ V ≥ E

Conclusions:

I. T > N

II. R ≥ E

III. M < T

IV. T ≥ U

A. All are true

B. None is true

C. Only II is true

D. Only I and either II or IV are true

E. Only I and II are true

Q.36 In a row of students, Ramesh is ninth from the left and Suman is sixth from the right. When Ramesh and Suman interchange their places, Ramesh becomes fifteenth from the left. Tell what will be the position of Suman from the right after the interchange?

A. 6th   B. 13th   C. 15th   D. 12th

E. 14th

Q.37 In a class of 60 students in which the number of girls is twice the number of boys, Kamal's rank is 17th from the top. If there are 9 girls ahead of Kamal then how many boys are behind him in the rank?

A. 3   B. 7   C. 12   D. 23

E. 20

Ques (38-42):Direction: Study the following information carefully and answer the question that follows:

Eight persons Fiona, Liz, Cody, Zack, Ashley, Betty, Derek and Patrick are sitting on a circular table facing away from centre but not necessarily in the same order.

Betty is sitting third to the left of Cody. Patrick is sitting second to the right of Ashley. Derek is sitting second to the left of Cody. Zack is not a neighbour of Ashley or Patrick. Fiona does not sit opposite to Derek. Ashley is sitting opposite to Betty.

Q.38 Which of the following pair is the immediate neighbour of Liz?

A. Patrick and Betty   B. Ashley and Patrick

C. Derek and Zack   D. Ashley and Cody

E. Betty and Zack

Q.39 Which of the following statements is/are definitely true?

I. Derek sits opposite to Ashley.

II. Betty sits second to the right of Zack.

III. Fiona sits opposite to Cody.

A. Only statement I is true

B. Only statement II is true

C. Only statement III is true

D. None is true

E. All are true

Q.40 How many persons are sitting between Liz and Zack when counted from right of Liz?

A. 2   B. 1   C. 3   D. 4

E. 5

Q.41 If Betty exchanges her position with Patrick then who is sitting third to the left of Betty?

A. Ashley   B. Zack   C. Derek   D. Cody

E. Liz

Q.42 Who sits opposite to Cody?

A. Derek   B. Fiona   C. Liz   D. Zack

E. Patrick

Ques (43-47):Directions: Read the instructions carefully and answer the question below.

Nine people – L, N, O, P, Q, R, S, T and W, are sitting in a row. Five of them are facing north while the remaining four are facing south. No three consecutive people are facing the same direction.

N is sitting fifth to the right of W and N is not facing the same direction as W. Two people are sitting to the left of W and both of them are facing north. P is sitting sixth to the left of T who is an immediate neighbour of N. Q is sitting fourth to the left of S who is facing the same direction as P. S is not sitting next to P. O is sitting fourth to the left of R and they are facing opposite directions. O is an immediate neighbour of T. People sitting at the extreme ends are facing opposite directions.

Q.43 Who is sitting second to the right of W?

A. O   B. S   C. L   D. R

E. Q

Q.44 Who is sitting third to the left of L?

A. S   B. P   C. Q   D. N

E. T

Q.45 Who are the immediate neighbours of R?

A. LS   B. ON   C. PL   D. PW

E. TO

Q.46 Who are the immediate neighbours of N?

A. QT   B. OS   C. LW   D. RP

E. SW

Q.47 Who is sitting third to the right of L?

A. N   B. T   C. R   D. W

E. P

Ques (48-49):Directions: In the question below are given some statements followed by two conclusions numbered I and

II. You have to take the given statements to be true even if they seem to be at variance with commonly known facts. Read all the conclusions and then decide which of the given conclusions logically follows from the given statements disregarding commonly known facts.

Q.48 Statements:

Some C are D.

No C is a E.

All E are F.

Conclusions:

I. No F is a C.

II. At least some D are F.

A. Neither I nor II follows

B. Only I follows

C. Only II follows

D. Either I or II follows

E. Both I and II follow

Q.49 Statement:

No Bad are Good.

All Good are Nice.

Only a few Nice are Sagar.

Conclusions:

I. All Sagar can be Good.

II. Some Nice are not Bad.

A. Only conclusion I follow

B. Only conclusion II follows

C. Either conclusion I or conclusion II follows

D. Neither conclusion I nor conclusion II follows

E. Both conclusion I and conclusion II follows

Ques (50-52):Direction: In the question below are given two statements followed by two conclusions numbered I and II .You have to take the given statements to be true even if they seem to be at variance with commonly known facts. Read all the conclusions and then decide which of the given conclusions logically follows from the given statements disregarding commonly known facts.

Q.50 Statements:

Only a few animal are cat

Some animal are dog

Conclusions:

I. All Cat are animal

II. Some cat are Dog

[SBI Clerk, 2021]

A. Only II follow

B. Both I and II follow

C. Either I or II follow

D. Only I follow

E. Neither I nor II follow

Q.51 Statement:

Only a few Sea are River

All River are Water bodies

Conclusion:

I. Some Sea are Water bodies

II. All sea are River

[SBI Clerk, 2021]

A. Both I and II follows

B. Neither I and II follows

C. Either I or II follows

D. Only I follow

E. Only II follows

Q.52 Statements:

All Desk are Jungle.

All Jungle are Mountain.

Conclusions:

I. No Jungle is Mountain.

II. Some Mountain are Desk.

[SBI Clerk, 2021]

A. Both I and II follow

B. Only I follows

C. Only II follows

D. Either I or II follow

E. None of these

Q.53 In the word 'LAVISLY', replace each vowel with the next letter in the alphabetical series and each consonant with the previous letter in the Alphabetical Series. How many letters occur more than once in this newly formed word?

[IBPS PO, 2021]

A. One   **B.** Two   **C.** Three   **D.** Four

E. Zero

Q.54 How many such pairs of letters are there in the word 'ENTHUSIASM', each of which has as many letters between them in the word (both forward and backward direction) as they have between them in the English alphabetical series?

[SBI Clerk, 2021]

A. One   **B.** Two

C. Three   **D.** Four

E. More than Four

Ques (55-59):Direction: Study the following information carefully to answer the given question.

2 # C D 6 % F I M K H 8 © @ T U V 4 € 2 7 8 $ H O K W 5 Y 4 ¥ Y A P @

Q.55 Which of the following is the sixth to the left of the twenty-fourth element from the left end of the above arrangement?

[SBI Clerk, 2021]

A. 4   **B.** V

C. @   **D.** H

E. None of these

Q.56 If all the even numbers are dropped from the given series, then which of the following element will be 10th from the right end?

[SBI Clerk, 2021]

A. # **B.** O
C. Y **D.** 7
E. None of these

Q.57 How many such vowels are there in the above arrangement each of which is immediately followed by a consonant but not immediately preceded by a number?

[SBI Clerk, 2021]

A. One **B.** Two
C. Three **D.** More than three
E. None

Q.58 Which of the following is the ninth to the right of the twenty third element from the right end of the above arrangement?

[SBI Clerk, 2021]

A. 8 **B.** @
C. © **D.** 4
E. None of these

Q.59 Four of the following five are alike in a certain way based on their positions in the above arrangement and so form a group. Which is the one that does not belong to that group?

[SBI Clerk, 2021]

A. C6F **B.** H©T **C.** 7\$O **D.** V€7
E. 4YA

Ques (60-62):Direction: Study the following information and answer the given questions.

Eight members of a family are living in a house, in which two are married couples. N is the father of D. E is married to N. G and D are siblings. C is married to G. N has no son. K is the father of E. Q is the only son of C. A is the brother-in-law of N.

Q.60 Who among the following is the son-in-law of N?

[IBPS PO, 2021]

A. G **B.** K
C. C **D.** Q
E. None of these

Q.61 How K is related to D?

[IBPS PO, 2021]

A. Father **B.** Uncle
C. Grand Mother **D.** Grand Father
E. None of these

Q.62 Which of the following statement is true?

[IBPS PO, 2021]

A. K is the mother of A
B. D and C are Sibling
C. Q is the son of A
D. N is the husband of E
E. None of these

Q.63 In a code language, 'SERVICE' is written as 'RESVECI'. How will 'NAUGHTY' be written as in that language?

[SSC Selection Post Phase IX, 2019]

A. UANGTYH **B.** GUANYTH

C. UANGYTH **D.** UNAGYHT
E. NNAGYHG

Q.64 If ACNE can be coded as $3 - 7 - 29 - 11$, then BOIL will be coded as:

[Territorial Army Officer, 2019]

A. $5 - 29 - 19 - 17$ **B.** $5 - 29 - 19 - 25$
C. $2 - 31 - 21 - 25$ **D.** $5 - 31 - 19 - 25$
E. $5 - 31 - 19 - 95$

Q.65 In a code language, 'SURGE' is written as 'GITWU'. How will 'LIGHT' be written as in that language?
A. VJIKN **B.** UJIMN **C.** VKIJM **D.** VJILM
E. MJILV

Quantitative Aptitude

Ques (66-70):Direction: What should come in place of question mark '?' in the following number series?

Q.66 $10212, 10631, 11482, 11925, 12824, ?$
A. 16195 **B.** 13178 **C.** 18822 **D.** 20002
E. 14555

Q.67 $16, 87, 103, 135, 151, 183, ?$
A. 119 **B.** 238 **C.** 231 **D.** 115
E. 230

Q.68 $12, 12, 18, 36, 90, ?$
A. 270 **B.** 280 **C.** 250 **D.** 235
E. 275

Q.69 $163, 150, 134, 112, 81, ?$

[IBPS Clerk, 2021]

A. 58 **B.** 42 **C.** 38 **D.** 30
E. 26

Q.70 $3, 4, 10, 33, 136, ?, 4116$

[IBPS Clerk, 2021]

A. 580 **B.** 685 **C.** 680 **D.** 612
E. 548

Ques (71-75):Direction: In the given question, two equations numbered I and II are given. Solve both the equations and mark the appropriate answer.

Q.71 I. $x^2 - 50x + 225 = 0$
II. $y^2 + 32y - 105 = 0$
A. x > y
B. y > x
C. x ≥ y
D. y ≥ x
E. x = 0 or relationship between x and y can't be established

Q.72 I. $24x^2 + 38x + 15 = 0$
II. $54y^2 + 123y + 65 = 0$
A. x > y
B. y > x

C. $x \geq y$

D. $y \geq x$

E. $x = y$ or relationship between x and y can not be established

Q.73 I. $2x^2 - 19x + 45 = 0$

II. $3y^2 - 17y + 20 = 0$

A. $x > y$

B. $y > x$

C. $x \geq y$

D. $y \geq x$

E. $x = y$ or relationship between x and y can not be established

Q.74 I. $x^2 + 13x - 140 = 0$

II. $y^2 - 13y - 140 = 0$

A. $x > y$

B. $y > x$

C. $x \geq y$

D. $y \geq x$

E. $x = y$ or relationship between x and y cannot be established

Q.75 I. $2x^2 + 23x + 56 = 0$

II. $12y^2 + 41y + 35 = 0$

A. $x > y$

B. $y > x$

C. $x \geq y$

D. $y \geq x$

E. $x = y$ or relationship between x and y can not be established

Q.76 A, B and C invested respectively Rs. 5000, Rs. 7000 and Rs. 6000 in a business. If at the end of two years, they got a profit of Rs. 10,800. The share of B in this total profit is:

A. Rs. 4500   **B.** Rs. 4200   **C.** Rs. 1800   **D.** Rs. 1500

E. Rs. 3600

Q.77 A dishonest shopkeeper professes to sell his goods at the cost price but use faulty measure. His $1kg$ weight measures $950gms$ only. Find his gain percent.

A. $7\frac{3}{19}\%$ **B.** $5\frac{7}{19}\%$ **C.** $5\frac{5}{19}\%$ **D.** $4\frac{5}{19}\%$

E. $3\frac{2}{19}\%$

Q.78 The average of 26 articles was found to be 40. On detecting, it was found that two items were wrongly taken as 20 and 18 instead of 40 and 24. Find the correct average.

A. 39   **B.** 40

C. 42   **D.** 41

E. None of these

Q.79 Sanju, Suraj and Sanjay can complete a work in 12 days, 16 days and 24 days respectively. In how many days will the three of them to do the same work together?

[IBPS Clerk, 2021]

A. $\frac{16}{3}$ days   **B.** $\frac{58}{9}$ days

C. 6 days   **D.** 8 days

E. None of these

Q.80 Two different type of cleaning liquid of Rs. 80 per litre and other is at certain price are mixed in the ratio of $\frac{6}{4}$. If mixture is formed is sold at Rs. 90 per kg then, find the price of a mixture when two liquids are mixed in same ratio.

A. Rs. 85.5   **B.** Rs. 91.2   **C.** Rs. 92.5   **D.** Rs. 95.5

E. Rs. 96

Q.81 Three taps A, B and C can fill a tank in 12,15 and 20 hours respectively. If A is open all the time and B and C are open for one hour each alternately, the tank will be full in:

A. 6 hours   **B.** $6\frac{2}{3}$ hours

C. 7 hours   **D.** $7\frac{1}{2}$ hours

E. $7\frac{3}{2}$ hours

Ques (82-86):Direction: Study the following line graph which gives the number of students who joined and left the school in the beginning of year for six years, from 1996 to 2001.

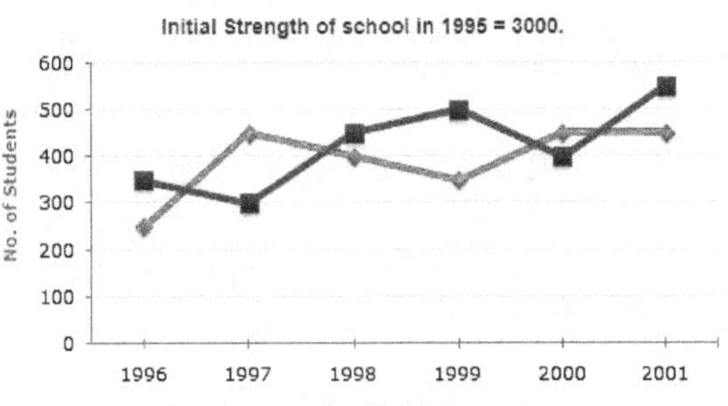

Q.82 The number of students studying in the school during 1999 was?

A. 2950   **B.** 3000   **C.** 3100   **D.** 3150

E. 3200

Q.83 For which year, the percentage rise/fall in the number of students who left the school compared to the previous year is maximum?

A. 1997   **B.** 1998   **C.** 1999   **D.** 2000

E. 2001

Q.84 The strength of the school increased/decreased from 1997 to 1998 by approximately what percent?

A. 1.2%   **B.** 1.7%   **C.** 1%   **D.** 2.1%

E. 2.5%

Q.85 The number of students studying in the school in 1998 was what percent of the number of students studying in the school in 2001?

A. 92.13%   **B.** 93.75%   **C.** 96.88%   **D.** 97.25%

E. 95.44%

Q.86 The ratio of the least number of students who joined the school to the maximum number of students who left the school in any of the years during the given period is?

A. 7:9 **B.** 4:5 **C.** 3:4 **D.** 2:3
E. 8:9

Ques (87-89):Direction: Given below are two quantities named A and B. Based on the given information, you have to determine the relationship between the two quantities. You should use the given data and your knowledge of Mathematics to choose between the possible answers.

Q.87 Quantity A: In a 63 liters mixture of alcohol and water, the ratio of alcohol to water is 5 : 4. In order to make the ratio of alcohol to water 3 : 2, some quantity of alcohol is to be added to the mixture. The quantity of alcohol present in the new mixture is?

Quantity B: 43 Liters

A. Quantity A > Quantity B
B. Quantity A < Quantity B
C. Quantity A ≥ Quantity B
D. Quantity A ≤ Quantity B
E. Quantity A = Quantity B or No relation

Q.88 Quantity A: A man sitting in a car noticed that a bus is 200 meters ahead of him, after 63 seconds he noticed that the bus is 150 meters behind him. If the speed of the car is 78 km/h then find the speed of the bus.

Quantity B: 60 km/h

A. Quantity A > Quantity B
B. Quantity A < Quantity B
C. Quantity A ≥ Quantity B
D. Quantity A ≤ Quantity B
E. Quantity A = Quantity B or No relation

Q.89 Quantity A: The profit made by selling an article for Rs. 19972 is equal to the amount of loss incurred on selling the same article at Rs. 17228. What will be the profit percentage if it is sold for Rs. 20088.

Quantity B: 10%

A. Quantity A > Quantity B
B. Quantity A < Quantity B
C. Quantity A ≥ Quantity B
D. Quantity A ≤ Quantity B
E. Quantity A = Quantity B or No relation

Q.90 The sum of the radius and height of a cylinder is $19m$. The total surface area of the cylinder is $1672m^2$. What is the volume of the cylinder?

[IBPS Clerk, 2021]

A. $3080m^3$ **B.** $2940m^3$
C. $3420m^3$ **D.** $2860m^3$
E. None of these

Ques (91-93):Direction: What will come in the place of the question mark '?' in the following question?

Q.91 $? = 40\%$ of $320 + 4^3 \div 16 \times 108 \div 8$

[SBI Clerk, 2021]

A. 176 **B.** 172 **C.** 168 **D.** 166
E. 182

Q.92 35% of $180 + 18^2 = (27)^{\frac{5}{3}} + ?^2$

[SBI Clerk, 2021]

A. 18 **B.** 15 **C.** 12 **D.** 13
E. 14

Q.93 $38 + 41 \times (441 \div 21) - 17^2 = ?$

[SBI Clerk, 2021]

A. 605 **B.** 206
C. 610 **D.** 508
E. None of these

Ques (94-100):Directions: What will come in the place of the question mark (?) in the following question?

Q.94 $(25^2 - 106) \div 3 - 13^2 + 35 = ?$

[SBI Clerk, 2021]

A. 39 **B.** 41
C. 43 **D.** 35
E. None of these

Q.95 6.67% of $225 + 6.25\%$ of $1120 = (?)^3 + 3$

A. $(-76)^{\frac{1}{2}}$ **B.** $(76)^{\frac{1}{2}}$
C. $(-76)^{\frac{1}{3}}$ **D.** $(76)^{\frac{1}{3}}$
E. None of these

Q.96 (999 + 99 + 9) + 5.55% of 90 = ?
A. 1202 **B.** 1022
C. 1122 **D.** 1112
E. None of these

Q.97 $32 + 65 - 16\frac{2}{3}\%$ of $96 = ? + 33\frac{1}{3}\%$ of 120
A. 32 **B.** 52 **C.** 41 **D.** 46
E. 64

Q.98 25% of $7428 + 71.5 \times 2 = 14\frac{2}{7}\%$ of ?
A. 2000 **B.** 5000 **C.** 4000 **D.** 14000
E. 12000

Q.99 31% of $200 + 21\%$ of $300 = 25 \times 5 + ?^2 - 40\%$ of 90
A. 7 **B.** 4 **C.** 6 **D.** 5
E. 8

Q.100 $\sqrt[3]{6859} + \sqrt{441} - \sqrt[3]{4096} - \sqrt{576} = ?$
A. 1 **B.** 48
C. 0 **D.** -42
E. None of these

// Smart Answer Sheet //

Correct — Indicates percentage of students who answered questions correctly.

Skipped — Indicates percentage of students who skipped questions.

Q.	Ans.	Correct / Skipped
1	C	51.07 % / 30.4 %
2	C	43.13 % / 33.15 %
3	C	47.58 % / 40.79 %
4	D	41.63 % / 32.25 %
5	A	12.61 % / 74.08 %
6	B	89.29 % / 10.25 %
7	D	86.6 % / 10.51 %
8	E	85.19 % / 12.3 %
9	C	45.76 % / 40.49 %
10	C	56.08 % / 41.56 %
11	B	64.61 % / 35.36 %
12	C	52.96 % / 36.8 %
13	A	63.12 % / 34.11 %
14	C	83.59 % / 16.36 %
15	B	79.19 % / 14.87 %
16	A	77.55 % / 18.3 %

Q.	Ans.	Correct / Skipped
17	A	89.15 % / 10.69 %
18	A	76.67 % / 16.45 %
19	A	85.2 % / 10.11 %
20	D	77.48 % / 17.52 %
21	A	85.91 % / 12.75 %
22	B	84.53 % / 10.65 %
23	D	84.79 % / 11.19 %
24	B	82.88 % / 15.82 %
25	D	77.1 % / 19.52 %
26	A	88.75 % / 11.14 %
27	B	62.19 % / 32.53 %
28	A	78.64 % / 11.32 %
29	E	57.71 % / 31.81 %
30	C	69.07 % / 30.63 %
31	D	58.08 % / 31.15 %
32	B	62.28 % / 35.38 %

Q.	Ans.	Correct / Skipped
33	C	56.92 % / 38.58 %
34	A	44.93 % / 41.57 %
35	A	54.68 % / 36.43 %
36	A	26.34 % / 71.28 %
37	C	44.03 % / 55.67 %
38	B	45.45 % / 47.95 %
39	C	19.61 % / 69.29 %
40	D	45.6 % / 39.02 %
41	D	16.51 % / 67.08 %
42	B	81.88 % / 14.63 %
43	B	67.17 % / 30.64 %
44	E	58.3 % / 30.02 %
45	D	54.87 % / 39.42 %
46	A	61.04 % / 33.34 %
47	E	41.11 % / 37.94 %
48	A	63.76 % / 30.4 %

Q.	Ans.	Correct / Skipped
49	E	41.35 % / 54.49 %
50	E	67.12 % / 31.31 %
51	D	49.86 % / 42.01 %
52	C	55.79 % / 39.34 %
53	A	87.06 % / 12.64 %
54	C	79.32 % / 17.47 %
55	A	87.94 % / 10.5 %
56	B	81.1 % / 17.01 %
57	D	57.17 % / 40.18 %
58	A	78.17 % / 14.18 %
59	E	80.26 % / 18.85 %
60	C	87.4 % / 10.61 %
61	D	61.49 % / 34.91 %
62	D	28.96 % / 69.41 %
63	C	83.34 % / 12.19 %
64	D	41.99 % / 54.17 %

Q.	Ans.	Correct / Skipped
65	A	87.97 % / 10.52 %
66	A	56.49 % / 40.27 %
67	C	63.96 % / 35.98 %
68	A	44.46 % / 46.82 %
69	C	77.38 % / 10.41 %
70	B	78.79 % / 18.02 %
71	A	42.28 % / 51.94 %
72	C	50.8 % / 47.04 %
73	A	52.43 % / 31.82 %
74	E	57.07 % / 33.81 %
75	B	56.32 % / 38.33 %
76	B	42.51 % / 46.79 %
77	C	83.22 % / 10.18 %
78	D	89.08 % / 10.84 %
79	A	52.43 % / 31.91 %
80	C	62.1 % / 33.14 %

Q.	Ans.	Correct / Skipped
81	C	55.74 %
		35.21 %
82	D	80.79 %
		16.56 %
83	A	82.72 %
		16.6 %
84	B	25.32 %
		68.63 %

Q.	Ans.	Correct / Skipped
85	B	86.01 %
		13.74 %
86	D	76.11 %
		19.56 %
87	B	63.65 %
		31.97 %
88	B	52.76 %
		37.69 %

Q.	Ans.	Correct / Skipped
89	B	60.8 %
		38.29 %
90	A	78.71 %
		15.27 %
91	E	45.31 %
		50.27 %
92	C	89.7 %
		10.03 %

Q.	Ans.	Correct / Skipped
93	C	69.88 %
		30.11 %
94	A	30.5 %
		67.15 %
95	E	52.54 %
		32.27 %
96	D	82.36 %
		11.35 %

Q.	Ans.	Correct / Skipped
97	C	54.71 %
		37.87 %
98	D	89.05 %
		10.41 %
99	C	59.0 %
		37.99 %
100	C	52.11 %
		36.87 %

Performance Analysis

Avg. Score (%)	55.0%
Toppers Score (%)	71.0%
Your Score	

//Hints and Solutions//

1. Pisiculture has the incorrectly spelt word. The correct spelling is pisciculture.

Pisciculture involves raising fish commercially in tanks or enclosures such as fish ponds, usually for food.

The meanings of the other words are:

Deliquescence means tending to melt or dissolve especially.

Pertinacious means holding firmly to an opinion or a course of action.

Renaissance means a new growth of activity or interest in something, especially art, literature, or music.

Renegade means someone or something that causes trouble and cannot be controlled.

Hence, the correct option is (C).

2. Millenerian has the wrongly spelt word. The correct spelling is millenarian. It is a belief in Christian millenarianism.

The meaning of the other words are:

Millennium means a period of a thousand years, especially when calculated from the traditional date of the birth of Christ.

A millionaire means a person whose assets are worth one million pounds or dollars or more.

Manageable means are able to be controlled or dealt with without difficulty.

Hence, the correct option is (C).

3. The correctly spelt word is disorientation means a feeling of being confused about where you are, where you are going, or what is happening.

Hence, the correct option is (C).

4. The first sentence after rearrangement is (B).

The sentence are arranged in the following pattern: (B)-(D)-(C)-(A)-(F)-(E)

- The subject that is being discussed in the passage is the successful launch of 104 satellites in a single mission by the Indian Space Research Organisation and sentence (B) sets the tone by mentioning this achievement in brief.
- (D) follows as it elaborates the details of the satellites launched.
- (C) follows next as it states the further details of the satellites launched.
- 'The United States', 'Israel', 'the UAE', 'the Netherlands', 'Kazakhstan' and 'Switzerland' are foreign countries and keyword that links (C) to (D) is "foreign".
- Now, if we pick sentence (E) as the next sentence, the position of sentence A as either the fifth or the sixth sentence would create absurdity and hence the

only available choice for the fourth sentence is sentence (A).

- The sequence made so far is (B)-(D)-(C)-(A).
- The next sentence that should follow is sentence (F) that describes the real purpose of the launch of satellites. Now, the only sentence that is left is (E).

Hence, the correct option is (D).

5. The second sentence after rearrangement is (D).

The sentence are arranged in the following pattern: (B)-(D)-(C)-(A)-(F)-(E)

- The subject that is being discussed in the passage is the successful launch of 104 satellites in a single mission by the Indian Space Research Organisation and sentence (B) sets the tone by mentioning this achievement in brief.
- (D) follows as it elaborates the details of the satellites launched.
- (C) follows next as it states the further details of the satellites launched.
- 'The United States', 'Israel', 'the UAE', 'the Netherlands', 'Kazakhstan' and 'Switzerland' are foreign countries and keyword that links (C) to (D) is "foreign".
- Now, if we pick sentence (E) as the next sentence, the position of sentence A as either the fifth or the sixth sentence would create absurdity and hence the only available choice for the fourth sentence is sentence (A).
- The sequence made so far is (B)-(D)-(C)-(A).
- The next sentence that should follow is sentence (F) that describes the real purpose of the launch of satellites. Now, the only sentence that is left is (E).

Hence, the correct option is (A).

6. The third sentence after rearrangement is (C).

The sentence are arranged in the following pattern: (B)-(D)-(C)-(A)-(F)-(E)

- The subject t\hat is being discussed in the passage is the successful launch of 104 satellites in a single mission by the Indian Space Research Organisation and sentence (B) sets the tone by mentioning this achievement in brief.
- (D) follows as it elaborates the details of the satellites launched.
- (C) follows next as it states the further details of the satellites launched.
- 'The United States', 'Israel', 'the UAE', 'the Netherlands', 'Kazakhstan' and 'Switzerland' are foreign countries and keyword that links (C) to (D) is "foreign".
- Now, if we pick sentence (E) as the next sentence, the position of sentence A as either the fifth or the sixth sentence would create absurdity and hence the only available choice for the fourth sentence is sentence (A).

- The sequence made so far is (B)-(D)-(C)-(A).

- The next sentence that should follow is sentence (F) that describes the real purpose of the launch of satellites. Now, the only sentence that is left is (E).

Hence, the correct option is (B).

7. The fourth sentence after rearrangement is (A).

The sentence are arranged in the following pattern: (B)-(D)-(C)-(A)-(F)-(E)

- The subject that is being discussed in the passage is the successful launch of 104 satellites in a single mission by the Indian Space Research Organisation and sentence (B) sets the tone by mentioning this achievement in brief.

- (D) follows as it elaborates the details of the satellites launched.

- (C) follows next as it states the further details of the satellites launched.

- 'The United States', 'Israel', 'the UAE', 'the Netherlands', 'Kazakhstan' and 'Switzerland' are foreign countries and keyword that links (C) to (D) is "foreign".

- Now, if we pick sentence (E) as the next sentence, the position of sentence A as either the fifth or the sixth sentence would create absurdity and hence the only available choice for the fourth sentence is sentence (A).

- The sequence made so far is (B)-(D)-(C)-(A).

- The next sentence that should follow is sentence (F) that describes the real purpose of the launch of satellites. Now, the only sentence that is left is (E).

Hence, the correct option is (D).

8. The last sentence after rearrangement is (F).

The sentence are arranged in the following pattern: (B)-(D)-(C)-(A)-(F)-(E)

- The subject that is being discussed in the passage is the successful launch of 104 satellites in a single mission by the Indian Space Research Organisation and sentence (B) sets the tone by mentioning this achievement in brief.

- (D) follows as it elaborates the details of the satellites launched.

- (C) follows next as it states the further details of the satellites launched.

- 'The United States', 'Israel', 'the UAE', 'the Netherlands', 'Kazakhstan' and 'Switzerland' are foreign countries and keyword that links (C) to (D) is "foreign".

- Now, if we pick sentence (E) as the next sentence, the position of sentence A as either the fifth or the sixth sentence would create absurdity and hence the only available choice for the fourth sentence is sentence (A).

- The sequence made so far is (B)-(D)-(C)-(A).

- The next sentence that should follow is sentence (F) that describes the real purpose of the launch of satellites. Now, the only sentence that is left is (E).

Hence, the correct option is (E).

9. Let's look at the meaning of the correct word:

Crippling: causing a severe and almost insuperable problem.

The blank requires an adjective that can be used to describe the quality of the third wave of the virus.

The sentence mentions that the current wave of the virus is more deadly than the previous waves as it is killing people at a faster rate.

This means that it would be seriously damaging to the country - for the people and the economy.

Complete sentence:

South Africa finds itself in the middle of a **crippling** third-wave of the COVID with people losing their lives faster than any wave before.

Hence, the correct option is (C).

10. Here the sentence is talking about the Louvre pyramid which is a famous monument in France.

Keeping this in mind let's look at the meaning of the given option.

Iconic: widely recognized and well-established; famous as an icon.

Example: He became an iconic figure for directors around the world.

Thus from the given meaning and example, it is evident that the correct answer is iconic.

Complete sentence:

The Louvre pyramid is one of the most **iconic** landmarks in France.

Hence, the correct option is (C).

11. Let's look at the meaning of the correct answer:

A computing machine 20000 times faster can increase the processing power of supercomputers.

boost - help or encourage (something) to increase or improve.

Example - We have to adopt a range of measures to boost tourism.

From the given meaning we can conclude that the correct answer is a boost.

Complete sentence:

China's computing machine is 20000 times faster than its international counterparts and may **boost** the processing power of supercomputers.

Hence, the correct option is (B).

12. Indolent: lazy or lackadaisical.

The context talks about the boss' frustration with the lazy employee.

Complete sentence:

The **indolent** nature of the employee was unacceptable to the boss because the work kept piling up with time.

Hence, the correct option is (C).

13. Garrulous: excessively talkative, especially on trivial matters.

The context talks about the reason the speaker hates talkative people.

Blow one's own trumpet: talk boastfully about one's achievements.

Complete sentence:

I despise **garrulous** people as they have a tendency to blow their own trumpet.

Hence, the correct option is (A).

14. The meaning of the given words:

- Occult: having seemingly supernatural qualities or powers
- Supernatural: being so extraordinary or abnormal as to suggest powers which violate the laws of nature
- Religious: of, relating to or used in the practice or worship services of a religion
- Unnatural: departing from some accepted standard of what is normal
- Strong: having muscles capable of exerting great physical force

So from the given meanings, we find that supernatural and Occult are synonyms.

Hence, the correct option is (C).

15. The meaning of the given words:

- Counterfeit: made in imitation of something else with intent to deceive
- Genuine: being exactly as appears or as claimed
- Destructive: causing great and irreparable damage
- Affirm: state emphatically or publicly
- Harmonize: add notes to (a melody) to produce harmony

So, from the given meanings, we find that genuine and Counterfeit are antonyms.

Hence, the correct option is (B).

16. In the given sentence, the error lies in part (A) where Despite of is an incorrect usage.

- The sentence talks the Republic Day celebrations going on uninterrupted, even though it was raining. Thus, in simple words, the festivities continued without being influenced or hindered by the rain.

- 'Despite' means without taking any notice of or being influenced by. It is most appropriate in the context of the given sentence.

- It is important to note that 'despite' should be not be followed by 'of'. Rather, it should be directly followed by the time-dependent clause which tells about the fact.

Thus, the correct sentence is: Despite the rain, the parade went on uninterrupted which was followed by the President's address and other formal festivities of the Republic Day.

Hence, the correct option is (A).

17. In the given sentence, the error is part (A) where more stronger than is an incorrect usage.

- Here, the coach says that Lisa is stronger than her opponent. There is a comparison between Lisa and her opponent and thus a comparative adjective stronger is used.

- The adjective 'strong' when used in a comparative form becomes 'stronger'. There is no need of using more along with this comparative adjective. Therefore, usage of 'more stronger' is a repetition mistake or redundancy.

Thus, the correct sentence is: "Lisa is stronger than her opponent", said the coach during the press briefing ahead of the Asian Games.

Hence, the correct option is (A).

18. Part (A) has an error.

According to the rule, before possessives, determiners such as 'all', 'both', 'half', etc. are used.

Example: She loves both her daughters equally and distributed the property evenly between them.

So, 'all my documents' should be used instead of 'my all documents' to make the sentence correct.

So, the correct sentence is: I lost the bag in which I had all my documents, certificates, and academic records. I have a job interview tomorrow where I need all these things, and I have no clue what will happen. I lodged a police complaint, but within this short time, nothing is possible.

Hence, the correct option is (A).

19. Part (A) has an error.

According to the rule, if 'as.....as' is used in a sentence, the adjective or adverb used in-between 'as' should always be in the Positive Degree.

Example: He is as brave as his father, who is a police officer.

So, 'as soft as' should be used to make the sentence correct.

So, the correct sentence is: The fabric is as soft as cotton, but it is not pure cotton. That's why she got so many allergic reactions on her face after using that mask and is now under proper medication and care.

Hence, the correct option is (A).

20. Error is in part (D) of the sentence.

- The adverbial phrase for 2005 used in part (D) is incorrect.
- We don't use for with a point in time (2005).
- The sentence can be made correct if we use since.

The correct sentence will be: Kiva has loaned out nearly a quarter of a billion dollars to small and medium businesses since 2005.

Hence, the correct option is (D).

21. Correct sentence: Covid treatment in this hospital is quite expensive and they had to sell off their land to pay for it.

- Option (A) replaces the bold part appropriately and thus becomes the best replacement among all.
- Option (B) can be eliminated because 'too' must be followed by an infinitive (to + verb1) which is not the case here.
- Option (C) gets eliminated too because 'so' must be followed by 'that' which is again not the case here.
- Option (D) gets eliminated because no comparison is made in the sentence and it gets confirmed by the absence of the preposition 'than' in the sentence.

Hence, the correct option is (A).

22. Set (someone) by the ears: To cause (someone, generally a group of two or more people) to engage in a squabble, dispute, or altercation. Ex: Jatin likes to set his classmates by the ears as a means of getting attention.

Correct sentence: The entire town was set by the ears when it was announced that a giant megastore would be closing itself.

Hence, the correct option is (B).

23. In the sentence, more leisure pace is grammatically incorrect.

- In the emboldened part, the word leisure is a noun that is followed by another noun pace.
- Here, the adjective of leisure i.e. leisurely which means acting, proceeding, or done without haste must be used to describe the noun pace.

Correct sentence: He slapped the team into action and they headed for the town at a more leisurely pace.

Hence, the correct option is (D).

24. The word 'later' means 'at a time in the near future' and is unsuitable in this sentence. The correct word to be used here is 'latter' which means 'denoting the second or second mentioned of two people or things.'

So, 'latter' should be used in place of 'later' to make the sentence grammatically correct.

Correct sentence: Although both the United States and China are formidable world powers, India should side with the latter.

Hence, the correct option is (B).

25. The underlined part of the sentence is grammatically incorrect. The preposition 'for' used here is wrong. The correct preposition should be 'to'.

Gauge means to judge or assess (a situation, mood, etc.). So, 'assess' is a synonym of 'gauge'.

Hence, the correct option is (D).

26. We need an adverb, and here the only adverb is 'significantly'.

- Significantly: having or likely to have influence or effect.
- Obsessed: preoccupied with or haunted by some idea, interest, etc
- Aggravated: to make something worse or more serious
- Mitigating: providing a reason that explains somebody's actions or why he/she committed a crime, which makes it easier to understand so that the punishment may be less harsh.

Hence, the correct option is (A).

27. The meaning of the given words:

- Restrictions: something (sometimes a rule or law) that limits the number, amount, size, freedom, etc. of somebody/something
- Limitation: the act of limiting or controlling something; a condition that puts a limit on something
- Liberation: an occasion when something or someone is released or made free.
- Freedom: the state of not being held prisoner or controlled by somebody else.
- Permission: the act of allowing somebody to do something, especially when this is done by somebody in a position of authority.

From the meanings of the given words, we can conclude that the word most similar in meaning to restrictions is limitation.

Hence, the correct option is (B).

28. According to passage, "Fall in employment also means large income losses for workers."

So, it is concluded that the fall in employment mean large income losses for workers.

Hence, the correct option is (A).

29. According to passage, "The economic and labour crisis created by the COVID-19 pandemic could increase global unemployment by almost 25 million, according to a new assessment by the International Labour Organization (ILO)."

So, it is concluded that a new assessment by the International Labour Organization (ILO), unemployment could globally increase by 25 million.

Hence, the correct option is (E).

30. According to passage, "Based on different scenarios for the impact of COVID-19 on global GDP growth, the ILO estimates indicate a rise in global unemployment of between 5.3 million ("low" scenario) and 24.7 million ("high" scenario) from a base level of 188 million in 2019."

Hence, the correct option is (C).

31. Statement: $B < S \leq Q < Y = X > C \geq J$

I. S < Y ⇒ True (as S ≤ Q < Y ⇒ S < Y)

II. X > B ⇒ True (as B < S ≤ Q < Y = X ⇒ B < X ⇒ X > B)

So, Both I and II are true.

Hence, the correct option is (D).

32. Given statements: A < C = D < E; B = A > F

On combining: F < B = A < C = D < E

I. D > F → True (as F < A < C = D → D > F)

II. B > E → False (as B < C = D < E → B < E)

Thus, the only conclusion I is true.

Hence, the correct option is (B).

33. Given statements: D = X ≥ C > S = F; D > Y ≥ H ≥ G

On combination: G ≤ H ≤ Y < D = X ≥ C > S = F

Conclusions:

I. G ≤ X → False (as G ≤ H ≤ Y < D = X)

II. D > F → True (as D = X ≥ C > S = F)

So, only conclusion II follows.

Hence, the correct option is (C).

34. Given statements: G ≥ M = P > C; Q < R = B < C

On combining above two statements: G ≥ M = P > C > B = R > Q

Conclusions:

I. M > R → True (as M = P > C > B = R)

II. G ≥ B → False (as G ≥ M = P > C > B → G > B)

So, only conclusion I follows.

Hence, the correct option is (A).

35. Given statements: M < N < U; R = T; U ≤ R ≥ V ≥ E

On combining: M < N < U ≤ R = T ≥ V ≥ E

I. T > N → True (as N < U ≤ R = T)

II. R ≥ E → True (as R ≥ V ≥ E)

III. M < T → True (as M < N < U ≤ R = T)

IV. T ≥ U → True (as U ≤ R = T)

Therefore, all are true.

Hence, the correct option is (A).

36. Given,

In a row of students, Ramesh is ninth from the left and Suman is sixth from the right. When Ramesh and Suman interchange their places, Ramesh becomes fifteenth from the left.

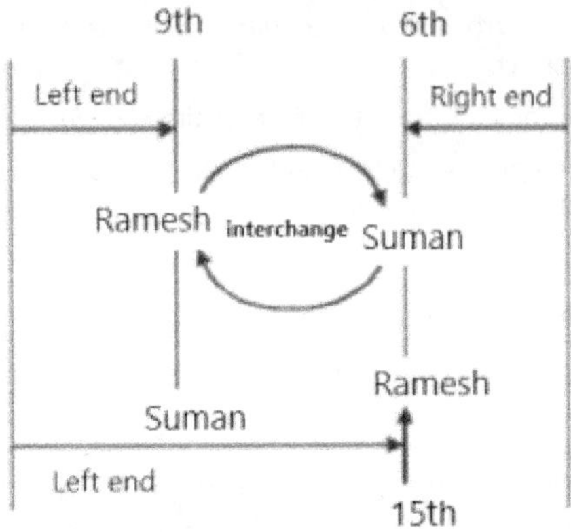

Thus the position of Suman changed from right to Suman $= 6 + 5 +$

$= 6 + 5 + 1 = 12$

Thus Suman will be 12th from the right.

Hence, the correct option is (A).

37. Let the number of boys be x.

Then, the number of girls $= 2x$

According to the question,

$\therefore x + 2x = 60$

$\Rightarrow 3x = 60$

$\Rightarrow x = 20$

Hence, the number of boys $= 20$

And the number of girls $= 40$

Number of students behind Kamal in rank $= (60 - 17) = 43$

Number of girls ahead of Kamal in rank $= 9$

Number of girls behind Kamal in rank $= (40 - 9) = 31$

$\therefore$ Number of boys behind Kamal in rank $= (43 - 31) = 12$

Hence, the correct option is (C).

Ques (38-42):8 persons - Fiona, Liz, Chad, Zack, Ashley, Betty, Derek and Patrick.

1) Betty sits third to the left of Cody.

2) Derek is sitting second to the left of Cody.

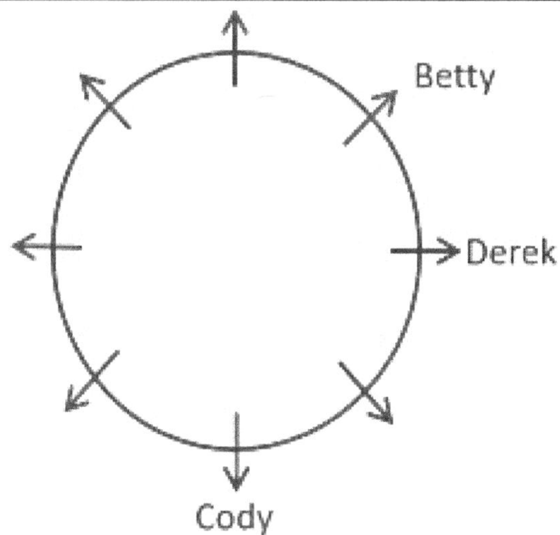

3) Ashley is sitting opposite to Betty.

4) Patrick is sitting second to the right of Ashley.

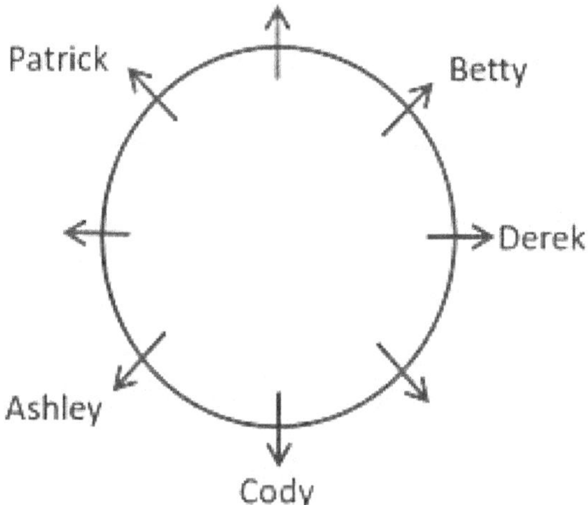

5) Zack is not a neighbour of Ashley or Patrick. Thus, Zack sits between Derek and Cody.

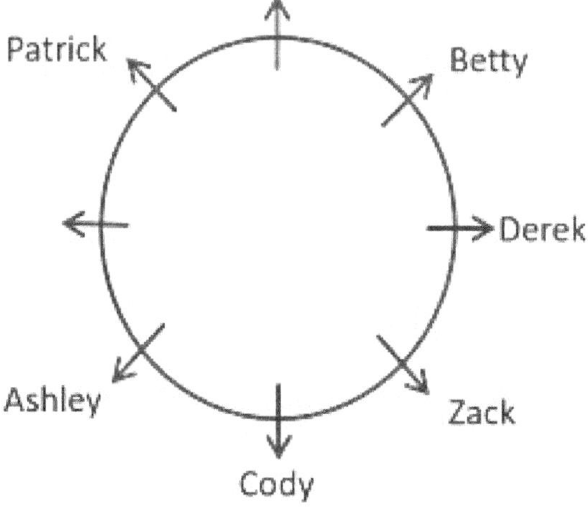

6) Fiona does not sit opposite to Derek. Thus, Fiona sits opposite to Cody. Liz sits opposite to Derek.

The final arrangement will be:

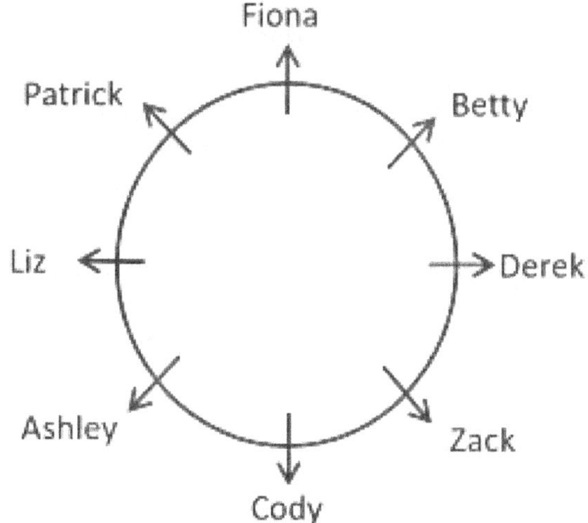

38. So, 'Ashley and Patrick' are immediate neighbors of Liz.

Hence, the correct option is (B).

39. If Betty exchanges her position with Patrick the arrangement will be as follows:

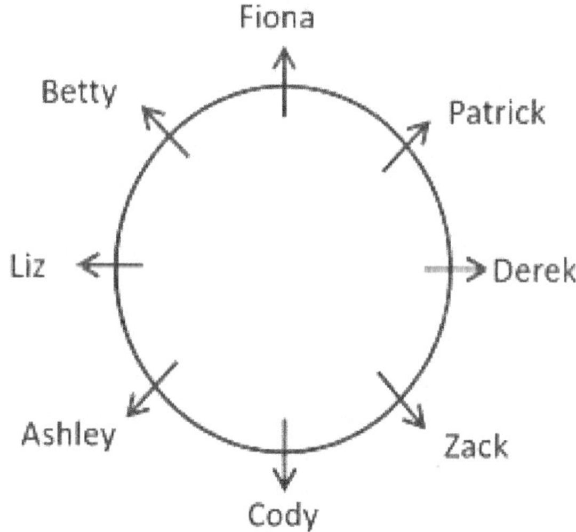

I. Derek sits opposite to Ashley → False.

II. Betty site second to the right of Zack → False.

III. Fiona sits opposite to Cody → True.

So, 'Only statement III is true' is the correct answer.

Hence, the correct option is (C).

40. If Betty exchanges her position with Patrick the arrangement will be as follows:

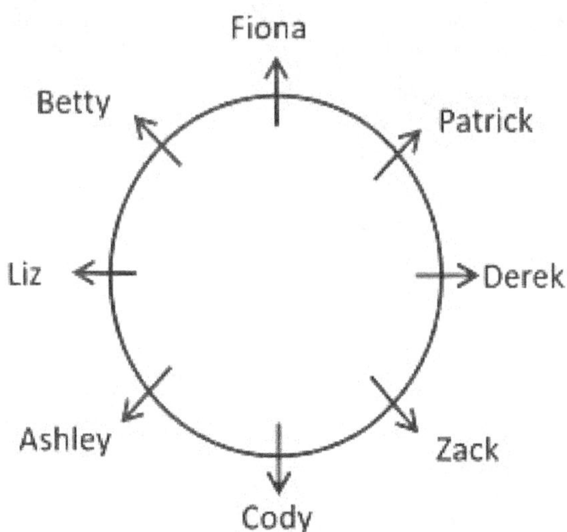

So, '4' persons are sitting between Liz and Zack when counted from right of Liz.

Hence, the correct option is (D).

41. If Betty exchanges her position with Patrick the arrangement will be as follows:

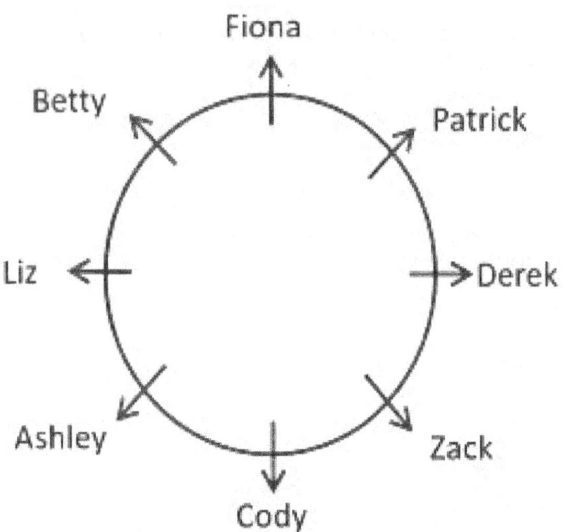

So, 'Cody' is the correct answer.

Hence, the correct option is (D).

42. So, 'Fiona' is the correct answer..

Hence, the correct option is (B).

Ques (43-47):1) N is sitting fifth to the right of W and N is not facing the same direction as W.

2) Two people are sitting to the left of W and both of them are facing north.

(Implies, W must be facing south as three consecutive people can't face the same direction. It further implies that N is facing north.)

3) P is sitting sixth to the left of T who is an immediate neighbour of N.

4) People sitting at the extreme ends are facing opposite directions.

(T must be facing south if he is an immediate neighbour of N because only then we can place P sixth to his left. Also, if we place T to the immediate left of N then W will be sitting sixth to the left of T which is not possible. Thus, T is sitting to the immediate right of N and P is sitting second to the left of W.

Also, the person sitting to the immediate left of N is facing south because P is facing north.)

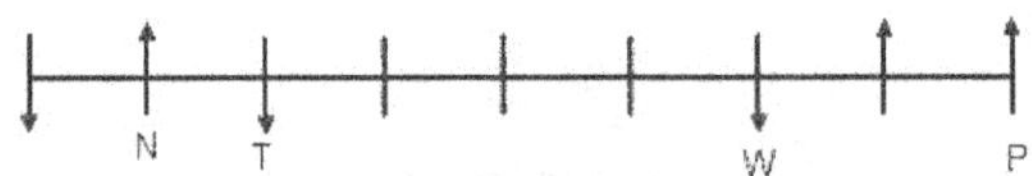

5) Q is sitting fourth to the left of S who is facing the same direction as P.

6) S is not sitting next to P.

(If S is not sitting next to P, implies, he is sitting second to the right of W because only then we can place Q fourth to the left S who is facing north.)

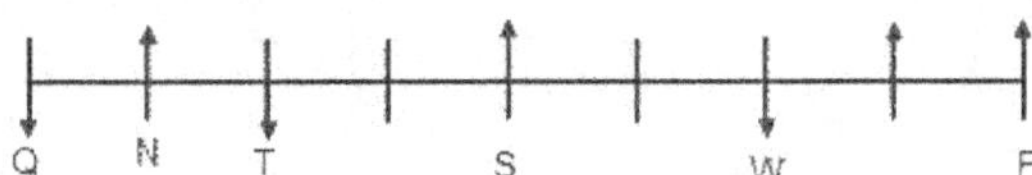

7) O is sitting fourth to the left of R and they are facing opposite directions.

8) O is an immediate neighbour of T.

(Implies, R is sitting between W and P. O is sitting between T and S and he is facing south because R is facing north. Also, now that only L is left to be placed, we can place him between S and W and he must be facing north as we have already identified the four people who are facing south.)

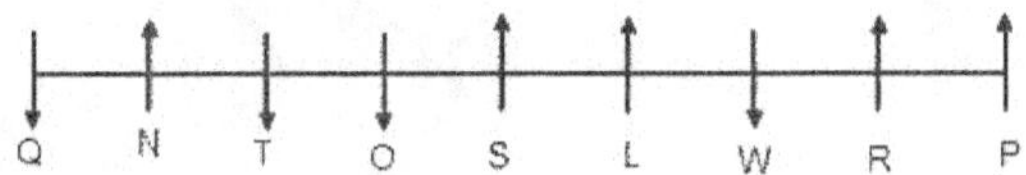

43. So, S is sitting second to the right of W.

Hence, the correct option is (B).

44. So, T is sitting third to the left of L.

Hence, the correct option is (E).

45. So, P and W are the immediate neighbours of R.

Hence, the correct option is (D).

46. So, Q and T are the immediate neighbours of N.

Hence, the correct option is (A).

47. So, P is sitting third to the right of L.

Hence, the correct option is (E).

48. The least possible Venn diagram for the given statements is as follows:

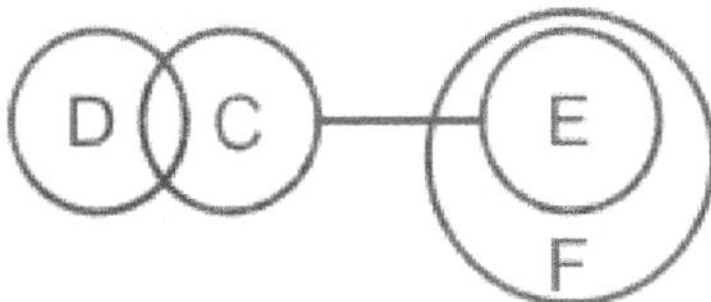

Conclusions:

I. No F is a C → False (It is possible but not definite so its false)

II. At least some D are F → False (It is possible but not definite so its false)

So, Neither I nor II follows.

Hence, the correct option is (A).

49. The least possible diagram is given below:

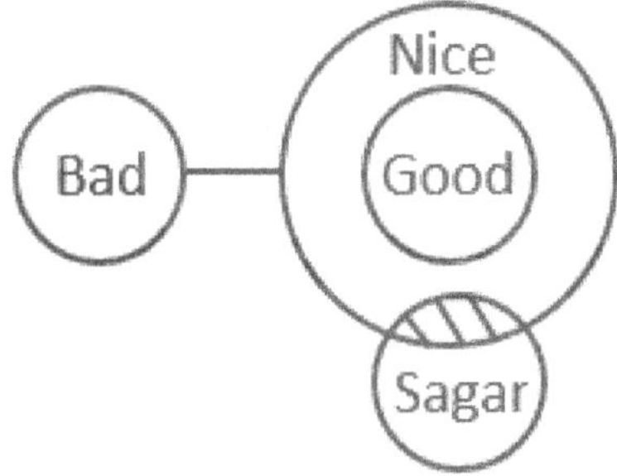

I. All Sagar can be Good → True (In statement it is clearly says Only a few Nice are Sagar and all Good are Nice)

II. Some Nice are not Bad → True (in statement it is clearly says No Bad are Good)

So, Both conclusion I and conclusion II follows.

Hence, the correct option is (E).

50. Statements:

Only a few animal are cat → Some part of Animal are overlapping with Cat and some part of animal are not cat

Some animal are dog → Some part of animal are overlapping with dog

Venn diagram for the given statements are follows.

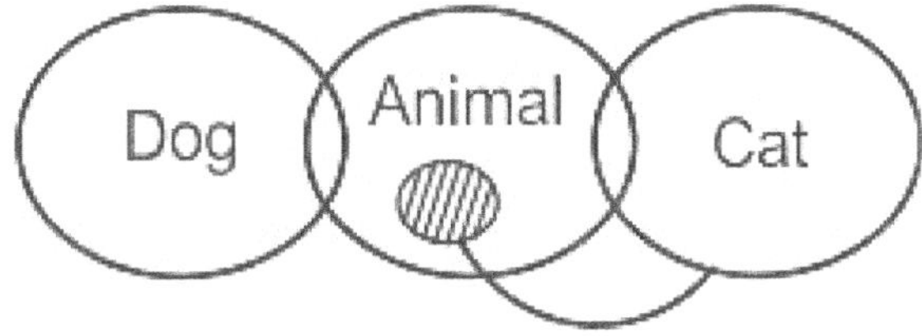

Conclusions:

I. All Cat are animal → False (some part of animal are not cat but remaining part of the animal can be cat so, this possible statement not definite hence false)

II. Some cat are Dog → False(some dog are cat or not is definite it can be a possible case but not definite)

So, Neither I nor II follows.

Hence, the correct option is (E).

51. Statement:

Only a few Sea are River → Some parts of Sea are River and Some parts of sea are not River

All River are Water bodies → All river will be part of Waterbodies

The least possible venn diagram will be:

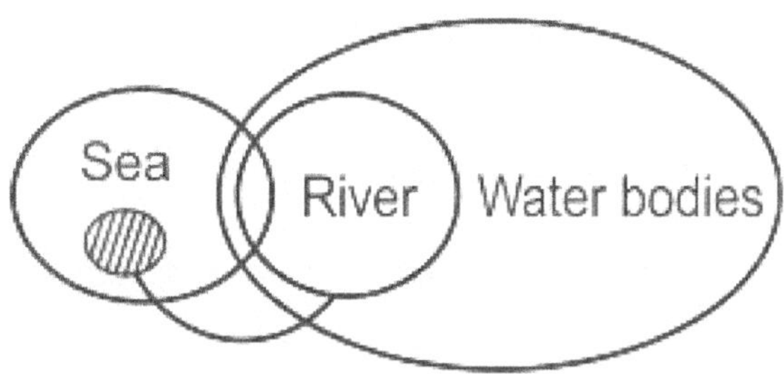

Conclusion:

I. Some Sea are Water bodies → True (Some parts of Sea are River and All River are water bodies hence some sea are water bodies)

II. All sea are River → False (Some parts of Sea are River and Some parts of the sea are not River hence all sea are river is False)

So, Only I follow.

Hence, the correct option is (D).

52. The least possible Venn diagram for the given statements is as follows:

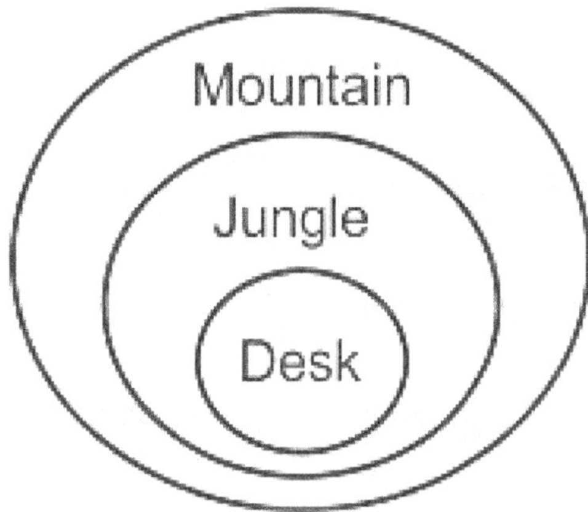

Conclusions:

I. No Jungle is Mountain → False(All Desk are Jungle and All Jungle are Mountain hence all the statements are positive this conclusion is False.)

II. Some Mountain are Desk → True (All Desk are Jungle and All Jungle are Mountain hence Some Mountain are desk)

So, only II follows.

Hence, the correct option is (C).

53. Given word: LAVISLY

After replacing each vowel with the next letter in the alphabetical series and each consonant with the previous letter in the Alphabetical Series, we get:

Given	L	A	V	I	S	L	Y
After Replacement	K	B	U	J	R	K	X

Here, one letter, K occurred twice.

Hence, the correct option is (A).

54.

Alpha bets	A	B	C	D	E	F	G	H	I	J	K	L	M
Positional value	1	2	3	4	5	6	7	8	9	10	11	12	13
Positional value	26	25	24	23	22	21	20	19	18	17	16	15	14
Alpha bets	Z	Y	X	W	V	U	T	S	R	Q	P	O	N

E	N	T	H	U	S	I	A	S	M
5	14	20	8	21	19	9	1	19	13

Forward Pair - EH

Backward Pair - NI, TM

So, there are three such pair which has as many letters between them in the word as they have between them in the English alphabetical series.

Hence, the correct option is (C).

55. Given series:

Left side 2 # C D 6 % F I M K H 8 © @ T U V 4 € 2 7 8 $ H O K W 5 Y 4 ¥ Y A P @ Right side

As Left side - Left side = Left side

24th from the left - 6th from the left = 18 from the left

Clearly, 18th from the left is 4.

Hence, the correct option is (A).

56. Given series:

Left side 2 # C D 6 % F I M K H 8 © @ T U V 4 € 2 7 8 $ H O K W 5 Y 4 ¥ Y A P @ Right side

1) If all the even numbers are dropped:

C D % F I M K H © @ T U V € 7 $ H O K W 5 Y ¥ Y A P @

2) 10th element from the right end is O.

So, the element that is 10th from the right end is 'O'.

Hence, the correct option is (B).

57. Given series:

Left side 2 # C D 6 % F I M K H 8 © @ T U V 4 € 2 7 8 $ H O K W 5 Y 4 ¥ Y A P @ Right side

First of All, mark the Vowels:

2 # C D 6 % F I M K H 8 © @ T **U** V 4 € 2 7 8 $ H **O** K W 5 Y 4 ¥ Y **A** P @

Required order: Not number → vowel → Consonant

2 # C D 6 % **F I M** K H 8 © @ **T U V** 4 € 2 7 8 $ **H O K** W 5 Y 4 ¥ **Y A P** @

So, there are more than 3 vowels (FIM, TUV, HOK, YAP) that are immediately followed by a consonant but not immediately preceded by a number.

Hence, the correct option is (D).

58. Given series:

2 # C D 6 % F I M K H 8 © @ T U V 4 € 2 7 8 $ H O K W 5 Y 4 ¥ Y A P @

As, Right - Right = Right

23rd from the Right - 9th from the Right = 14 from the Right

Clearly, 14th from the Right is '8'.

Hence, the correct option is (A).

59. Given series:

Left side 2 # C D 6 % F I M K H 8 © @ T U V 4 € 2 7 8 $ H O K W 5 Y 4 ¥ Y A P @ Right side

According to the positions of the elements in the series:

(A) C6F → C + 2 = 6 and 6 + 2 = F

(B) H©T → H + 2 = © and © + 2 = T

(C) 7$O → 7 + 2 = $ and $ + 2 = O

(D) V€7 → V + 2 = € and € + 2 = 7

(E) 4YA → 4 + 2 = Y and Y + 1 = A

So, 4YA does not belong to the group.

Hence, the correct option is (E).

Ques (60-62): The table is drawn describing symbols and their meanings,

Symbol in Diagram	Meaning
◯	Female
▢	Male
=	Married Couple
—	Siblings
│	Difference of A Generation

1. N is the father of D. E is married to N. G and D are siblings. C is married to G. N has no son.

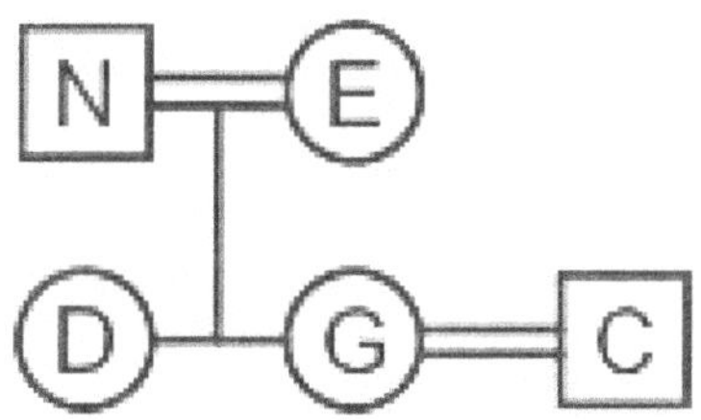

2. Eight members of a family are living in a house, in which two are married couples. K is the father of E. Q is the only son of C. A is the brother-in-law of N.

Therefore, the final arrangement will be,

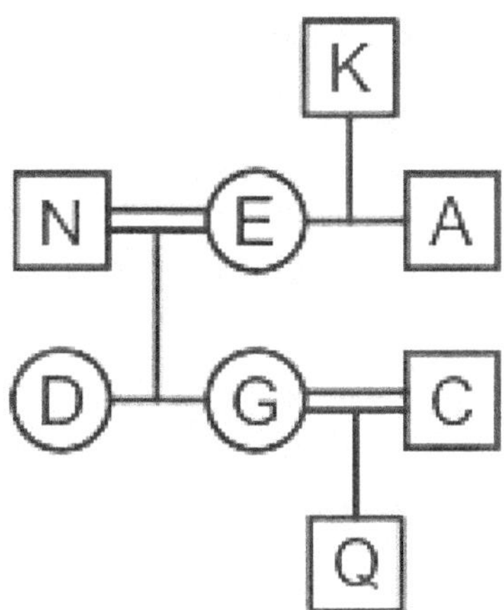

60. So, C is the son-in-law of N.

Hence, the correct option is (C).

61. So, K is the grandfather of D.

Hence, the correct option is (D).

62. So, N is the husband of E.

Hence, the correct option is (D).

63. The logic followed here is as follows:

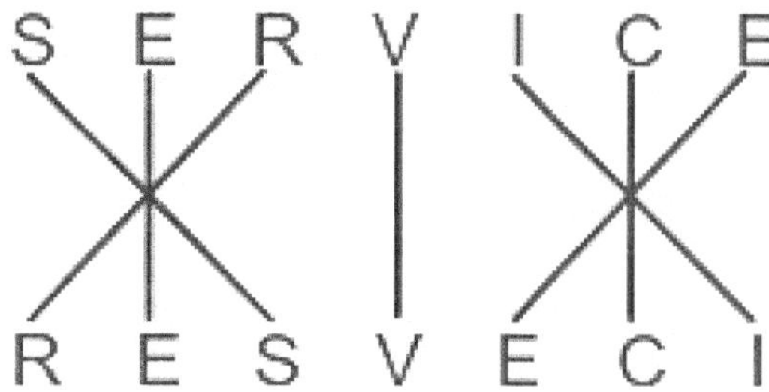

Similarly,

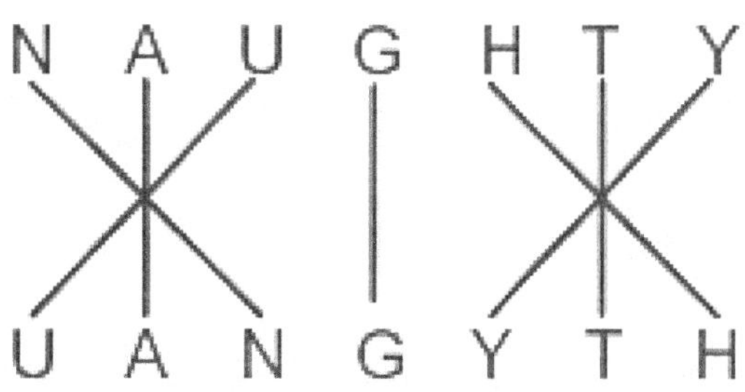

So, 'NAUGHTY' will be written as UANGYTH in that language.

Hence, the correct option is (C).

64. According to English Alphabet series with positional value:

Alphabet	A	B	C	D	E	F	G	H	I	J	K	L	M
Positional value	1	2	3	4	5	6	7	8	9	10	11	12	13
Positional value	26	25	24	23	22	21	20	19	18	17	16	15	14
Alphabet	Z	Y	X	W	V	U	T	S	R	Q	P	O	N

In a certain code;

$A = 1, 1 \times 2 + 1 = 3$

$C = 3, 3 \times 2 + 1 = 7$

$N = 14, 14 \times 2 + 1 = 29$

$E = 5, 5 \times 2 + 1 = 11$

Similarly,

B $= 2, 2 \times 2 + 1 = 5$

O $= 15, 15 \times 2 + 1 = 31$

I $= 9, 9 \times 2 + 1 = 19$

L $= 12, 12 \times 2 + 1 = 25$

So, the BOIL will be coded as $5 - 31 - 19 - 25$.

Hence, the correct option is (D).

65. The logic followed here is as follows:

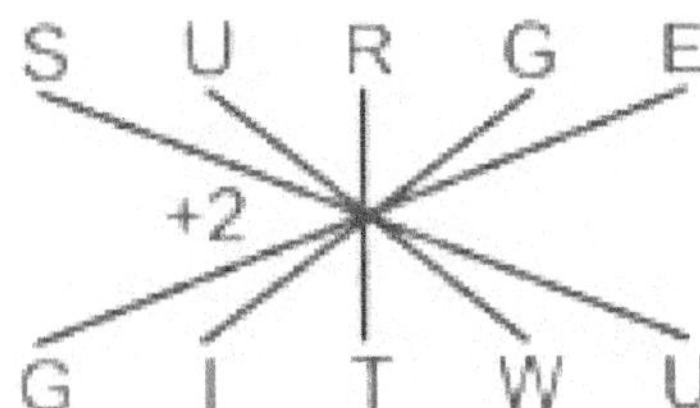

Similarly,

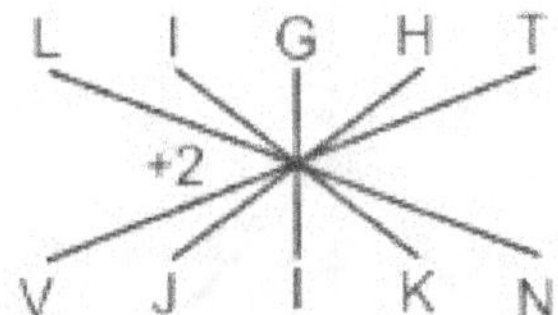

So, 'LIGHT' will be written as VJIKN in that language.

Hence, the correct option is (A).

66. The series follows the following pattern:

$101^2 + 11 = 10212$

$103^2 + 22 = 10631$

$107^2 + 33 = 11482$

$109^2 + 44 = 11925$

$113^2 + 55 = 12824$

We can see that $101, 103, 107, 109$ & 113 are prime numbers.

According to the logic the next number after 12824 is $127^2 + 66 = 16195$

Hence, the correct option is (A).

67. The series follows the following pattern:

$\left(16 \times \frac{11}{2}\right) - 1 = 87$

$\left(16 \times \frac{13}{2}\right) - 1 = 103$

$\left(16 \times \frac{17}{2}\right) - 1 = 135$

$\left(16 \times \frac{19}{2}\right) - 1 = 151$

$\left(16 \times \frac{23}{2}\right) - 1 = 183$

$\Rightarrow$ According to the logic the next number after 183 is

$\left(16 \times \frac{29}{2}\right) - 1 = 231$.

Hence, the correct option is (C).

68. The pattern of the given series is:

$\Rightarrow 12 \times 1 = 12$

$\Rightarrow 12 \times 1.5 = 18$

$\Rightarrow 18 \times 2 = 36$

$\Rightarrow 36 \times 2.5 = 90$

$\Rightarrow 90 \times 3 = 270$

Hence, the correct option is (A).

69. The logic of the series can be explained as:

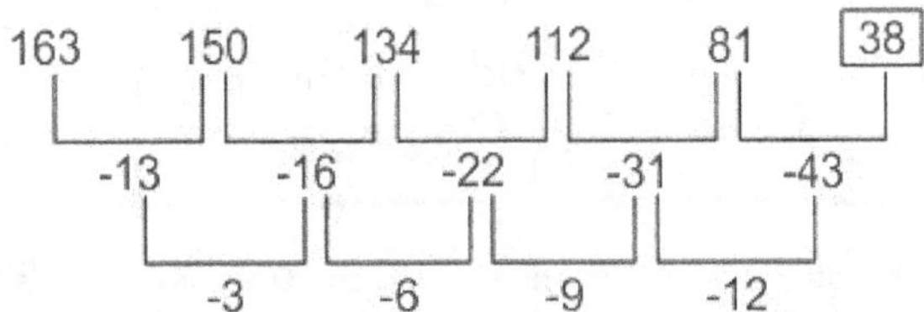

$\therefore$ The value of $?$ is 38.

Hence, the correct option is (C).

70. The series follows the following pattern:

$\Rightarrow 3 \times 1 + 1 = 4$

$\Rightarrow 4 \times 2 + 2 = 10$

$\Rightarrow 10 \times 3 + 3 = 33$

$\Rightarrow 33 \times 4 + 4 = 136$

$\Rightarrow 136 \times 5 + 5 = 685$

$\Rightarrow 685 \times 6 + 6 = 4116$

$\therefore$ The value of $?$ is 685.

Hence, the correct option is (B).

71. I. $x^2 - 50x + 225 = 0$

$\Rightarrow x^2 - 45x - 5x + 225 = 0$

$\Rightarrow x(x - 45) - 5(x - 45) = 0$

$\Rightarrow (x - 5)(x - 45) = 0$

$\Rightarrow x = 5, 45$

II. $y^2 + 32y - 105 = 0$

$\Rightarrow y^2 + 35y - 3y - 105 = 0$

$\Rightarrow y(y + 35) - 3(y + 35) = 0$

$\Rightarrow (y - 3)(y + 35)$

$\Rightarrow y = 3, -35$

$\therefore x > y$

Hence, the correct option is (A).

72. I. $24x^2 + 38x + 15 = 0$

$\Rightarrow 24x^2 + 18x + 20x + 15 = 0$

$\Rightarrow 6x(4x + 3) + 5(4x + 3) = 0$

$\Rightarrow (6x + 5)(4x + 3) = 0$

$\Rightarrow x = -\dfrac{5}{6}, -\dfrac{3}{4}$

II. $54y^2 + 123y + 65 = 0$

$\Rightarrow 54y^2 + 78y + 45y + 65 = 0$

$\Rightarrow 6y(9y + 13) + 5(9y + 13) = 0$

$\Rightarrow (6y + 5)(9y + 13) = 0$

$\Rightarrow y = -\dfrac{5}{6}, -\dfrac{13}{9}$

$\therefore x \geq y$

Hence, the correct option is (C).

73. I. $2x^2 - 19x + 45 = 0$

$\Rightarrow 2x^2 - 10x - 9x + 45 = 0$

$\Rightarrow 2x(x - 5) - 9(x - 5) = 0$

$\Rightarrow (2x - 9)(x - 5) = 0$

$\Rightarrow x = \dfrac{9}{2}, 5$

II. $3y^2 - 17y + 20 = 0$

$\Rightarrow 3y^2 - 12y - 5y + 20 = 0$

$\Rightarrow 3y(y - 4) - 5(y - 4) = 0$

$\Rightarrow (3y - 5)(y - 4) = 0$

$\Rightarrow y = \dfrac{5}{3}, 4$

$\therefore x > y$

Hence, the correct option is (A).

74. I. $x^2 + 13x - 140 = 0$

$\Rightarrow x^2 + 20x - 7x - 140 = 0$

$\Rightarrow x(x + 20) - 7(x + 20) = 0$

$\Rightarrow (x + 20)(x - 7) = 0$

$\Rightarrow x = -20, 7$

II. $y^2 - 13y - 140 = 0$

$\Rightarrow y^2 - 20y + 7y - 140 = 0$

$\Rightarrow y(y - 20) + 7(y - 20) = 0$

$\Rightarrow (y - 20)(y + 7)$

$\Rightarrow v = 20 - 7$

$\therefore$ x = y or relationship between x and y cannot be established.

Hence, the correct option is (E).

75. I. $2x^2 + 23x + 56 = 0$

$\Rightarrow 2x^2 + 16x + 7x + 56 = 0$

$\Rightarrow 2x(x + 8) + 7(x + 8) = 0$

$\Rightarrow (2x + 7)(x + 8) = 0$

$\Rightarrow x = -\dfrac{7}{2}, -8$

II. $12y^2 + 41y + 35 = 0$

$\Rightarrow 12y^2 + 21y + 20y + 35 = 0$

$\Rightarrow 3y(4y + 7) + 5(4y + 7) = 0$

$\Rightarrow (3y + 5)(4y + 7) = 0$

$\Rightarrow y = -\dfrac{5}{3}, -\dfrac{7}{4}$

$\therefore$ y > x

Hence, the correct option is (B).

76. Ratio of shares of A, B and C = Ratio of their investments for 2 years

= [(5000 × 2): (7000 × 2): (6000 × 2)]

= [10000: 14000: 12000]

= 5: 7: 6

Given: Net profit earned = Rs. 10,800

$\therefore$ B's share = $\dfrac{7}{18}$ × 10800 = Rs. 4,200

Hence, the correct option is (B).

77. Let, the cost price of $1g$ sugar be $Rs.\,1$

Assume he sells $1000g$ sugar.

Since he uses false weight he actually sells only $950g$ sugar. Therefore, the actual cost price for him is Rs. 950.

Selling price $=$ Rs. 1000

Profit percentage $= \dfrac{(1000-950)}{950} \times 100$

$$= \frac{100}{19}\%$$

$$= 5\frac{5}{19}\%$$

Hence, the correct option is (C).

78. We know that,

Sum of observations = Average × Number of Observations

Correct sum of observations = [sum of the observations – (wrong observation) + (correct observation)]

According to the question,

Calculated average of 26 articles = 40

Incorrect sum of 26 articles = 40 × 26 = 1040

Correct sum of 26 articles = Incorrect sum – sum of incorrect articles + sum of correct articles

Correct sum = 1040 – (20 + 18) + (40 + 24)

= 1040 – 38 + 64

= 1066

Correct average = $\frac{1066}{26}$ = 41

Hence, the correct option is (D).

79. Given:

Sanju complete a work $= 12$ days

Suraj complete a work $= 16$ days

Sanjay complete a work $= 24$ days

As we know,

Total Wok Done $=$ Number of Days $\times$ Efficiency

Let the efficiencies (work is done per day) of Sanju, Suraj and Sanjay be ' a ', ' b ' and ' c ' respectively.

Let total work be 1 unit.

Then, $(a \times 12) = 1$

$$\Rightarrow a = \frac{1}{12}$$

Then, $(b \times 16) = 1$

$$\Rightarrow b = \frac{1}{16}$$

Then, $(c \times 24) = 1$

$$c = \frac{1}{24}$$

Time Taken by Sanju, Suraj and Sanjay together $= \frac{\text{Total work done}}{\text{Efficiency}}$

$$= \frac{1}{\left\{\left(\frac{1}{12}\right)+\left(\frac{1}{16}\right)+\left(\frac{1}{24}\right)\right\}}$$

$$= \frac{48}{(4+3+2)}$$

$$= \frac{48}{9} \text{ days}$$

$$= \frac{16}{3} \text{days}$$

∴ Sanju, Suraj and Sanjay together complete the whole work in $\frac{16}{3}$ days.

Hence, the correct option is (A).

80. Given,

Let price of other type liquid be Rs. N per litre.

Using allegation rule,

$$\Rightarrow \frac{6}{4} = \frac{(N-90)}{(90-80)}$$

$$\Rightarrow \frac{6}{4} = \frac{(N-90)}{10}$$

$$\Rightarrow 4N - 360 = 60$$

$$\Rightarrow N = 105$$

Price of other type liquid is Rs. 105.

Given,

Let the price of new mixture be Rs. M.

$$\Rightarrow (M - 80) = (105 - M)$$

$$\Rightarrow 2M = 185$$

$$\Rightarrow M = 92.5$$

∴ The price of new mixture is Rs. 92.5.

Hence, the correct option is (C).

81. Given,

Time taken by tap A to fill the tank =12 hours

Part filled by tap A in 1 hour = $\frac{1}{12}$

Time taken by tap B to fill the tank = 15 hours

Part filled by tap A in 1 hour = $\frac{1}{15}$

Time taken by tap C to fill the tank = 20 hours

Part filled by tap C in 1 hour = $\frac{1}{20}$

(A + B) 's 1 hour work $= \frac{1}{12} + \frac{1}{15}$

$$= \frac{9}{60}$$

$$= \frac{3}{20}$$

(A + C) 's 1 hour work $= \frac{1}{12} + \frac{1}{20}$

$$= \frac{8}{60}$$

$$= \frac{2}{15}$$

Part filled in 2 hours $= \frac{3}{20} + \frac{2}{15}$

$$= \frac{17}{60}$$

Part filled in 6 hours $= 3 \times \frac{17}{60}$

$$= \frac{17}{20}$$

Remaining part $= 1 - \frac{17}{20}$

$$= \frac{3}{20}$$

Since the remaining part is $\frac{3}{20}$ and this part can be filled by tap A and B in 1 hour.

So, total time taken = 6 + 1

= 7 hours

$\therefore$ The total time taken for the tank is 7 hours.

Hence, the correct option is (C).

82. Given:

In the year 1995 = 3000

Number of students studying in the school in different years:

In the year 1996 = 3000 - 250 + 350 = 3100

In the year 1997 = 3100 - 450 + 300 = 2950

In the year 1998 = 2950 - 400 + 450 = 3000

In the year 1999 = 3000 - 350 + 500 = 3150

In the year 2000 = 3150 - 450 + 400 = 3100

In the year 2001 = 3100 - 450 + 550 = 3200

So, the number of students studying in the school during the year 1999 = 3150

Hence, the correct option is (D).

83. The percentage rise/fall in the number of students who left the school (compared to the previous year) during various years are:

For $1997 = [\frac{(450-250)}{250} \times 100]\% = 80\%$ (rise)

For $1998 = [\frac{(450-400)}{450} \times 100]\% = 11.11\%$ (fall)

For $1999 = [\frac{(400-350)}{400} \times 100]\% = 12.5\%$ (fall)

For $2000 = [\frac{(450-350)}{350} \times 100]\% = 28.57\%$ (rise)

For $2001 = [\frac{(450-450)}{450} \times 100]\% = 0\%$

Clearly, the maximum percentage rise/fall is for 1997.

Hence, the correct option is (A).

84. Important data noted from the given graph:

In 1996 : Number of students left = 250 and students joined = 350.

In 1997 : Number of students left = 450 and students joined = 300.

In 1998 : Number of students left = 400 and students joined = 450.

In 1999 : Number of students left = 350 and students joined = 500.

In 2000 : Number of students left = 450 and students joined = 400.

In 2001 : Number of students left = 450 and students joined = 550.

Therefore, the numbers of students studying in the school (i.e., strength of the school) in various years:

In 1995 = 3000 (given)

In 1996 = 3000 - 250 + 350 = 3100

In 1997 = 3100 - 450 + 300 = 2950

In 1998 = 2950 - 400 + 450 = 3000

In 1999 = 3000 - 350 + 500 = 3150

In 2000 = 3150 - 450 + 400 = 3100

In 2001 = 3100 - 450 + 550 = 3200

Percentage increase in the strength of the school from 1997 to 1998 $= [\frac{(3000-2950)}{2950} \times 100]\%$

$$= 1.69\% \approx 1.7\%$$

Hence, the correct option is (B).

85. Required percentage $= \left(\frac{3000}{3200} \times 100\right)\%$

$$= 93.75\%$$

Hence, the correct option is (B).

86. Required ratio= 300 : 450

= 2 : 3

Hence, the correct option is (D).

87. Quantity A:

Given,

Quantity = 63 liters

Initial ratio (alcohol : water) = 5 : 4

Final ratio (alcohol : water) = 3 : 2

Total mixture (ratio) = 5 + 4 = 9 ratio

9 ratio = 63 liters

→ 1 ratio = 7 liters

∴ Alcohol = 5 ratio = 35 liters

and, water = 4 ratio = 28 liters

Since the amount of water will remain same,

For final ratio, 2 ratio = 28 liters

∴ 3 ratio = 42 liters

So, alcohol quantity in the new mixture = 42 liters

Quantity B: 43 Liters

∴ Quantity A < Quantity B

Hence, the correct option is (B).

88. Quantity A:

Given,

Initial distance = 200 m (Bus ahead)

Distance after 63 seconds = 150 m (car ahead)

Car's speed = 78 km/h

When two objects are moving in the same direction the relative speed is the difference of their individual speeds.

Formula used:

$$\text{Speed} = \frac{Distance}{Time}$$

$$\text{Relative speed} = \frac{(200+150)}{63}$$

$$= \frac{350}{63}$$

$$\Rightarrow \frac{50}{9} \text{ m/s}$$

$$\Rightarrow \frac{50}{9} \times \frac{18}{5}$$

$$= 20 \text{ km/hr}$$

Also, Relative speed = Car's speed - Bus's speed

$$\therefore 20 = 78 \text{ - Bus's speed}$$

$$\Rightarrow \text{Bus's speed} = 58 \text{ km/hr}$$

∴ Speed of the bus is 58 km/hr.

Quantity B: 60 km/h

∴ Quantity A < Quantity B

Hence, the correct option is (B).

89. Quantity A:

Given,

Selling Price 1 = Rs. 19972

Selling Price 2 = Rs. 17228

Desired S.P = Rs. 20088

Formula used:

$$\text{Profit\%} = \frac{Profit}{\text{Cost Price}} \times 100$$

Let the Cost Price be Rs. x.

According to the question:

19972 - x = x - 17228

⇒ 2x = 37200

⇒ x = Rs. 18600

Now, Profit = 20088 - 18600

= Rs. 1488

$$\therefore \text{Profit\%} = \frac{1488}{18600} \times 100$$

= 8%

Quantity B: 10%

∴ Quantity A < Quantity B

Hence, the correct option is (B).

90. Given,

Surface area of the cylinder $= 1672m^2$

As we know,

Surface area of the cylinder $= 2\pi r(r + h)$

According to the question,

$$\Rightarrow 2\pi r(r + h) = 1672m^2$$

$$\Rightarrow 2 \times \frac{22}{7} \times r \times 19 = 1672m^2$$

$$\Rightarrow r = \frac{(1672 \times 7)}{(2 \times 22 \times 19)}$$

$$\Rightarrow r = 14$$

$$\therefore h = 19 - 14 = 5m$$

Volume of the cylinder $= \pi r^2 h$

$$= \frac{22}{7} \times 14 \times 14 \times 5$$

$$= 3080m^3$$

Hence, the correct option is (A).

91. Given,

$$? = 40\% \text{ of } 320 + 4^3 \div 16 \times 108 \div 8$$

$$\Rightarrow ? = \frac{40}{100} \times 320 + 4^3 \div 16 \times 108 \div 8$$

$$\Rightarrow ? = 128 + 64 \div 16 \times 108 \div 8$$

$$\Rightarrow ? = 128 + 4 \times \left(\frac{27}{2}\right)$$

$$\Rightarrow ? = 128 + 54$$

$$\Rightarrow ? = 182$$

$\therefore$ The value of ? is 182.

Hence, the correct option is (E).

92. Given,

$$35\% \text{ of } 180 + 18^2 = (27)^{\frac{5}{3}} + ?^2$$

$$\Rightarrow \frac{35}{100} \times 180 + 324 = 3^5 + ?^2$$

$$\Rightarrow 63 + 324 = 243 + ?^2$$

$$\Rightarrow ? = \sqrt{(324 + 63 - 243)}$$

$$\Rightarrow ? = \sqrt{(387 - 243)}$$

$$\Rightarrow ? = \sqrt{(144)}$$

$$\Rightarrow ? = 12$$

$\therefore$ The value of ? is 12.

Hence, the correct option is (C).

93. Given,

$$38 + 41 \times (441 \div 21) - 17^2 = ?$$

$$\Rightarrow 38 + 41 \times 21 - 289 = ?$$

$$\Rightarrow 38 + 861 - 289 = ?$$

$$\Rightarrow ? = 610$$

$\therefore$ The value of ? is 610.

Hence, the correct option is (C).

94. Given,

$$(25^2 - 106) \div 3 - 13^2 + 35 = ?$$

$$\Rightarrow (625 - 106) \div 3 - 169 + 35 = ?$$

$$\Rightarrow 519 \div 3 - 169 + 35 = ?$$

$$\Rightarrow 173 - 169 + 35 = ?$$

$$\Rightarrow ? = 39$$

$\therefore$ The value of ? is 39.

Hence, the correct option is (A).

95. Given:

$$6.67\% \text{ of } 225 + 6.25\% \text{ of } 1120 = (?)^3 + 3$$

$$\Rightarrow \frac{1}{15} \times 225 + \frac{1}{16} \times 1120 = (?)^3 + 3$$

$$\Rightarrow 15 + 70 = (?)^3 + 3$$

$$\Rightarrow 85 = (?)^3 + 3$$

$$\Rightarrow (?)^3 = 82$$

$$\Rightarrow ? = (82)^{\frac{1}{3}}$$

The value of ? is $(82)^{\frac{1}{3}}$.

Hence, the correct option is (E).

96. Given:

$$(999 + 99 + 9) + 5.55\% \text{ of } 90 = ?$$

We know that value of 5.55% is $\frac{1}{18}$

$$1107 + \frac{1}{18} \text{ of } 90 = ?$$

$$\Rightarrow 1107 + 5 = ?$$

$$\Rightarrow 1112 = ?$$

$\therefore$ The value of ? is 1112.

Hence, the correct option is (D).

97. Given:

$$32 + 65 - 16\frac{2}{3}\% \text{ of } 96 = ? + 33\frac{1}{3}\% \text{ of } 120$$

$$\Rightarrow 97 - \frac{50}{3}\% \text{ of } 96 = ? + \frac{100}{3}\% \text{ of } 120$$

$$\Rightarrow 97 - \frac{50}{(3 \times 100)} \times 96 = ? + \frac{100}{(3 \times 100)} \times 120$$

$$\Rightarrow 97 - 16 = ? + 40$$

$$\Rightarrow ? = 97 - 56$$

$$\Rightarrow ? = 41$$

$\therefore$ The value of ? is 41.

Hence, the correct option is (C).

98. As we know,

$$25\% = \frac{1}{4} \text{ and } 14\frac{2}{7}\% = \frac{1}{7}$$

Given:

$$25\% \text{ of } 7428 + 71.5 \times 2 = 14\frac{2}{7}\% \text{ of } ?$$

$$\Rightarrow \frac{1}{4} \times 7428 + 143 = \frac{1}{7} \times ?$$

$$\Rightarrow 1857 + 143 = \frac{1}{7} \times ?$$

$$\Rightarrow 2000 = \frac{1}{7} \times ?$$

$$\Rightarrow ? = 7 \times 2000$$

$\Rightarrow ? = 14000$

Hence, the correct option is (D).

99. Given:

31% of $200 + 21\%$ of $300 = 25 \times 5 + ?^2 - 40\%$ of 90

$\Rightarrow \dfrac{31}{100} \times 200 + \dfrac{21}{100} \times 300 = 125 + ?^2 - \dfrac{40}{100} \times 90$

$\Rightarrow 62 + 63 = 125 + ?^2 - 36$

$\Rightarrow ?^2 = 36$

$\Rightarrow ? = 6$

$\therefore$ The value of $?$ is 6.

Hence, the correct option is (C).

100. Given:

$\sqrt[3]{6859} + \sqrt{441} - \sqrt[3]{4096} - \sqrt{576} = ?$

$\Rightarrow 19 + 21 - 16 - 24 = ?$

$\Rightarrow 19 + 21 - 16 - 24 = ?$

$\Rightarrow 40 - 40 = ?$

$\Rightarrow ? = 0$

$\therefore$ The value of $?$ is 0.

Hence, the correct option is (C).

Ques (1-5):Direction: Below, a set of eight statements is given, out of which the first sentence, given in bold, is fixed. The rest are jumbled in any random order. Out of the remaining seven statements, one does not belong to the passage. Rearrange the remaining sentences in the correct order and then answer the question.

A. Until the early 2000s, Bollywood remained the main source of entertainment for the Himalayan monarchy of Bhutan.

B. As the industry continues to boom, a new parallel cinema movement, made mostly for an international audience, is emerging.

C. Arun Bhattarai's The Next Guardian, a bittersweet documentary set in a remote monastery, also features a character going through a sexual identity crisis.

D. Passionate, self-taught film-makers, armed with themes ranging from magical realism to social justice and sexual identity, have begun to appear in major international film festivals in recent years.

E. The advent of the internet brought along a tidal wave of new content and a nascent parallel voice has also begun taking shape.

F. It was a love triangle about two college boys falling for the same girl, that birthed the commercial Bhutanese film industry.

G. Two decades later, commercial Bhutanese films continue to ride on Bollywood influences, with staple themes of mawkish drama, syrupy duets and acrobatic action sequences featuring prominently.

H. It was in 1999 when the late Tshering Wangyel released the first Dzongkha-language movie called Rewaa (Hope).

Q.1 Which of the following sentences is SECOND in the correct order?
A. B   B. G   C. E   D. H
E. F

Q.2 Which of the following sentences is FOURTH in the correct order?
A. E   B. C   C. G   D. B
E. H

Q.3 Which of the following sentences does not belong in the given passage?
A. E   B. F   C. G   D. H
E. C

Q.4 Which of the following sentences is FIFTH in the correct order?
A. C   B. E   C. B   D. F
E. H

Q.5 Which of the following sentences is SIXTH in the correct order?
A. E   B. D   C. C   D. B
E. G

Ques (6-10):Direction: Read the passage and answer the following question.

Mother Teresa is famous in the history of mankind for her charity work toward the poor, sick, helpless, homeless, and downtrodden people of the society. She was born on 27th August, 1910 in Yugoslavia, as Agnes Gonxha Bojaxhin, to Albanian parents.

Agnes Gonxha became a nun of the Order of the Sisters of Our Lady of Loreto in Ireland at an early age of 18 years. She came to India and commenced her novitiate (a beginner becoming a nun) in 1928 in Darjeeling, a hill station in the Indian State of West Bengal. She soon became the principal of the institution. Agnes Gonxha adopted the name "Teresa" in 1931, in memory of Saint Thérèse of Lisieux. In 1946 Agnes felt an inner calling to serve the poor, sick, old, and helpless people. Accordingly, she obtained permission from Pope Pius XII in 1948 to leave the convent and serve the people living in the slums and in the streets.

In 1948 Agnes Gonxha managed to secure Indian citizenship and started to drape herself in a sari. In 1950 she started her own order "Missionaries of Charity" to look after the **unloved**, abandoned, and unwanted people. She also ran many children's homes to look after the orphaned, retarded and sick children. Gradually she came to be known as Mother Teresa. Mother Teresa's Missionaries of Charity founded "Nirmal Hriday", which is a home for the dying, at an abandoned Kali temple in Kalighat in West Bengal. In 1953 Mother Teresa founded her first orphanage. She also started a home for the lepers in the year 1957 in Kolkata. Gradually she **established** around 570 homes for the poor in more than 125 countries, both in the East and in the West.

Mother Teresa was **honored** with several awards for her contributions to the human society. These awards include the Nobel Prize for Peace in 1979, Bharat Ratna (Highest Civilian Award in India) in 1980, Templeton Award (Britain), Magsaysay Award (The Philippines), Presidential Medal of Freedom from President Ronald Reagan, etc. However, fame and recognitions mattered very little to her. Mother Teresa breathed her last on September 5, 1997, in Kolkata, India. She was buried within the premises of Missionaries of Charity in Kolkata. She has been beatified by the Catholic Church. This is a step towards becoming a Saint. Now she is referred to as Blessed Teresa of Calcutta.

Q.6 Mother Teresa is currently referred to as:
A.   Teresa
B.   Saint Teresa
C.   Blessed Teresa of Calcutta

D. Agnes Gonxha

E. None of these

Q.7 Which were some of the awards that Mother Teresa received?

(A). Nobel Prize for Peace in 1979

(B). Bharat Ratna in 1980 (India)

(C). Magsaysay Award (The Philippines)

A. Only (A) **B.** Only (B)

C. Only (C) **D.** All of the above

E. None of these

Q.8 What was the name of the home set up by the Missionaries of Charity for the dying?

A. Kalighat

B. Missionaries of Charity

C. Nirmal Hriday

D. Home for the dying

E. Order of the Sisters of Our Lady of Loreto

Q.9 Which children did Mother Teresa look after?

(A). Orphaned

(B). Sick

(C). Active

A. Only (A) **B.** Only (B)

C. Only (C) **D.** All except (C)

E. All of the above

Q.10 What does the word 'unloved' mean in the passage?

A. Uncared for

B. An intense feeling of deep affection

C. A great interest and pleasure in something

D. Love, loyalty, or enthusiasm for a person or activity

E. Not having or showing the necessary skills to do something successfully

Ques (11-15):Direction: A passage is given below with the blanks labeled (A)-(J). Below the passage, five options are given for each blank. Choose the word that fits each blank most appropriately in the context of the passage, and mark the corresponding answer.

The heatwave conditions in India will be "serious" before monsoon hits various parts of the country, said the World Meteorological Organisation (WMO), as global temperature records were smashed yet again in April, 2016.

Though heatwaves are common in India from April through June, this year ___(A)___ [contains] seen an exceptionally powerful one. The climate pattern sits well with the general global experience this year of record high temperatures in most parts of the world.

Last year, El Niño, a climactic occurrence ___(B)___ **[above]** the Pacific Ocean that unusually spikes up the ocean temperatures was ___(C)___ **[interrogated]** for severe droughts and dry spells over southern Africa, South and South-east Asia, the US and the western Pacific. The event also ___(D)___ **[accelerating]** powerful west Pacific typhoons.

El Nino that has a significant impact on the Asian monsoon has a high probability of becoming a La Nina weather system, the opposite of El Niño towards the end of the year. La Niña brings cooler temperatures, ___(E)___ **[greater]** rainfall, including to the South East Asian region, sometimes even flooding countries.

Frequent deficit monsoons are ___(F)___ **[developing]** common in India as well as in other parts of the subcontinent. An increase in extreme rainfall events have occurred at the expense of ___(G)___ **[inadequate]** rainfall events over the central Indian region and in many other areas, according to the Intergovernmental Panel on Climate Change (IPCC) findings.

___(H)___ **[Expeditious]** climate change and thinning snow covers may also have ___(I)___ **[hold]** an impact on the increasing Indian temperatures, like for most other parts of the world. The threats on health from rising temperatures are real. Last month, the WMO and WHO hosted a climate and health forum to ___(J)___**[encourage]** heat-health early warning systems to encourage countries to respond better.

Q.11 Which of the following fits in the blank labelled (A)?

A. Have **B.** were **C.** Has **D.** was

E. had

Q.12 Which of the following fits in the blank labelled (B)?

A. Over **B.** on **C.** At **D.** For

E. of

Q.13 Which of the following fits in the blank labelled (C)?

A. Question **B.** Asked **C.** say **D.** Blamed

E. praised

Q.14 Which of the following fits in the blank labelled (F)?

A. coming **B.** becoming

C. become **D.** Approaching

E. became

Q.15 Which of the following fits in the blank labelled (G)?

A. weak **B.** strong **C.** fewer **D.** stronger

E. Weaker

Ques (16-20):Direction: Which of the phrases given below the sentence should replace the word/phrase given below in bold in the sentence to make it grammatically correct? If the sentence is correct as it is given and no correction is required, mark 'No correction required' as the answer.

Q.16 I have great **antipathy towards** the people who are born with a silver spoon.

A. antipathy for

B. antipathy to

C. antipathy on

D. antipathy against

E. No correction required

Q.17 The technician **impressed on** the need for focus and innovation, which were necessary for the upcoming project.

A. impressed upon

B. impressed into

C. impressed onto

D. impressed with

E. No correction required

Q.18 The unfortunate husband **pined off** in the memory of his lost wife, who had died an untimely death.

A. pined away

B. pined

C. pined down

D. pined up

E. No correction required

Q.19 Mahatma Gandhi **say that** honesty is the best policy.

A. speak

B. were saying

C. says that

D. say

E. No correction required

Q.20 The aeroplane **alighted at the airport and it was ahead of its** scheduled time.

A. alighted on the airport and it was ahead of its

B. alighted at the airport and it was ahead of it's

C. alighted in the airport and it was ahead of its

D. alighted the airport and it was ahead of its

E. No correction required

Q.21 Choose the correctly spelt word from the options.

A. Sacriligeous **B.** Sacrilegious

C. Sacriligious **D.** Sacrilegeous

E. Sacrilegeuos

Q.22 Choose the correctly spelt word from the options.

A. Puritanical **B.** Puirtanical

C. Pruitanical **D.** Pirutanical

E. Piurtanical

Q.23 Choose the correctly spelt word from the options.

A. Schrizophenia **B.** Schizophenia

C. Schyzophrenia **D.** Schizophrenia

E. Schiozphrenia

Q.24 Direction: Select the most appropriate synonym of the given word.

Embezzle

A. Misappropriate **B.** Balance

C. Remunerate **D.** Clear

E. None of these

Q.25 Direction: Select the most appropriate antonym of the given word.

Persuasion

A. Dislike **B.** Discouraging

C. Convincing **D.** Induce

E. None of these

Ques (26-30):Direction: In the following question, a sentence is divided into five parts; (A), (B), (C), (D) and (E). There may be an error in one of the parts, which makes the sentence grammatically or contextually incorrect. Choose the option with the part containing error.

Q.26 It brings with it issues not only of cultural and (A) / managerial alterations, but rather various financial conflicts, (B) / such as internal disputes between the banks (C) / that could affect lending as well as recovery. (D) / No error (E)

A. A **B.** B **C.** C **D.** D

E. E

Q.27 Issues could include something as simple as an internal (A) / hierarchical muddle to more direct and large conflicts like priority (B)/ of charge on securities in cases of common stressed assets, (C) / and the different recovery process being followed by each bank. (D) / No error (E)

A. A **B.** B **C.** C **D.** D

E. E

Q.28 It is necessary that resources be dedicated (A) / towards engaging competent teams (B) / from oversee and resolve issues arising (C) out of such a transition phase. (D) / No error (E)

A. A **B.** B **C.** C **D.** D

E. E

Q.29 Global oil demand is muted against the backdrop in economic uncertainty (A) / and continuing trade frictions, and there has been (B) / a surge in petroleum output in the US and elsewhere, (C) / which should ease oil prices sooner rather than later. (D) / No error (E)

A. A **B.** B **C.** C **D.** D

E. E

Q.30 The way ahead is for the government to (A) / fast forward long pending reform of (B) / oil marketing, so as to purposefully shore on (C) / investments and revamp market design in oil. / No error (E)

A. A **B.** B **C.** C **D.** D

E. E

// Smart Answer Sheet //

Correct   Indicates percentage of students who answered questions correctly.

Skipped   Indicates percentage of students who skipped questions.

Q.	Ans.	Correct / Skipped
1	D	69.96 % / 30.03 %
2	C	30.69 % / 67.21 %
3	E	68.26 % / 31.11 %
4	B	60.68 % / 34.15 %
5	D	26.71 % / 70.03 %
6	C	46.01 % / 39.13 %

Q.	Ans.	Correct / Skipped
7	D	15.69 % / 67.57 %
8	C	55.81 % / 36.94 %
9	C	56.4 % / 32.39 %
10	A	81.98 % / 14.82 %
11	C	54.48 % / 34.3 %
12	A	62.02 % / 37.55 %

Q.	Ans.	Correct / Skipped
13	D	45.46 % / 31.17 %
14	B	30.81 % / 67.82 %
15	E	46.02 % / 49.84 %
16	D	19.37 % / 70.41 %
17	A	49.53 % / 36.78 %
18	A	56.07 % / 38.01 %

Q.	Ans.	Correct / Skipped
19	C	26.19 % / 70.79 %
20	E	29.82 % / 67.28 %
21	B	26.62 % / 67.58 %
22	A	48.94 % / 47.9 %
23	D	52.49 % / 38.44 %
24	A	87.37 % / 12.39 %

Q.	Ans.	Correct / Skipped
25	B	68.66 % / 30.9 %
26	B	19.34 % / 78.01 %
27	B	55.4 % / 42.83 %
28	C	53.42 % / 35.83 %
29	A	55.06 % / 36.09 %
30	C	58.45 % / 34.95 %

Performance Analysis	
Avg. Score (%)	50.0%
Toppers Score (%)	63.33%
Your Score	

//Hints and Solutions//

1. The first sentence of a paragraph gives an introduction, which is then elaborated in the following sentences.

A is given as the first, introductory sentence. So, logically, the next sentence must give more information about the Bhutanese cinema circa 2000.

This is only shown by H, which talks about the first commercially successful Bhutanese film. **So, H is the second sentence.**

Sentence F gives more information about the film in H. **So, F is the third sentence.**

The next sentences talk about the current state of commercial cinema. **So, G must be fourth.**

E talks about the emergence of current parallel cinema. **So, E must be fifth.**

It is followed logically by B, which talks about its audience. **So, B is the sixth sentence.**

The remaining sentence, **D, is then, the seventh.**

The correct order is : **AHFGEBD**

Hence, the correct option is (D).

2. The first sentence of a paragraph gives an introduction, which is then elaborated in the following sentences.

A is given as the first, introductory sentence. So, logically, the next sentence must give more information about the Bhutanese cinema circa 2000.

This is only shown by H, which talks about the first commercially successful Bhutanese film. **So, H is the second sentence.**

Sentence F gives more information about the film in H. **So, F is the third sentence.**

The next sentences talk about the current state of commercial cinema. **So, G must be fourth.**

E talks about the emergence of current parallel cinema. **So, E must be fifth.**

It is followed logically by B, which talks about its audience. **So, B is the sixth sentence.**

The remaining sentence, **D, is then, the seventh.**

The correct order is : **AHFGEBD**

Hence, the correct option is (C).

3. The context of most sentences is the emergence of Bhutanese cinema.

Only C talks about Anil Bhattarai's documentary. **So, C is out of context.**

The first sentence of a paragraph gives an introduction, which is then elaborated in the following sentences.

A is given as the first, introductory sentence. So, logically, the next sentence must give more information about the Bhutanese cinema circa 2000.

This is only shown by H, which talks about the first commercially successful Bhutanese film. **So, H is the second sentence.**

Sentence F gives more information about the film in H. **So, F is the third sentence.**

The next sentences talk about the current state of commercial cinema. **So, G must be fourth.**

E talks about the emergence of current parallel cinema. **So, E must be fifth.**

It is followed logically by B, which talks about its audience. **So, B is the sixth sentence.**

The remaining sentence, **D, is then, the seventh.**

The correct order is : **AHFGEBD**

Hence, the correct option is (E).

4. The first sentence of a paragraph gives an introduction, which is then elaborated in the following sentences.

A is given as the first, introductory sentence. So, logically, the next sentence must give more information about the Bhutanese cinema circa 2000.

This is only shown by H, which talks about the first commercially successful Bhutanese film. **So, H is the second sentence.**

Sentence F gives more information about the film in H. **So, F is the third sentence.**

The next sentences talk about the current state of commercial cinema. **So, G must be fourth.**

E talks about the emergence of current parallel cinema. **So, E must be fifth.**

It is followed logically by B, which talks about its audience. **So, B is the sixth sentence.**

The remaining sentence, **D, is then, the seventh.**

The correct order is : **AHFGEBD**

Hence, the correct option is (B).

5. The first sentence of a paragraph gives an introduction, which is then elaborated in the following sentences.

A is given as the first, introductory sentence. So, logically, the next sentence must give more information about the Bhutanese cinema circa 2000.

This is only shown by H, which talks about the first commercially successful Bhutanese film. **So, H is the second sentence.**

Sentence F gives more information about the film in H. **So, F is the third sentence.**

The next sentences talk about the current state of commercial cinema. **So, G must be fourth.**

E talks about the emergence of current parallel cinema. **So, E must be fifth.**

It is followed logically by B, which talks about its audience. **So, B is the sixth sentence.**

The remaining sentence, **D, is then, the seventh.**

The correct order is : **AHFGEBD**

Hence, the correct option is (D).

6. The passage is about Mother Teresa and her charitable work.

Important point:

The following is stated in the passage: "Now she is referred to as Blessed Teresa of Calcutta."

Her major work was in Kolkata (also known as Calcutta). She spent most of her life serving the less privileged people of West Bengal.

Therefore, now she is also known as Blessed Teresa of Calcutta.

Hence, the correct option is (C).

7. The passage is about Mother Teresa and her charitable work.

Important point:

The following is stated in the passage: "Mother Teresa was honored with several awards for her contributions to human society. These awards include the Nobel Prize for Peace in 1979, Bharat Ratna (Highest Civilian Award in India) in 1980, Templeton Award (Britain), Magsaysay Award (The Philippines), Presidential Medal of Freedom from President Ronald Reagan, etc".

Hence, the correct option is (D).

8. The passage is about Mother Teresa and her charitable work.

Important point:

The following is stated in the passage: "Mother Teresa's Missionaries of Charity founded the "Nirmal Hriday", which is a home for the dying, at an abandoned Kali temple in Kalighat in West Bengal".

Hence, the correct option is (C).

9. The passage is about Mother Teresa and her charitable work.

Important point:

The following is stated in the passage: " She also ran many children's homes to look after the orphaned, retarded and sick children".

Out of all the points, only point (C) is not mentioned in the passage.

Hence, the correct option is (C).

10. The passage is about Mother Teresa and her charitable work.

Important point:

The sentence in the passage containing the above word is: "In 1950 she started her own order "Missionaries of Charity" to look after the unloved, abandoned, and unwanted people".

In this context, it refers to those who didn't receive any love or care and were left to fend for themselves. Mother Teresa set up the organization to look after these people.

Example: "The most terrible thing is the feeling of being unloved".

Hence, the correct option is (A).

11. The context implies that this year exceptionally powerful heatwaves are being seen. It shows an action or situation that started in the past, but continues in the present. This implies the use of present perfect tense. Therefore, 'has' should be used with 'seen'.

Hence, the correct option is (C).

12. By observing the given options, the most obvious option is 'over'. 'On' is used to show a surface of something. 'At' is used to indicate a place or destination. 'For' is used to indicate the use of something. 'Of' is used to show certain relation or connection. The preposition 'over' is used to show a place covered by something. In the given context, El Niño, is a climactic occurrence that is not static in nature and is used to cover the Pacific Ocean. Therefore, we can select option (A) as the most suitable answer.

Hence, the correct option is (A).

13. By observing the given options, we can remove options (A) and (C). This is because; the sentence is written in past tense while option (A) and (C) represent tense consistency error. Therefore, we can eliminate these options. The sentence says that El Niño was responsible for severe droughts. Therefore, 'praised' could not be the correct option. Option (B) is also incorrect as El Niño would not ask for severe droughts. Now as we are left with option (D), we can select it as the most suitable answer.

Hence, the correct option is (D).

14.

The context implies that recurrent deficit of monsoon is becoming common in India. As the action is showing the prevailing trend, the present continuous tense of the given options should be used. Also, here we are talking about a phenomenon that is coming into being. Therefore, a synonym of 'being' will be suitable. Hence, 'becoming' appears as the most suitable option for the given blank.

Hence, the correct option is (B).

15. The context implies that increase in extreme rainfall events has occurred due to feebler rainfall events over the central Indian region. The sentence comprises a sense of comparison as due to feebler rainfall in some regions, increase in extreme rainfall events has occurred. While eliminating the options on this basis, we can eliminate options (A) (B) and (D) directly as they do not fit into the context. Considering the rest of the options, i.e. 'weaker' and 'fewer'; 'weaker' appears as the most suitable option as 'fewer' applies to countable objects.

Hence, the correct option is (E).

16. 'antipathy against' will replace 'antipathy towards'

- antipathy means hatred or scorn.
- Preposition against is used with antipathy, when the object of antipathy is a human being.
- Therefore, the correct answer is: I have great antipathy against the people who are born with a silver spoon.

Hence, the correct option is (D).

17. 'Impressed upon' will replace 'impressed on'.

- impressed upon means advised.
- Therefore, the correct answer is: The technician impressed upon the need for focus and innovation, which were necessary for the upcoming project.

Hence, the correct option is (A).

18. 'pined away' will replace 'pined off'.

- 'pine' takes the preposition 'away'
- pined away means died with grief.
- Therefore, the correct answer is: The unfortunate husband pined away in the memory of his lost wife, who had died an untimely death.

Hence, the correct option is (A).

19. The Plural verb say does not appear to agree with the singular subject Mahatma Gandhi.

- According to the Subject-Verb agreement rule, a verb must be in accordance with the noun. A singular noun must be followed by a singular verb and a plural noun by a plural verb.
- The correct sentence will be "Mahatma Gandhi says that honesty is the best policy."

Hence, the correct option is (C).

20. 'Alighted at' means land at a site or place.

- 'it's' will not be used (see option B) because 'it's' means 'it is' or 'it has'.
- Therefore, the correct answer is: The aeroplane alighted at the airport and it was ahead of its scheduled time.

Hence, the correct option is (E).

21. The correctly spelt word among the given options is 'Sacrilegious'.

- The word 'Sacrilegious' means 'treating something holy or important without respect'.
- Example: The performance is not sacrilegious or blasphemous.

Hence, the correct option is (B).

22. The correct answer is 'Puritanical.'

The correctly spelled word is 'Puritanical' and it means believing or involving the belief that it is important to work hard and control yourself, and that pleasure is wrong or unnecessary.

Hence, the correct option is (A).

23. The correctly spelt word is 'Schizophrenia' and it means a serious mental illness in which a person confuses the real world and the world of the imagination and often behaves in strange and unexpected ways.

Hence, the correct option is (D).

24. Embezzle - steal or misappropriate money placed in one's trust or belonging to the organization for which one works

Misappropriate - dishonestly or unfairly take

Balance - an even distribution of weight enabling someone or something to remain upright and steady

Remunerate - pay (someone) for services rendered or work done

Clear - easy to perceive, understand or interpret

Thus, 'Misappropriate' is the synonym of the word 'Embezzle'.

Hence, the correct option is (A).

25. Persuasion: the action or fact of persuading someone or of being persuaded to do or believe something

Discouraging: causing someone to lose confidence or enthusiasm; depressing

Dislike: feel distaste for or hostility toward

Convincing: capable of causing someone to believe that something is true or real

Induce: to cause something to happen

Thus, from the given meanings, we find that Persuasion and Discouraging are antonyms.

Hence, the correct option is (B).

26. The error lies in the fragment B of the sentence.

'Not only - but also' is a correlative conjunction. In fragment B, 'rather' should be replaced with 'also' in order to make it a grammatically correct sentence.

Correct Sentence:

It brings with it issues not only of cultural and managerial alterations, but also various financial conflicts, such as internal disputes between the banks that could affect lending as well as recovery.

Hence, the correct option is (B).

27. The error lies in the fragment B of the sentence.

The comparative form of the adjective 'large' should be used to describe the conflicts because the accompanying adjective 'more direct' is also in comparative form.

Instead of 'large', 'larger' should be used to make it a grammatically correct sentence.

Correct Sentence :

Issues could include something as simple as an internal hierarchical muddle to more direct and larger conflicts like priority of charge on securities in cases of common stressed assets, and the different recovery process being followed by each bank.

Hence, the correct option is (B).

28. The error lies in the fragment C of the sentence.

The use of preposition 'from' in the fragment C is incorrect. Instead of the preposition 'from', the preposition 'to' should be used to make it a grammatically correct sentence.

Correct Sentence:

It is necessary that resources be dedicated towards engaging competent teams to oversee and resolve issues arising out of such a transition phase.

Hence, the correct option is (C).

29. The error lies in the fragment A of the sentence.

The use of preposition 'in' in the fragment A is incorrect. Instead of the preposition 'in', the preposition 'of' should be used to make it a grammatically correct sentence.

Correct Sentence:

Global oil demand is muted against the backdrop of economic uncertainty and continuing trade frictions, and there's been a surge in petroleum output in the US and elsewhere, which should ease oil prices sooner rather than later.

Hence, the correct option is (A).

30. The error lies in the fragment C of the sentence.

The correct phrasal verb of 'shore' appropriate for this sentence is 'shore up'.

Shore up (phrasal verb)

Meaning : to make something stronger by supporting it.

E.g.: After the earthquake we had to shore up ceilings and walls.

Instead of 'on', 'up' should be used to make it a grammatically correct sentence.

Correct Sentence:

The way ahead is for the government to fast-forward long pending reform of oil marketing, so as to purposefully shore up investments and revamp market design in oil.

Hence, the correct option is (C).

Ques (1-5):Direction: Rearrange the following eight sentences P, Q, R, S, T, U, V and W in the proper sequence to form a meaningful paragraph and answer the question accordingly.

P. What was until then a sport predominantly of the hinterlands received wider recognition as television and newspapers began discovering it.

Q. The Aamir Khan-starrer Dangal, which narrates the story of Mahavir Singh Phogat and his daughters Geeta Phogat and Babita Kumari, was perhaps the icing on the cake.

R. Ever since Sushil Kumar won a bronze medal at the 2008 Beijing Olympics, wrestling has, without doubt, grown by leaps and bounds.

S. Now, it has reached a stage where Sakshi's Olympic bronze is expected to do to women's wrestling what Sushil's did to wrestling in general.

T. Also, independent India's first individual Olympic medal winner was a wrestler: Khashaba Dadasaheb Jadhav, who bagged a bronze in the 1952 Helsinki Games. This aided wrestling in securing a prominent place both in the minds of the country's citizenry as well as in its yet-to-thrive sporting ecosystem.

U. That Sakshi and the Phogats came from Haryana, a State infamous for its skewed gender ratio, even boosted the narrative of the sport now being a tool for breaking gender stereotypes.

V. Even to the uninitiated, the sport's rich moral, philosophical and mystical heritage — with links first to the Ramayana and the Mahabharata through the likes of Hanuman and Bhima, and then to the Mughals and Maratha kings, who were huge patrons of the sport — has always appealed.

W. A series of successes followed, from Yogeshwar Dutt to the Phogat sisters to Sakshi Malik.

Q.1 Which of the following would be the FIFTH sentence after rearrangement?
A. P   **B.** Q   **C.** U   **D.** V
E. S

Q.2 Which of the following would be the SECOND sentence after rearrangement?
A. S   **B.** T   **C.** W   **D.** R
E. U

Q.3 Which of the following would be the SEVENTH sentence after rearrangement?
A. Q   **B.** P   **C.** V   **D.** S
E. W

Q.4 Which of the following would be the FIRST sentence after rearrangement?
A. T   **B.** P   **C.** Q   **D.** R

E. S

Q.5 Which of the following would be the FOURTH sentence after rearrangement?
A. W   **B.** S   **C.** U   **D.** Q
E. T

Ques (6-10):Direction: Read the passage and answer the following question.

Child labor is an important topic that is being debated as a serious social issue all around the world. Keeping the society aware of this issue will help to avoid such illegal and **inhuman** activity from destroying the lives of many children. Child labor is something that replaces the normal activities of a child, like education, playing, etc., with economic activities. These economic activities may be paid or unpaid work, which benefits the family of the child or the owner the child works for. The age limit is restricted to fourteen years or even seventeen years in case of dangerous works.

Children may be forced to do child labor because of poverty and financial problems in their family. Many owners accept child labors since they only need a less amount as salary or even some accept non-monetary jobs too. Children are often made to do such hard jobs by their irresponsible parents. They send their kids for domestic works for the money as well as for the food they get through these works. These demanding works often spoil the childhood and give a harder way of living to the kid.

Parents allow their children for such jobs because of lack of awareness too. When they are too poor to take admissions in schools and the lack of good schools in their locality may also lead to such activities. Not all forms of jobs done by children are considered as child labor, but there are some things to note while categorizing them. Whether the job is done mentally, morally, physically and socially, does it affects the child in a dangerous way? Does the job done affect their education and other childhood activities like playing? The job they do shouldn't be both tiring and excessive that they are forced to avoid other activities they should be doing in their age. These are the characteristics of Child Labor.

In extreme ways, there are owners who treat children like slaves and separate them from their families to do such hard jobs. Whatever be the job done, child labor depends on the age of the kid involved, type of activity and hours of work they do per day. As a conclusion, children are meant to be enjoying their childhood and should be allowed to educate themselves at early ages. There are many **schemes** introduced by the government to reduce such child labors like providing free education and taking severe actions against those who promote child labor.

Q.6 Which of the following statements is true in terms of child labor?

A.   Children cannot get admissions to school and should

continue earning money through labor

B. Children are meant to be enjoying their childhood and should not be allowed to do these jobs

C. Children below 17 are more active and can provide better productivity as laborers.

D. Since they only need a less amount as salary, they should continue to do these jobs

E. None of these is true

Q.7 What do the government schemes include to reduce child labor?

(A). Providing free education.

(B). Taking severe actions against those who promote child labor.

(C). Encouraging more wages for child laborers.

A. Only (A)   **B.** Only (B)

C. All except (A)   **D.** All except (C)

E. None of these

Q.8 What are the characteristics to look for to identify child labor?

(A). Whether the job affects the child in a dangerous way

(B). Whether the jobs done affect their education and other childhood activities like playing.

(C). Whether the jobs are fun and not risky.

A. Only (A)   **B.** Only (B)

C. Only (C)   **D.** All except (B)

E. All except (C)

Q.9 Why do parents push their children into doing child labor?

(A). lack of awareness

(B). lack of good schools in the area

(C). too poor to admit their children to schools

A. All of these   **B.** All except (A)

C. All except (B)   **D.** All except (C)

E. None of these

Q.10 According to the passage, **'schemes'** refers to:

A. Make plans, especially in a devious way or with intent to do something illegal or wrong

B. Not properly planned and controlled

C. Involving or contributing to a breakdown of peaceful and law-abiding behavior

D. A large-scale systematic plan or arrangement for putting a particular idea into effect

E. Not done or acting according to a fixed plan or system

Q.11 Direction: In the following the question choose the word which is the synonym of the given word.

Emancipate

A. Liberate   **B.** Release

C. Acquit   **D.** Conformist

E. Eccentric

Q.12 Direction: In the following the question choose the word which is the antonym of the given word.

Haggard

A. Exuberant   **B.** Vile

C. Emaciated   **D.** Exquisite

E. None of these

Ques (13-17):Direction : In the question below, a sentence has been given with some of its part in bold. To make the sentence grammatically and idiomatically correct, you have to replace the bold part with one of the correct alternatives stated below. If the sentence is correct, mark the option 'no improvement required' as the answer.

Q.13 It is about time we **tell you that** you should start preparing for the exam carefully.

A. told you that

B. tell you that

C. will tell you that

D. have told you that

E. No improvement required

Q.14 Mr. Subhash is eclipsed by his wife who is **much lively and more intelligent** than he is.

A. more lively and much intelligent

B. much more lively and much more intelligent

C. much livelier and more intelligent

D. much liveliest and most intelligent

E. No improvement required

Q.15 Indian farmers have been reeling under financial stress **from immemorial time.**

A. since immemorial time

B. for immemorial time

C. for time immemorial

D. from time immemorial

E. No improvement required

Q.16 The brilliant administrator **was destined for** the post of Assistant Commissioner; there was no one to challenge his caliber.

A. were destined for

B. was destined of

C. were destined of

D. was destined with

E. No improvement required

Q.17 The young man bought **a pair of branded trouser** from the new mall.

A. a pair of branded trousers

B. pair of branded trouser

C. pair of branded trousers

D. a pair for branded trousers

E. No improvement required

Ques (18-22):Direction: In the question given below, a blank has been provided for each and needs to be filled with the appropriate word. Choose the best option among the given ones.

Q.18 Higher input costs have squeezed profits for companies and further_______ these worries, the yield on 10-year U.S. Treasuries hit 3% for the first time in more than four years, indicating that companies would require more cash to service company their debt.

A. ameliorating   B. aggravate
C. compounding   D. relieving
E. None of these

Q.19 The Reserve Bank of India has further liberalised the norms for external commercial borrowing (ECB) that will allow Indian companies to access _______ funds from overseas markets.
A. cheaper   B. dearer
C. expensive   D. poor
E. ordinary

Q.20 The government _______ up to Rs 1.03 lakh crore in GST collection in April, indicating stabilization of the new indirect tax regime which was rolled out on July 1 last year.
A. moped   B. collected
C. mopped   D. Both (A) and (B)
E. Both (B) and (C)

Q.21 With increasing adoption of digital payments and reliance on electronic banking ecosystem, India must have a data localization mandate to avoid data _______.
A. safety   B. pilferage
C. thief   D. reduction
E. substantiate

Q.22 Paytm has said that no payment system should be allowed to roll out services unless they _______ with the regulations.
A. refer   B. flout   C. adhere   D. comply
E. abide

Ques (23-27):Direction: In the following question, a sentence is divided into five parts; (A), (B), (C), (D) and (E). There may be an error in one of the parts, which makes the sentence grammatically or contextually incorrect. Choose the option with the part containing error.

Q.23 It is the job of the political executive to (A) / release the economy's fate from the thrall of (B) / civil servant's perception that doing their (C) / work is a threat to their future liberty. (D) / No error (E)
A. A   B. B   C. C   D. D
E. E

Q.24 Not only is the reintroduction of driving restrictions (A) / ineffective in terms of improving air quality, but it also ignores (B) / Delhi residents' mobility recourse in the absence of reliable, (C) / affordable and accessibility mass public transport. (D) / No error (E)
A. A   B. B   C. C   D. D
E. E

Q.25 Reports say New Delhi has begin (A) / making a list of the products and (B) / tariff lines on which it can offer duty (C) / concessions to the other 15 Asia-Pacific members. (D) / No error (E)
A. A   B. B   C. C   D. D
E. E

Q.26 The reported advisory by the Centre to (A) / the states to ban production of certain kind of (B) / articles of single-use plastic before October 2 (C) / represents the wrong way to go about the job. (D) / No error (E)
A. A   B. B   C. C   D. D
E. E

Q.27 It is far better to leave lending rates (A) / to competition among lenders and increase (B) / the potential competition by licensing more banks (C) / and giving a large role to fin-tech companies. (D) / No error (E)
A. A   B. B   C. C   D. D
E. E

Q.28 Find the correctly spelt word.
A. Vaccinetion   B. Vacination
C. Vaccination   D. Veccinetion
E. Vecinetion

Q.29 Find the correctly spelt word.
A. Lieutenant   B. Leftinant
C. Leiutnant   D. Lieotenant
E. Lieoteant

Q.30 Find the correctly spelt word.
A. Acsessibility   B. Accessibility
C. Accessebility   D. Accessiblity
E. Accessibity

// Smart Answer Sheet //

Correct Indicates percentage of students who answered questions correctly.

Skipped Indicates percentage of students who skipped questions.

Q.	Ans.	Correct / Skipped
1	D	62.14 % / 35.29 %
2	C	19.61 % / 73.41 %
3	A	50.76 % / 36.22 %
4	D	63.82 % / 33.84 %
5	B	69.83 % / 30.1 %
6	B	81.25 % / 14.36 %

Q.	Ans.	Correct / Skipped
7	D	23.23 % / 71.73 %
8	E	24.61 % / 68.75 %
9	A	49.17 % / 42.09 %
10	D	63.8 % / 30.3 %
11	A	78.9 % / 17.08 %
12	A	59.88 % / 30.21 %

Q.	Ans.	Correct / Skipped
13	A	45.19 % / 34.79 %
14	C	45.05 % / 41.31 %
15	D	47.2 % / 43.19 %
16	E	61.06 % / 31.23 %
17	A	82.71 % / 16.89 %
18	C	31.61 % / 67.96 %

Q.	Ans.	Correct / Skipped
19	A	42.62 % / 38.56 %
20	E	55.26 % / 43.62 %
21	B	50.19 % / 39.83 %
22	D	40.65 % / 40.41 %
23	C	56.4 % / 38.37 %
24	D	14.73 % / 81.95 %

Q.	Ans.	Correct / Skipped
25	B	58.96 % / 34.68 %
26	B	55.11 % / 36.94 %
27	D	50.15 % / 31.68 %
28	C	77.6 % / 13.19 %
29	A	46.7 % / 39.0 %
30	B	78.62 % / 14.74 %

Performance Analysis

Avg. Score (%)	50.0%
Toppers Score (%)	60.0%
Your Score	

//Hints and Solutions//

1. The correct sequence of the sentences is R-W-P-S-V-T-Q-U and the fifth sentence clearly is V.

The passage clearly describes changing perception towards Wrestling in India and how the sport has received recognition in recent times.

Sentence R clearly sets the tone of the passage by mentioning the phenomenal growth the sport has achieved since 2008.

Sentence W immediately follows as it quotes a few more recent successes to strengthen the idea stated in sentence R.

Keywords/phrases that link W to R:

'A series of successes' (W) – 'won' (R)

Sentence P clearly seems to follow next as it takes the description forward.

Keyword/phrase that links P to W:

'Recognition' (P) – 'A series of successes followed' (W)

Sentence S follows next as it augments the idea stated so far.

Keyword/phrase that links S to P:

'Now' (S) – 'then' (P)

The sequence made so far is R - W – P - S

From here, though it becomes a bit complex to pick the next sentence in sequence yet we can pair up the remaining sentences.

For instance,

Between Q and U, sentence U clearly follows Q and hence they get paired up as Q – U.

Keyword/phrase that links U to Q:

'narrative' (U) – 'narrates' (Q)

Similarly, between T and V, sentence V must precede T keeping the chronology of events happened in mind. This forms another pair as V – T.

If we observe further we can infer that sentence T links to sentence Q.

Keywords/phrases that link T to Q:

'This added wrestling', 'a prominent place' (T) – 'icing on the cake' (Q)

The complete sequence of the sentences thus formed is R-W-P-S-V-T-Q-U.

Hence, the correct option is (D).

2. The correct sequence of the sentences is R-W-P-S-V-T-Q-U and the fifth sentence clearly is V.

The passage clearly describes changing perception towards Wrestling in India and how the sport has received recognition in recent times.

Sentence R clearly sets the tone of the passage by mentioning the phenomenal growth the sport has achieved since 2008.

Sentence W immediately follows as it quotes a few more recent successes to strengthen the idea stated in sentence R.

Keywords/phrases that link W to R:

'A series of successes' (W) – 'won' (R)

Sentence P clearly seems to follow next as it takes the description forward.

Keyword/phrase that links P to W:

'Recognition' (P) – 'A series of successes followed' (W)

Sentence S follows next as it augments the idea stated so far.

Keyword/phrase that links S to P:

'Now' (S) – 'then' (P)

The sequence made so far is R - W – P - S

From here, though it becomes a bit complex to pick the next sentence in sequence yet we can pair up the remaining sentences.

For instance,

Between Q and U, sentence U clearly follows Q and hence they get paired up as Q – U.

Keyword/phrase that links U to Q:

'narrative' (U) – 'narrates' (Q)

Similarly, between T and V, sentence V must precede T keeping the chronology of events happened in mind. This forms another pair as V – T.

If we observe further we can infer that sentence T links to sentence Q.

Keywords/phrases that link T to Q:

'This added wrestling', 'a prominent place' (T) – 'icing on the cake' (Q)

The complete sequence of the sentences thus formed is R-W-P-S-V-T-Q-U.

Hence, the correct option is (C).

3. The correct sequence of the sentences is R-W-P-S-V-T-Q-U and the fifth sentence clearly is V.

The passage clearly describes changing perception towards Wrestling in India and how the sport has received recognition in recent times.

Sentence R clearly sets the tone of the passage by mentioning the phenomenal growth the sport has achieved since 2008.

Sentence W immediately follows as it quotes a few more recent successes to strengthen the idea stated in sentence R.

Keywords/phrases that link W to R:

'A series of successes' (W) – 'won' (R)

Sentence P clearly seems to follow next as it takes the description forward.

Keyword/phrase that links P to W:

'Recognition' (P) – 'A series of successes followed' (W)

Sentence S follows next as it augments the idea stated so far.

Keyword/phrase that links S to P:

'Now' (S) – 'then' (P)

The sequence made so far is R - W – P - S

From here, though it becomes a bit complex to pick the next sentence in sequence yet we can pair up the remaining sentences.

For instance,

Between Q and U, sentence U clearly follows Q and hence they get paired up as Q – U.

Keyword/phrase that links U to Q:

'narrative' (U) – 'narrates' (Q)

Similarly, between T and V, sentence V must precede T keeping the chronology of events happened in mind. This forms another pair as V – T.

If we observe further we can infer that sentence T links to sentence Q.

Keywords/phrases that link T to Q:

'This added wrestling', 'a prominent place' (T) – 'icing on the cake' (Q)

The complete sequence of the sentences thus formed is R-W-P-S-V-T-Q-U.

Hence, the correct option is (A).

4. The correct sequence of the sentences is R-W-P-S-V-T-Q-U and the fifth sentence clearly is V.

The passage clearly describes changing perception towards Wrestling in India and how the sport has received recognition in recent times.

Sentence R clearly sets the tone of the passage by mentioning the phenomenal growth the sport has achieved since 2008.

Sentence W immediately follows as it quotes a few more recent successes to strengthen the idea stated in sentence R.

Keywords/phrases that link W to R:

'A series of successes' (W) – 'won' (R)

Sentence P clearly seems to follow next as it takes the description forward.

Keyword/phrase that links P to W:

'Recognition' (P) – 'A series of successes followed' (W)

Sentence S follows next as it augments the idea stated so far.

Keyword/phrase that links S to P:

'Now' (S) – 'then' (P)

The sequence made so far is R - W – P - S

From here, though it becomes a bit complex to pick the next sentence in sequence yet we can pair up the remaining sentences.

For instance,

Between Q and U, sentence U clearly follows Q and hence they get paired up as Q – U.

Keyword/phrase that links U to Q:

'narrative' (U) – 'narrates' (Q)

Similarly, between T and V, sentence V must precede T keeping the chronology of events happened in mind. This forms another pair as V – T.

If we observe further we can infer that sentence T links to sentence Q.

Keywords/phrases that link T to Q:

'This added wrestling', 'a prominent place' (T) – 'icing on the cake' (Q)

The complete sequence of the sentences thus formed is R-W-P-S-V-T-Q-U.

Hence, the correct option is (D).

5. The correct sequence of the sentences is R-W-P-S-V-T-Q-U and the fifth sentence clearly is V.

The passage clearly describes changing perception towards Wrestling in India and how the sport has received recognition in recent times.

Sentence R clearly sets the tone of the passage by mentioning the phenomenal growth the sport has achieved since 2008.

Sentence W immediately follows as it quotes a few more recent successes to strengthen the idea stated in sentence R.

Keywords/phrases that link W to R:

'A series of successes' (W) – 'won' (R)

Sentence P clearly seems to follow next as it takes the description forward.

Keyword/phrase that links P to W:

'Recognition' (P) – 'A series of successes followed' (W)

Sentence S follows next as it augments the idea stated so far.

Keyword/phrase that links S to P:

'Now' (S) – 'then' (P)

The sequence made so far is R - W – P - S

From here, though it becomes a bit complex to pick the next sentence in sequence yet we can pair up the remaining sentences.

For instance,

Between Q and U, sentence U clearly follows Q and hence they get paired up as Q – U.

Keyword/phrase that links U to Q:

'narrative' (U) – 'narrates' (Q)

Similarly, between T and V, sentence V must precede T keeping the chronology of events happened in mind. This forms another pair as V – T.

If we observe further we can infer that sentence T links to sentence Q.

Keywords/phrases that link T to Q:

'This added wrestling', 'a prominent place' (T) – 'icing on the cake' (Q)

The complete sequence of the sentences thus formed is R-W-P-S-V-T-Q-U.

Hence, the correct option is (B).

6. The passage speaks of child labor as an inhuman aspect.

It generally describes the reasons as well as the effects of child labor.

Hence, the correct option is (B).

7. According to the passage, there are many schemes introduced by the government to reduce such child labors like providing free education and taking severe actions against those who promote child labor.

Hence, the correct option is (D).

8. The passage speaks of child labor as an inhuman aspect.

It generally describes the reasons as well as the effects of child labor.

The sentences in the passage clearly mention "...does it affects the child in a dangerous way?" and "Does the job done attect their education and other childhood activities?"

The job they do shouldn't be both tiring and excessive that they are forced to avoid other activities they should be doing in their age.

Other than point (C), the rest are mentioned in the passage.

Hence, the correct option is (E).

9. The passage speaks of child labor as an inhuman aspect.

It generally describes the reasons as well as the effects of child labor.

The sentences in the passage clearly mention "Parents allow their children for such jobs because of lack of awareness too. When they are too poor to take admissions in schools and the lack of good schools in their locality may also lead to such activities".

These demanding works often spoil their childhood and give a harder way of living to the kid.

Hence, the correct option is (A).

10. The passage speaks of child labor as an inhuman aspect.

It generally describes the reasons as well as the effects of child labor.

The sentence in the passage containing the above word is "There are many schemes introduced by the government to reduce such child labors like providing free education and taking severe actions against those who promote child labor".

Here, it refers to the planning or arrangement of putting a law into action against the people who employee child laborers.

An example of 'schemes' is: The government is dusting off schemes for supporting creative industries.

Hence, the correct option is (D).

11. Emancipate: set free, especially from legal, social, or political restrictions

Liberate: set (someone) free from imprisonment, slavery, or oppression

Release: allow or enable to escape from confinement

Acquit: free (someone) from a criminal charge by a verdict of not guilty

Conformist: a person who conforms to accepted behaviour or established practices

Eccentric: unconventional and slightly strange

Thus, 'Liberate' is the synonym of the given word 'Emancipate'.

Hence, the correct option is (A).

12. Haggard: Someone who looks haggard has a tired expression and shadows under their eyes, especially because they are ill or have not had enough sleep.

Exuberant: If you are exuberant, you are full of energy, excitement, and cheerfulness.

Vile: If you say that someone or something is vile, you mean that they are very unpleasant.

Emaciated: A person or animal that is emaciated is extremely thin and weak because of illness or lack of food.

Exquisite: Something that is exquisite is extremely beautiful or pleasant, especially in a delicate way.

Thus, 'Exuberant' is the antonym of the word 'Haggard'.

Hence, the correct option is (A).

13. Here,

It's time + subject + past verb form.

Therefore, the sentence would be correct if "tell you that" is replaced by "told you that".

Correct Sentence :

It is about time we told you that you should start preparing for the exam carefully.

Hence, the correct option is (A).

14. Here, a comparison is made between Mr. Subhash and his wife.

So, the comparative degree of the adjectives has to be used.

Though "more intelligent" is the comparative degree of "intelligent", "lively" is the positive degree.

So, the sentence would be correct if "lively" is replaced by its comparative degree "livelier".

Correct Sentence :

Mr. Subhash is eclipsed by his wife who is much livelier and more intelligent than he is.

Hence, the correct option is (C).

15. "From time immemorial" is a standard English expression/ phrase.

It cannot be changed whimsically.

The sentence would be correct if "from immemorial time" is replaced by "from time immemorial".

Correct Sentence:

Indian farmers have been reeling under financial stress from time immemorial.

Hence, the correct option is (D).

16. "For" is the correct preposition after "destined" in this context.

"Destined for" means 'headed for/ bound for/ intended for'.

The subject of the statement "the brilliant administrator" is singular. Hence the verb would also be "was" (=singular).

So, the sentence is absolutely correct from every aspect.

Hence, the correct option is (E).

17. Here "Trouser" is always used in the plural (=trousers).

So, "a pair of branded trousers" is the correct expression.

Correct Sentence :

The young man bought a pair of branded trousers from the new mall.

Hence, the correct option is (A).

18. The tone of the statement is negative and it conveys that higher prices lead to less profits and then goes on to talk about another negative issue. Thus, clearly, the second would add to the stress and not reduce it. Hence, we can eliminate ameliorating and relieving, both of which mean to make a situation better.

Aggravate is correct in terms of meaning (to worsen) but incorrect grammatically as aggravating should have been used.

Compounding means to make (something bad) worse and is a perfect fit.

Then the sentence is,

Higher input costs have squeezed profits for companies and further compounding these worries, the yield on 10-year U.S. Treasuries hit 3% for the first time in more than four years, indicating that companies would require more cash to service company their debt.

Hence, the correct option is (C).

19. If the RBI has eased ECB norms, it would lead to borrowing on cheaper rates.

The other options do not fit in.

Dearer and expensive are opposite of what is needed.

Poor and ordinary are both irrelevant here.

Then the sentence is,

The Reserve Bank of India has further liberalised the norms for external commercial borrowing (ECB) that will allow Indian companies to access cheaper funds from overseas markets.

Hence, the correct option is (A).

20. Moped means to feel dejected and apathetic.

Collected and mopped both mean the same and fit in well.

Then the sentence is,

The government mopped (collected) up to Rs 1.03 lakh crore in GST collection in April, indicating stabilization of the new indirect tax regime which was rolled out on July 1 last year.

Hence, the correct option is (E).

21. The statement wants India to store its data domestically. One of the obvious reasons could be to avoid data leak. This eliminates safety as it is the opposite of the correct meaning.

Thief is incorrect as it is the action of stealing i.e. theft that is to be avoided here.

Reduction clearly does not fit in while substantiate means to provide evidence to support and does not fit in the blank.

Only pilferage meaning leakage fits in well.

Then the sentence is,

With increasing adoption of digital payments and reliance on electronic banking ecosystem, India must have a data localization mandate to avoid data pilferage.

Hence, the correct option is (B).

22. Adhere is always followed by to and is thus incorrect here.

Similarly, abide is to be followed by 'by' which is not the case here. This can also be eliminated.

Flout meaning to defy is the opposite of what is needed.

Refer does not make sense in the statement.

Only Comply which means to follow/abide by/adhere to is correct.

Then the sentence is,

Paytm has said that no payment system should be allowed to roll out services unless they comply with the regulations.

Hence, the correct option is (D).

23. The error lies in the fragment C of the sentence.

The use of singular possessive form "servant's" in the fragment C is incorrect. Here the reference has been made to all civil servants in general.

Instead of "servant's", the plural possessive form "servants'" should be used to make it a grammatically correct sentence.

Correct Sentence:

It is the job of the political executive to release the economy's fate from the thrall of civil servants' perception that doing their work is a threat to their future liberty.

Hence, the correct option is (C).

24. The error lies in the fragment D of the sentence.

Usage of 'accessibility' given in fragment D is incorrect.

Instead of 'accessibility', the form 'accessible' should be used to make it a grammatically correct sentence.

Correct Sentence:

Not only is the reintroduction of driving restrictions ineffective in terms of improving air quality, but it also ignores Delhi residents' mobility recourse in the absence of reliable, affordable and accessible mass public transport.

Hence, the correct option is (D).

25. The error lies in the fragment B of the sentence.

The presence of 'has' before 'begin' indicates that it should be in the past perfect form.

'Begin' should be replaced with 'begun' in order to make it a grammatically correct sentence.

Correct Sentence:

Reports say New Delhi has begun making a list of the products and tariff lines on which it can offer duty concessions to the other 15 Asia-Pacific members.

Hence, the correct option is (B).

26. The error lies in the fragment B of the sentence.

The absence of the singular article 'a' before 'kind of' indicates that several types of articles are being referred to.

Instead of 'kind', 'kinds' should be used to make it a grammatically correct sentence.

Correct Sentence:

The reported advisory by the Centre to the states to ban production of certain kinds of articles of single-use plastic before October 2 represents the wrong way to go about the job.

Hence, the correct option is (B).

27. The error lies in the fragment D of the sentence.

The comparative form of the adjective 'large' should be used to describe the role given to fin-tech companies just as 'more' banks are to be licensed.

Instead of 'large', 'larger' should be used to make it a grammatically correct sentence.

Correct Sentence:

It is far better to leave lending rates to competition among lenders and increase the potential competition by licensing more banks and giving a larger role to fin-tech companies.

Hence, the correct option is (D).

28. Vaccination is correctly spelt word. It means treatment with a vaccine to produce immunity against a disease.

Example:

Routine smallpox vaccination in the United States ended in 1972.

Hence, the correct option is (C).

29. Lieutenant is correctly spelt word. A lieutenant is a person who holds a junior officer's rank in the army, navy, marines, or air force, or in the American police force.

Example: Lieutenant Campbell ordered the man at the wheel to steer for the gunboat.

Hence, the correct option is (A).

30. Accessibility is correctly spelt word. Accessibility is the quality of being able to be reached or entered.

Hence, the correct option is (B).

Ques (1-5):Direction: In the following question assuming the given statements to be true, find which of the conclusion(s) among given conclusions is/are definitely true and then give your answers accordingly.

Q.1 Statements: Z > Y ≥ X ≥ K; K = L ≥ M;
Which of the following are definitely true?

A. X > L

B. Z > L

C. K = Z

D. K < Y

E. None of the above

Q.2 Statements: T ≥ C ≥ F; E = A < D; X > T; D < F = T

Conclusions:

I. F < E

II. C = F

III. A > T

A. Only I is True

B. Only II is True

C. Only III is True

D. Only I and III are True

E. None is True

Q.3 Statements: Y < Z > X; W > D < R; Y > T = R; X > W

Conclusions:

I. R < Z

II. X > D

III. T < W

A. Only I is True

B. Only II is True

C. Only I and II are True

D. Only II and III are True

E. Only III and I are True

Q.4 Statements: E ≥ U = D; R < A < F; W ≤ D; W > F

Conclusions:

I. U < R

II. E = W

III. E > W

A. Only II is True

B. Only III is True

C. Only I and II are True

D. Either I or II is True

E. Either II or III is True

Q.5 Statements: $M \leq K < L; N \leq M < P < Q$

Conclusions:

I. $L > P$

II. $N < L$

A. Either conclusion I or II is true

B. Only conclusion II is true

C. Only conclusion I is true

D. Both conclusions I and II are true

E. None of the conclusions is true

Q.6 How many such pairs of letters are there in the word 'DISCOVERY' which has as many letters between them as in the alphabetical series?

A. Six   **B.** Five   **C.** Four   **D.** Seven

E. Three

Q.7 Each consonant of the word 'INSURANCE' is changed to the previous letter in the English alphabetical series and each vowel is changed to the next letter in the English alphabetical series. If the new alphabet thus formed are arranged in alphabetical order (from left to right), which of the following will be the third from the right?

A. M

B. B

C. Q

D. V

E. None of these

Ques (8-10):Direction: Study the following information carefully and answer the given questions.

In a certain code language,

'fa ga ba ha' means 'idli has low calories',

'ta ya ha va' means 'idli diet reduces fat',

'wa va ta ha' means 'idli reduces more fat',

'fa xa ba va' means 'chapati has low fat'.

Q.8 Which of the following means 'reduces' in that code language?

A. ya

B. va

C. ta

D. Either (A) or (B) or (C)

E. Either (B) or (C)

Q.9 Code 'wa' is for which word in the given language?

A. idli

B. reduces

C. more

D. fat

E. Either (A) or (B)

Q.10 What would be the possible code for 'low calories food reduces weight'?

A. ta ba ga va wa

B. wa ta ga ba ya

C. ta ba ma ga va

D. ta ja ba ma ga

E. Either (A) or (C)

Q.11 Among five person A, B, C, D and E, D is taller than only C and A. A is not as tall as C or B. E is shorter than B but taller than D. Find the tallest person.

A. B   **B.** E   **C.** D   **D.** C

E. A

Q.12 D is taller than C and E. A is not as tall as E. C is taller than A. D is not as tall as B. Who among them is next to the tallest one?

A. A   **B.** D   **C.** B & D   **D.** C
E. E

Ques (13-15):Directions: These questions are based on the following information.

There are 7 members K, L, T, W, S, Q, and Y in a family of three-generation. There is no single parent in the family. W is the mother-in-law of K, who is the mother of L. Q is the father-in-law of Y. L is the niece of T, who is the son of S.

Q.13 How Q is related to T?
A. Brother   **B.** Father   **C.** Mother   **D.** Sister
E. Son

Q.14 Find odd one out:
A. S   **B.** Y   **C.** K   **D.** Q
E. T

Q.15 How L is related to S?
A. Son   **B.** Daughter
C. Father   **D.** Granddaughter
E. Grandson

Q.16 Direction: In the following question three statements are given and these statements are followed by two conclusions numbered I and II. Taking the given statements to be true even if they seem to be at variance from commonly known facts. Read the conclusions and then decide which of the given conclusions logically follows from the two given statements.

Statement:

All mango are papaya

No papaya is apple

Some papaya are watermelon

Conclusions:

I. Some apple are mango

II. Some watermelon are not papaya

[SBI PO, 2021]

A. Only I follows   **B.** Only II follows
C. Both follow   **D.** Either I or II follow
E. None follow

Ques (17-20):Direction: In the question below are given two statements followed by two conclusions numbered I and II. You have to take the given statements to be true even if they seem to be at variance with commonly known facts. Read all the conclusions and then decide which of the given conclusions logically follows from the given statements disregarding commonly known facts.

Q.17 Statement:

Some huts are mud.

No mud is iron.

Conclusion:

I. Some huts are iron.

II. Some huts are not iron.

A. Only I follows
B. Only II follows
C. Either I or II follows
D. Neither I nor II follows
E. Both I and II follow

Q.18 Statement:

Some oranges are lemons.

Only a few lemons are sweet.

Conclusion:

I. Some oranges are sweet.

II. No orange is sweet.

A. Only I follows
B. Only II follows
C. Either I or II follows
D. Neither I nor II follows
E. Both I and II follow

Q.19 Statement:

All fighters are women.

All women are mothers.

Conclusion:

I. All mothers are fighters.

II. All women are fighters.

A. Only I follows
B. Only II follows
C. Either I or II follows
D. Neither I nor II follows
E. Both I and II follow

Q.20 Statement:

All trams are trains.

Only a few trains are bullet.

Conclusion:

I. Some trams can be bullet.

II. All bullet can be trains.

A. Only I follows
B. Only II follows
C. Either I or II follows
D. Neither I nor II follows
E. Both I and II follow

Ques (21-25):Direction: Study the following information to answer the given questions:

Eight students P, Q, R, S, T, U, V and W are sitting in a horizontal row. All face in north direction. V sits third to the left of S. Q sits immediate left of R. Four students sit between R and T. W sits to the left of U, who is not adjacent to V. At least three students sit to the left of V. P does not sit at extreme end. T neither sits at the extreme left nor at the second extreme left position.

Q.21 Who sits at extreme left end?
A. Q   **B.** R   **C.** W   **D.** U
E. S

Q.22 How many persons sit to the right of P?

| A. Three | B. Four | C. Five | D. Two |
| E. One | | | |

| A. 1W? | B. 3$6 | C. RT5 | D. M97 |
| E. WEC | | | |

Q.23 Which of the following statement is correct?
A.   T sits immediate right of U
B.   One person sits between Q and U
C.   Q sits second to the left of V
D.   S sits third to the right of R
E.   All are correct

Q.33 How many such letters are there in the above arrangement, each of which is immediately preceded by a number and immediately followed by a consonant?
A. None   B. One
C. Two   D. Three
E. More than three

Q.24 How many students sit between Q and U?
A. Two   B. One   C. Four   D. Three
E. Five

Q.34 Which of the following element is eighth to the right of thirteenth element from left end?
A. J   B. U   C. 7   D. M
E. S

Q.25 Who sits at extreme right end?
A. S   B. U   C. W   D. R
E. T

Q.35 If a meaningful word is to form using only first vowels from both left and right end and the consonants which are between first and second symbol from left end then how many meaningful words can be formed?
A. None   B. One
C. Two   D. Three
E. More than three

Ques (26-30):Directions: Study the information given below carefully and answer the questions that follow.

Eight people, P, Q, R, S, T, U, V, and W, are sitting around a circular table facing the centre. P is sitting third to the left of R. S is sitting opposite U. P is an immediate neighbor of S. Q is sitting second to the right of W. W is not an immediate neighbor of S. V is not sitting opposite R.

Q.26 Who is sitting third to the right of W?
A. P   B. U   C. V   D. R
E. T

Q.27 How many people are sitting between V and T if we start counting from V in anti-clockwise direction?
A. More than four   B. Four
C. Three   D. Two
E. Zero

Q.28 Who is sitting opposite P?
A. V   B. Q   C. S   D. W
E. T

Q.29 Who are the immediate neighbors of U?
A. TQ   B. PS   C. WR   D. VR
E. QW

Q.30 Who is sitting to the immediate left of P?
A. T   B. U   C. V   D. W
E. S

Ques (31-35):Directions: Study the following information carefully and answer the questions given beside:

1 W E 3 $ R T % M 9 4 L S C 8 & F J 2 @ U P 7 D 5 * 6 Z C ? A

Q.31 If all the elements which are on the prime position in the above sequence are to be dropped then which of the following element will be 13th from the left end?
A. F   B. J   C. 2   D. @
E. U

Q.32 Four of the following five are alike in a certain way and hence form a group. Which of the following is the one that does not belong to the group?

// Smart Answer Sheet //

| Correct | Indicates percentage of students who answered questions correctly. |

| Skipped | Indicates percentage of students who skipped questions. |

Q.	Ans.	Correct / Skipped	Q.	Ans.	Correct / Skipped	Q.	Ans.	Correct / Skipped	Q.	Ans.	Correct / Skipped	Q.	Ans.	Correct / Skipped
1	B	41.95 % / 32.35 %	8	C	48.18 % / 36.22 %	15	D	57.2 % / 34.68 %	22	A	46.9 % / 39.58 %	29	E	15.85 % / 67.84 %
2	E	63.97 % / 30.97 %	9	C	58.04 % / 39.92 %	16	E	50.49 % / 40.17 %	23	C	23.07 % / 75.88 %	30	A	44.16 % / 53.59 %
3	C	49.52 % / 30.1 %	10	D	63.47 % / 34.84 %	17	B	78.34 % / 11.79 %	24	D	64.1 % / 31.17 %	31	E	66.04 % / 30.06 %
4	E	69.27 % / 30.33 %	11	A	61.17 % / 31.48 %	18	C	52.95 % / 45.19 %	25	E	83.68 % / 15.65 %	32	D	50.61 % / 40.51 %
5	B	82.85 % / 12.83 %	12	B	43.05 % / 49.5 %	19	D	69.22 % / 30.28 %	26	E	50.19 % / 39.29 %	33	C	53.03 % / 42.13 %
6	C	13.43 % / 75.13 %	13	A	41.02 % / 52.21 %	20	E	23.62 % / 72.09 %	27	B	69.53 % / 30.14 %	34	B	56.89 % / 36.55 %
7	C	82.53 % / 13.56 %	14	C	62.69 % / 37.02 %	21	C	54.28 % / 35.46 %	28	D	47.98 % / 49.05 %	35	C	61.08 % / 37.97 %

Performance Analysis

Avg. Score (%)	54.29%
Toppers Score (%)	54.29%
Your Score	

//Hints and Solutions//

1. Given statements: Z > Y ≥ X ≥ K; K = L ≥ M;

On combining: Z > Y ≥ X ≥ K = L ≥ M;

Conclusions:

I. X > L → False (as X ≥ K and K = L implies X ≥ L, thus a clear relation cannot be determined)

II. Z > L → True (as Z > Y ≥ X ≥ K; K = L implies Z > L)

III. K = Z → False (as Z > Y ≥ X ≥ K implies K < Z)

IV. K < Y → False (as Z > Y ≥ X ≥ K implies Y ≥ K, thus a clear relation cannot be determined)

Hence, the correct option is (B).

2. Given statements: T ≥ C ≥ F; E = A < D; X > T; D < F = T

On combining: E = A < D < F ≤ C ≤ T < X; F = T

Conclusions:

I. F < E → False (as E = A < D < F → E < F)

II. C = F → False (as per the given information F = T & T ≥ C ≥ F)

III. A > T → False (as A < D < F ≤ C ≤ T → A < F ≤ C ≤ T → A < C ≤ T → A < T)

Hence, the correct option is (E).

3. Given statements: Y < Z > X; W > D < R; Y > T = R; X > W

On combining: D < R = T < Y < Z > X > W > D

Conclusions:

I. R < Z → True (as R = T < Y < Z → R < Z)

II. X > D → True (as X > W > D → X > D)

III. T < W → False (as T < Y < Z > X > W → T < Z > W → thus clear relation between T and W cannot be determined)

Hence, the correct option is (C).

4. Given statements: E ≥ U = D; R < A < F; W ≤ D; W > F

On combining: E ≥ U = D ≥ W > F > A > R

Conclusions:

I. U < R → False (as U = D ≥ W > F > A > R → U ≥ W > R → U > R)

II. E = W → False (as E ≥ U = D ≥ W → E ≥ D ≥ W → E ≥ W)

III. E > W → False (as E ≥ U = D ≥ W → E ≥ D ≥ W → E ≥ W)

Since, conclusion II and III form complementary pair and E ≥ W.

Hence, the correct option is (E).

5. Given statements: $M \leq K < L; N \leq M < P < Q$

On combining, we get

$$L > K \geq M < P < Q; N \leq M \leq K < L$$

Conclusions:

I. $L > P$ → False (As $L > K \geq M < P < Q$ thus, the relation between L and P cannot be determined)

II. $N < L$ → True (As $N \leq M \leq K < L$, so $N < L$)

Hence, the correct option is (B).

6. The given word:

DISCOVERY

Possible pair of letters in the above word which has as many letters between them as in the English alphabetical series:

Pair 1:

Letters in the word	S	C	O	V
Letters in the alphabetical series	S	T	U	V

Pair 2:

Letters in the word	O	V	E	R
Letters in the alphabetical series	O	P	Q	R

Pair 3:

Letters in the word	V	E	R	Y
Letters in the alphabetical series	V	W	X	Y

Pair 4:

Letters in the word	S	C	O	V	E	R	Y
Letters in the alphabetical series	S	T	U	V	W	X	Y

Here, we can observe that there are four such possible pairs of letters satisfy the above conditions.

Hence, the correct option is (C).

7. The given word:

I N S U R A N C E

Applying the above condition, we have new word:

J M R V Q B M B F

Now, arranging in alphabetical order (from left to right)

B B F J M M Q R V

So, Q is third from the right.

Hence, the correct option is (C).

Ques (8-10): In the given coding language,

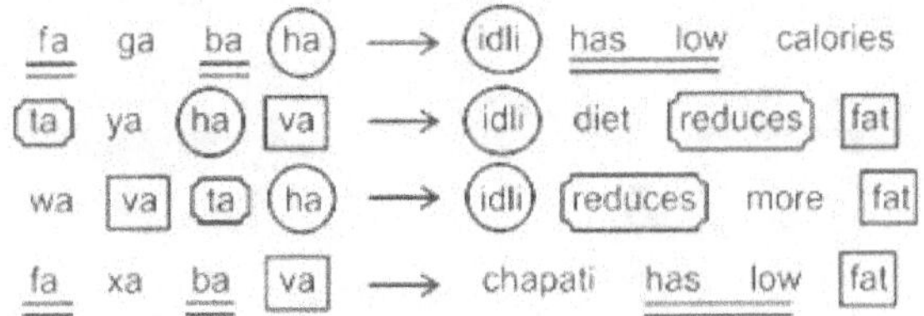

8. So, 'reduces' is coded as 'ta'.

Hence, the correct option is (C).

9. So, 'wa' is the code for 'more'.

Hence, the correct option is (C).

10. Code for 'low' is 'ba' or 'fa',

Code for 'calories' is 'ga',

Code for 'food' is either 'ma' or 'ja', as code for 'food' is not given.

Code for 'reduces' is 'ta',

Code for 'weight' is either 'ma' or 'ja', as code for 'weight' is not given.

So, the possible answer is 'ta ja ba ma ga'.

Hence, the correct option is (D).

11. 1. D is taller than only C and A

_ > D > C & A

2. A is not as tall as C or B

C / B > A

3. E is shorter than B but taller than C.

B > E > D

On combining 1, 2 & 3, we get:

B > E > D > C > A

So, 'B' is the tallest person.

Hence, the correct option is (A).

12. (1) D is taller than C and E.

D > C/E

(2) A is not as tall as E.

E > A

(3) C is taller than A.

C > A

(4) D is not as tall as B.

B > D

By combining all the above statements together, we get:

B > D > C/E > C/E > A

Thus, D is the second tallest.

Hence, the correct option is (B).

Ques (13-15): From the given information,

Symbol in Diagram	Meaning
○	Female
□	Male
═	Married couple
—	Siblings
|	Difference of a generation

1) W is the mother-in-law of K, who is the mother of L.

2) Q is the father-in-law of Y.

3) L is the niece of T, who is the son of S.

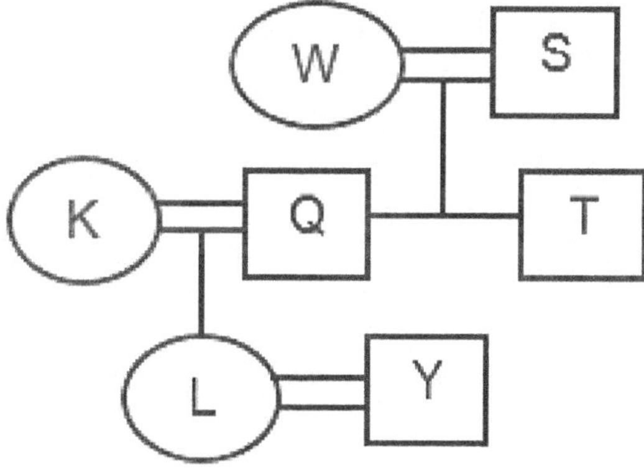

13. So, Q is the brother of T.

Hence, the correct option is (A).

14. S → Male

Y → Male

K → Female

Q → Male

T → Male

So, K is odd among the given options.

Hence, the correct option is (C).

15. So, L is the granddaughter of S.

Hence, the correct option is (D).

16.

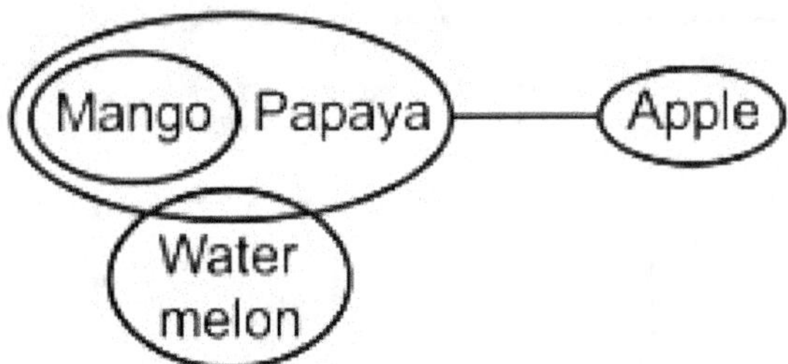

Conclusions:

I. Some apple are mango → False (All mango are papaya and No papaya is apple. So, apple cannot be mango)

II. Some watermelon are not papaya → False (As given some watermelon are papaya. So negative conclusion not follow)

Thus, None of the conclusion are follow.

Hence, the correct option is (E).

17. The least possible diagram for the given statements is as follows:

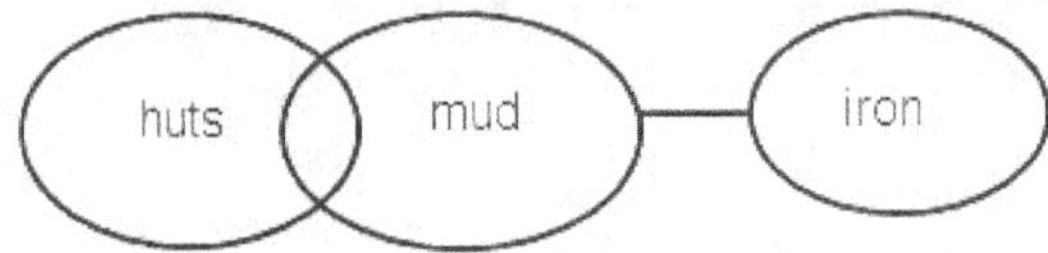

Conclusions:

I. Some huts are iron. → False (It is possible but not definite).

II. Some huts are not iron. → True (Part of huts which is mud is definitely not iron).

Hence, the correct option is (B).

18. The least possible diagram for the given statements is as follows:

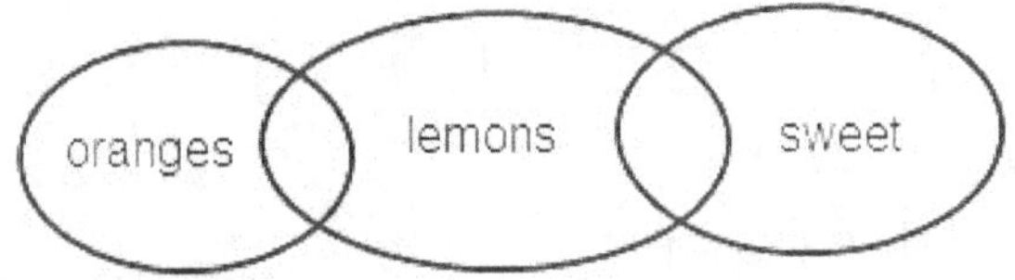

Conclusions:

I. Some oranges are sweet → False (It is possible but not definite).

II. No orange is sweet → False (It is possible but not definite)

Both are complementary conclusions.

Hence, the correct option is (C).

19. The least possible diagram for the given statements is as follows:

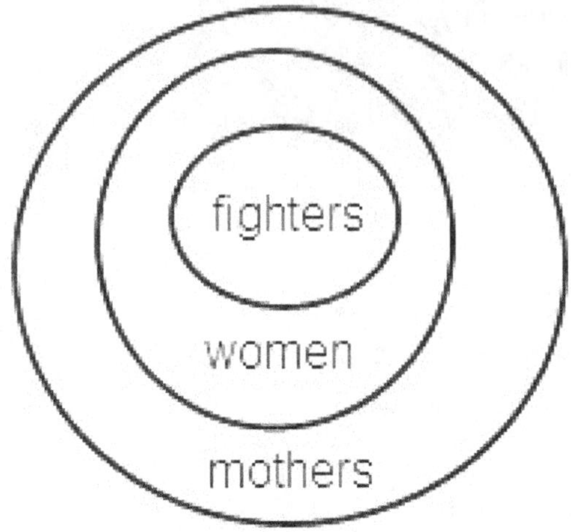

Conclusions:

I. All mothers are fighters → False (It is possible but not definite).

II. All women are fighters → False (It is possible but not definite).

Hence, the correct option is (D).

20. The least possible diagram for the given statements is as follows:

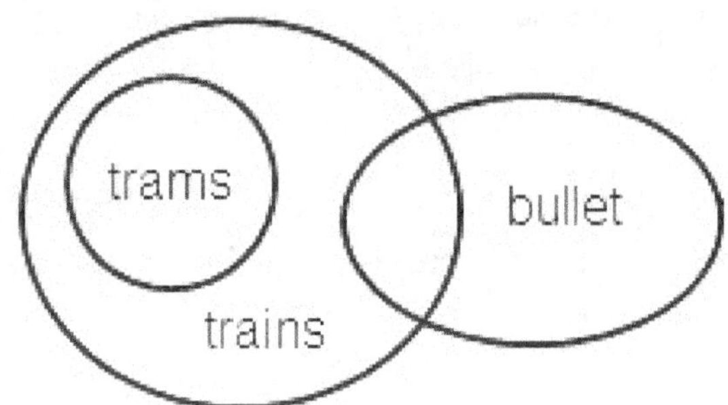

Conclusions:

I. Some trams can be bullet → True (It is not definite. Possibility with non definite conclusion makes conclusion true).

II. All bullet can be trains → True (It is not definite. Possibility with non definite conclusion makes conclusion true).

Hence, the correct option is (E).

Ques (21-25): Students: P, Q, R, S, T, U, V and W.

1) V sits third to the left of S.

2) At least three students sit to the left of V.

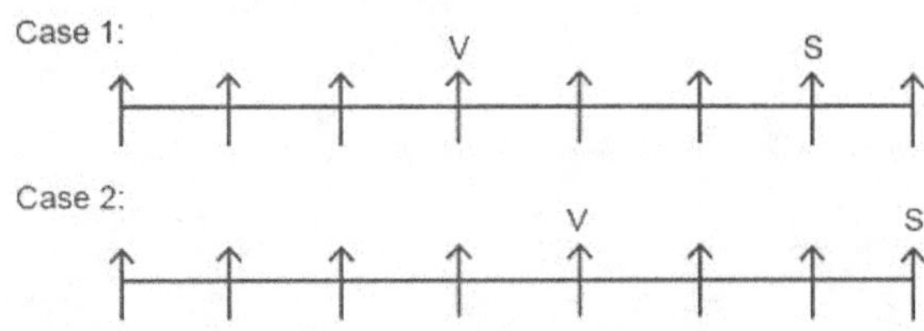

3) Four students sit between R and T.

4) Q sits immediate left of R.

5) T neither sits at the extreme left nor at the second extreme left position.

Case 1:

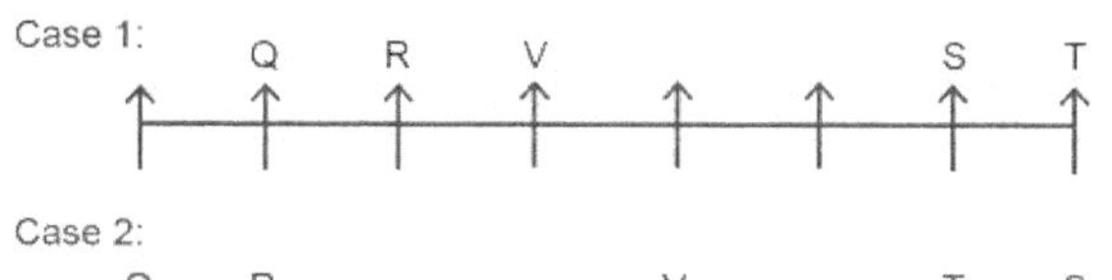

Case 2:

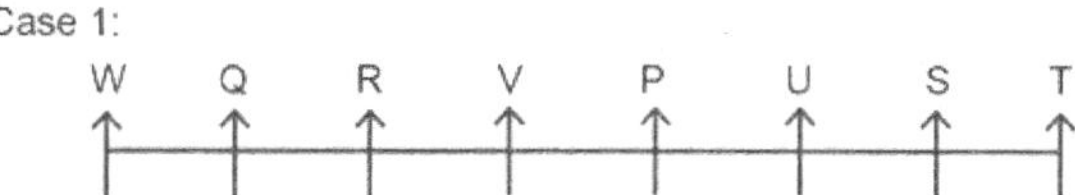

5) W sits to the left of U, who is not adjacent to V. So, case 2 would be invalid as V cannot sit adjacent to U.

6) P does not sit at extreme end. So, W must sit at extreme left end.

Case 1:

21. So, W sits at extreme left end.

Hence, the correct option is (C).

22. So, three persons sit to the right of P.

Hence, the correct option is (A).

23. Statement 'S sits third to the right of R' is correct.

Hence, the correct option is (C).

24. So, three students sit between Q and U.

Hence, the correct option is (D).

25. So, T sits at extreme right end.

Hence, the correct option is (E).

Ques (26-30): People = P, Q, R, S, T, U, V, and W

1) P is sitting third to the left of R.

(As it is a circular arrangement, we can randomly select a seat for R and then place P accordingly.)

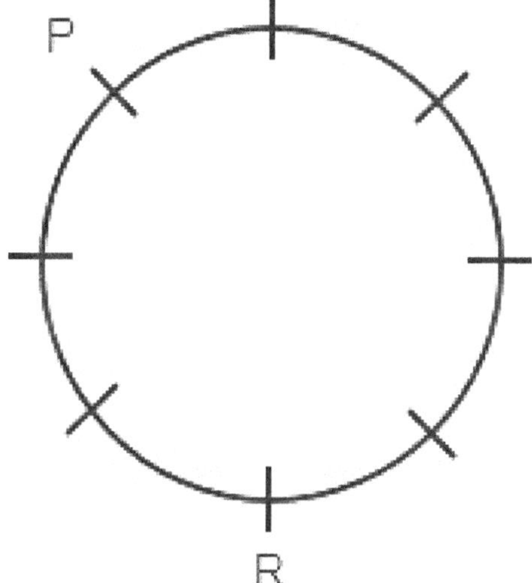

2) S is sitting opposite U.

3) P is an immediate neighbor of S.

(Clearly, we cannot place S to the immediate left of P as R is sitting opposite to that seat. Implies, S is sitting to the immediate right of P and U is sitting second to the right of R.)

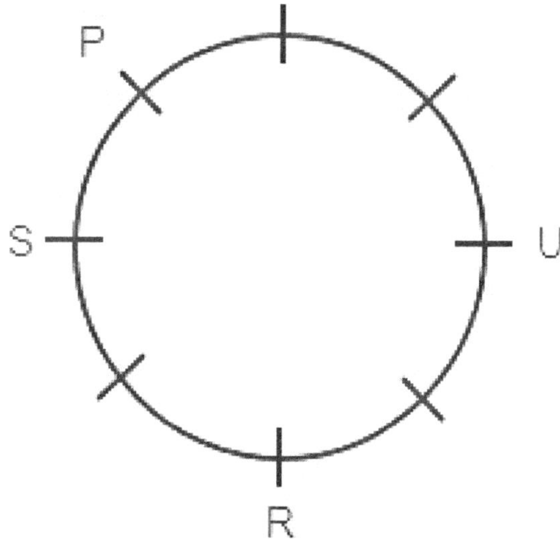

4) Q is sitting second to the right of W.

(There are two possibilities to place Q and W. In the first case we can place W to the immediate right of S and Q to the immediate right of R and in the second case we can place W to the immediate right of R and W to the immediate right of U.)

5) W is not an immediate neighbor of S.

(Implies, the first case of the previous statement is not true. Thus, W is sitting to the immediate right of R and Q is sitting to the immediate right of U.)

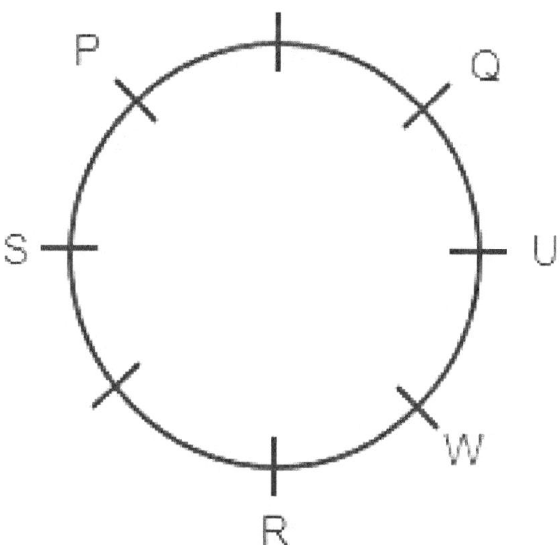

6) V is not sitting opposite R.

(If V is not sitting opposite R then he must be sitting to the immediate left of R as it is the only seat left. Also, now that only

one person is left to be placed i.e. T, we can place T opposite R as it is the only seat left to be filled.)

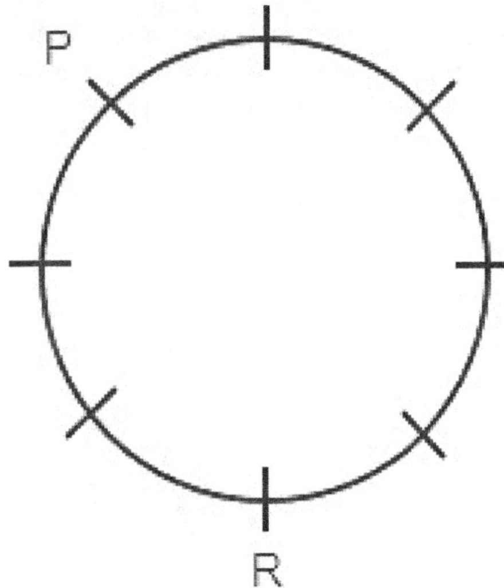

26. Clearly, T is sitting third to the right of W.

Hence, the correct option is (E).

27. Clearly, four people are sitting between V and T if we start from V and move towards the anti-clockwise direction.

Hence, the correct option is (B).

28. Clearly, W is sitting opposite P.

Hence, the correct option is (D).

29. Clearly, Q and W are the immediate neighbors of U.

Hence, the correct option is (E).

30. Clearly, T is sitting to the immediate left of P.

Hence, the correct option is (A).

31. The given sequence:

1 W E 3 $ R T % M 9 4 L S C 8 & F J 2 @ U P 7 D 5 * 6 Z C ? A

After dropping all the elements which are on the prime position in the above sequence, we have

1 3 R % M 9 L C 8 & J @ **U** P D 5 * 6 Z ?

Here, the element which is 13th from the left end is U.

Hence, the correct option is (E).

32. The given sequence:

1 W E 3 $ R T % M 9 4 L S C 8 & F J 2 @ U P 7 D 5 * 6 Z C ? A

After comparing the given options with the given sequence.

We can say that the pattern is second element is the immediate next element of first element and third element which has same rank from right end as the second element from left end.

Here, only option which is not following the pattern is M97.

Hence, the correct option is (D).

33. The given sequence:

1 W E 3 $ R T % M 9 4 L S C 8 & F J 2 @ U P 7 D 5 * 6 Z C ? A

Here, we have 2 such letters in the given sequence which are immediately preceded by a number and immediately followed by a consonant.

1 W E 3 $ R T % M 9 4 **L** S C 8 & F J 2 @ U P 7 D 5 * 6 **Z** C ? A

Hence, the correct option is (C).

34. The given sequence:

1 W E 3 $ R T % M 9 4 L S C 8 & F J 2 @ U P 7 D 5 * 6 Z C ? A

Now, the element which is eighth to right of thirteenth from left end i.e. 8 + 13 = 21st element from left end.

1 W E 3 $ R T % M 9 4 L S C 8 & F J 2 @ **U** P 7 D 5 * 6 Z C ? A

Here, the element which is 21st from the left end is U.

Hence, the correct option is (B).

35. The given sequence:

1 W E 3 $ R T % M 9 4 L S C 8 & F J 2 @ U P 7 D 5 * 6 Z C ? A

Here, the first vowels from both left and right end and the consonants which are between first and second symbol from left end are E, A, R and T respectively.

1 W **E** 3 $ **R T** % M 9 4 L S C 8 & F J 2 @ U P 7 D 5 * 6 Z C ? **A**

At this point only 2 meaningful words can be formed using E, A, R and T.

'Rate' and 'Tear' are two meaningful words.

Hence, the correct option is (C).

Ques (1-3):Direction: In the following question assuming the given statements to be true, find which of the conclusion among given conclusions is/are definitely true and then give your answers accordingly.

Q.1 Statements: Y ≥ R < E; R > P ≥ C = A

Conclusions:

I. Y > A

II. E ≥ C

A. Only I is True

B. Neither I nor II is True

C. Both I and II are True

D. Either I or II is True

E. Only II is True

Q.2 Statements: W > Q ≥ M; H ≤ T = M

Conclusions:

I. H ≤ Q

II. W > T

A. Only I is True

B. Neither I nor II is True

C. Both I and II are True

D. Either I or II is True

E. Only II is True

Q.3 Statements: J < E ≥ O; Y < P ≤ H < O

Conclusions:

I. J > P

II. Y < E

A. Only II is True

B. Neither I nor II is True

C. Both I and II are True

D. Either I or II is True

E. Only I is True

Ques (4-5):Direction: In the following question assuming the given statements to be True, find which of the conclusion among given conclusions is/are definitely true and then give your answers accordingly.

Q.4 Statements: C ≤ D ≤ X; K > V ≥ I; C = O ≥ K

Conclusions:

I. D ≤ V

II. X > K

III. I < O

A. Only III is True

B. Both I and III are True

C. Either I or II is True

D. Both II and III are True

E. Only II is True

Q.5 Statements: X < N ≤ W; B ≥ L ≥ O; O = X

Conclusions:

I. B > N

II. N ≥ B

III. L < W

A. Only III is True

B. Both I and III are True

C. Either I or II is True

D. Both II and III are True

E. Only II is True

Q.6 How many meaningful English words can be formed using the second, third, fifth and seventh letters of the word 'KITCHEN' using each letter once in each word?

A. One
B. Three
C. Two
D. Four
E. None of these

Q.7 If the letters in the word 'CREATION' are rearranged as they appear in the English alphabet then the position of how many letters will remain unchanged after the rearrangement?

A. Two
B. One
C. Three
D. Zero
E. Four

Ques (8-10):Direction: Read the following information carefully and answer the question given beside.

"Backlog disc live heavily" is coded as " 2$A 4#I 8$E 12#I ".

"Innocent band actress salute" is coded as " 2#A 1$C 9%N 19&A".

"Notify selfish model change" is coded as "14&O 13!O 19$E 3&H".

"Langer hill external limelight" is coded as "12&A 12@I 8#I 5%X".

Q.8 Find the code for "Take advance receipt".

A. 20#A 1$D 18$E
B. 2#A 1$D 7$E
C. 20#A 11#D 17$E
D. 20$A 1$D 17$E
E. None of these

Q.9 Find the code for "Advertise your product".

A. 1@D 5#O 6$R
B. 1@D 25#O 16$R
C. 1@D 25#O 16#R
D. 1@D 25#O 16@R
E. None of these

Q.10 Find the code for "Travel with wander".

A. 20&R 23#I 23#A
B. 20&R 23&I 23&A
C. 23&R 23#I 23&A
D. 20&R 23#I 23&A
E. None of these

Q.11 In a row where all are facing north, Riya is 15th from the left end and Garima is 19th from the right end. They interchange their positions, and Shyam who sits 24th from the left end sits at the 5th place to the left of Riya's new position. How many persons were there in the row?

A. 36
B. 42
C. 47
D. 56

E. 57

Q.12 In a row of 40 girls, when Komal moves four places to the left from her position, her position becomes 10th from the left end of the row. What was Swati's position from the right end of the row, if Swati was three places to the right of Komal's original position.

A. 7   **B.** 21   **C.** 22   **D.** 24
E. 25

Ques (13-16):Direction: In the question below are given three statements followed by two conclusions. You have to take the given statements to be true even if they seem to be at variance with commonly known facts. Read all the conclusions and then decide which of the given conclusions logically follows from the given statements disregarding commonly known facts.

Q.13 Statement:

I. All cars are bikes

II. No bikes are track

III. Only few tracks are laps

Conclusions:

I. Some cars are laps.

II. No cars are track.

A. Only conclusion I follows

B. Only conclusion II follows

C. Either conclusion I or II follows

D. Neither conclusion I nor II follows

E. Both conclusion I and II follows

Q.14 Statement:

I. Only a few switches are USB.

II. Only a few USB are wires.

III. Some switches are not chargers.

Conclusion:

I. Some chargers are wires.

II. Few USB are chargers.

A. Only I follows

B. Only II follows

C. Either I or II follows

D. Neither I nor II follows

E. Both I and II follows

Q.15 Statement:

I. No brick is cement.

II. All cement is soil.

III. No soil is a rod.

Conclusion:

I. Some soil is not brick.

II. No rod is brick.

A. Only I follows

B. Only II follows

C. Either I or II follows

D. Neither I nor II follows

E. Both I and II follows

Q.16 Statement:

I. Only a few caps are hats.

II. All hats are masks.

III. Some masks are covers.

Conclusion:

I. Some masks are hats.

II. No caps are covers is a possibility.

A. Only I follows

B. Only II follows

C. Either I or II follows

D. Neither I nor II follows

E. Both I and II follow

Q.17 Direction: In the question given below, three conclusions of I, II, and III are followed by four statements. You have to take the given statements to be true even if they are in variance with commonly known facts. Read all the conclusions and then decide which of the given conclusions logically follows from the given statement disregarding commonly known facts.

Statements:

1) No Poet is Artist.

2) All Artist are Singer.

3) All Singers are Writer.

4) No Writer is Father.

Conclusion:

I) Only Writers are Artists.

II) No Singer is a Poet.

III) Only Artist is Writer.

A. Only conclusion II follows

B. Only conclusion III follows

C. Both conclusion I and III follow

D. Only Conclusion I follows

E. None follows

Ques (18-22):Direction: Read the following information carefully and answer the question given below.

Eight persons Ds, Fg, Lm, Ms, Nd, Pe, Ps, and Xy are sitting around a circular table but not necessarily in the same order. Some of them are facing away from centre and some of them are facing towards the centre.

Pe is sitting third to the left of Lm who is facing towards the centre. Ms and Fg are immediate neighbour of Pe. Nd is second to the right of Fg. Fg and Ms face the same direction but opposite to Pe. Ds is not an immediate neighbour of Nd. Xy is second to the right of Ds. Both the immediate neighbour of Nd face the same direction as Ms. Lm faces the same direction as the person who is sitting second to his right.

Q.18 How many persons are sitting between Fg and Xy when counting from the left of Xy?

A. Two   **B.** One   **C.** Five   **D.** Three
E. Four

Q.19 How many persons are facing away from centre between Nd and Ds counting from right of Nd?

A. One   **B.** Three   **C.** Four   **D.** Two
E. Zero

Q.20 Who is sitting opposite to Ds?

A. Xy   **B.** Fg   **C.** Pe   **D.** Lm
E. Ps

Q.21 Who sits second to the left of Ps?

A. Pe   **B.** Ms
C. Lm   **D.** Xy
E. None of the above

Q.22 How many persons are facing away from the centre?

A. Five   **B.** Three   **C.** Four   **D.** Two
E. One

Ques (23-27):Direction: Study the following information and answer the question given below:

8 persons Amar, Bikram, Charan, Deepak, Edward, Flint, Gautham and Hari are sitting in 2 parallel rows. Both the rows are facing the north and 4 persons are sitting in each of the rows. The rows are arranged such that exactly one person from the second row sits behind a person from the first row. Each one of them likes a different colour among yellow, blue, orange, red, green, white, black and cyan. Further, the following information is known about them.

Amar sits behind the person who likes yellow. The person who likes blue is sitting to the left of Bikram and he is the only neighbour of Bikram. Amar and Bikram are not sitting in the same row. The person who likes yellow is sitting adjacent to the person who likes blue. Amar is sitting adjacent to the person who likes green. The person who likes green is not sitting behind the person who likes blue. Charan is sitting behind the person who likes cyan. Charan does not like green. The persons who like red and orange are sitting adjacent to each other. None of them is a neighbour of the person who likes green. Charan does not like red. Deepak likes white. Flint is sitting adjacent to the person who likes blue. Edward does not like red but he is a neighbour of Amar. Gautham does not like blue.

Q.23 Who likes red?

A. Amar   **B.** Harish   **C.** Gautham   **D.** Bikram
E. Charan

Q.24 Who is sitting behind Flint?

A. Edward   **B.** Amar   **C.** Gautham   **D.** Charan
E. Deepak

Q.25 What colour does the person sitting behind the person who likes white like?

A. Red   **B.** Orange   **C.** Black   **D.** White
E. Green

Q.26 Who likes cyan?

A. Bikram   **B.** Harish   **C.** Gautham   **D.** Amar
E. Edward

Q.27 What colour does Amar like?

A. Green   **B.** Red   **C.** Black   **D.** Orange
E. Cyan

Ques (28-30):Direction: Read the following information carefully and answer the question given beside.

G is the mother of F, who is the spouse of D. M is the daughter of D, who is the only brother of C. E is the son of G, who is married to H. A is the niece of C, who has no sister and is unmarried. T is the father of D and has no daughter. V is the sister-in-law of F. G has only two children. M is the granddaughter of O.

Q.28 How is V related to M?

A. Paternal aunt   **B.** Maternal aunt
C. Sister   **D.** Either (A) or (B)
E. None of these

Q.29 How many female members are there in the family?

A. 7   **B.** 4   **C.** 5   **D.** 6
E. 7

Q.30 How is F's mother-in-law related to T?

A. Sister   **B.** Mother
C. Wife   **D.** Aunt
E. None of these

Ques (31-35):Direction: Read the following symbolic series carefully and answer the question based on it.

S $ 6 U K 7 % * 4 J O @ 2 3 L P 9 8 A # Y ^ 5 W &

Q.31 If all the even digits are skipped from the sequence then which one of the following elements is fifth to the right of '@'?

A. A   **B.** U   **C.** W   **D.** Y
E. #

Q.32 What is the sum of the second prime number from the right end and the third composite number from the left end?

A. 18   **B.** 16
C. 11   **D.** 20
E. None of these

Q.33 Which of the following elements is the 17th from the left end?

A. %   **B.** 9   **C.** #   **D.** 8
E. A

Q.34 Four of the following five are alike in a certain way and thus form a group. Which one of the following does not belong to that group?

A. 7*K   **B.** L93   **C.** J@4   **D.** $US
E. Y^A

Q.35 If all the letters are skipped from given sequence then which of the following is exactly between '%' and '#'?

A. @   **B.** 4   **C.** 3   **D.** 2
E. 1

// Smart Answer Sheet //

Correct   Indicates percentage of students who answered questions correctly.

Skipped   Indicates percentage of students who skipped questions.

Q.	Ans.	Correct / Skipped
1	A	64.31 % / 32.38 %
2	C	43.65 % / 53.64 %
3	A	40.67 % / 55.88 %
4	A	52.96 % / 38.76 %
5	C	19.13 % / 75.92 %
6	C	87.63 % / 12.13 %
7	B	83.86 % / 15.13 %

Q.	Ans.	Correct / Skipped
8	A	51.92 % / 42.15 %
9	B	47.67 % / 35.23 %
10	D	63.77 % / 32.58 %
11	C	65.87 % / 31.22 %
12	E	60.19 % / 37.63 %
13	B	53.93 % / 30.03 %
14	D	55.28 % / 37.15 %

Q.	Ans.	Correct / Skipped
15	A	59.97 % / 39.62 %
16	E	77.07 % / 17.69 %
17	E	10.5 % / 70.11 %
18	A	41.21 % / 50.43 %
19	B	46.22 % / 43.69 %
20	E	56.0 % / 36.06 %
21	A	49.85 % / 40.0 %

Q.	Ans.	Correct / Skipped
22	C	59.19 % / 31.8 %
23	C	18.89 % / 71.93 %
24	B	56.15 % / 40.81 %
25	E	60.91 % / 32.51 %
26	A	60.61 % / 33.18 %
27	C	60.2 % / 37.16 %
28	B	69.61 % / 30.13 %

Q.	Ans.	Correct / Skipped
29	D	55.54 % / 30.97 %
30	C	58.3 % / 37.66 %
31	A	55.37 % / 40.19 %
32	E	31.97 % / 67.29 %
33	B	52.41 % / 42.92 %
34	E	59.48 % / 40.17 %
35	D	58.23 % / 34.9 %

Performance Analysis

Avg. Score (%)	40.0%
Toppers Score (%)	68.57%
Your Score	

//Hints and Solutions//

1. Given statements: Y ≥ R < E; R > P ≥ C = A

On combining: Y ≥ R > P ≥ C = A; E > R > P ≥ C = A

Conclusions:

I. Y > A → True (as Y ≥ R > P ≥ C = A → Y > A)

II. E ≥ C → False (as E > R > P ≥ C → E > C)

Hence, the correct option is (A).

2. Given statements: W > Q ≥ M; H ≤ T = M

On combining: W > Q ≥ M = T ≥ H

Conclusions:

I. H ≤ Q → True (as Q ≥ M = T ≥ H → Q ≥ H)

II. W > T → True (as W > Q ≥ M = T → W > T)

Hence, the correct option is (C).

3. Given statements: J < E ≥ O; Y < P ≤ H < O.

On combining: J < E ≥ O > H ≥ P > Y.

Conclusions:

I. J > P → False (as J < E ≥ O > H ≥ P thus clear relation between J and P cannot be determined).

II. Y < E → True (as E ≥ O > H ≥ P > Y → E > Y).

Hence, the correct option is (A).

4. Given statements: C ≤ D ≤ X; K > V ≥ I; C = O ≥ K

On combining: X ≥ D ≥ C = O ≥ K > V ≥ I

Conclusions:

I. D ≤ V → False (D > C = O ≥ K > V → D > V)

II. X > K → False (X ≥ D > C = O ≥ K → X > K)

III. I ≤ O → True (O ≥ K > V ≥ I → O > I)

Thus, Only III is True.

Hence, the correct option is (A).

5. Given statements: X < N ≤ W; B ≥ L ≥ O; O = X

On combining: B ≥ L ≥ O = X; W ≥ N > O = X

Conclusions:

I. B > N → False (B ≥ L ≥ O and N > O → relation between B and M cannot be determined.)

II. N ≥ B → False (B ≥ L ≥ O and N > O → relation between B and M cannot be determined.)

III. L < W → False (L ≥ O and W ≥ N > O → relation between L and W can't be determined.)

None of the conclusions are true but conclusions I and II form a complementary pair.

Thus, either conclusion I or conclusion II is true.

6. The given word:

KITCHEN

Second, third, fifth and seventh letters of the word are I, T, H and N respectively.

The words formed from the letters:

HINT and THIN

So, two words can be formed from the given letters above.

Hence, the correct option is (C).

7. The given word:

C R E A T I O N

After arranging the letters of the given word as they appear in the English alphabet, we have:

A C E I N O R T

Only 'E' remains at the same position after rearrangement.

Hence, the correct option is (B).

Ques (8-10): The first element of the code represents the numerical value of first letter, considering A-Z as 1-26.

For Example: Disk

The first element would be 4, which represents the numeric value of D.

The second element of the code represents the codes as per number of letters as shown in the following table.

Number of letters Code:

Number of letters	Code
4	#
5	!
6	&
7	$
8	%
9	@

Disk has 4 letters, so its middle code would be # as per the table.

The third element represents the second letter of the respective word.

Second letter in the word Disk is 'i', so the last element would be 'I'.

Thus code for Disk would be 4#I.

8. By following the above explanation, we can get the code for "Take advance receipt" as 20#A 1$D 18$E.

Hence, the correct option is (A).

9. By following the above explanation, we can get the code for "Advertise your product" as 1@D 25#O 16$R.

Hence, the correct option is (B).

10. By following the above explanation, we can get the code for "Travel with wander" as 20&R 23#I 23&A.

Hence, the correct option is (D).

11. Using the given information we can create a following figure:

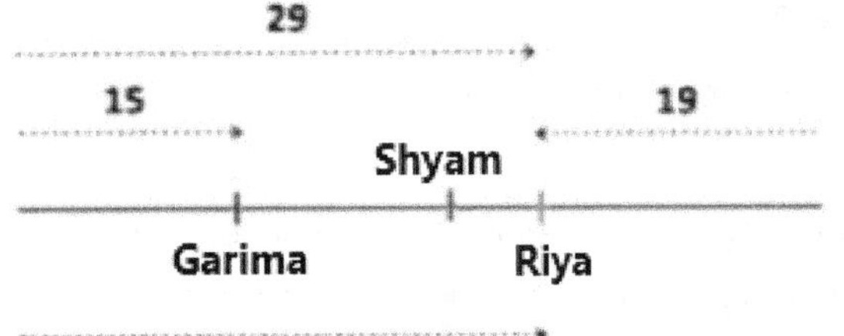

Here the total number of persons in the queue = (29 + 19 - 1)

= 47

Here, 29 is derived by adding Shyam's position from left end of the row (24) and his position with respect to Riya (5).

Hence, the correct option is (C).

12. Given,

In a row of 40 girls, when Komal moves four places to the left from her position, her position becomes 10th from the left end of the row.

Komal is 10th from the left end of the row by shifting 4.

Thus Komal's original position was 14th from the left end. Swati is 3rd to the right of Komal's original place.

Clearly, Swati is $14 + 3 = 17$ th from the left end.

Number of girls $= (40 - 17) = 23$ to the right of Swati

Thus, Swati is 24th from the right end of the row.

Hence, the correct option is (D).

13. The least possible Venn diagram for the given statements is as follows:

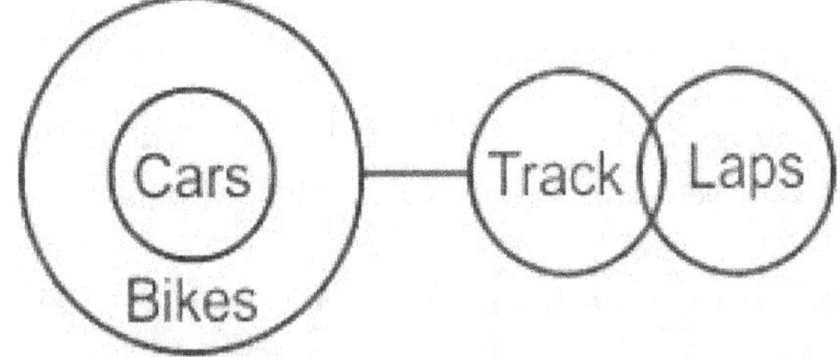

Conclusions:

I. Some cars are laps → False (It is possible, but there is no definite positive or negative relation is given between the elements, therefore it is false)

II. No cars are track → True (Because all cars are bikes and no bikes are track → no cars are track)

So, only conclusion II follows.

Hence, the correct option is (B).

14. The least possible Venn diagram for the given statements is as follows:

Conclusion:

I. Some chargers are wires → False (As there is no definite relation between chargers and wires, We cannot determine some chargers are wires or not)

II. Few USB are chargers → False (As there is no definite relation between chargers and USB, We cannot determine few USB are chargers or not)

So, Neither I nor II follows.

Hence, the correct option is (D).

15. The least possible Venn diagram for the given statements is as follows:

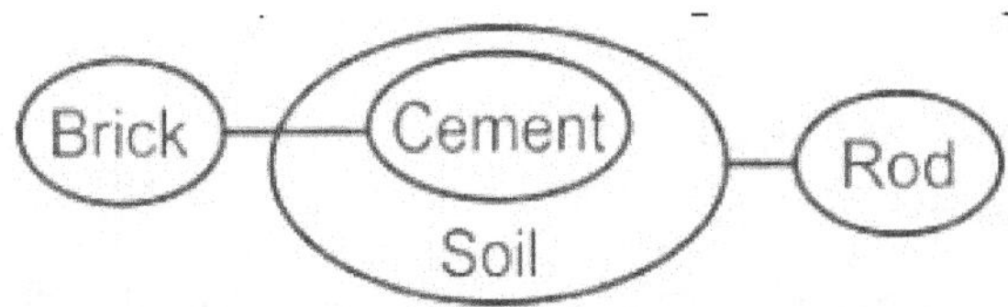

Conclusion:

I. Some soil is not brick → True (As all cement is oil and no cement is brick so the part of the soil which is cement is not brick, So, it is true)

II. No rod is brick → False (As there is no relation between rod and brick)

So, Only I follows.

Hence, the correct option is (A).

16. The least possible Venn diagram for the given statements is as follows:

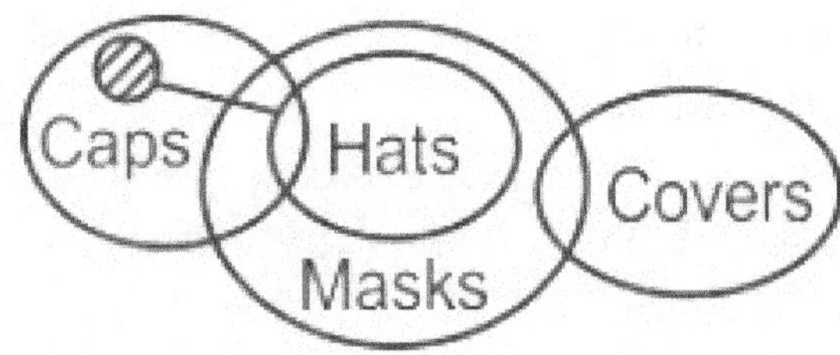

Conclusion:

I. Some masks are hats → True (As all hats are masks so, Some hats are definitely masks)

II. No caps are covers is a possibility → True (As there is no relation between caps and covers so we cannot say anything here but any possibility can follow here, So it is true)

So, Both I and II follow.

Hence, the correct option is (E).

17.

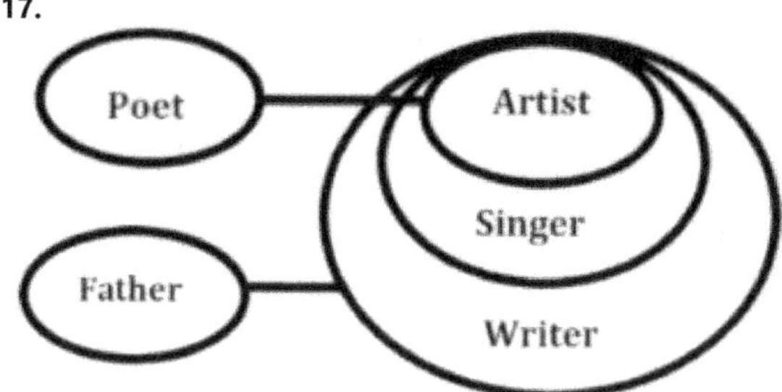

Conclusion:

(I) Only Writers are artists means Except Writer nothing can be Artist. So, This Conclusion doesn't follow.

(II) No Singer is a Poet. False (As It is possible but not definite).

(III) Only artists are Writer means Except Artist nothing can be writers. So, This Conclusion doesn't follow.

Hence, the correct option is (E).

Ques (18-22):Persons: Ds, Fg, Lm, Ms, Nd, Pe, Ps, and Xy

i) Pe is sitting third to the left of Lm who is facing towards the centre.

ii Ms and Fg are immediate neighbour of Pe.

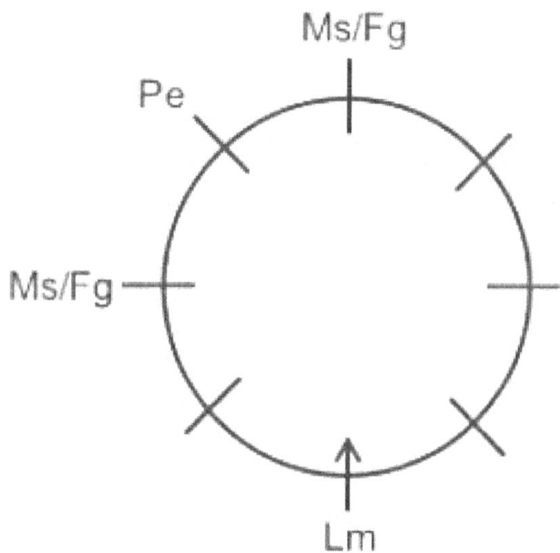

iii) Fg and Ms face the same direction but opposite to Pe.

iv) Nd is second to the right of Fg.

v) Ds is not an immediate neighbour of Nd.

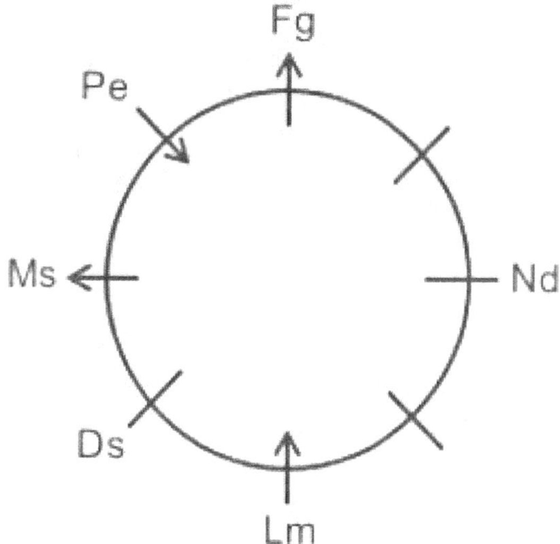

vi) Xy is second to the right of Ds.

vii) Both the immediate neighbour of Nd face the same direction as Ms.

viii) Lm faces the same direction as the person who is sitting second to his right.

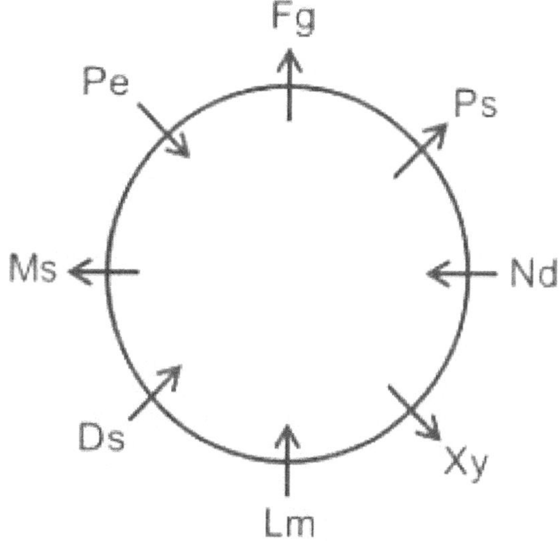

18. So, "Two" persons are sitting between Fg and Xy when counting from the left of Xy.

Hence, the correct option is (A).

19. So, three persons are facing away from centre between Nd and Ds counting from right of Nd.

Hence, the correct option is (B).

20. So, "Ps" is sitting opposite to Ds.

Hence, the correct option is (E).

21. So, "Pe" sits second to the left of Ps.

Hence, the correct option is (A).

22. So, Four persons are facing away from the centre.

Hence, the correct option is (C).

Ques (23-27): The person who likes blue is the only neighbour of Bikram and he is sitting to the left of Bikram. Therefore, Bikram must be sitting at the right corner. Bikram and Amar are not sitting in the same row. Therefore, Amar must be sitting in row 2. Amar sits behind the person who likes yellow. The person who likes yellow is sitting adjacent to the person who likes blue.

	Yellow	Blue	
			Bikram
——	——	——	——
——	——	——	——
	Amar		

Amar is sitting adjacent to the person who likes green. The person who likes green is not sitting behind the person who likes blue. Therefore, the person who likes green must be sitting at the left corner of row 2. Charan is sitting behind the person who likes cyan. Charan does not like green. Therefore, Charan must be sitting behind B and B must be liking cyan.

	Yellow	Blue	Cyan
			Bikram
——	——	——	——
——	——	——	——
	Amar		Charan
Green			

The persons who like red and orange are sitting adjacent to each other. None of them is a neighbour of the person who likes green. Therefore, Charan and his neighbour must be liking red and orange. Charan does not like red. Therefore, Charan must be liking orange and his neighbour must be liking red. Deepak likes white. Therefore, Deepak must be sitting at the left corner of row 1. Amar must be liking black.

White	Yellow	Blue	Cyan
Deepak			Bikram
——	——	——	——
——	——	——	——
	Amar		Charan
Green	Black	Red	Orange

Flint is sitting adjacent to the person who likes blue. Therefore, Flint must be liking yellow. Edward does not like red but he is a neighbour of A. Therefore, Edward must be liking green. Gautham does not like blue. Therefore, Gautham must be liking red and Harish must be liking blue. The final arrangement is as follows:

White	Yellow	Blue	Cyan
Deepak	Flint	Hari	Bikram
——	——	——	——
——	——	——	——
Edward	Amar	Gautham	Charan
Green	Black	Red	Orange

23. Gautham likes red.

Hence, the correct option is (C).

24. Amar is sitting behind Flint.

Hence, the correct option is (B).

25. Edward is the person sitting behind the person who likes white. Edward likes green.

Hence, the correct option is (E).

26. Bikram likes cyan.

Hence, the correct option is (A).

27. Amar likes black.

Hence, the correct option is (C).

Ques (28-30): According to the given information, the family tree is,

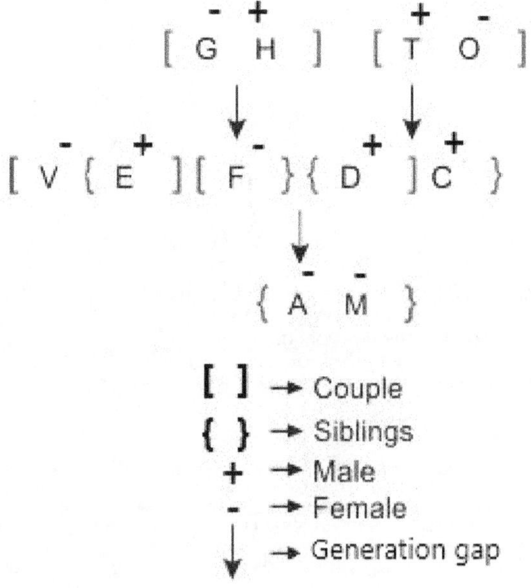

28. Thus, V is the maternal aunt of M.

Hence, the correct option is (B).

29. Thus, There are 6 female members in the family.

Hence, the correct option is (D).

30. Thus, F's mother-in-law is O, who is the wife of T.

Hence, the correct option is (C).

31. Given Sequence: S $ 6 U K 7 % * 4 J O @ 2 3 L P 9 8 A # Y ^ 5 W &

New Sequence: S $ U K 7 % * J O @ 3 L P 9 A # Y ^ 5 W &

Clearly 'A' is fifth to the right of '@'.

Hence, the correct option is (A).

32. Given Sequence: S $ 6 U K 7 % * 4 J O @ 2 3 L P 9 8 A # Y ^ 5 W &

Second prime number from right end is 3.

Third composite number from left end is 9.

Required sum = 12

Hence, the correct option is (E).

33. Given Sequence: S $ 6 U K 7 % * 4 J O @ 2 3 L P 9 8 A # Y ^ 5 W &

Evidently, 9 is 17th from the left end.

Hence, the correct option is (B).

34. Given Sequence: S $ 6 U K 7 % * 4 J O @ 2 3 L P 9 8 A # Y ^ 5 W &

Logic: Second element is second to the right of first element and third element is immediate left of the first element.

Thus option (E) 'Y^A' does not follow the logic.

Hence, the correct option is (E).

35. Given Sequence: S $ 6 U K 7 % * 4 J O @ 2 3 L P 9 8 A # Y ^ 5 W &

New Sequence: $ 6 7 % * 4 @ 2 3 9 8 # ^ 5 &

Thus, 2 is exactly between % and #.

Hence, the correct option is (D).

Q.1 The average price of 10 books is Rs. 12 while the average price of 8 of these books is Rs. 11.75. Of the remaining two books, if the price of one book is 60 % more than the price of the other, what is the price of each of these two books?

A. Rs. 5, Rs.7.50

B. Rs. 8, Rs. 12

C. Rs. 10, Rs. 16

D. Rs. 12, Rs. 14

E. Rs. 12, Rs. 15

Q.2

A motorboat, whose speed is 15 km/hr in still water goes 30 km downstream and comes back in a total of 4 hours 30 minutes. The speed of the stream (in km/hr) is:

A. 4   **B.** 5   **C.** 6   **D.** 10

E. 12

Ques (3-7):Direction: Given below pie chart show the percentage distribution of accounts opened by five different banks under 'Jan Dhan Yojana'. Read the data carefully and answer the question.

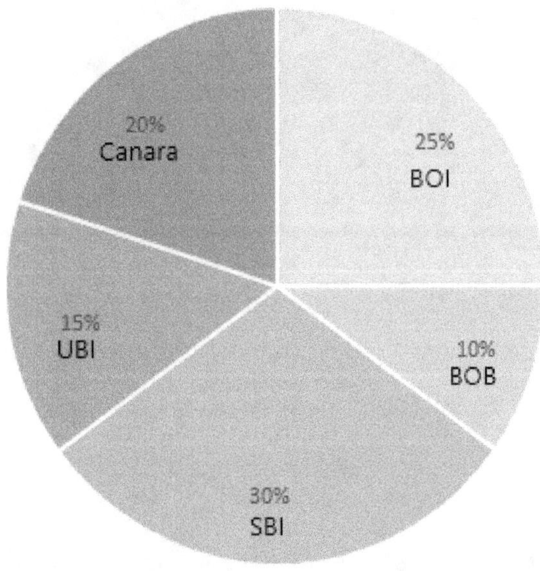

Q.3 If the difference between total accounts opened by SBI and Canara is 2.1 crores, then find the total account opened by UBI?

A. 2.15 crores

B. 3.15 crores

C. 3.25 crores

D. 3.05 crores

E. 3.75 crores

Q.4 Find the ratio between total accounts opened by SBI & BOI together to total accounts opened by Canara?

A. 11 : 4   **B.** 3 : 1   **C.** 4 : 1   **D.** 5 : 1

E. 1 : 1

Q.5 Total accounts opened by BOI is what percent more than total accounts opened by BOB?

A. 200%   **B.** 125%   **C.** 75%   **D.** 100%

E. 150%

Q.6 If the total accounts opened by UBI and BOI is 3.6 crores, then find the difference between accounts opened by Canara and BOB?

A. 0.64 crores

B. 0.9 crores

C. 0.56 crores

D. 0.48 crores

E. 0.42 crores

Q.7 If total 24 crores accounts opened by all five bank then find average number of accounts opened by SBI and UBI?

A. 5.6 crores

B. 5.4 crores

C. 5.2 crores

D. 6.4 crores

E. 7.2 crores

Ques (8-12):Direction: In the following question, two equations numbered I and II are given. You have to solve both the equations and give the answer.

Q.8 I. $x^2 = 169$

II. $y^2 - 30y + 221 = 0$

A. $x > y$

B. $x < y$

C. $x \geq y$

D. $x \leq y$

E. $x = y$ or no relation can be obtained

Q.9 I. $3x^2 + 32x + 85 = 0$

II. $2y^2 + 19y + 45 = 0$

A. If $x > y$

B. If $x < y$

C. If $x \geq y$

D. If $x \leq y$

E. If $x = y$ or no relation can be established

Q.10 I. $x^2 - 10x + 24 = 0$

II. $y^2 - 20y + 96 = 0$

A. $x > y$

B. $x \geq y$

C. $x < y$

D. $x \leq y$

E. $x = y$ or no relation can be established between x and y

Q.11 I. $x^2 - 2x - 15 = 0$

II. $y^2 - 4y - 12 = 0$

A. $x > y$

B. $x \geq y$

C. $x < y$

D. $x \leq y$

E. $x = y$ or no relation can be established between x and y

Q.12 I. $12x^2 + 29x + 14 = 0$

II. $3y^2 + 14y + 16 = 0$

A. If $x > y$
B. If $x < y$
C. If $x \geq y$
D. If $x \leq y$
E. If $x = y$ or no relation can be established

Q.13 What will come in place of question mark (?) in the following equation?

$950 + 50 \times 15 - 14 \times 22 + \sqrt{?} = 11^3 + 9^2$

A. 200   B. 240   C. 320   D. 400
E. 420

Q.14 What will come in place of question mark '?' in the following question?
74% of 159 – [36.5% of 142 + 25.4% of 203] = 13.5% of ? – 10.5% of 120

A. 129.05   B. 149.22
C. 179.03   D. 199.02
E. None of the above

Q.15 What should come in place of question mark (?) in the following questions? (You do not have to calculate the exact value.)

$17^4 + \sqrt{2400.5} + 50.67 + 17\%$ of $400 + \sqrt{528.9} = (?) + 44$

A. 38128   B. 98728
C. 50488   D. 83668
E. None of these

Q.16 What should come in place of the question mark '?' in the following question?

$9\frac{10}{2} \times \left(\frac{3}{8} \times \frac{16}{9}\right) - 6\frac{5}{3} = 5\frac{5}{2} + 4\frac{1}{2} - ?$

A. $\frac{14}{3}$ B. $\frac{31}{3}$ C. $\frac{28}{3}$ D. $\frac{33}{5}$
E. $\frac{31}{5}$

Q.17 What should come in place of the question mark (?) in the following question?

$\sqrt[3]{12167} \times \sqrt[3]{5832} = ?$

A. 416   B. 394
C. 414   D. 396
E. None of these

Q.18 What should come in place of the question mark (?) in the following question?
(8.2% of 365) – (1.75% of 108) = ?

A. 16.02   B. 28.04
C. 42.34   D. 53.76
E. None of these

Q.19 What should come in place of the question mark (?) in the following question?
$36^2 \times 5^2 - 2400^2 = ?$

A. 520   B. 7200000
C. 5727600   D. -5727600
E. None of these

Q.20 What should come in place of the question mark (?) in the following question?

$\frac{2}{3} \times \dfrac{3}{\frac{5}{6} \div \frac{2}{3} \times 1\frac{1}{4}} = ?$

A. 2   B. $1\frac{11}{2.5}$
C. $2\frac{7}{25}$ D. $3\frac{1}{29}$
E. None of these

Q.21 What should come in place of the question mark (?) in the following question?

$\sqrt{64 \times 49} \div (4)^2 \times 12 = ?$

A. 56   B. 49
C. 63   D. 42
E. None of these

Q.22 What should come in place of the question mark (?) in the following question?
3 - [6 - {4 + (-4 + 5 - 2)4}] = ?

A. 3   B. -6
C. -3   D. 4
E. None of these

Q.23 A man sells two books for Rs. 1110. He earns 15% loss on the first book and 25% profit on the second book. If the cost price of the first book is equal to the selling price of the second book, find the cost price of the two books.

A. Rs. 700 and Rs. 400   B. Rs. 600 and Rs. 480
C. Rs. 450 and Rs. 650   D. Rs. 500 and Rs. 600
E. Rs. 800 and Rs. 300

Ques (24-28):Direction: What will come in the place of question mark(?).

Q.24 2,8,26,?,242

A. 78   B. 72
C. 82   D. 84
E. None of these

Q.25 3,13,39,89,?,293
A. 172   B. 171   C. 182   D. 181
E. 201

Q.26 1,3,4,7,11,18,?,47
A. 25   B. 28   C. 29   D. 31
E. 33

Q.27 3,2,3,6,?,37.5,115.5
A. 11   B. 3   C. 6   D. 12
E. 14

Q.28 26,32,58,90,?,238,386
A. 110   B. 130   C. 148   D. 160
E. 150

Q.29 5 liters of milk is drawn from a tank that has 50 liters of milk. The taken milk is replaced by water and the process is repeated 3 times. The mixture is sold at Rs. $\dfrac{100}{L}$ and cost price of milk is Rs. $\dfrac{100}{L}$, then find the profit (In Rs.).

A. Rs. 1455   **B.** Rs. 1355   **C.** Rs. 1255   **D.** Rs. 2000
E. Rs. 1555

Ques (30-31):Direction: The question below consists of a question and two statements numbered I and II given below it. You have to decide whether the data provided in the statements are sufficient to answer the question. Read both the statements and give answer.

Q.30 At present, the age of Ram and Shyam is in the ratio of 5 : 6 respectively. What is the age of Ram?

Statement I: At present, the respective ratio of the age of the age of Shyam and Mohan is 3 : 4.

Statement II: 5 years hence, the ratio of the age of Ram and Mohan will become 2 : 3.

A. The data in statements I alone is sufficient to answer the question, while the data in statement II alone is not sufficient to answer the question.

B. The data in statements II alone is sufficient to answer the question, while the data in statement I alone is not sufficient to answer the question.

C. Either Statement I or Statement II alone is sufficient to answer the question.

D. The data in both the statements I and II is not sufficient to answer the question.

E. The data in both the statements I and II together is necessary to answer the question.

Q.31 Is 'A' is an odd number?

Statement I: When A is multiplied with a number then the product is an even number.

Statement II: When 'A' is added with the product of two odd numbers then the number thus obtained is an even number.

A. The data in statements I alone is sufficient to answer the question, while the data in statement II alone is not sufficient to answer the question.

B. The data in statements II alone is sufficient to answer the question, while the data in statement I alone is not sufficient to answer the question.

C. Either Statement I or Statement II alone is sufficient to answer the question.

D. The data in both the statements I and II is not sufficient to answer the question.

E. The data in both the statements I and II together is necessary to answer the question.

Q.32 Direction: Each of the questions below consists of a question and three statements numbered I, II and III given below it. You have to decide whether the data provided in the statements are sufficient to answer the question. Read all the statements and give answer:

How much profit did the company earn in the year 2002?

Statement I: The company earned 40% more profit in the year 2003 than that in the year 2001.

Statement II: The company earned a total profit of Rs. 20 crores in the years 2001 and 2002 taken together.

Statement III: In the year 2003, the company earned 80% of the profit earned in 2002.

A. Either statement III alone or statements I and II together are sufficient.

B. Only statement III is sufficient.

C. Statement I and Statement II together are sufficient.

D. Only statement I, II, and III together are sufficient.

E. None of these

Ques (33-34):Direction: Below given a question and three statements numbered I, II and III. You have to decide whether the data provided in the statements are sufficient to answer the question. Read all the statements and give answer:

Q.33 A person can purchase three articles in Rs. 49. What is the price of costliest article?

Statement I: The cost price of two articles each is Rs. 1 less than the cost price of costliest article.

Statement II: The cost price of two articles is same.

Statement III: The cost price of costliest article is 6.25% more than the cost price of cheapest article.

A. Either statement I alone or statements II and III together are sufficient.

B. Only statement III is sufficient.

C. Only statement I and II together are sufficient.

D. Only statement I and III together are sufficient.

E. None of these

Q.34 A metal block of density 'D' and mass 'M', in the form of a cuboid, is beaten into a thin square sheet of thickness 't', and rolled to form a cylinder of the same thickness. Find the inner radius of the cylinder –

Statement I: Cuboid has dimensions 10cm x 5 cm x 12 cm

Statement II: Thickness 't' = 1.5cm

Statement III: Mass of block, M = 216kg

A. Either statement III alone or statements I and II together are sufficient.

B. Only statement III is sufficient.

C. Statement I and Statement II together are sufficient.

D. Only statement I, II, and III together are sufficient.

E. None of these

Q.35 In a class, the number of girls is 20 % more than that of the boys. The strength of the class is 66. If 4 more girls are admitted to the class, the ratio of the number of boys to that of the girls is:

A. 1: 2   **B.** 1: 4   **C.** 3: 4   **D.** 5: 7
E. 1: 7

// Smart Answer Sheet //

| Correct | Indicates percentage of students who answered questions correctly. |

| Skipped | Indicates percentage of students who skipped questions. |

Q.	Ans.	Correct / Skipped	Q.	Ans.	Correct / Skipped	Q.	Ans.	Correct / Skipped	Q.	Ans.	Correct / Skipped	Q.	Ans.	Correct / Skipped
1	C	58.59 % / 40.27 %	8	D	76.88 % / 15.37 %	15	D	58.75 % / 40.62 %	22	C	83.1 % / 16.83 %	29	B	30.1 % / 68.58 %
2	B	59.07 % / 38.85 %	9	D	60.43 % / 35.5 %	16	B	63.38 % / 30.73 %	23	B	18.33 % / 73.23 %	30	E	12.22 % / 83.73 %
3	B	13.94 % / 74.67 %	10	C	77.11 % / 13.07 %	17	C	83.58 % / 16.27 %	24	E	69.18 % / 30.24 %	31	B	76.55 % / 15.1 %
4	A	11.35 % / 68.32 %	11	E	46.07 % / 39.82 %	18	B	23.46 % / 76.14 %	25	B	59.0 % / 36.5 %	32	D	62.23 % / 36.22 %
5	E	53.76 % / 35.93 %	12	A	64.72 % / 34.86 %	19	D	83.36 % / 11.17 %	26	C	47.79 % / 48.06 %	33	A	88.85 % / 10.11 %
6	B	29.94 % / 68.83 %	13	D	44.71 % / 43.5 %	20	A	40.85 % / 35.28 %	27	E	44.65 % / 38.65 %	34	C	48.85 % / 48.96 %
7	B	42.65 % / 38.04 %	14	D	59.47 % / 33.79 %	21	D	17.73 % / 68.45 %	28	C	41.35 % / 50.01 %	35	C	64.88 % / 33.65 %

Performance Analysis

Avg. Score (%)	28.57%
Toppers Score (%)	54.29%
Your Score	

//Hints and Solutions//

1. Given:

Total cost of 10 books = Rs. 120

Total cost of 8 books = Rs. 94

⇒ The cost of 2 books = Rs. 26

Let the price of each book be x and y.

⇒ x + y = 26 - - - - - -(1)

Given that the price of 1 book is 60% more than the other price

$$\left(\frac{160}{100}\right)y + y = 26$$

$$\Rightarrow y\left(\frac{160}{100} + 1\right) = 26$$

$$\Rightarrow y\left(\frac{160+100}{100}\right) = 26$$

$$\Rightarrow y = \frac{(26\times100)}{260}$$

$$\Rightarrow y = 10$$

Substituting y = 10 in equation (1), we get

$$x + 10 = 26$$

$$x = 16$$

Hence, the correct option is (C).

2. Given,

Speed of motorboat in still water = 15 km/hr

Distance covered by motorboat in downstream = 30 km

Let the speed of the stream be x km/hr.

Then, Speed in downstream = (15 + x) km/hr.

Speed in upstream = (15 - x) km/hr.

Therefore,

$$\frac{30}{(15+x)} + \frac{30}{(15-x)} = 4\frac{1}{2}$$

$$\Rightarrow \frac{30\times(15-x)+30\times(15+x)}{(15+x)\times(15-x)} = \frac{9}{2}$$

$$\Rightarrow \frac{900}{225-x^2} = \frac{9}{2}$$

$$\Rightarrow 9x^2 = 225$$

$$\Rightarrow x^2 = 25$$

$$\Rightarrow x = 5km/hr$$

Hence, the correct option is (B).

3. Given:

The value of the difference between total accounts opened by SBI and Canara = 2.1 crores

The percentage value of the difference between total accounts opened by SBI and Canara Bank, as per the pie chart = 30% - 20%

⇒ 10% = 2.1 crores

⇒ 1% = 0.21 crores

UBI percentage value = 15%

= 0.21 crores × 15

= 3.15 crores

∴ The total account opened by UBI is 3.15 crores.

Hence, the correct option is (B).

4. Given:

Distribution of accounts opened by SBI = 30%

Distribution of accounts opened by BOI = 25%

Distribution of accounts opened by Canara = 20%

Let the total number of accounts opened by all five banks = $100x$

$$\therefore \text{Required ratio} = \frac{100x\times\frac{(25+30)}{100}}{100x\times\frac{20}{100}}$$

$$= \frac{55x}{20x}$$

$$= 11:4$$

Hence, the correct option is (A).

5. Given:

Percentage distribution of accounts opened by BOI = 25%

Percentage distribution of accounts opened by BOB = 10%

Let the total accounts opened by all five banks = 100x

$$\text{Total accounts opened by BOI} = \frac{100x\times25}{100}$$

$$= 25x$$

$$\text{Total accounts opened by BOB} = \frac{100x\times10}{100}$$

$$= 10x$$

$$\therefore \text{Required percentage} = \frac{25x-10x}{10x} \times 100$$

$$= 150\%$$

Hence, the correct option is (E).

6. Given:

Percentage distribution of accounts opened by UBI = 15%

Percentage distribution of accounts opened by BOI = 25%

Percentage distribution of accounts opened by Canara = 20%

Percentage distribution of accounts opened by BOB = 10%

Let the total accounts opened by all five banks = $100x$

According to the question,

Total accounts opened by UBI and BOI = $\dfrac{100x \times (15+25)}{100}$ = 3.6 crores

$\Rightarrow \dfrac{100x \times 40}{100}$ = 3.6 crores

$\Rightarrow 40x$ = 3.6 crores

$\Rightarrow x$ = 0.09 crores

Difference between Canara and BOB = $20x - 10x$

= $10x$

Putting value of (x)

= 10 × 0.09

= 0.9 crores

∴ Difference between accounts opened by Canara and BOB is 0.9 crores.

Hence, the correct option is (B).

7. Given:

Distribution of accounts opened by SBI = 30%

Distribution of accounts opened by UBI = 15%

Accounts opened by all five bank = 24 crores

Total number of accounts opened by SBI and UBI

= $24 \times \dfrac{(30+15)}{100}$

= $24 \times \dfrac{45}{100}$

= $\dfrac{1080}{100}$

= 10.8 crores

∴ Required average = $\dfrac{Total\ amount}{Number\ of\ Banks}$

= $\dfrac{10.8}{2}$

= 5.4 crores

Hence, the correct option is (B).

8. Given,

I. $x^2 = 169$

$\Rightarrow x = \sqrt{169}$

$\Rightarrow x = 13, -13$

II. $y^2 - 30y + 221 = 0$

$\Rightarrow y^2 - 13y - 17y + 221 = 0$

$\Rightarrow y(y - 13) - 17(y - 13) = 0$

$\Rightarrow (y - 13)(y - 17) = 0$

$\Rightarrow y = 13, 17$

When $x = 13$, for $y = 13$ or 17, $x \le y$

When $x = -13$, for $y = 13$ or 17, $x < y$

∴ $x \le y$

Hence, the correct option is (D).

9. I. $3x^2 + 32x + 85 = 0$

$\Rightarrow 3x^2 + 15x + 17x + 85 = 0$

$\Rightarrow 3x(x + 5) + 17(x + 5) = 0$

$\Rightarrow (x + 5)(3x + 17)$

∴ $x = -5, \dfrac{-17}{3}$

II. $2y^2 + 19y + 45 = 0$

$\Rightarrow 2y^2 + 10y + 9y + 45 = 0$

$\Rightarrow 2y(y + 5) + 9(y + 5) = 0$

$\Rightarrow (y + 5)(2y + 9) = 0$

∴ $y = -5, \dfrac{-9}{2}$

When $x = -5$, for $y = -5, x = y$ and for $y = \dfrac{-9}{2}, x < y$

When $x = \dfrac{-17}{3}$, for $y = -5, x < y$ and for $y = \dfrac{-9}{2}, x < y$

∴ $x \le y$

Hence, the correct option is (D).

10. Given,

$x^2 - 10x + 24 = 0$

$x^2 - 6x - 4x + 24 = 0$

$(x - 6)(x - 4) = 0$

Solving we get, $x = 4, 6$

$y^2 - 20y + 96 = 0$

$y^2 - 8y - 12y + 96 = 0$

$(y - 8)(y - 12) = 0$

Solving we get, $y = 8, 12$

So, y is greater than x

Hence, the correct option is (C).

11. Given,

I. $x^2 - 2x - 15 = 0$

$\Rightarrow x^2 - 5x + 3x - 15 = 0$

$\Rightarrow x(x-5) + 3(x-5) = 0$

$\Rightarrow (x-5)(x+3) = 0$

Then, $x = (5)$ or $x = (-3)$

II. $y^2 - 4y - 12 = 0$

$\Rightarrow y^2 - 6y + 2y - 12 = 0$

$\Rightarrow y(y-6) + 2(y-6) = 0$

$\Rightarrow (y+2)(y-6) = 0$

Then, $y = (6)$ or $y = (-2)$

So, when $x = (5)$, $x < y$ for $y = (6)$ and $x > y$ for $y = (-2)$

And when $x = (-3)$, $x < y$ for $y = (6)$ and $x < y$ for $y = (-2)$

$\therefore$ So, the relationship cannot be determined.

Hence, the correct option is (E).

12. Given,

I. $12x^2 + 29x + 14 = 0$

$\Rightarrow 12x^2 + 8x + 21x + 14 = 0$

$\Rightarrow 4x(3x+2) + 7(3x+2) = 0$

$\Rightarrow (4x+7)(3x+2)$

$\therefore x = -\dfrac{2}{3}, \dfrac{-7}{4}$

II. $3y^2 + 14y + 16 = 0$

$\Rightarrow 3y^2 + 6y + 8y + 16 = 0$

$\Rightarrow 3y(y+2) + 8(y+2) = 0$

$\Rightarrow (y+2)(3y+8) = 0$

$\therefore y = -2, \dfrac{-8}{2}$

The value of x lies between $\dfrac{-2}{3}$ and $\dfrac{-7}{4}$ whereas the value of y is lies between -2 and $\dfrac{-8}{3}$.

We see that the minimum value of $x \left(\dfrac{-7}{4}\right)$ is greater than maximum value of $y(-2)$.

Therefore, $x > y$.

Hence, the correct option is (A).

13. Given:

$950 + 50 \times 15 - 14 \times 22 + \sqrt{?} = 11^3 + 9^2$

$\Rightarrow 950 + 750 - 308 + \sqrt{?} = 1331 + 81$

$\Rightarrow 1392 + \sqrt{?} = 1412$

$\Rightarrow \sqrt{?} = 20$

$\Rightarrow ? = 400$

Hence, the correct option is (D).

14. Follow the BODMAS rule to solve the question,

Step-1: Parts of an equation enclosed in 'Brackets' must be solved first, and in the bracket, the BODMAS rule must be followed,

74% of 159 – [36.5% of 142 + 25.4% of 203] = 13.5% of ? – 10.5% of 120

$\Rightarrow$ 74% of 159 –
$\left\{ \left[\left(\frac{36.5}{100}\right) \times 142 \right] + \left[\left(\frac{25.4}{100}\right) \times 203 \right] \right\} = \left[\left(\frac{13.5}{100}\right) \times ? \right] - \left[\left(\frac{10.5}{100}\right) \times 120 \right]$

$\Rightarrow$ 74% of 159 – [51.83 + 51.56] = [0.135 × ?] – 12.6

$\Rightarrow$ 74% of 159 – 103.39 = 0.135 × ? – 12.6

Any mathematical 'Of' or 'Exponent' must be solved,

$\Rightarrow \left[\left(\frac{74}{100}\right) \times 159 \right] - 103.39 = 0.135 \times ? - 12.6$

$\Rightarrow$ 117.66 – 103.39 = 0.135 × ? – 12.6

$\Rightarrow$ 14.27 = 0.135 × ? – 12.6

$\Rightarrow$ 14.27 + 12.6 = 0.135 × ?

$\Rightarrow$ 26.87 = 0.135 × ?

$\therefore$? = 199.02

Hence, the correct option is (D).

15. Given:

$17^4 + \sqrt{2400.5} + 50.67 + 17\% \text{ of } 400 + \sqrt{528.9} = (?) + 44$

Approximating the value to the nearest integer:

$\Rightarrow 17^4 + \sqrt{2400} + 51 + 17\% \text{ of } 400 + \sqrt{529} = (?) + 44$

$\Rightarrow$ 83521 + 49 + 51 + 68 + 23 = (?) + 44

$\Rightarrow$ 83521 + 191 – 44 = (?)

$\Rightarrow$ (?) = 83668

Hence, the correct option is (D).

16. Given expression is,

$9\dfrac{10}{2} \times \left(\dfrac{3}{8} \times \dfrac{16}{9}\right) - 6\dfrac{5}{3} = 5\dfrac{5}{2} + 4\dfrac{1}{2} - ?$

$\Rightarrow \left(\dfrac{28}{2}\right) \times \left[\left(\dfrac{3}{8}\right) \times \left(\dfrac{16}{9}\right) \right] - \dfrac{23}{3} = \dfrac{15}{2} + \dfrac{9}{2} - ?$

$$\Rightarrow 14 \times \left(\frac{2}{3}\right) - \frac{23}{3} = \frac{15}{2} + \frac{9}{2} - ?$$

$$\Rightarrow \frac{28}{3} - \frac{23}{3} = \frac{15}{2} + \frac{9}{2} - ?$$

$$\Rightarrow \frac{28}{3} - \frac{23}{3} = \frac{24}{2} - ?$$

$$\Rightarrow \frac{5}{3} = 12 - ?$$

$$\Rightarrow ? = 12 - \frac{5}{3}$$

$$\Rightarrow ? = \frac{31}{3}$$

Hence, the correct option is (B).

17. Given: $\sqrt[3]{12167} \times \sqrt[3]{5832} = ?$

$\sqrt[3]{12167} = 23$

Also $\sqrt[3]{5832} = 18$

So, $\sqrt[3]{12167} \times \sqrt[3]{5832} = 23 \times 18$

$= 414$

Hence, the correct option is (C).

18. Given:

(8.2% of 365) – (1.75% of 108) = ?

$$\Rightarrow \left[\left(\frac{8.2}{100}\right) \times 365\right] - \left[\left(\frac{1.75}{100}\right) \times 108\right] = ?$$

$$\Rightarrow \frac{[(8.2 \times 365) - (1.75 \times 108)]}{100} = ?$$

$$\Rightarrow \frac{(2993 - 189)}{100} = ?$$

$$\Rightarrow ? = \frac{2804}{100} = 28.04$$

Hence, the correct option is (B).

19. Given:

$36^2 \times 5^2 - 2400^2 = ?$

$\Rightarrow 180^2 - 2400^2 = ?$

$\Rightarrow (180 + 2400)(180 - 2400) = ?$

$\Rightarrow 2580 \times (-2220) = ?$

$\Rightarrow ? = -5727600$

Hence, the correct option is (D).

20. Given:

$$\frac{2}{3} \times \frac{3}{\frac{5}{6} \div \frac{2}{3} \times 1\frac{1}{4}} = ?$$

$$\Rightarrow ? = \frac{2}{3} \times \frac{3}{\frac{5}{6} \div \frac{2}{3} \times 1\frac{1}{4}}$$

$$\Rightarrow ? = \frac{2}{3} \times \frac{3}{\frac{5}{6} \div \frac{2}{3} \times \frac{5}{4}}$$

$$\Rightarrow ? = \frac{2}{3} \times \frac{3}{\frac{5}{6} \div \frac{5}{6}}$$

$$\Rightarrow ? = 2 \times \frac{1}{1} = 2$$

Hence, the correct option is (A).

21. Let the unknown be x.

$$\sqrt{64 \times 49} \div (4)^2 \times 12 = ?$$

Factoring the terms under the square root and squaring 4 we get,

$$x = \sqrt{(8 \times 8 \times 7 \times 7)} \div 16 \times 12$$

Square rooting the given term, we get,

$x = 8 \times 7 \div 16 \times 12$

Applying BODMAS rule and simplifying we get,

$$x = \frac{(8 \times 7 \times 12)}{16} = 42$$

Hence, the correct option is (D).

22. Given:

3 - [6 - {4 + (-4 + 5 - 2)4}] = ?

$\Rightarrow$ 3 - [6 - {4 + (-1)4}] = ?

$\Rightarrow$ 3 - [6 - {4 - 4}] = ?

$\Rightarrow$ 3 - [6 - 0] = ?

$\Rightarrow$? = -3

Hence, the correct option is (C).

23. Given:

Selling price two books = Rs. 1110

Loss % on 1st book = 15%

Profit % on 2nd book = 25%

Concept used:

SP = [CP + (CP × profit%)]

SP = [CP – (CP × loss%)]

SP = selling price

CP = cost price

Let CP of two books be Rs. 20x and Rs. 20y

SP of 1st book = Rs. 20x × $\dfrac{85}{100}$

= Rs. 17x

SP of 2nd book = Rs. 20y × $\dfrac{125}{100}$

= Rs. 25y

According to the question,

20x = 25y

$$\Rightarrow \frac{x}{y} = \frac{5}{4}$$

CP of 1st book = 20 × 5 = Rs. 100

SP of 1st book = 17 × 5 = Rs. 85

CP of 2nd book = 20 × 4 = Rs. 80

SP of 2nd book = 25 × 4 = Rs. 100

Total CP = 180

Total SP = 185

According to the question,

The value of 185 is 1110

6 × 185 = 1110

= 1 → 6

So, CP of 1st book = 100 × 6

= 600

So, CP of 2nd book = 80 × 6

= 480

∴ Cost price of both the books is Rs. 600 and Rs. 480.

Hence, the correct option is (B).

24. The pattern is,

$$8 = 2 \times 3 + 2$$

$$26 = 8 \times 3 + 2$$

$$80 = 26 \times 3 + 2$$

$$242 = 80 \times 3 + 2$$

Hence, the correct option is (E).

25. The pattern is,

$$13 = 3 + (3^2 + 1)$$

$$39 = 13 + (5^2 + 1)$$

$$89 = 39 + (7^2 + 1)$$

$$171 = 89 + (9^2 + 1)$$

$$293 = 171 + (11^2 + 1)$$

Hence, the correct option is (B).

26. The pattern is,

$$4 = 1 + 3$$

$$7 = 4 + 3$$

$$11 = 7 + 4$$

$$18 = 11 + 7$$

$$29 = 18 + 11$$

$$47 = 29 + 18$$

Hence, the correct option is (C).

27. The pattern is,

$$2 = 3 \times 0.5 + 0.5$$

$$3 = 2 \times 1 + 1$$

$$6 = 3 \times 1.5 + 1.5$$

$$14 = 6 \times 2 + 2 = 14$$

$$37.5 = 14 \times 2.5 + 2.$$

$$115.5 = 37.5 \times 3 + 3$$

Hence, the correct option is (E).

28. The pattern is,

$$58 = 32 + 26$$

$$90 = 58 + 32$$

$$148 = 90 + 58$$

$$238 = 148 + 90$$

$$386 = 238 + 148$$

So, there should be 148 in place of ?.

Hence, the correct option is (C).

29. Milk left = Capacity × (1 – fraction of milk withdrawn)^n, where n is the no of process

$$\Rightarrow \text{Milk left} = 50 \times \left(\frac{1-5}{50}\right)^3 = 50 \times \left(\frac{45}{50}\right)^3 = 36.45 \text{ L}$$

⇒ Total cost price = 36.45 × 100 = Rs. 3645

⇒ Total selling price = 50 × 100 = Rs. 5000

∴ Required profit = 5000 – 3645 = Rs. 1355

Hence, the correct option is (B).

30. Given:

Ram : Shyam = 5 : 6

From the statement I:

Ram : Shyam : Mohan = 2.5 : 3 : 4

From the statement II, after 5 years, hence,

Ram : Mohan = 2 : 3

If we combine both the statement then we will get R's present age = 25 years

Shayam's present age = 30 years and Mohan's present age = 40 years

Hence, the correct option is (E).

31. From the statement I, we could not conclude our answer because even × even = even and even × odd = even.

From the statement II, we can conclude our answer because

even + odd × odd = odd

But odd + odd × odd = even

Therefore, the data in statements II alone is sufficient to answer the question, while the data in statement I alone is not sufficient to answer the question.

Hence, the correct option is (B).

32. Taking all statement together,

Let the profit earned by company in $2001 =$ Rs. x and in $2002 =$ Rs. y

Profit earned in $2003 = 1.4x$

$x + y =$ Rs. 20 crore ..... (i)

From statement (III),

$$1.4x = y \times \frac{80}{100}$$

$$x = \frac{4}{5} \times \frac{1}{1.4} y$$

$$x = \frac{4}{7} y \;.....\; (ii)$$

From equation (i) and (ii), we can get the required profit.

So all the statements are required to find profit in the year $2002.$

Hence, the correct option is (D).

33. Let the CP of each of two cheapest articles = x and the CP of costliest article = x + 1

Then, x + x + x + 1 = 49,

x = 16

therefore, the CP of costliest article = 16 + 1 = 17

From the Statement II, we can say that the cost price of two articles is same

i.e., the cost price of first article = cost price of second article= x

And from Statement III, we can say that the cost price of costliest article is 6.25% more than the cost price of cheapest article

Therefore, the cost price of costliest article $= x + x \times 6.25\%$

$$= 1.0625x$$

According to question,

$$x + x + 1.0625x = 49$$

$$x = 16$$

Therefore, cost price of costliest article $= 1.0625x$

$$= 1.0625 \times 16 = 17$$

Therefore, by combining both the statement we can also get our answer.

Hence, the correct option is (A).

34. If we have the dimensions, from Statement a,

Volume of cuboid $= 10 \times 5 \times 12 = 600 \; cm^3$

If thickness is ' t ' and let side of square sheet be S, then,

$$600 = (S^2) \times (t)$$

If $t = 1.5 \; cm$ is taken from Statement II,

$$\frac{600}{1.5} = (S^2) = 400$$

$$S = 20 \; cm$$

Height of cylinder $= S = 20 \; cm$ [As square sheet is rolled so the side of the cylinder will be equal to side of square]

Outer circumference $= S = 20 \; cm = 2\pi r$

Or, $r = \frac{10}{\pi} \approx 3.185$

Thickness taken, $t = 1.5 \; cm$

So inner radius $= 3.185 - 1.5 = 1.685 \; cm$

Whereas Statement III has no significance anywhere.

But none of the statement alone can answer the question individually.

Hence, answer is using statement I and II together is sufficient

Hence, the correct option is (C).

35. Let the number of boys be x.

Then, number of girls $= x + x \times \frac{20}{100} = x \left(1 + \frac{20}{100}\right) = \frac{120x}{100} = \frac{6x}{5}$

As Given,

$$x + \frac{6x}{5} = 66$$

$$\Rightarrow \frac{11x}{5} = 66$$

$$\Rightarrow x = 30$$

∴Number of boys = 30

Number of girls $= \frac{6 \times 30}{5} = 36$

∴ Required ratio = 30: 40 = 3: 4

Hence, the correct option is (C).

Q.1 A certain sum of money amounts to Rs. 720 in 2 years and Rs. 870 in 4.5 years, with same rate of simple interest. Find the rate of interest.

A. 12%   **B.** 15%   **C.** 10%   **D.** 8%

E. 11%

Q.2 Two pipes A and B can fill a tank in 15 min and 20 min respectively. Both the pipes are opened together but after 4 min, pipe A is turned off. What is the total time required to fill the tank?

A. 10 min 20 sec   **B.** 11 min 45 sec

C. 12 min 30 sec   **D.** 14 min 40 sec

E. 12 min 40 sec

Q.3 Direction: In the given question, two equations numbered I and II are given. Solve both the equations and give the appropriate answer.

I. $x^2 - 15x + 54 = 0$

II. $y^2 - 13y + 36 = 0$

A.   x > y

B.   x < y

C.   x ≥ y

D.   x ≤ y

E.   Relation can't be established or x = y

Q.4 Direction: In the given question, two equations numbered I and II are given. Solve both the equations and mark the appropriate answer.

I. $x^2 - 13x + 40 = 0$

II. $y^2 - 11y + 24 = 0$

A.   x > y

B.   x < y

C.   x ≥ y

D.   x ≤ y

E.   Relation can't be established or x = y

Q.5 Direction: In the given question, two equations numbered I and II are given. You have to solve both the equations and mark the appropriate answer.

I. $x^2 - 7x + 10 = 0$

II. $y^2 - 11y + 24 = 0$

A.   If x > y

B.   If x ≥ y

C.   If x < y

D.   If x ≤ y

E.   If x = y or the relationship cannot be established

Q.6 Direction: In the given question, two equations numbered I and II are given. You have to solve both the equations and mark the appropriate answer.

I. $x^2 - 50x + 225 = 0$

II. $y^2 + 32y - 105 = 0$

A.   x > y

B.   y > x

C.   x ≥ y

D.   y ≥ x

E.   x = 0 or relationship between x and y can't be established

Q.7 Direction: In the given question, two equations numbered I and II are given. Solve both the equations and mark the appropriate answer.

I. $2x^2 - 11x + 15 = 0$

II. $9y^2 - 12y + 4 = 0$

A.   x > y

B.   x < y

C.   x ≥ y

D.   x ≤ y

E.   x = y or relation between x and y can not be established

Q.8 Direction: What will come in place of question mark(?) in the following question?

$$6153 \div \sqrt{?} \times 53 = 4028$$

A. 6889   **B.** 6241

C. 5929   **D.** 6561

E. None of these

Ques (9-10):Direction: What will come in place of the question mark (?) in the following equation?

Q.9 $? \%$ of $(15360 \div 4) = 2^{11} - 2^9$

A. 6   **B.** 60

C. 40   **D.** 80

E. None of these

Q.10 $27 - [16^2 - (273 + 281) \div 2] = ?$

A. 52   **B.** 58   **C.** 32   **D.** 48

E. 38

Q.11 Two sports bikes were sold for Rs. 18,750 each, gaining 25% on one and losing 25% on the other. The gain or loss percent on the whole transaction is:

A. 6.25% profit   **B.** 6% profit

C. $7\frac{1}{4}$% profit   **D.** 6% loss

E. 6.25% loss

Ques (12-16):Direction: The given table shows the prices of various garments and the discount offered on them by a branded garment company. Study the table and answer the question that follow.

	Marked price	Discount %	Selling price
Sweatshirt	Rs. 3999	-	-
T-shirt	-	30%	-
Jeans	Rs. 4999	-	Rs. 2749
Trouser	Rs. 3499	-	-
Shorts	-	20% + 20%	Rs. 4159

Q.12 A boy bought a Sweatshirt and trousers by paying Rs. 4698. If the discount $\%$ on a trouser is 5 more than that on a Sweatshirt, find the discount $\%$ on a Sweatshirt

A. 20%   **B.** 35%   **C.** 25%   **D.** 40%
E. 45%

Q.13 If the price of a Shorts is marked 66% above its cost price, find the profit $\%$ (approximate) earned by the company on a Shorts.

A. 6.3%   **B.** 5.8%   **C.** 6.1%   **D.** 6.7%
E. 7.5%

Q.14 When a boy buys 4 t-shirts, he saves a total of Rs. 2400. If the price of a t-shirt is marked 55% above its cost price, find the approximate cost price of a t-shirt

A. Rs. 1100   **B.** Rs. 1450   **C.** Rs. 1290   **D.** Rs. 2000
E. Rs. 1180

Q.15 If the company earns a profit of 4.5% on a jeans, at what percentage above the cost price did the company marked its price?

A. 80%   **B.** 100%   **C.** 60%   **D.** 70%
E. 90%

Q.16 The discount $\%$ on jeans is what percentage more than the discount $\%$ on a t-shirt?

A. 50%   **B.** 60%   **C.** 40%   **D.** 35%
E. 72%

Q.17 The average age of a mother and her son is 45 year. The ratio of their ages is 3 : 2. Find the age of the son.

A. 36 year   **B.** 46 year   **C.** 54 year   **D.** 12 year
E. 20 year

Q.18 The average salary of male workers in a firm is Rs 4100 and that of the female workers is Rs 4800. If the mean salary of all the employees is Rs 4345, Then find the percentage of male employees in the firm.

A. 35%   **B.** 65%   **C.** 45%   **D.** 55%
E. 40%

Ques (19-21):Direction: Given below are two quantities named A and B. Based on the given information, you have to determine the relationship between the two quantities. You should use the given data and your knowledge of Mathematics to choose between the possible answers.

Q.19 Quantity A: 42 workers can do a piece of work in 17 days, 10 days after they started the work half the workers left the job. The remaining work is completed by the remaining workers in how many days?

Quantity B: 15 days

A. Quantity A > Quantity B
B. Quantity A < Quantity B
C. Quantity A ≥ Quantity B
D. Quantity A ≤ Quantity B
E. Quantity A = Quantity B or No relation

Q.20 Quantity A: If 6 liters of water is evaporated on boiling from 18 liters of sugar solution containing 9% sugar, then find the percentage of sugar in the remaining solution.

Quantity B: 13%

A. Quantity A > Quantity B
B. Quantity A < Quantity B
C. Quantity A ≥ Quantity B
D. Quantity A ≤ Quantity B
E. Quantity A = Quantity B or No relation

Q.21 Quantity A: Aman goes to the office at a speed of 50 km/h and reaches 10 minutes late. The next day he goes at a speed of 75 km/h and reaches the office 10 minutes early. Find the distance from his home to the office.

Quantity B: 40 km

A. Quantity A > Quantity B
B. Quantity A < Quantity B
C. Quantity A ≥ Quantity B
D. Quantity A ≤ Quantity B
E. Quantity A = Quantity B or No relation

Ques (22-26):Direction: Find the missing number in place of the question mark (?) in the given series.

Q.22 2, 8, 28, 102, 432, ?
A. 1860   **B.** 1296
C. 2190   **D.** 2490
E. None of these

Q.23 6, 16, 44, 126, 370, ?
A. 1100   **B.** 1050
C. 1400   **D.** 1260
E. None of these

Q.24 51, 77, 175, 250, 279, ?
A. 313   **B.** 413
C. 512   **D.** 616
E. None of these

Q.25 2, 2, 5, 15.5, ?, 267.125
A. 58.25   **B.** 65.25
C. 56.25   **D.** 62.25
E. None of these

Q.26 219, 223, 232, 248, ?
A. 296   **B.** 284   **C.** 257   **D.** 273
E. 267

Ques (27-32):Direction: Simplify the given expression.

Q.27 $\sqrt{1024} \times 40 + 20^2 + 0.5\%$ of $9600 + 469 = ?^3$

[IBPS Clerk, 2021]

A. 23   **B.** 13   **C.** 17   **D.** 19
E. 21

Q.28 $4\frac{3}{5}\%$ of $6500 + 3\frac{2}{7}\%$ of $3500 = ?$
A. 424   **B.** 414   **C.** 418   **D.** 404
E. 401

Q.29 $3\frac{1}{2} \times \frac{7\frac{2}{5}}{9\frac{3}{5}} \times 8^2 \times 60 = 2^4 \times ?$

A. 624   **B.** 2364   **C.** 647.5   **D.** 1864

E. 1946

Q.30 $\left(\frac{?}{37}\right) = \left(\frac{15}{?}\right) \times \left(\frac{1}{2145}\right) \times \left(\frac{1}{9.25}\right) \times 676 \times 143$

A. 36   **B.** 26   **C.** 69   **D.** 55

E. 52

Q.31 $\left[\frac{3}{2} + \frac{1}{2}\left\{\frac{3}{4} - \frac{1}{2}\left(\frac{7}{8} - \frac{3}{4}\right)\right\}\right] = ?$

A. $\frac{59}{15}$ **B.** $\frac{59}{32}$ **C.** $\frac{59}{37}$ **D.** $\frac{58}{11}$

E. $\frac{60}{11}$

Q.32 $\frac{1}{3}$ of $2529 + 42\%$ of $1450 = (?)^2 - 949$

A. 51   **B.** 41   **C.** 39   **D.** 49

E. 59

Q.33 P is twice efficient than Q, Q is is thrice efficient than R and R does the whole work in 54 days then in how many days P and Q together complete work?

A. 9 days   **B.** 5 days   **C.** 8 days   **D.** 6 days

E. 7 days

Q.34 Direction: Simplify the given expression.

$$\frac{\sqrt{576}+(14\times8)}{\sqrt{289}} + \frac{3}{7} \times 168 = ?$$

A. 110   **B.** 80   **C.** 90   **D.** 116

E. 100

Q.35 How many litres of water should be added to a 30 litre mixture of milk and water containing milk and water in the ratio of $7:3$ such that the resultant mixture has 40% water in it?

A. 2 litres   **B.** 5 litres   **C.** 6 litres   **D.** 9 litres

E. 12 litres

// Smart Answer Sheet //

| Correct | | Indicates percentage of students who answered questions correctly. |

| Skipped | | Indicates percentage of students who skipped questions. |

Q.	Ans.	Correct / Skipped	Q.	Ans.	Correct / Skipped	Q.	Ans.	Correct / Skipped	Q.	Ans.	Correct / Skipped	Q.	Ans.	Correct / Skipped
1	C	52.36 % / 42.56 %	8	D	85.46 % / 12.75 %	15	E	50.65 % / 49.16 %	22	C	69.02 % / 30.6 %	29	C	52.92 % / 30.11 %
2	D	44.49 % / 40.27 %	9	C	45.88 % / 44.88 %	16	A	62.04 % / 30.43 %	23	A	45.32 % / 49.79 %	30	E	64.27 % / 31.15 %
3	E	65.32 % / 31.48 %	10	D	16.7 % / 67.54 %	17	A	81.74 % / 17.36 %	24	B	69.01 % / 30.47 %	31	B	52.89 % / 34.8 %
4	E	49.97 % / 31.78 %	11	E	55.52 % / 34.65 %	18	B	53.02 % / 41.53 %	25	A	50.82 % / 31.52 %	32	D	58.92 % / 36.19 %
5	E	50.3 % / 38.86 %	12	B	58.63 % / 40.5 %	19	B	58.16 % / 36.62 %	26	D	21.01 % / 72.94 %	33	D	50.42 % / 32.76 %
6	A	40.74 % / 58.3 %	13	A	64.55 % / 33.05 %	20	A	54.75 % / 31.72 %	27	B	64.63 % / 34.48 %	34	B	43.72 % / 49.77 %
7	A	63.93 % / 35.81 %	14	C	69.79 % / 30.21 %	21	A	17.62 % / 76.5 %	28	B	68.0 % / 30.95 %	35	B	68.13 % / 31.82 %

Performance Analysis	
Avg. Score (%)	45.71%
Toppers Score (%)	65.71%
Your Score	

//Hints and Solutions//

1. Given:

Amount in 2 years $=$ Rs. 720

Amount in 4.5 years = Rs. 870

Formula:

Simple interest(SI) $= \dfrac{[\text{ Principal }(P)\times \text{ Rate }\times \text{ Time }]}{100}$

And Amount = Principal + SI

Let the sum(principal) be P and the rate of interest be R

So, $720 =$ Principal $+SI$

$\Rightarrow 720 = P + \dfrac{(P \times R \times 2)}{100}$ ... (i)

And $870 = P + SI$

$\Rightarrow 870 = P + \dfrac{(P \times R \times 4.5)}{100}$ ... (ii)

Equation (ii) - (i)

$\dfrac{(2.5 \times P \times R)}{100} = 150$

$\Rightarrow P \times R = 6000$ ... (iii)

Now, from eq.(i),

$720 = P + \dfrac{(6000 \times 2)}{100}$

$\Rightarrow P = 720 - 120 = \text{ Rs. } 600$

From eq. (iii)

$600 \times R = 6000$

$\Rightarrow R = 10\%$

∴ The rate of interest is 10%.

Hence, the correct option is (C).

2. Given,

Time taken by pipe A to fill the tank = 15 min

Part filled by A in 1 minutes $= \dfrac{1}{15}$

Time taken by pipe B to fill the tank = 20 min

Part filled by B in 1 minutes $= \dfrac{1}{20}$

Pipe A is off after 4 min.

Part filled by A and B in 4 min $= 4\left(\dfrac{1}{15} + \dfrac{1}{20}\right)$

$= \dfrac{7}{15}$

Remaining part $= 1 - \dfrac{7}{15}$

$= \dfrac{8}{15}$

Time taken to fill the remaining part $= \dfrac{\text{Remaining part}}{\text{Part filled by B in 1 min}}$

$= \dfrac{\left(\dfrac{8}{15}\right)}{\left(\dfrac{1}{20}\right)}$

$= \dfrac{32}{3}$

$= 10\dfrac{2}{3}$ min

$= 10\dfrac{2}{3} \times 60$ min

= 10 min 40 sec

Total time required to fill the tank = 4 min + 10 min 40 sec

= 14 min 40 sec

∴ Total time required to fill the tank is 14 min 40 sec.

Hence, the correct option is (D).

3. I. $x^2 - 15x + 54 = 0$

$\Rightarrow x^2 - 6x - 9x + 54 = 0$

$\Rightarrow x(x - 6) - 9(x - 6) = 0$

$\Rightarrow (x - 6)(x - 9) = 0$

$\Rightarrow x = 6$ or 9

II. $y^2 - 13y + 36 = 0$

$\Rightarrow y^2 - 9y - 4y + 36 = 0$

$\Rightarrow y(y - 9) - 4(y - 9) = 0$

$\Rightarrow (y - 9)(y - 4) = 0$

$\Rightarrow Y = 9$ or 4

x	sign	y
6	<	9
6	>	4
9	=	9
9	>	4

∴ Relation can't be established or x = y

Hence, the correct option is (E).

4. I. $x^2 - 13x + 40 = 0$

$\Rightarrow x^2 - 8x - 5x + 40 = 0$

$\Rightarrow x(x - 8) - 5(x - 8) = 0$

$\Rightarrow (x - 8)(x - 5) = 0$

$\Rightarrow x = 5$ or 8

II. $y^2 - 11y + 24 = 0$

$\Rightarrow y^2 - 3y - 8y + 24 = 0$

$\Rightarrow y(y - 3) - 8(y - 3) = 0$

$\Rightarrow (y - 3)(y - 8) = 0$

$\Rightarrow y = 3$ or 8

x	sign	y
5	>	3
5	<	8
8	>	3
8	=	8

$\therefore$ Relation can't be established or $x = y$

Hence, the correct option is (E).

5. I. $x^2 - 7x + 10 = 0$

$\Rightarrow x^2 - 5x - 2x + 10 = 0$

$\Rightarrow x(x - 5) - 2(x - 5) = 0$

$\Rightarrow (x - 5)(x - 2) = 0$

$\Rightarrow x = 5$ or $x = 2$

II. $y^2 - 11y + 24 = 0$

$\Rightarrow y^2 - 8y - 3y + 24 = 0$

$\Rightarrow y(y - 8) - 3(y - 8) = 0$

$\Rightarrow (y - 8)(y - 3) = 0$

$\Rightarrow y = 8$ or $y = 3$

Value of x	Relation	Value of y
5	<	8
2	<	8
5	>	3
2	<	3

$\therefore$ The relationship cannot be established between x and y.

Hence, the correct option is (E).

6. 1. $x^2 - 50x + 225 = 0$

$\Rightarrow x^2 - 45x - 5x + 225 = 0$

$\Rightarrow x(x - 45) - 5(x - 45) = 0$

$\Rightarrow (x - 5)(x - 45) = 0$

$\Rightarrow x = 5, 45$

II. $y^2 + 32y - 105 = 0$

$\Rightarrow y^2 + 35y - 3y - 105 = 0$

$\Rightarrow y(y + 35) - 3(y + 35) = 0$

$\Rightarrow (y - 3)(y + 35)$

$\Rightarrow y = 3, -35$

$\therefore x > y$

Hence, the correct option is (A).

7. Given:

I. $2x^2 - 11x + 15 = 0$

II. $9y^2 - 12y + 4 = 0$

From I,

$2x^2 - 11x + 15 = 0$

$\Rightarrow 2x^2 - 6x - 5x + 15 = 0$

$\Rightarrow 2x(x - 3) - 5(x - 3) = 0$

$\Rightarrow (x - 3)(2x - 5) = 0$

Taking,

$\Rightarrow (x - 3) = 0$ or $(2x - 5) = 0$

$\Rightarrow x = 3$ or $\left(\dfrac{5}{2}\right)$

From II,

$9y^2 - 12y + 4 = 0$

$\Rightarrow 9y^2 - 6y - 6y + 4 = 0$

$\Rightarrow 3y(3y - 2) - 2(3y - 2) = 0$

$\Rightarrow (3y - 2)(3y - 2) = 0$

Taking,

$\Rightarrow (3y - 2) = 0$

$\Rightarrow y = \dfrac{2}{3}$

Comparison between x and y (via Tabulation):

Value of x	Value of y	Relation
3	$\dfrac{2}{3}$	x > y
$\dfrac{5}{2}$	$\dfrac{2}{3}$	x > y

$\therefore x > y.$

Hence, the correct option is (A).

8. Given,

$6153 \div \sqrt{?} \times 53 = 4028$

$\Rightarrow \dfrac{(6153 \times 53)}{\sqrt{?}} = 4028$

$\Rightarrow \sqrt{?} = 80.96 \approx 81$

$\Rightarrow ? = 6561$

Hence, the correct option is (D).

9. Given:

$? \% \text{ of } (15360 \div 4) = 2^{11} - 2^9$

$\left(\dfrac{?}{100}\right) \times 3840 = 2^9 \times (4 - 1)$

$\left(\dfrac{?}{100}\right) \times 3840 = 512 \times 3 = 1536$

$? = 1536 \times \left(\dfrac{100}{3840}\right)$

? = 40

Hence, the correct option is (C).

10. Follow BODMAS rule to solve this question, as per the order given below,

$$27 - [16^2 - (273 + 281) \div 2]$$

$$= 27 - [256 - \frac{554}{2}]$$

$$= 27 - 256 + 277$$

$$= 48$$

Hence, the correct option is (D).

11. Let the two sports bikes be A & B.

Total S.P. of the two sports bikes = 18750 × 2 = Rs. 37,500

C.P. of sports bike A (C.P.$_1$) = S.P. of sports bike A – Profit

$\Rightarrow$ C.P.$_1$ = 18750 – (25% of C.P.$_1$)

$\Rightarrow$ C.P.$_1$ + 0.25 C.P.$_1$ = 18750

$\Rightarrow$ C.P.$_1$ = $\frac{18750}{1.25}$ = Rs. 15,000

$\therefore$ C.P. of sports bike A = C.P.$_1$ = Rs. 15,000

C.P. of sports bike B (C.P.$_2$) = S.P. of sports bike B + Loss

$\Rightarrow$ C.P.$_2$ = 18750 + (25% of C.P.$_2$)

$\Rightarrow$ C.P.$_2$ – 0.25C.P.$_2$ = 18750

$\Rightarrow$ C.P.$_2$ = $\frac{18750}{0.75}$ = Rs. 25,000

$\therefore$ C.P. of sports bike B = C.P.$_2$ = Rs. 25,000

C.P. of the two sports bikes = 15000 + 25000 = Rs. 40,000

$\because$ S.P. of the whole transaction < C.P. of the whole transaction, there is loss.

$\therefore$ Loss % on the whole transaction = $\frac{C.P. - S.P.}{C.P.} \times 100 =$

$\frac{40,000 - 37,500}{40,000} \times 100 = 6.25$

Hence, the correct option is (E).

12. Let the discount % on a Sweatshirt be $'x'\%$

Discount % on trouser = $(x + 5)\%$

$\because$ Selling price = Marked price – discount

$\Rightarrow$ Selling price of Sweatshirt = $[\frac{(100-x)}{100}] \times 3999$

$\Rightarrow$ Selling price of trouser = $[\frac{(100-x-5)}{100}] \times 3499$

Now, total selling price = 4698

$\Rightarrow [\frac{(100-x)}{100}] \times 3999 + [\frac{(95-x)}{100}] \times 3499 = 4698$

$\Rightarrow 399900 - 3999x + 332405 - 3499x = 469800$

$\Rightarrow 7498x = 732305 - 469800 = 262505$

$\Rightarrow x = \frac{262505}{7498} \cong 35\%$

The discount % on a Sweatshirt is 35%

Hence, the correct option is (B).

13. $\because$ The discount on a Shorts is a successive discount of 20%, followed by 20%

Selling price of a Shorts = $(100 - 20)\%$ of $(100 - 20)\%$ of the Marked price

$\Rightarrow$ Marked price of a Shorts = $\frac{4159}{(0.8 \times 0.8)} \cong$ Rs. 6498

Also, Marked price of a Shorts = $(100 + 66)\%$ of Cost price

$\Rightarrow$ Cost price of a Shorts = $\frac{6498}{1.66} \cong$ Rs. 3914

$\therefore$ Profit % = $[\frac{(4159-3914)}{3914}] \times 100 \cong 6.3\%$

Hence, the correct option is (A).

14. Discount price on 4 t-shirts = Rs. 2400

Discount price on 1 t-shirt = $\frac{2400}{4}$ = Rs. 600

Also,

Discount price on 1 t-shirt = 30% of the Marked price

$\Rightarrow$ Marked price of 1 t-shirt = $\frac{600}{0.3}$ = Rs. 2000

Also, Marked price of a t-shirt = $(100 + 55)\%$ of Cost price

$\therefore$ Cost price of a t-shirt = $\frac{2000}{1.55} \cong$ Rs. 1290

Hence, the corretc option is (C).

15. Let the required percentage be $'x'\%$

As we know,

Selling price = Cost price + profit

$\Rightarrow$ Cost price of a jeans = $\frac{2749}{(100+4.5)}\% = \frac{2749}{1.045}$ = Rs. 2631

Now,

Marked price of jeans = $(100 + x)\%$ of Cost price of jeans

$\Rightarrow 4999 = [\frac{(100+x)}{100}] \times 2631$

$\Rightarrow 100 + x \cong 190$

$\Rightarrow x = 190 - 100 = 90\%$

∴ The price of jeans is marked 90% above its cost price

Hence, the correct option is (E).

16. Let the discount $\%$ on a jeans be $'d'\%$.

Marked price of jeans $-$ discount price $=$ Selling price of jeans

$\Rightarrow (100 - d)\%$ of $4999 = 2749$

$\Rightarrow 100 - d = \dfrac{274900}{4999}$

$\Rightarrow 100 - d \cong 55$

$\Rightarrow d = 100 - 55 = 45\%$

Discount $\%$ on a t-shirt $= 30\%$

∴ Required percentage $= [\dfrac{(45-30)}{30}] \times 100 = 50\%$

Hence, the correct option is (A).

17. Given:

The average age of Mother and son = 45 year

Mother and son's age ratio = 3 : 2

Let the age of Mother be 3x.

Let the age of the son be 2x.

According to the question

$\Rightarrow \dfrac{(3x + 2x)}{2} = 45$

$\Rightarrow 5x = 90$

$\Rightarrow x = 18$

Son's age = 2 × 18 = 36 year.

∴ Son's age Is 36 year.

Hence, the correct option is (A).

18. Given:

Average salary of Males = Rs 4100

Average salary of Females = Rs 4800

Average salary of all the workers = Rs 4345

We know that,

$$\text{Average} = \dfrac{\text{Sum of observations}}{\text{Total number of observations}}$$

Let the males be x and the females be y

Total salary of males $= 4100x$

Total salary of females $= 4800y$

Total salary of all the workers $= 4345(x + y)$

So, $4100x + 4800y = 4345x + 4345y$

$\Rightarrow 245x = 455y$

$\Rightarrow \dfrac{x}{y} = \dfrac{13}{7}$

So, percentage of males $= \dfrac{13}{20} \times 100 = 65\%$

∴ The males are 65%.

Hence, the correct option is (B).

19. Quantity A:

Given:

42 workers' time = 17 days

Half workers left after 10 days

Let the remaining work is done in x days.

Work = Efficiency × time

Work = 42 × 17

Also, work $= (42 \times 10) + (21 \times x)$

Equating both equations,

$$(42 \times 17) - (42 \times 10) = (21 \times x)$$

$\Rightarrow (42 \times 17) - (42 \times 10) = (21 \times x)$

$\Rightarrow 42(17 - 10) = (21 \times x)$

$\Rightarrow 42 \times 7 = 21 \times x$

$\Rightarrow$ x = 14 days

Quantity B: 15 days

∴ Quantity A < Quantity B

Hence, the correct option is (B).

20. Quantity A:

Given,

Initial solution = 18 liters

Water evaporated = 6 liters

Sugar % = 9%

When the solution is boiled only water evaporates and the amount of sugar remains the same.

Amount of sugar,

9% of 18 = 1.62

After evaporation,

Remaining solution = 18 liters - 6 liters

= 12 liters

% of sugar in remaining solution,

$\Rightarrow \dfrac{1.62}{12} \times 100$

= 13.5%

Quantity B: 13%

∴ Quantity A > Quantity B

Hence, the correct option is (A).

21. Quantity A:

Given,

Speed = 50 km/h; reaches 10 minutes late

Speed = 75 km/h; reaches 10 minutes early

We know,

$$\text{Speed} = \frac{\text{Distance}}{\text{Time}}$$

Let the distance be x km.

Difference in time = 10 + 10 = 20 min = $\frac{1}{3}$ hr

According to the question:

$$\frac{x}{50} - \frac{x}{75} = \frac{1}{3}$$

$$\Rightarrow \frac{(3x - 2x)}{150} = \frac{1}{3}$$

$$\Rightarrow x = 50 \text{ km}$$

∴ The distance is 50 km.

Quantity B: 40 km

∴ Quantity A > Quantity B

Hence, the correct option is (A).

22. Given series:

2, 8, 28, 102, 432, ?

The pattern is:

2 × 1 + 6 = 8

8 × 2 + 12 = 28

28 × 3 + 18 = 102

102 × 4 + 24 = 432

432 × 5 + 30 = 2190

So, the missing number is 2190.

Hence, the correct option is (C).

23. Given series:

6, 16, 44, 126, 370, ?

The pattern is:

6 × 3 − 2 = 16

16 × 3 − 4 = 44

44 × 3 − 6 = 126

126 × 3 − 8 = 370

370 × 3 − 10 = 1100

So, the missing number is 1100.

Hence, the correct option is (A)

24. Given series:

51, 77, 175, 250, 279, ?

The pattern is:

$$51 + (5^2 + 1^2) = 77$$

$$77 + (7^2 + 7^2) = 175$$

$$175 + (1^2 + 7^2 + 5^2) = 250$$

$$250 + (2^2 + 5^2 + 0^2) = 279$$

$$279 + (2^2 + 7^2 + 9^2) = 413$$

So, the missing number is 413.

Hence, the correct option is (B).

25. Given series:

2, 2, 5, 15.5, ?, 267.125

The pattern is:

2 × 0.5 + 1 = 2

2 × 1.5 + 2 = 5

5 × 2.5 + 3 = 15.5

15.5 × 3.5 + 4 = 58.25

58.25 × 4.5 + 5 = 267.125

So, the missing number is 58.25.

Hence, the correct option is (A).

26. Given series:

219, 223, 232, 248, ?

The pattern is:

$$219 + (1^2 + 1 + 2) = 223$$

$$223 + (2^2 + 2 + 3) = 232$$

$$232 + (3^2 + 3 + 4) = 248$$

$$248 + (4^2 + 4 + 5) = 273$$

So, the missing number is 273.

Hence, the correct option is (D).

27. Given:

$$\sqrt{1024} \times 40 + 20^2 + 0.5\% \text{ of } 9600 + 469 = ?^3$$

$$\Rightarrow 32 \times 40 + 400 + 9600 \times \frac{0.5}{100} + 469 = ?^3$$

$$\Rightarrow 32 \times 40 + 400 + 48 + 469 = ?^3$$

$$\Rightarrow 1280 + 400 + 48 + 469 = ?^3$$

$\Rightarrow 1280 + 448 + 469 = ?^3$

$\Rightarrow 2197 = ?^3$

$\Rightarrow ? = \sqrt[3]{2197}$

$\Rightarrow ? = 13$

Hence, the correct option is (B).

28. Given:

$4\frac{3}{5}\%$ of $6500 + 3\frac{2}{7}\%$ of $3500 = ?$

$\Rightarrow \frac{23}{5}\%$ of $6500 + \frac{23}{7}\%$ of $3500 = ?$

$\Rightarrow \left(\frac{23}{500}\right) \times 6500 + \left(\frac{23}{700}\right) \times 3500 = ?$

$\Rightarrow 23 \times 13 + 23 \times 5 = ?$

$\Rightarrow ? = 23 \times (13 + 5)$

$\Rightarrow ? = 23 \times 18$

$\Rightarrow ? = 414$

Hence, the correct option is (B).

29. Given:

$3\frac{1}{2} \times \dfrac{7\frac{2}{5}}{9\frac{3}{5}} \times 8^2 \times 60 = 2^4 \times ?$

$\Rightarrow \dfrac{7}{2} \times \dfrac{\frac{37}{5}}{\frac{48}{5}} \times 8^2 \times 60 = 2^4 \times ?$

$\Rightarrow \dfrac{7}{2} \times \dfrac{37}{5} \times \dfrac{5}{48} \times 64 \times 60 = 16 \times ?$

$\Rightarrow \dfrac{7 \times 37 \times 64 \times 60}{18 \times 2} = 16 \times ?$

$\Rightarrow ? \times 16 = 7 \times 37 \times 8 \times 5$

$\Rightarrow ? \times 16 = 10360$

$\Rightarrow ? = \dfrac{10360}{16}$

$\Rightarrow ? = 647.5$

Hence, the correct option is (C).

30. Given:

$\left(\dfrac{?}{37}\right) = \left(\dfrac{15}{?}\right) \times \left(\dfrac{1}{2145}\right) \times \left(\dfrac{1}{9.25}\right) \times 676 \times 143$

$\Rightarrow ?^2 = \left(37 \times 15 \times 676 \times 143 \times \dfrac{1}{2145} \times \dfrac{1}{9.25}\right)$

$\Rightarrow ?^2 = \left(37 \times 15 \times 676 \times \dfrac{143}{2145} \times \dfrac{1}{9.25}\right)$

$\Rightarrow ?^2 = \left(37 \times 15 \times 676 \times \dfrac{1}{15} \times \dfrac{1}{9.25}\right)$

$\Rightarrow ?^2 = \left(37 \times 676 \times \dfrac{1}{9.25}\right)$

$\Rightarrow ?^2 = 4 \times 676$

$\Rightarrow ? = \sqrt{4 \times 676}$

$\Rightarrow ? = \sqrt{4} \times \sqrt{676}$

$\Rightarrow ? = 2 \times 26$

$\Rightarrow ? = 52$

Hence, the correct option is (E).

31. Given:

$[\frac{3}{2} + \frac{1}{2}\{\frac{3}{4} - \frac{1}{2}\left(\frac{7}{8} - \frac{3}{4}\right)\}] = ?$

$\Rightarrow ? = [\frac{3}{2} + \frac{1}{2}\{\frac{3}{4} - \frac{1}{2}\left(\frac{7-6}{8}\right)\}]$

$\Rightarrow ? = [\frac{3}{2} + \frac{1}{2}\{\frac{3}{4} - \frac{1}{2}\left(\frac{1}{8}\right)\}]$

$\Rightarrow ? = [\frac{3}{2} + \frac{1}{2}\{\frac{3}{4} - \frac{1}{16}\}]$

$\Rightarrow ? = [\frac{3}{2} + \frac{1}{2}\{\frac{12-1}{16}\}]$

$\Rightarrow ? = [\frac{3}{2} + \frac{1}{2}\{\frac{11}{16}\}]$

$\Rightarrow ? = \frac{3}{2} + \frac{11}{32}$

$\Rightarrow ? = \frac{48+11}{32}$

$\Rightarrow ? = \frac{59}{32}$

Hence, the correct option is (B).

32. Given:

$\frac{1}{3}$ of $2529 + 42\%$ of $1450 = (?)^2 - 949$

$\Rightarrow \frac{1}{3} \times 2529 + \frac{1450 \times 42}{100} = (?)^2 - 949$

$\Rightarrow 843 + 29 \times 21 = (?)^2 - 949$

$\Rightarrow 843 + 609 + 949 = (?)^2$

$\Rightarrow (?)^2 = 2401$

$\Rightarrow ? = \sqrt{2401}$

$\Rightarrow ? = 49$

Hence, the correct option is (D).

33. Given:

P = 2Q

Q = 3R

R can complete a work in 54 days

Concept:

If A does a work in n days then 1-day work of A is $\dfrac{1}{n}$

Calculation:

According to question,

Let, P's one day work = 6 unit

⇒ Q's one day work = 3 unit

⇒ R's one day work = 1 unit

C can complete work in 54 days

⇒ Total work = 1 × 54 = 54 unit

⇒ (P + Q) can complete work in = $\dfrac{54}{(6+3)}$

⇒ $\dfrac{54}{9}$

⇒ 6 days

∴ P and Q together can complete work in 6 days.

Hence, the correct option is (D).

34. Given:

$$\dfrac{\sqrt{576}+(14\times8)}{\sqrt{289}} + \dfrac{3}{7} \times 168 =?$$

$$\Rightarrow \dfrac{24+112}{17} + 3 \times 24 =?$$

$$\Rightarrow \dfrac{146}{17} + 72 =?$$

$$\Rightarrow 8 + 72 =?$$

$$\Rightarrow ? = 80$$

Hence, the correct option is (B).

35. Given:

30 litres of the mixture has milk and water in the ratio $7:3$.

The solution has 21 litres of milk and 9 litres of water.

When you add more water, the amount of milk in the mixture remains constant at 21 litres.

In the first case, before addition of further water, 21 litres of milk accounts for 70% by the volume.

After water is added, the new mixture contains 60% milk and 40% water.

The 21 litres of milk accounts for 60% by volume.

$$100\% \text{ volume } = \dfrac{21}{0.6} = 35 \text{ litres}$$

∴ 5 litres of water was added.

Hence, the correct option is (B).

// Notes //

// Notes //

www.ingramcontent.com/pod-product-compliance
Lightning Source LLC
Chambersburg PA
CBHW082016160726
47999CB00008B/2842